Design and Analysis of Piled Raft Foundations - 2017

Editors

Der-Wen Chang, Tatsunori Matsumoto and Deepankar Choudhury

Tamkang University Press

Design and Analysis of Piled Raft Foundations – 2017

Editors
Der-Wen Chang, Tatsunori Matsumoto and Deepankar Choudhury

ISBN: 978-986-5608-73-6

Published in Taiwan by
Tamkang University Press
151, Yingzhuan Rd., Tamsui Dist., New Taipei City 25137, R.O.C.
Tel: 886-2-8631-8661; Fax: 886-2-8631-8660
http://www.tkupress.tku.edu.tw/
E-mail: tkupress@www2.tku.edu.tw

Preface

Piled raft foundation has been widely used as the foundation system for high-rise buildings and mega structures located on sites consisting of soft soils. Considerable research efforts on such structural system have been made even since 1960s. Overview of the analysis and design methods of piled raft foundations can be found in the works of Randolph (1994) and Poulos (2001). With the developments of modern technologies, the piled raft foundation can be now analyzed rigorously using the three dimensional Finite Element Method (FEM). Until recent years, the design principles for the Combined Pile-raft Foundation (CPRF) considering the structural performances on both capacity and serviceability were suggested in ISSMGE design guideline of TC 212 (Katzenbach and Choudhury, 2013). The analytical and numerical analyses with practical approaches which are able to model rationally such structural system nowadays became very important to geotechnical engineers as outlined in the book of Katzenbach et al. (2016). The modeling needs to be verified with the material testing and the field measurements to better improve the applicability and reliability. Material laws which are able to model the foundation behaviors are always the key to the success of the numerical modeling of piled raft.

Although FEM is powerful, for simplicity in routine design practice and time concern in Performance Based Design (PBD), the methods of approximate computer modeling became typically important to the engineers. There are still a lot of research work in need to establish the goals of completeness and excellence. With these concerns, the co-editors decide to host an International Symposium on Design and Analysis of Piled Raft Foundations. The date of the Symposium is September 12-13, 2017 and the venue of the Symposium is at the Int. Convention center of Tamkang University in Taiwan. There are 19 papers invited which includes the works of ISSMGE TC212/TC305/ATC18 Chairs. Eleven of the articles are related to Design and Analysis, seven of them are related to Testing, Construction and Monitoring. The last one is a special report on advance of Japanese geotechnical technologies on this topic. All the articles collected are presented by Chapters in this book entitled Design and Analysis of Piled Raft Foundations - 2017. It is our sincere gratitude towards the great efforts and contributions of the authors. We believe that this book presents the updated research on the task and it can provide very useful information to the geotechnical engineers in dealing with the piled raft foundations.

The co-editors would also like to express their thankfulness to towards Tamkang University (TKU) and Ministry of Science and Technology (MOST) in Taiwan to support the Symposium.

The logistics helps provided by Taiwan Geotechnical Society (or Chinese Taipei Geotechnical Society) and AGSSEA as well as Alliance of Geotechnical Engineering in Taiwan are sincerely appreciated. There are a number of sponsors, including Diagnostic Engineering Consultants, Ltd./DECL Singapore PTE. Ltd., Ground Master Construction Co., Ltd./MICE Consultant Company, Ltd., KGS-Astana, LLP/Kazakhstan Geotechnical Society, PAH ASIA Co., Sino Geotechnology, Inc., and Tang Yuang Construction Engineer, Inc., who helped greatly to make this event successful and remarkable, their kind supports are highly acknowledged by the editors.

Der-Wen Chang
Professor, Tamkang University, Taiwan

Tatsunori Matsumoto
Professor, Kanazawa University, Japan

Deepankar Choudhury
Professor, Indian Institute of Technology Bombay, India

Contents

Testing, Construction and Monitoring   167

Special Report   257

Acknowledgements   275

Design and Analysis

CHAPTER 1

PILED RAFT CONCEPT: A VIRTUOUS EXAMPLE TO GET MORE WITH LESS

Alessandro Mandolini*
Raffaele Di Laora
Chiara Iodice
Department of Civil Engineering, Design, Building and Environment, Università degli Studi della Campania "Luigi Vanvitelli", Aversa, Italy
*alessandro.mandolini@unicampania.it

ABSTRACT: In this work the concept of 'piled raft' is applied to a well-documented case history of the main pier of the bridge over the river Garigliano, in Southern Italy. A recently published simplified method able to estimate the nonlinear load-settlement curve as well as the load sharing between piles and raft is applied first to reproduce the observed behavior in the original pile group configuration. Then, the same procedure has been utilized to optimize the design using different piles' layout. It is proved that large savings may be achieved through the exploitation of the 'piled raft' concept. In addition, a seismic analysis has been performed. It is shown that the layout optimized for vertical loads possesses adequate safety margins also against earthquake action.

1. INTRODUCTION

A group of piles is always surmounted by a cap connecting piles' heads. If this cap is in direct contact with the ground, it will contribute to carry a portion of the applied loads. In the latter case, the full system involving piles, cap and soil constitute a mixed foundation system and is generally referred in literature to as 'piled raft'. In order to describe the portion of the total load Q_{pr} taken by the horizontal cap in contact with the ground (termed in the ensuing as 'raft'), it is possible to refer to the load sharing ratio α_r defined as (Fig. 1):

$$\alpha_r = Q_r/Q_{pr} \qquad (1)$$

where Q_r is the load taken by the raft. A load sharing ratio $\alpha_r = 1$ represents a shallow foundation with no piles, while $\alpha_r = 0$ represents a pile group with a raft not in contact with ground; piled raft foundations cover the range $0 < \alpha_r < 1$.

In principle, there is no need to use piles if a shallow foundation guarantees a sufficient safety margin against bearing capacity failure and contemporarily experiences settlements under working loads which are tolerable in light of structure serviceability. When the raft alone does not guarantee a satisfactory performance, the adoption of piles underneath the shallow foundation represent a common design option to increase bearing capacity and/or reduce settlement. However, once the decision of adopting piles has been made, it is common assumption that the design loads are carried solely by the piles, thus neglecting the contribution of the raft-soil contact. This traditional design approach is clearly conflicting with the collected experimental evidence (see for example Mandolini et al. 2005) which proves that the load taken by the raft is not less than 20% and increases up to 60-70% depending essentially on piles' geometrical layout. The traditional approach of considering piles the only elements able to transfer loads to the ground (implicitly assuming $\alpha_r = 0$) may be definitely over-conservative when piles are required to increase the foundation

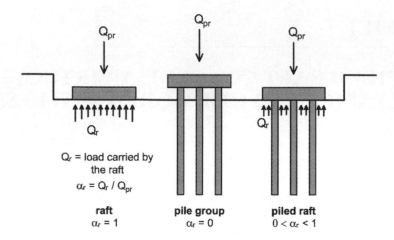

Figure 1. Definition of different foundation systems.

bearing capacity. Moreover, such an approach is totally erroneous from a conceptual standpoint when the raft alone possesses a bearing capacity larger than the one provided by the pile group, the latter having the mere role of decreasing and/or regulating settlements.

In the last decades, many specialists focused on this field, either from theoretical or experimental point of view (for a more comprehensive coverage, reference may be made to Randolph 1994; Poulos et al. 2001). Mandolini (2003) proposed a schematic chart for choosing the foundation type and the proper 'geotechnical' design approach (Fig. 2). In the figure, the center, A, represents an ideal condition or optimum for which, under a certain applied vertical load Q_{pr}, an unpiled raft having width B_R and bearing capacity $Q_{r,u}$, has a global factor of safety FS_{UR} equal to some fixed minimum value (arbitrarily assumed as 3 in the figure) and, at the same time, experiences an overall displacement w_{UR} equal to some admissible value ($w_{UR}/w_{adm} = 1$).

From a general point of view, three design situations may occur:

a) both the estimated values of FS_{UR} and w_{UR} are acceptable (Location [1]): the adoption of an unpiled raft is possible and therefore piles could be required to reduce the state of

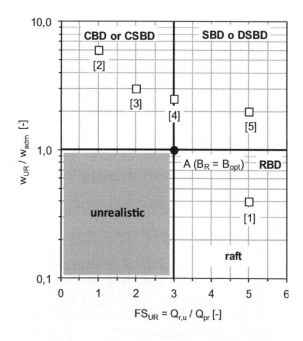

Figure 2. Chart for selection of the design approach (modified from Mandolini 2003).

the stress and deformation into the raft;

b) both the estimated values of FS_{UR} and w_{UR} are not acceptable (Locations [2] and [3]); piles have to be added in order to increase the value of FS_{UR} and to reduce the displacement w_{UR} (CSBD);

c) although the factor of safety is equal (Location [4]) or larger (Location [5]) than the minimum admissible value, the displacement under working loads is greater than w_{adm}. Piles have thus to be added with the aim of reducing average and/or differential settlement (SBD and/or DSBD).

Note that it is quite rare that a shallow foundation possesses unsatisfactory safety margins against a bearing capacity failure while experiencing acceptable settlements. This could be the case of a small plinth equipped with few piles, where the raft contribution is negligible and therefore the foundation system cannot be listed in the category of 'piled rafts'.

2. SIMPLIFIED DESIGN TOOLS FOR PILED RAFT

Besides complex numerical analyses, capable to take into account in detail peculiar aspects of the soil behaviour, limited simplified yet reliable procedures are available for a preliminary geotechnical design of piled rafts.

A very simple approach to the problem is the so-called PDR method (Poulos and Davis 1980; Randolph 1994; Poulos 2000), which provides the bi-linear load-settlement relationship for the piled raft and the load sharing between pile group and raft under the following assumptions: (1) piles and raft behave as linearly elastic systems until failure; (2) the raft is rigid and subjected to a vertical central load, hence only a uniform vertical displacement can occur. Due to the hypotheses about the raft rigidity, in principle, the method is applicable only to small piled rafts ($B_R/L < 1$) for which CSBD or SBD approaches are of relevance (Fig. 2) and relevant differential settlements would not occur (Russo and Viggiani 1998). However, if the aim is the assessment of load sharing between pile group and raft and the estimation of the load-average settlement curve, the method can be still applied to furnish useful information for design

purposes. Starting from the knowledge of the behavior of pile group and raft considered as individual systems, the PDR method combines them to predict the behavior of the piled raft system.

An enhanced version of the method has been recently proposed by Mandolini et al. (2017). The procedure employs arbitrary non-linear load-settlement curves for both pile group and raft considered as stand-alone system and combines them to get the non-linear piled raft behavior, both in terms of load-settlement curve and load sharing. For example, tangent stiffnesses may be expressed as:

$$\frac{dQ_p}{dw_p} = K_p = K_p(Q_p) = K_{p,0}\left(1 - \frac{Q_p}{Q_{p,u}}\right)^{np}$$

$$\frac{dQ_r}{dw_r} = K_r = K_r(Q_r) = K_{r,0}\left(1 - \frac{Q_r}{Q_{r,u}}\right)^{nr}$$

(2a,b)

where K_p and K_r are the tangent stiffnesses of pile group and raft (with $K_{p,0}$ and $K_{r,0}$ their initial value), $Q_{p,u}$ and $Q_{r,u}$ the ultimate loads, np and nr real positive numbers regulating the shape of the curves. It is easy to verify that np [nr] = 0 corresponds to the assumption of elastic behavior of the piles [raft] until failure. In matrix form, the method assumes:

$$\begin{bmatrix} dw_p \\ dw_r \end{bmatrix} = \begin{bmatrix} \dfrac{1}{K_p} & \dfrac{\alpha_{rp}}{K_{p,0}} \\ \dfrac{\alpha_{rp}}{K_{p,0}} & \dfrac{1}{K_r} \end{bmatrix} \cdot \begin{bmatrix} dQ_p \\ dQ_r \end{bmatrix}$$

(3)

Forces equilibrium and displacements compatibility requires that:

$$\begin{cases} dQ_{pr} = dQ_p + dQ_r \\ dw = dw_p = dw_r \end{cases}$$

(4)

The stiffness of the piled raft is then obtained as:

$$K_{pr} = \frac{K_{p,0} \cdot \left\{ K_p \cdot \left[K_p - \left(2 \cdot \alpha_{rp} \cdot K_r \right) \right] + \left(K_{p,0} \cdot K_r \right) \right\}}{K_{p,0}^2 - \left[\alpha_{rp}^2 \cdot \left(K_p \cdot K_r \right) \right]}$$

(5)

while the raft/piles load ratio is given by:

$$\beta = \frac{dQ_r}{dQ_p} = \frac{K_r \cdot \left[K_{p,0} - \left(\alpha_{rp} \cdot K_p \right) \right]}{K_p \cdot \left[K_{p,0} - \left(\alpha_{rp} \cdot K_r \right) \right]} \qquad (6)$$

Additional details about the method, including its implementation in a spreadsheet, are available in the abovementioned reference.

3. CASE HISTORY: THE MAIN PIER OF THE GARIGLIANO BRIDGE OVER THE GARIGLIANO RIVER

The above procedure is first applied to reproduce the actual measured behaviour for the case history of the main pier of the cable stayed bridge over the river Garigliano, situated in Southern Italy along Rome to Naples direction (Fig. 3). Then, a simple exercise of optimization is reported, showing that the application of the 'piled raft' concept may lead to substantial saving in design. In the second part of this section, seismic design is also analysed, evaluating the performance of original and optimized configurations under lateral loads coming from earthquake forces.

The viaduct over the Garigliano river is located in the central region of Italy, 1 km far from the seacoast. It was built in order to improve the existing road network between Naples and Rome by modifying a portion of the Appia highway (SS7).

The project had to face different issues: from one side the local network imposed several crossroads; from the other, closer to the SS7 there was an old Bourbon bridge that forced to select an alternative route. Thus, owing to all these constrains, the final project was a viaduct, crossing the Garigliano in a point where it flows into the Ausente river, having two roadways. Its total length is of about 1100 m, and it is composed by 21 × 2 spans of 37.7 m in length, supported by precast prestressed concrete beams; 4 spans made with steel beams, 2 of which covering 55 m and the other 2 covering 80 m; a cable stayed bridge with 2 spans of 90 m each (Fig. 3).

Since the viaduct is by the sea, the ground was essentially a coastal marsh made of clayey silt and silty clay deposits, rich in organic matter. The subsoil stratigraphy was obtained through soil investigation, in particular performing core sampling and CPTs (Fig. 4). At a depth of about 50 m a sand and gravel deposit was found; it can

be considered as a base formation since it is at least of about 12 m in thickness. Finally, some irregular sandy and peaty layers have been recognized. The water table is at the ground surface.

Some site results (CPT profiles) and soil properties (over-consolidation ratio, OCR; small strain stiffness, G0) are shown in Figure 4. Further

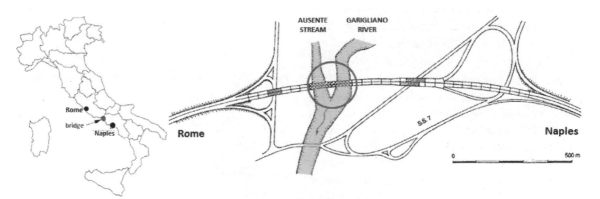

Figure 3. Bridge layout. The metallic spans are highlighted with dashed lines and the cables stayed bridge with crosses (adapted from Mandolini and Viggiani 1992).

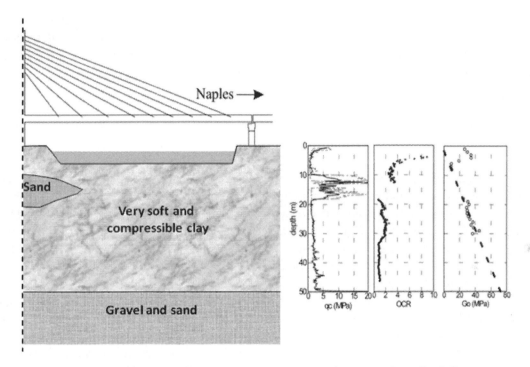

Figure 4. Subsoil sketch for the cable stayed bridge over the river Garigliano.

details are available in other scientific works (e.g. Mandolini and Viggiani, 1992; Mandolini et al. 2005; Viggiani et al. 2012).

With reference to the central pier of the Garigliano bridge, the original design lead to a foundation made up by a 4 m thick, 10.6 × 19 m raft and 144 driven tubular steel piles, filled with concrete, having length of 48 m (upper 24 m section with diameter 0.406 m; lower 24 m section with diameter 0.356).

4. PREDICTION OF LOAD-SETTLEMENT CURVE UNDER VERTICAL LOAD FOR THE ORIGINAL CONFIGURATION

To simulate the evolution of the loads during construction process, 4 stages have been considered: (1) undrained settlement due to raft weight; (2) settlement in drained conditions after consolidation; (3) bridge load acting on the piled raft in undrained conditions; (4) bridge load considering long term conditions.

For stage (1), the raft weight, equal to 22 MN, due to the concrete in the fluid state has been considered as a uniformly distributed load acting only the soil. The undrained settlement has been evaluated through the formula proposed by Mayne and Poulos (1999), considering a Gibson soil profile within a layer of depth equal to 6 meters below foundation level, where the sandy layer is encountered. The calculations have been performed employing a low-strain stiffness of the soil varying according to the law $G_0(z^*) = 3.8 + 1.5z^*$, with z^* the depth of the raft base (4 m from soil surface) and shear modulus expressed in MPa, as suggested by soil investigations reported in the abovementioned references. For stage (2) the same formula has been employed, with the exception that Poisson coefficient for the soil has been assumed equal to 0.3 instead of 0.5. The stiffness of the raft-soil system has been therefore estimated as 2100 MN/m and 1770 MN/m, for undrained and drained conditions, respectively.

For stage (3) the procedure by Mandolini et al. (2017) has been adopted. Linear elastic behaviour of the raft has been assumed. This choice has been made considering that it plays a minor role due to the limited raft load in the combined system and that some previous studies adopted the same assumption although the analyses were performed through a computer program (Viggiani et al. 2012). The axial capacity of the individual pile has been assumed to be 4150 kN, following the data reported in Mandolini and Viggiani (1992). To account for group effects the ultimate axial capacity of the pile group has been taken as the sum of the individual contributions of the single piles multiplied by an efficiency factor of 0.8, following the indications by De Mello (1969). Bearing capacity of pile group has been found to be 480 MN. Pile

group stiffness has been assessed by summing the elastic contribution due to the pile-to-pile interaction to the nonlinear component of the settlement of the single pile. Initial stiffness of single pile has been estimated by the classical Randolph and Wroth (1978) as 211 MN/m,

therefore obtaining $K_{p0} = 3471$ MN/m by taking into account interaction effects through the formula proposed by Butterfield and Douglas (1981). Adopting the suggestion from Mandolini et al. (2017), a factor $np = 1.5$ has been utilized to describe the nonlinear behavior of the single pile. According to Clancy and Randolph (1993), raft-pile group interaction factor $\alpha_{rp} = 0.7$ has been adopted. To calculate the final settlement at the stage (4) a drained calculation has been performed in the same manner as for stage (3), with the exception that pile initial stiffness and pile-to-pile interaction are evaluated with a Poisson coefficient for the soil equal to 0.3.

The comparison between the results obtained by the proposed procedure and the experimental load-settlement curve is reported in Figure 5. Very good agreement between predictions and measurements can be observed, especially considering that the construction of the bridge had started before the end of consolidation, so that the meaningful comparison must be referred to undrained settlement due to raft weight (stage 1), slope of the load-settlement curve in stage 3 and final settlement at stage 4.

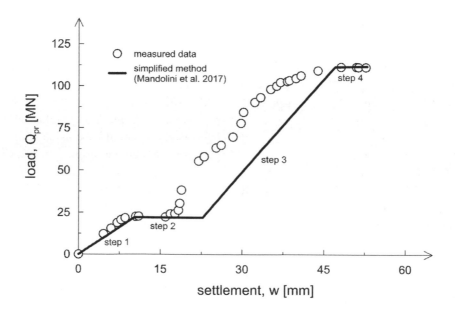

Figure 5. Comparison between measured data and results from the simplified method.

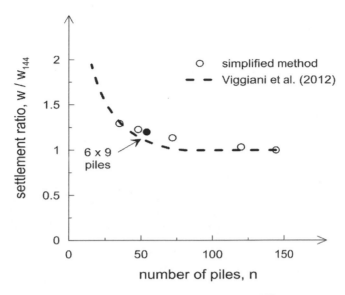

Figure 6. Long-term settlement of the piled raft for different number of piles.

4.1 Optimization of Pile Layout Under Vertical Load

The above simplified method may be therefore applied considering different pile group layouts. More specifically, the number of piles has been progressively reduced to calculate the final settlement of the piled raft with an optimized group configuration.

Figure 6 shows the increment of settlement w (related to that obtained with 144 pile group layout) due to a reduction in the piles' number. As it can be noticed, a 6 × 9 configuration (54 piles) still provides satisfactory performance. The same result has been obtained using computer program (Viggiani et al. 2012), as shown in Figure 6.

4.2 Consideration of Seismic Action

In the following, the geotechnical performance of the piled foundation under seismic loads will be also investigated.

The assessment of seismic action has been carried out according to the Italian Building Code (NTC, 2008) adopting soil classification defined by Eurocode 8 (CEN, 2003). Regarding the profile

of shear modulus at very low strain, results from direct measurement of shear wave velocity in the field shown in Figure 4 have been complemented with a value of G0 for the sand computed as an average between the upper and lower bound curve of the correlations with CPT tests proposed by Schnaid (2004):

$$G_0 = 110 \div 280 \cdot \sqrt[3]{q_c \sigma'_{v0} p_a} \cong 70 \text{MPa} \qquad (7)$$

Below 50 meters, an underlying elastic bedrock having shear wave velocity equal to 600 m/s has been considered. The unit weight has been set at 18 kN/m^3 for the fine-grained soil layers and 16 kN/m^3 for the sand. Seismic Site Response (SSR) analyses have been performed by means of the program EERA (Bardet et al. 2000). Shear modulus and damping degradation curves have been adopted to simulate non linearity in the soil in the realm of a linear-equivalent approach. More specifically clay curves refer to Seed and Sun (1989), upper range, for stiffness reduction and to Idriss (1990) for damping ratio. For the sandy layer, expressions from Seed and Idriss (1970) have been adopted. However, a preliminary parametric study showed that results are not very sensitive to the specific curves adopted to describe material nonlinearity.

Seven real earthquake records have been utilized as outcrop motion, selected through the program REXEL v3.5 (Iervolino et al. 2010) to be compatible with the spectrum prescribed by the code for rock within the range of periods [0, 0.5 s] given the very low fundamental period of the bridge. Figure 7 reports the elastic acceleration spectra of the signals adopted along with the code spectrum, derived in the hypotheses of supported structure of class III and nominal life equal to 100 years, for

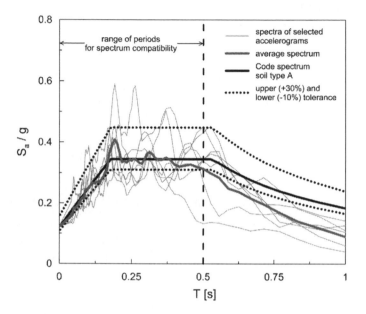

Figure 7. Selection of rock signals for SSR analyses.

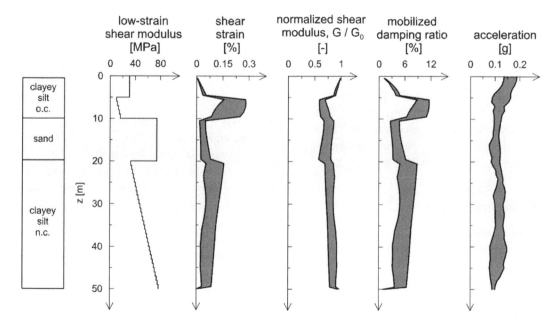

Figure 8. Results of SSR analyses: bounds of mobilized strain, shear modulus, damping ratio and acceleration with depth.

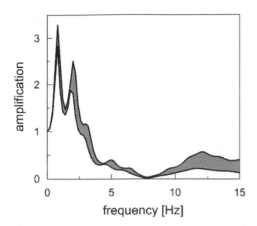

Figure 9. Results of SSR analyses: bounds of amplification function from outcrop to the foundation level.

the life safety limit state.

Results of SSR analyses are shown in Figure 8, in terms of upper and lower bounds of mobilized strain, shear modulus, damping ratio and acceleration with depth. Figure 9 depicts the bounds of the amplification function, from outcrop

to the foundation level ($z = 4$m), which varies with the specific accelerogram due to the different mobilized stiffness.

Acceleration spectra at foundation level are reported in Figure 10, together with the spectrum prescribed by NTC for subsoil type D. Note that while maximum acceleration (i.e. spectral acceleration at $T = 0$) at foundation level is about 15% larger than the rock acceleration according to SSR analyses, Codes impose larger magnification "soil factor" of 1.8 to take into account site amplification. At the fundamental period of the bridge, estimated as $T = 0.1$s, the average elastic spectral acceleration is about 0.15g. This value has been reduced of a behavior factor of 1.5 to take into account material over-strength. The design horizontal force H acting upon the piled raft has been thereby assumed as 10% of the total weight.

4.3   Piled Raft Lateral Capacity

The capacity of a single pile under lateral load is derived for free-head conditions starting from

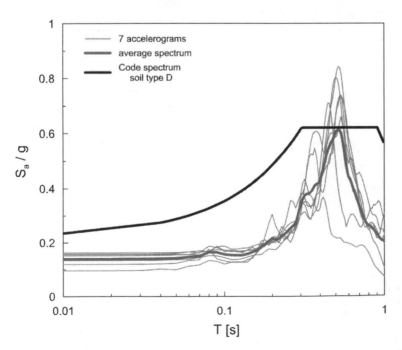

Figure 10. Elastic acceleration spectra at foundation level for structural damping ratio equal to 5%.

the load test reported in Mandolini and Viggiani (1992). By calibrating Broms' method to match the experimental results, it is possible to derive the lateral capacity of piles for different pile group layout, taking into account the increment in undrained shear strength due to the increment in vertical effective stress after consolidation due to the raft load, which increases with decreasing piles' number. To extrapolate such value to the capacity of the whole group ($H_{lim,g}$), a value of efficiency η_h, function of the average spacing of piles, has been multiplied to the sum of individual capacity of piles:

$$H_{lim,g} = \eta_h \cdot n \cdot H_{lim,s} \qquad (8)$$

More specifically, efficiency factor has been assumed equal to 0.5 when average spacing is 3 pile diameters (original configuration) and 1 for spacings larger than 5 pile diameters. A linear interpolation has been adopted for s/d values falling in between the above bounds.

Raft capacity, Hlim,r, has been simply estimated considering the undrained shear strength accounting for raft vertical load and multiplying such value by the raft area. This way, the passive

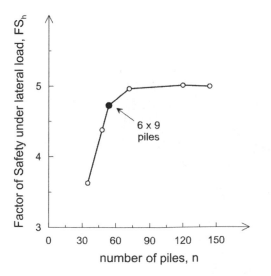

Figure 11. Factor of Safety under lateral loads for different number of piles.

resistance at raft sides has been conservatively neglected.

4.4 Safety Factor Under Seismic Actions

The simple assumption described above allow to define a safety factor FS_h against lateral loads as the ratio between capacity and demand:

$$FS_h = \frac{H_{lim,g} + H_{lim,r}}{H} \qquad (9)$$

Values of FS_h are depicted in Figure 11 as function of the number of piles. It can be noticed that a decrease in piles number from the original 144 will not produce a decrease in the safety factor. This should not come in surprise, as a decrease in piles' number will lead to a higher load transmitted directly from the raft to the ground and, therefore, to higher undrained shear strength. For $n < 72$ the effect of the decrement in number of piles will prevail over the increment in soil strength, resulting in a lower safety factor. However, it can be noticed that all the configurations examined possess adequate safety margins against lateral loads coming from seismic action.

It is worth highlighting that the whole foundation design should include structural considerations about internal forces along piles, coming from both kinematic loads, that is the distress arising from the deformations of the surrounding soil due to propagation of seismic waves (see for example Anoyatis et al. 2013 and Di Laora and Rovithis 2015) and inertial loads, i.e. the forces coming from the structure considered here for the geotechnical design. However, such topic lies beyond the scope of this work.

5. CONCLUSIONS

Scope of this contribution was to furnish an example demonstrating how the 'piled raft' concept may be very helpful in design, leading to substantial savings in the foundation cost while providing valuable insight into the actual behaviour of the foundation system. To this aim, a method recently proposed by the writers was applied to the case history of the main pier of the bridge over the river Garigliano, in South Italy. After having validated the method on the actual configuration by comparison with available experimental data, the same procedure was applied considering a progressively decreasing number of piles underneath the raft. A satisfactory performance was obtained for a layout of 6 × 9 piles (54 piles, that is one third of the original 144 piles) under vertical loads. To account for seismic loads, a ground response analysis was also performed to obtain design seismic actions. In the configuration optimized for vertical loads, the piled raft still possess an adequate safety factor against seismic loads.

REFERENCES

Anoyatis, G., Di Laora, R., Mandolini, A. and Mylonakis, G. (2013). Kinematic response of single piles for different boundary conditions: analytical solutions and normalization schemes. *Soil Dynamics and Earthquake Engineering*, 44, pp 183-195.

Bardet, J. P., Ichii, K. and Lin, C. H. (2000). EERA: a computer program for equivalent-linear earthquake site response analyses of layered soil deposits. *University of Southern California, Department of Civil Engineering*.

Butterfield, R. and Douglas, R. A. (1981). Flexibility coefficients for the design of piles and pile groups. *Construction Industry Research and Information Association*, Technical Note, 108.

Clancy, P. and Randolph, M. F. (1993). An approximate analysis procedure for piled raft foundations. *International Journal for Numerical and Analytical Methods in Geomechanics*, 17(12), pp 849-869.

De Mello, V. F. B. (1969). Foundations of buildings on clay. State of the Art Report, *Proc. VII Int. Conf. Soil Mech. Found. Eng.*, Mexico City, Vol. 1, pp 49-136.

Di Laora, R. and Rovithis, E. (2015). Kinematic Bending of Fixed-Head Piles in Nonhomogeneous Soil. *Journal of Geotechnical and Geoenvironmental Engineering*, 141(4), 04014126.

Eurocode 8 (CEN, 2003).

Idriss, I. M. (1990). Response of soft soil sites during earthquakes. *Proc. H. Bolton Seed Memorial Symposium* , Univ. of California, Berkeley, May, Vol. 2, No. 4.

Iervolino, I., Galasso, C. and Cosenza, E. (2010). REXEL: computer aided record selection for code-based seismic structural analysis. *Bulletin of Earthquake Engineering*, 8(2), pp 339-362.

Mandolini, A. (2003). Design of piled rafts foundations: practice and development. *Proc. 4th Int, Geotechnical Seminar on Deep Foundations on Bored and Auger Piles,* Millpress, Rotterdam, pp 59-80.

Mandolini, A., Di Laora, R. and Iodice, C. (2017). Simple approach to static and seismic design of piled rafts. *Accepted for the Third Bolivian International Conference on Deep Foundation.*

Mandolini, A., Russo, G. and Viggiani, C. (2005). Pile foundations: experimental investigations, analysis and design. *State of the Art Report at XVI ICSMFE*, Osaka, Japan, September 12-16. Vol. 1, pp 177-213.

Mandolini, A. and Viggiani, C. (1992). Terreni ed opere di fondazione di un viadotto sul fiume Garigliano. *Rivista Italiana di Geotecnica*, 26(2), pp 95-113.

Mayne, P. W. and Poulos, H. G. (1999). Approximate displacement influence factors for elastic shallow foundations. *Journal of Geotechnical and Geoenvironmental Engineering*, 125(6), pp 453-460.

NTC08, I. C. (2008). Norme tecniche per le costruzioni in zone sismiche. *Ministerial Decree DM*, 14(08), 9-04.

Poulos, H.G. (2000). Practical design procedures for piled raft foundations. *"Design applications of raft foundations", Hemsley J.A. ed., Thomas Telford*, pp 425-467.

Poulos, H.G., Carter, J.P. and Small, J.C. (2001). Foundations and retaining structures – Research and practice. *Proc. XV Int. Conf. Soil Mechanics and Foundation Engineering*, Istanbul, Vol. 4, pp 2527-2606.

Poulos, H.G. and Davis, E.H., *Pile Foundations Analysis and Design*. Wiley, New York, 1980.

Randolph, M.F. (1994). Design methods for pile groups and piled rafts. *State of the Art Report, XIII ICSMFE*, New Delhi, January 5-10, Vol. 5, pp 61-82.

Randolph, M.F. and Wroth, C.P. (1978). Analysis of vertical deformation of vertically loaded piles. *Journal of Geotechnical and Geoenviromental Engineering Div. ASCE*, 104(12), pp 1465-1488.

Russo, G. and Viggiani, C. (1998). Factors controlling soil-structure interaction for piled rafts. *Proc. Int. Conf. on Soil-Structure Interaction in Urban Civil Engineering*, Darmstadt, pp 297-322.

Schnaid F., Lehane B.N. and Fahey M. (2004). In situ test Characterization of unusual geomaterials. *Proc. 2nd Int. Conf. on Site Charact.*, Milpress, Porto, Vol. 1, pp 49-74.

Seed, H. B. and Idriss, I. M. (1970). Moduli and damping factors for dynamic response analysis. *Report No. EERC 70*, 10.

Seed, H. B. and Sun, J. I. (1989). Implications of Site Effects in the Mexico City Earthquake of September 19, 1985 for Earthquake-resistant Design Criteria in the San Francisco Bay Area of California. *Earthquake Engineering Research Center Report UCB/EERC-89-03*, 124p.

Viggiani, C., Mandolini, A. and Russo, G., *Piles and pile foundations*, CRC Press, 2012.

CHAPTER 2

PRACTICES OF PILE FOUNDATION DESIGN IN JAPAN, AND DEMONSTRATIVE ANALYSES OF PILED RAFTS COMPARED WITH PILE GROUPS

Tatsunori Matsumoto*

Graduate School of Science & Technology, Kanazawa University, Kanazawa, Japan
*matsumoto@se.kanazawa-u.ac.jp

Junji Hamada

Research & Development Institute, Takenaka Corporation, Chiba, Japan, hamada.junji@takenaka.co.jp

Mayumi Kawamori, Atsushi Morikage

Nihonkai Consultant Corp., Kanazawa, Japan, m-kawamori@nihonkai.co.jp, a-morikage@nihonkai.co.jp

ABSTRACT: This article, first, introduces four major design codes in Japan for seismic design of pile foundations for buildings, highway bridges, port and harbour structures, and railway structures. Only codes for building foundation explicitly describe the design of piled raft foundations, whereas the other codes still employ the conventional design method of pile group. Secondary, simple elastic FEM analyses of piled raft foundations subjected to vertical loading or horizontal loading or overturning moment loading are presented to demonstrate advantages of pile rafts over pile groups especially in cases of horizontal loading and overturning moment loading

1. INTRODUCTION

1.1 Brief review of history of application and research of piled rafts in Japan

Piled raft foundations have been used for building foundations since 1980s in Japan by Takenaka Corporation (Kakurai 1987, Kakurai et al. 1987, Tanaka et al. 1987, Yamashita and Kakurai 1991, Yamashita et al. 1994, Yamashita et al 1998, Yamada et al 2001, Kakurai 2003, Yamashita et al 2011a, Yamashita et al 2011b, Yamashita et al 2012, Yamashita et al 2016,). In most these applications of piled raft foundations, piles were bell-bottomed type and were designed as primarily end-bearing piles. Two cases of piled rafts using reverse (top-down) construction method were included in the above cases. Detail field observations including

settlements and load transfer to piles were carried in these cases (Kakurai 2003). Several general contractors started to use piled rafts from the end of the 1990s (for examples, Majima & Nagao 2000, Sonoda et al. 2009).

One of issues in design of a piled raft in Japan is estimation of behaviours of the piled raft subjected to horizontal external force and/or an earthquake. With an aim to investigate behaviours of pile raft models, Horikoshi et al. (2003a, 2003b) conducted a series of static and dynamic centrifuge model tests for piled raft foundation models in dry sand at a centrifugal field of 50g. An influence of the rigidity of the pile head connection on the horizontal behaviour of the foundation was investigated by designing two model piled rafts with two different pile head connections, i.e., rigidly fixed and hinged pile head connections. It was found that comparable behaviours of the piled rafts were obtained in the static and dynamic centrifuge model tests.

Matsumoto et al. (2004a, 2004b, 2005) carried out static horizontal load tests and shaking tests of model piled rafts in dry sand, in which rigid superstructures having the same mass but different heights of gravity centre were placed on the model raft. The results of their experiments showed that the height of gravity centre of the superstructure affects greatly the behaviour of the whole structure consisted of the superstructure and the piled raft during shaking.

Matsumoto et al. (2010) carried out a series of experimental and analytical studies on the behaviour of model piled rafts in dry sand subjected to static vertical load and static horizontal load, in order to investigate the influence of various pile head connection conditions on the behaviours of model pile groups and model piled rafts. Four different pile head connection conditions were modelled and denoted as 'rigid', 'semi-rigid', 'semi-hinged' and 'hinged'.

Unsever et al. (2014, 2015) carried out cyclic horizontal load tests of a model piled raft and a model pile group in a dry sand ground. Unsever et al. (2015) simulated the experiments using FEM. The experimental and analytical results showed advantages of the pile raft over the pile group in reducing settlement and inclination as well as horizontal displacement of the model foundations.

Vu et al. (2016) and Vu et al. (2017) carried out a series of cyclic horizontal load tests of 3-pile and 6-pile foundation models (piled raft and pile group) having batter piles or vertical piles alone in a dry sand ground. They also simulated the experiments well using FEM. Both the experimental and analytical results showed that (a) The pile foundations including pile groups and piled rafts with batter piles have considerably higher resistance and stiffness than the corresponding foundations with only vertical piles, in both vertical and horizontal directions. The results also obviously indicate that the piled rafts have much higher resistance and stiffness than the corresponding pile groups, in both vertical and horizontal directions; (b) Settlements of the foundations are effectively reduced by the inclusion of batter piles, particularly in the case of pile groups; (c) Larger axial forces and larger bending moments generated in the batter piles in the case of the batter pile group 3BPG compared with those in the corresponding vertical piles in the case of the pile group 3PG enhance the vertical resistance of the batter pile group 3BPG. The axial forces play the main role in the increase in vertical resistance at small normalised settlements. Meanwhile, bending moments play the main role in the increase in vertical resistance at large normalised settlements and contribute to the preserving behaviour of 3BPG.

Unsever et al (2015) carried out a series of shaking tests of a piled raft model and a pile group model in a model ground of dry sand, and showed that horizontal displacement, inclination and settlement of the piled raft model are largely suppressed, compared with those of the pile group model. Unsever et al (2016) extended their experiments and carried out a series of shaking tests of the piled raft model and the pile group model in a saturated sand ground, in which pore water pressures in the model ground were successfully measured. Advantages of the piled raft over the pile group were observed again even in the case of saturated ground. It was also shown that the load transferred to the ground from the raft base suppresses the occurrence of liquefaction of the ground beneath the foundation, and that the proportions of vertical load supported by the raft and the piles are not changed so much after the shaking.

It should be noted that the model piles used in the above-mentioned experimental studies were not end-bearing piles but friction piles.

Long-term field measurements of behaviour of piled raft foundations of buildings have been conducted by Takenaka Corporation since the 1990s. Behaviours of a piled raft foundation of a building during a huge earthquake were first measured during Kobe (Hanshin-Awaji) earthquake in 1995 (Yamada et al, 2001). Thereafter, piled raft foundations of several buildings have been monitored, and behaviours of the foundations during earthquakes including middle to huge size earthquakes (Yamashita et al, 2011a, 2011b, 2012, 2016). It is noticed that the piles of the foundations were designed as end-bearing bell-bottomed piles supported by hard bearing soil layers. In these field measurements, settlements of the raft, axial forces of some piles, earth pressures and pore water pressures beneath attribute areas of the raft are monitored. Hamada et al (2014, 2015) simulated the measured seismic responses of the piled raft foundations. The field monitoring and the numerical simulations showed that the average and/ or differential settlements during and after huge earthquakes are small, giving negligible damages (influences) on superstructures (buildings). It was also shown that the proportions of the vertical load supported by the raft (effective earth pressure and pore water pressure at the raft base) and the piles were not changed so much even after huge earthquakes, showing the pile raft foundations are stable and safe against huge earthquakes. From the field measurements, the raft supports from 30 to 60% of the vertical load of the building.

Owing to a relatively large number of the applications of pile raft design to building foundations, design concept of piled raft foundation has been implemented in Recommendations for Design of Building Foundations (Architectural Institute of Japan, 2001), and in Technical Standard Guideline of Building Structure (Editorial Committee for Technical Standard Guideline of Building Structure 2007).

For pile foundations of other structures such as bridges, port and harbour facilities and railway structures, piled raft design has not been employed so far and piled raft design concept has not been implemented in the corresponding codes.

1.2 Constitution of the present paper

In Section 2, standards or codes for design of pile foundations in Japan are briefly presented with an emphasis placed mainly on building foundations, because piled raft design concept is implemented in only building foundation codes. Essence of Specifications for highway bridges is also introduced briefly, because pile foundations of highway bridges are designed according to the specifications.

In Section 3, demonstrative analyses of piled rafts subjected to vertical or horizontal or overturning load are presented, being compared with pile groups. Assumed configurations of foundations considered in the analyses are typical for bridge foundations, intending to advocate the piled raft design for bridge foundations. The analytical results will show advantages of pile raft over pile group even for cases of horizontal and overturning loading.

2. PRACTICES OF SEISMIC DESIGN OF PILE FOUNDATIONS IN JAPAN

2.1 Pile Foundations for Buildings

Building Standard Law of Japan (BSLJ hereafter) and Recommendations for Design of Building Foundations (Architectural Institute of Japan 2001) (Recommendations for Foundations, hereafter) are the major seismic design codes of buildings in Japan. The BSLJ prescribes the minimum legal requirements.

Design of building foundations in Japan shall follow 1) the Building Standard Law of Japan (BSLJ), 2) cabinet order and notification of BSLJ, and 3) Technical Standard Guideline of Building Structure (Editorial Committee for Technical

Standard Guideline of Building Structure 2007).

As for the piled raft design, it is clearly prescribed in Article 38 of the cabinet order of BSLJ that design of piled raft is not allowed as a general rule. Exception of the order is allowed, if the structural calculation of the piled raft foundation is performed following the structural calculation procedure appointed by the Minister of Ministry of Land, Infrastructure, Transport and Tourism (MLIT, hereafter).

The structural calculation procedure appointed by the Minister of MLIT prescribes that it shall be confirmed that detrimental damages, deformations and settlements of the building are not caused, through the examination of the bearing capacity of the foundation against the design loads (such as self-weight of the building, live load, earth pressures, pore water pressure and so on), possible settlements of the foundation and deformation of the ground. However, any substantial design approach has not been implemented in BSLJ. Design of piled rafts is carried out on the basis of each designer's experience or approach, although Recommendations for Design of Building Foundations (Recommendations for Foundations) are often referred by designers.

The current Recommendations for Design of

Building Foundations is based on the criteria for Design of Building Foundations (Criteria for Foundations, hereafter) established in 1952. The Criteria for Foundations were revised in 1960 and 1974, and were renamed as Recommendations for Design of Building Foundations in 1988 to divide the Criteria for Foundations into administrative approval issues and technical issues. The Recommendations for Foundations involve or technical issues. The current Recommendations for Foundations revised in 2001 involve the performance-based design concept and introduce design concepts of piled raft foundations.

The current Recommendations for Foundations prescribe the following design concepts:

(a) General

   i) Explanation of piled raft foundation

   ii) Required performance of piled raft is basically similar to that of raft foundation, in which bearing capacity and settlement are main required performance.

(b) Design items to be examined

   i) Items to verify required performance of piled rafts are shown in Table 1. Three

Table 1 Items corresponding to required performance levels

Performance level (Limit state)	Verification items		
	Effects on super structure	Foundation members*	Ground
Ultimate limit state	(Deformation angle and inclination of foundations)	Stress of each foundation body and displacement	Vertical bearing capacity (Sliding resistance) (Settlement) Liquefaction
Reparability limit state	Deformation angle and inclination of foundations	Stress of each foundation body	Vertical bearing capacity Sliding resistance Settlement Liquefaction
Serviceability limit state	Deformation angle and inclination of foundations	Stress of each foundation body and crack width	Settlement Sliding resistance

Note: * foundation beam, foundation slab, pile top connection, pile body, pile joints
        Items shown inside brackets () should be verified as necessary.

performance levels such as ultimate limit state, reparability limit state and serviceability limit sate are defined based on the effects on superstructure, foundation members and ground.

(c) Methods to confirm the required performance

i) To verify the required performance, loads carried by the raft are firstly designed based on building loads and ground conditions. Then the loads carried by piles are designed. Pile properties, number of piles and pile allocation are designed based on the load carried by the piles.

ii) A piled raft foundation is appropriately modelled, and design responses related to required items under each loading condition are confirmed so that these are below the design limit value. It should be noted that an appropriate evaluation of ground properties is important in calculating design responses.

iii) For the seismic design of piled raft foundations, the seismic design of the raft should be referred.

As mentioned in the above, specific design approach for piled rafts has not been described in the Recommendations for Foundations, although only the design concept is presented. Hence, only limited designers and organizations which have field data, experiences of model tests and designs can design piled raft foundations in Japan.

When a building is planned to be constructed, the construction shall be approved by the examiner of building division of each local government. In the approval procedure, the design of the building is examined whether it matches with legal demands or not. In some cases, the structural design is approved by an evaluation committee which members consist of foundation engineers. As for piled rafts, the same procedure is required for approval.

2.2 Pile Foundations for Highway Bridges

Design of the pile foundation of a highway bridge follows Specifications for highway bridges, Part IV: Substructures (Japan Road Association, 2015). Performance-based design concept has been implemented in the Specifications.

(a) Required performance for a bridge foundation

Bridges are classified into important bridge (Type B) and usual bridge (Type A), according to number of traffics per day, importance in disaster prevention, influence of other facilities and so on. Design earthquake level is classified into two levels, Level I and Level II. Level I earthquake is expected to occur multiple times during the life time of a bridge. Level II earthquake includes offshore/subduction plate triggered quake and in-land/active faulting triggered quake having high seismic levels. Table 2 shows the performance matrix for a bridge, considering design earthquake level and bridge type (importance).

Table 2 Performance matrix for a bridge

Design earthquake		Bridge type	
		Type A (normal)	Type B (important)
Level I		Serviceability shall be secured. (Requirement No. 1)	
Level II	Type I: offshore/subduction plate triggered quake	No fatal damage shall be caused.(Requirement No. 2)	Damages shall be limited so that restoration of the bridge can be done quickly. (Requirement No. 3)
	Type II in-land/active faulting triggered quake		

(b) Analytical model

In case of Level I (usual) earthquake, seismic loads induced by an earthquake are converted to static equivalent loads, vertical load V_0, horizontal load H0 and overturning moment load M_0, acting on the raft (footing), as shown in Figure 1. FEM or beam-spring model may be used for modelling the foundation and the ground. It should be noted that even if the raft (footing) is embedded in the ground, the ground surface is assumed to exit below the raft base, as shown in Figure 1. In other words, the soil resistance acting directly on the raft, such as supporting resistance and shear resistance at the raft base, lateral earth pressure or shear resistance of the raft side walls, is completely ignored in the design, so that all the external loads are resistance by the piles alone.

In case of Level II (huge) earthquake, push-over type of analysis is conducted using a foundation model shown in Figure 2. Piles are modelled by beam elements, and the ground is expressed as horizontal soil springs having stiffness, k_{HE},

connected to the pile nodes. When the raft (footing) is embedded in the ground, horizontal earth pressure acting on the side wall of the raft may be considered. However, the friction resistance and vertical resistance at the raft base are not taken into account in design. An extreme and unrealistic assumption is used for the analytical model. That is, piles are assumed to be perfect end-bearing piles sat on very hard soil layer with negligible pile tip settlement. In other words, the pile head settlement is equal to compression of the pile body. Hence, the pile head stiffness, K_{VE}, is expressed as $K_{VE} = (E_p A_p)/L_p$ where E_p, A_p and L_p are Young's modulus, cross-sectional area and length of the pile. Vertical soil springs along the pile shaft are not considered, since the pile is a perfect end-bearing pile.

The horizontal soil spring stiffness, kHE, is usually estimated using SPT-N value through empirical equations in which several empirical parameters are contained. Interaction between the soil springs are not appropriately considered, but kHE is empirically adjusted to take into account "group efficiency" on empirical basis. The authors'

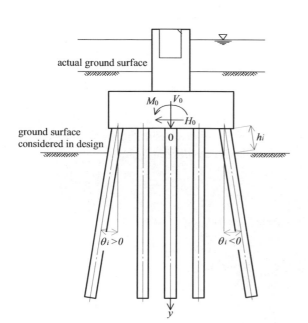

Fig. 1 Foundation model used for Level I earthquake

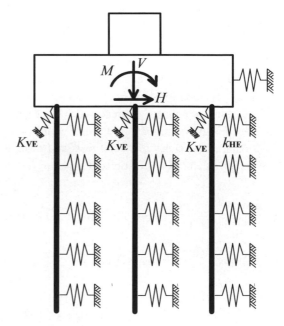

Fig. 2 Foundation model used for Level II earthquake

opinion, the analytical model in Figure 2 is only a very crude modelling.

3. DEMONSTRATIVE ANALYSES OF PILED RAFTS COMPARED WITH PILE GROUPS

3.1 Objective of Analyses

As mentioned earlier in this paper, application of a piled raft foundation to bridge foundations is not allowed in Japan at present. In order to improve the current design situation, it seems to be useful to show simple analyses of piled rafts compared with conventional pile groups, which

demonstrates several advantages of the piled rafts over the pile groups under various quasi-static loading conditions such as vertical or horizontal or overturning loading.

3.2 Analytical Methods

Figure 3 show the configurations of pile foundations considered (assumed) in these particular analyses. A rectangular concrete raft, 10 m width, 6 m depth and 2 m thickness, is supported by 6 concrete piles having a diameter, D, of 1 m. Centre-to-centre pile spacing ratio, s/D, is 4. Pile length, L_p, was varied from 2 m to 30 m in the analyses.

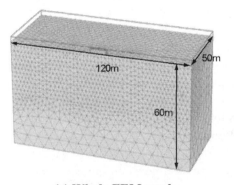

(a) Whole FEM mesh

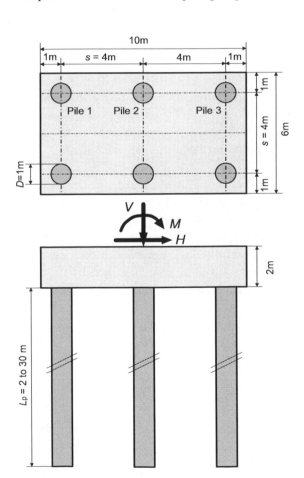

Fig. 3 Pile foundation models considered in the analyses

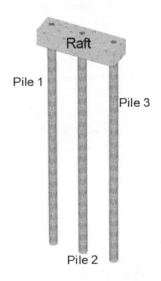

(b) Example of FEM mesh of foundation with $L = 30$m

Fig. 4 FEM mesh for the ground and foundation

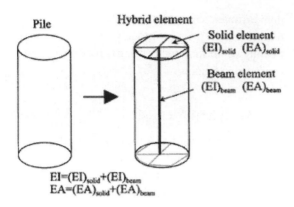

$$EI=(EI)_{solid}+(EI)_{beam}$$
$$EA=(EA)_{solid}+(EA)_{beam}$$

Fig. 5 Mechanism of the hybrid model (after Kimura and Zhang, 2000)

The FEM analyses were carried out using a software, PLAXIS 3D developed by Plaxis BV Netherlands (2013). Figure 4(a) shows the whole FEM mesh of the ground and a foundation, and Figure 4(b) shows an example of FEM mesh for a foundation with piles having L_p = 30 m. A half of the ground and the foundation was modelled due to symmetric conditions of the foundations and applied load. Vertical displacements at the bottom boundary were fixed. And, horizontal displacements perpendicular to the side wall boundaries were fixed. In cases of analyses of pile groups, a gap of 0.05 m between the raft base and the ground surface was considered.

All of the ground, the raft and the piles were considered as linear elastic materials. Young's modulus of the ground, E_s, was estimated using an empirical equation, E_s = 2800N (kPa) where N is SPT blow count, which is prescribed in Specifications for Highway Bridges (Japan Road

Association, 2015). The concrete raft and the concrete piles were assumed in the analyses. Mechanical properties of the ground, the raft and the piles are listed in Table 3. No interface elements were assigned along the pile shaft, which means that occurrence of the pile shaft slippage was not taken into account in the analyses.

In order to model the pile, a hybrid model in which beam element surrounded by solid elements is used, according to Kimura and Zhang (2000). Figure 5 shows the mechanism of the hybrid model. In the hybrid model of this paper, beam element carries a large proportion (90%) of the axial stiffness, EA, and bending stiffness, EI of the pile. The properties of the model pile, the beam pile and the solid pile are summarised in Table 4.

Analyses of three quasi-static loading types, such as vertical or horizontal or overturning moment loading (VL or HL or ML in short), were conducted separately. In each type of the analyses, vertical load V = 1000 kN or horizontal load H = 1000 kN or overturning moment M = 1000 kN m was applied on the raft, as shown in Figure 3.

The authors are fully aware that soils exhibit non-linear responses and elastic-plastic responses except for very small strain level. The authors are aware also that pile-soil-raft interactions depend on pile-soil interface behaviour of the pile shaft, configuration of pile foundation structure and stress-strain relations of soils. These aspects have been investigated by Russo & Viggiani (1998), Reul (2004), Mandolini et al (2005), Unsever et al (2015), Vu et al (2016), and so on.

Table 3 Mechanical properties (elastic modulus) of the ground, the raft and the piles

	SPT N-value	Young's modulus(kPa)	Poisson's ratio
Ground	20	$E_s = 5.6 \times 10^4$	$v_s = 0.30$
Raft and piles	—	$E = 2.8 \times 10^7$	$v = 0.17$

Table 4 Properties of the model pile, beam pile element and solid pile element

Property	Actual pile	Beam pile	Solid pile
Young's modulus (kPa)	2.8×10^7	2.52×10^7	2.8×10^6

However, simple analytical conditions mentioned earlier are intentionally employed in this particular paper, intending to show advantages of piled rafts over pile groups for small strain conditions where soil could be modelled as a liner-elastic material.

3.3 Analytical Results

3.3.1 Vertical loading (VL)

Figure 6 shows vertical displacement (settlement) of the raft w vs. pile length L_p in vertical loading (VL). The case of PR with $L_P = 0$ means the raft alone foundation. It is seen that w of the piled raft (PR) is smaller than that of the pile group (PG). However, this difference becomes minor for $L_p > 10$ m. The settlement of the foundation is effectively reduced in PR compared with PG for $L_p \leq 10$ m.

Figure 7 shows the proportion of vertical load supported by the piles vs. L_p. The load proportion by the piles rapidly increases with L_p until L_p increases to 10 m. However, for $L_p > 10$ m, further increase of L_p is not so efficient to increase the proportion of the vertical load supported by the piles.

Figure 8 shows the distributions of axial forces

in Piles 1 and 3 (corner piles) in cases of PR and PG with $L_p = 10$ and 30 m. If there is no raft resistance, the pile head load is 166.7 kN (=1000/6 kN) in average. Let us see the results for $L_p = 10$ m. The pile head load of Pile 1 in case of PG is 180.6

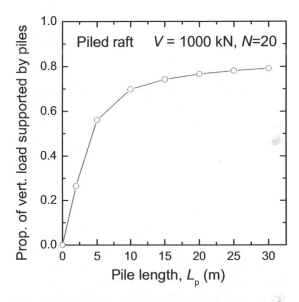

Fig. 7 Proportion of vertical load supported by piles vs. pile length L_p in VL

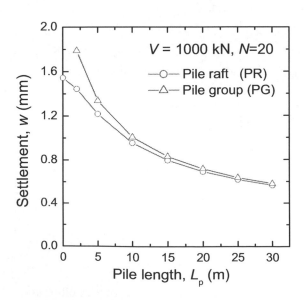

Fig. 6 Settlement w vs. pile length L_p in VL

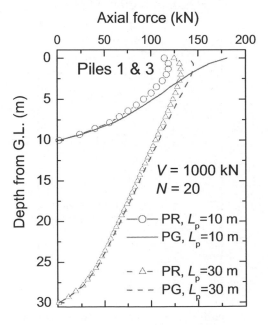

Fig. 8 Axial force distributions of Pile 1 (corner pile) in cases of pile length $L_p = 10$ and 30m in VL

kN that is larger than the average values of 166.7 kN. The pile head load of Pile 2 (centre pile) is 138.8 kN, although the result is not indicated in the figure. The difference between the pile head loads of Pile 1 (Pile 3) and Pile 2 clearly indicates that the interaction between the piles, in other words group effect, cannot be neglected even if $s/D \geq 4$. The pile head load of Pile 1 in case of PR is about 120 kN that is about 2/3 of that in case of PG.

It is also seen from Figure 8 that effect of the raft for reducing the pile axial force becomes less as the pile length becomes large ($L_p = 30$ m). Furthermore, it is seen that axial force transferred to the pile tip, that is the pile tip resistance, is very small in all 4 cases.

Figure 9 shows the distributions of bending moments in Pile 1 (corner pile) in cases of PR and PG with $L_p = 10$ and 30 m. Maximum bending moment is generated at the pile head in all cases. In both cases of $L_p = 10$ and 30 m, magnitudes of bending moments of the pile in PR are smaller

than those in PG. If we compare the results of each foundation type having $L_p = 10$ and 30 m, smaller magnitudes of the bending moments are generated in the pile having $L_p = 30$ m. It is interesting to note that the bending moments are almost zero for the pile section deeper than 10 m.

3.3.2 Horizontal loading (HL)

Figure 10 shows horizontal displacement of the raft u vs. pile length L_p in horizontal loading (HL). The case of PR with $L_p = 0$ means the raft alone foundation. It is clearly seen that the horizontal displacement of the foundation is considerably reduced by the existence of the raft base resistance. For an example, u of PR with $L_p = 3$ m is comparable to that of PG with $L_p = 30$ m. The horizontal displacement, u, of PG with $L_p = 0$ is infinity, whereas u of the raft alone (PR with $L_p = 0$) has a finite value.

In Figure 10, the analytical results according to Specifications for highway bridges, Part IV: Substructures (Japan Road Association, 2015) also are shown. The JRA approach gives considerably small displacements, due to the unrealistic assumptions which were mentioned earlier.

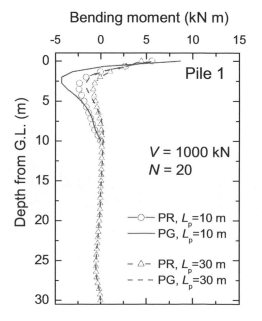

Fig. 9 Bending moment distributions of Pile 1 (corner pile) in cases of pile length $L_p = 10$ and 30m in VL

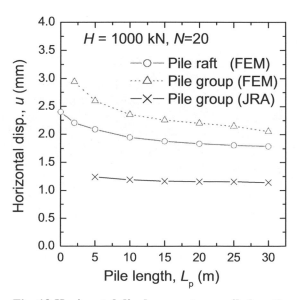

Fig. 10 Horizontal displacement u vs pile length L_p in HL

Figure 11 shows the proportion of horizontal load supported by the piles in the piled raft vs. L_p. The load proportion by the piles rapidly increases with L_p until L_p increases to 3 m. However, for $L_p > 5$ m, further increase of L_p is not so efficient to increase proportion of the horizontal load supported by the piles. Only about 20% of the horizontal load is supported by the piles even if L_p becomes very large.

Figure 12 shows the inclination of raft vs pile length L_p. Inclination of the raft in case of PR is smaller than that in case of PG for any L_p. This is more evident for PR and PG with shorter $L_P < 15$ m. That is, inclusion of shorter piles in a raft effectively suppresses the inclination (rocking) of the foundation.

Figure 13 shows the distributions of bending moments in Piles 1 and 3 (corner pile) and Pile 2 (centre pile) in cases of PR and PG with $L_p = 10$ and 30 m. Maximum bending moment is generated at the pile head in all cases. In both cases of $L_p = 10$ and 30 m, magnitudes of bending moments of the pile in PR are smaller than those in PG. If we compare the results of each foundation type having

$L_p = 10$ and 30 m, smaller magnitudes of the bending moments are generated in the pile having $L_p = 30$ m. The magnitudes of bending moments in Pile 2 are smaller than those in Piles 1 and 3, due to interaction between the piles and the raft through the elastic ground assumed in the analyses.

Figure 14 shows the distributions of shear forces in Piles 1 and 3 (corner pile) and Pile 2 (centre pile) in cases of PR and PG with $L_p = 10$ and 30 m. Similar to the bending moments, shear forces of the piles in PR are reduced compared with those in PG, and magnitudes of shear forces of Pile 2 are smaller than those of Piles 1 and 3 due to the interaction effects.

Figure 15 shows the distributions of axial forces in Pile 1 (rear corner pile) in cases of PR and PG with $L_p = 10$ and 30 m. Compression force is taken as positive. Although the results are not graphically indicated, compression axial forces having the same magnitudes of Figure 15 are generated in Pile 3 (front corner pile). Axial forces are not caused in Pile 2 (centre pile).

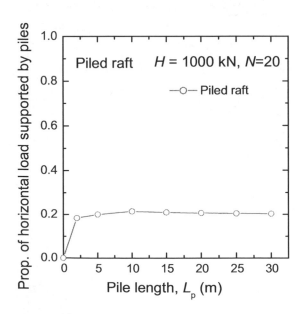

Fig. 11 Proportion of horizontal load carried by piles vs. pile length L_p in HL

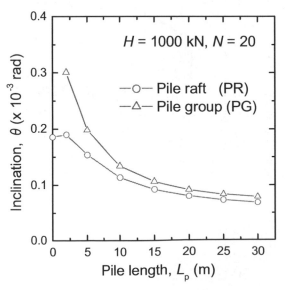

Fig. 12 Inclination of raft vs. pile length L_p in HL

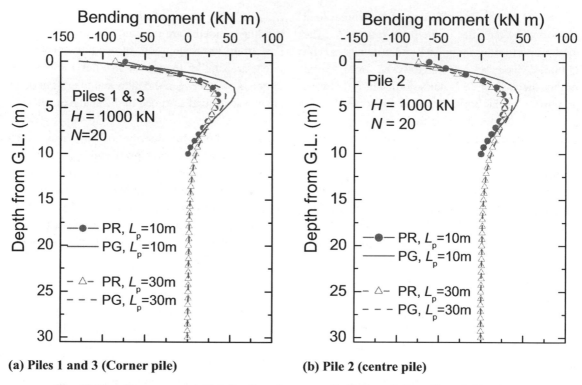

(a) Piles 1 and 3 (Corner pile)   **(b) Pile 2 (centre pile)**

Fig. 13 Bending moment distributions in cases of pile length L_p = 10 and 30m in HL

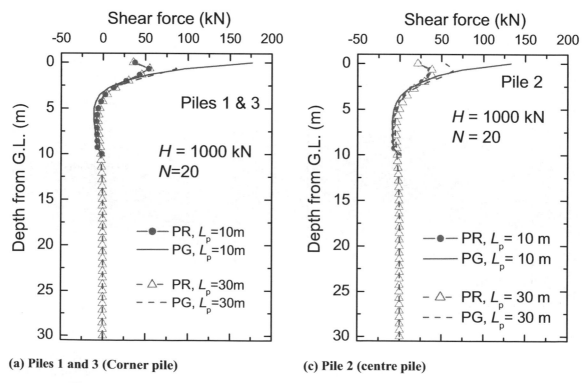

(a) Piles 1 and 3 (Corner pile)   **(c) Pile 2 (centre pile)**

Fig. 14 Shear force distributions in cases of pile length L_p = 10 and 30m in HL

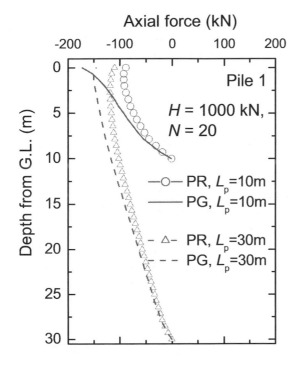

Fig. 15 Axial force distributions of Pile 1 (corner pile) in cases of pile length L_p = 10 and 30m in HL

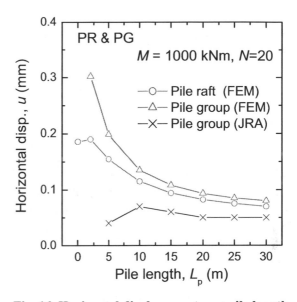

Fig. 16 Horizontal displacement u vs pile length L_p in ML

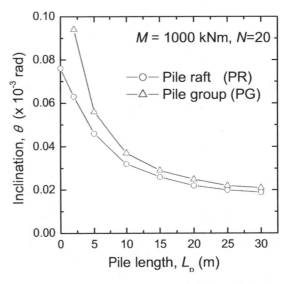

Fig. 17 Inclination of raft vs. pile length L_p in ML

It is seen from Figure 15 that magnitudes of axial forces are smaller in PR compared with PG. This aspect is more evident for shorter pile length.

3.3.3 Overturning moment loading (ML)

Figure 16 shows horizontal displacement of the raft u vs. pile length L_p in overturning moment loading (ML). The horizontal displacement, u, of the piled raft (PR) is smaller than that of the pile group (PG) for any L_p. This aspect is pronounced for L_p < 15 m.

The results calculated using the JRA approach (Fig. 2) are indicated also in Figure 16. The JRA approach gives extremely small horizontal displacements again as mentioned in 3.3.2, due to the unrealistic assumptions which were mentioned earlier.

Figure 17 shows the inclination of raft vs pile length L_p in case of overturning moment loading (ML). Inclination of the raft in case of PR is smaller than that in case of PG for any L_p. This is more evident for PR and PG with shorter L_P < 15 m. That is, inclusion of shorter piles in a raft effectively suppresses the inclination (rocking) of the foundation against also overturning moment loading.

Figure 18 shows the distributions of bending moments in Piles 1 and 3 (corner pile) and Pile 2 (centre pile) in cases of PR and PG having L_p = 10 and 30 m. Maximum bending moment is generated at the pile head in all cases. In both cases of L_p = 10 and 30 m, magnitudes of bending moments of the pile in PR are smaller than those in PG. If we compare the results of each foundation type having L_p = 10 and 30 m, smaller magnitudes of the bending moments are generated in the pile having L_p = 30 m. It should be noticed that bending moments are almost zero for the pile section deeper than 10 m in all the cases.

Figure 19 shows the distributions of shear forces in Piles 1 and 3 (corner pile) and Pile 2 (centre pile) in cases of PR and PG with L_p = 10 and 30 m.

Similar to the bending moments, shear forces of the piles in PR are reduced compared with those in PG. If we compare the results of each foundation type having L_p = 10 and 30 m, smaller magnitudes of the shear forces are generated in the pile having L_p = 30 m.

Figure 20 shows the distributions of axial forces in Pile 1 (rear corner pile) in cases of PR and PG with L_p = 10 and 30 m. Although the results are not graphically indicated, compression axial forces having the same magnitudes of Figure 20 are generated in Pile 3 (front corner pile). Axial forces are not caused in Pile 2 (centre pile). It is seen from Figure 20 that magnitudes of axial forces are smaller in PR compared with PG. This aspect is more evident for shorter pile length.

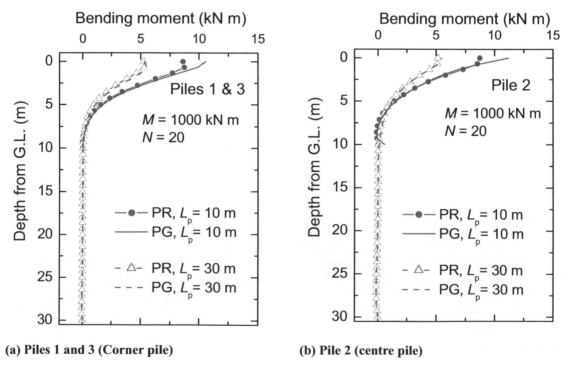

(a) Piles 1 and 3 (Corner pile)   (b) Pile 2 (centre pile)

Fig. 18 Bending moment distributions in cases of pile length L_p = 10 and 30m in ML

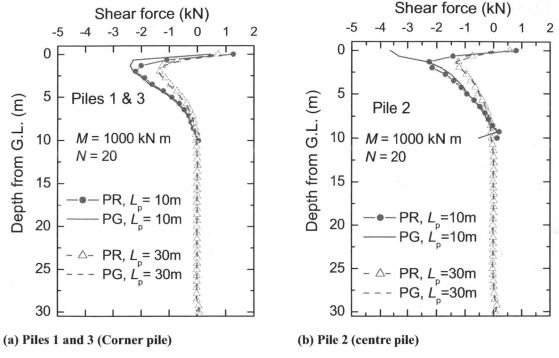

(a) Piles 1 and 3 (Corner pile)   **(b) Pile 2 (centre pile)**

Fig. 19 Shear force distributions in cases of pile length L_p = 10 and 30m in ML

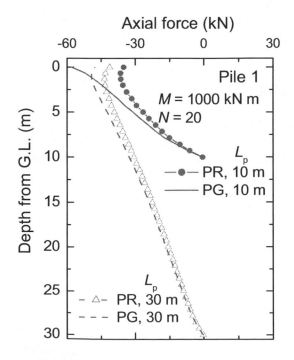

Fig. 20 Axial force distributions of Pile 1 (corner pile) in cases of pile length L_p = 10 and 30m in ML

3.3.4 Combination loading (CL)

Responses of the foundations subjected to any combination loading (CL) of vertical, horizontal and overturning moment loading are readily obtained from the analytical results mentioned above:

$$R(CL) = \alpha \cdot R(VL) + \beta \cdot R(HL) + \gamma \cdot R(ML) \qquad (1)$$

where $R(CL)$ is the response of the foundation subjected to combination loads. $R(VL)$, $R(HL)$ and $R(ML)$ are the responses subjected to vertical load (VL) alone, horizontal load (HL) alone and overturning moment load (ML) alone which were presented in 3.3.1, 3.3.2 and 3.3.3, respectively. α, β and γ are load ratios VL, HL and ML to V, H and M which were used in 3.3.1, 3.3.2 and 3.3.3, respectively.

It should be noted that Eq. (1) is valid only for the linear elastic response of the foundation subjected to combination loading.

4. CONCLUDING REMARKS

In this article, first, the history of application and research of piled rafts since the 1980s in Japan was briefly reviewed. One of things that should be mentioned specially is that long-term field observations of several piled raft foundations of actual buildings have been made. The behaviours of the piled rafts during strong earthquakes were observed. The field observations indicate that the pile rafts are safe and stable during and after the strong earthquakes.

Many experimental and numerical researches on piled rafts have been conducted in order to investigate resistance mechanisms of pile rafts subjected to vertical or horizontal or combined loading. These researches support the safety and the high stability of the piled raft foundations observed in the field.

Secondly, practices of seismic design of pile foundations in Japan were presented. Two major pile design codes, Recommendations for Design of Building Foundations and Specifications for highway bridges, Part IV: Substructures were picked up. Regardless of the above mentioned practical and academic researches, definite seismic design concept or design approach of piled rafts has not been implemented in any Japanese design standards or codes so far. It is difficult to apply piled raft design to pile foundations except building foundations.

Thirdly, demonstrative analyses of piled rafts subjected to vertical or horizontal or overturning moment loading were carried out, intending to widen the applications of piled raft foundations to bridge foundations. Analytical results were compared with the corresponding analytical results of pile groups. The analytical conditions were set simple such that foundation structure and ground were assumed to behave in linear elastic manner. Only static loads were applied to the foundation.

The useful aspects from the analyses are:

1) If relatively long piles are used in a piled raft, its behaviour is similar to that of the corresponding pile group.

2) If piles having moderate lengths are used in a piled raft, settlement, horizontal displacement and inclination of the piled raft are reasonably reduced, compared with those of the corresponding pile group.

3) If piles having moderate lengths are used in a piled raft, axial forces, bending moments and shear forces of the piles in the piled raft are reasonably reduced, compared with those of the corresponding pile group.

4) An analytical approach that can take into account the interaction between the foundation elements, raft and piles, through the ground should be employed in design.

Although the demonstrative analyses were static linear elastic analyses, the analytical results definitely indicate considerable advantages of pile rafts over pile groups during seismic loading.

REFERENCES

Architectural Institute of Japan (2001). Recommendations for Design of Building Foundations. Maruzen Print. Co., Tokyo (in Japanese).

Editorial Committee for Technical Standard Guideline of Building Structure (2007). Technical Standard Guideline of Building Structure. Government Publications Service Center (in Japanese).

Japan Road Association (2015). Specifications for highway bridges, Part IV: substructures. The Japan Road Association, Tokyo (in Japanese).

Kimura, M. and Zhang, F. (2000). Seismic evaluations of pile foundations with three different methods based on three-dimensional elasto-plastic finite element analysis. *Soil and Foundation*, Vol. 40, No. 5, pp 113-132.

Hamada, J., Shigeno, Y., Onimaru, S., Tanikawa, T., Nakamura, N. and Yamashita, K. (2014). Numerical analysis on seismic response of piled raft foundation with ground improvement based on seismic observation records, *Proc. of the 14th IACMAG*, Kyoto, Japan.

Hamada, J., Aso, N., Hanai, A. and Yamashita, K. (2015). Seismic performance of piled raft subjected to unsymmetrical earth pressure based on seismic observation records, *Proc. of the 6th Int. Conf. on Earthquake Geotechnical Engineering*, Christchurch.

Horikoshi, K., Matsumoto, T., Hashizume, Y., Watanabe, T. and Fukuyama, H. (2003a). Performance of piled raft foundations subjected to static vertical loading and horizontal loading, Int. *Journal of Physical Modelling in Geotechnics*, Vol. 3, No. 2, pp 37-50.

Horikoshi, K., Matsumoto, T., Hashizume, Y. and Watanabe, T. (2003b). Performance of piled raft foundations subjected to dynamic loading. Int. *Journal of Physical Modelling in Geotechnics*, Vol. 3, No. 2, pp 51-62.

Kakurai, M. (1987). Field measurements of load transfer in piled raft foundation. *Proc. of the 8th ARCSMFE*, Kyoto, Vol. 1, pp 327-329.

Kakurai, M., Yamashita, K. and Tomono, M. (1987). Settlement behavior of piled raft foundations on soft ground. *Proc. of the 8th ARCSMFE*, Kyoto, Vol. 1, pp 373-376.

Kakurai, M. (2003). Study on vertical load transfer of piles. *Dr. Thesis of Tokyo Institute of Technology*, 304pp. (in Japanese).

Tanaka, T., Segawa, T., Katoh, Y., Kakurai, M. and Tomono, M. (1987). A design of foundation and

the behaviour of a tall building at Kobe Port Island. *Proc. of the Int. Symp. on Geotechnical Engineering of Soft Soils*, pp 389-396.

Majima, M. and Nagao, T. (2000). Behaviour of piled raft foundation for tall building in Japan. *Design applications of raft foundations* (Hemsley, J.A., Ed.), Thomas Telford, pp 393-410.

Mandolini, A., Russo, G. and Viggiani, C. (2005). Pile foundations: experimental investigations, analysis and design. *State of the Art Report at XVI ICSMFE*, Osaka, Japan, Vol. 1: pp 177-213.

Matsumoto, T., Fukumura, K., Kitiyodom, P., Oki, A. and Horikoshi, K. (2004a). Experimental and analytical study on behaviour of model piled rafts in sand subjected to horizontal and moment loading. Int. *Journal of Physical Modelling in Geotechnics*, Vol. 4, No. 3, pp 1-19.

Matsumoto, T., Fukumura, K., Oki, A. and Horikoshi, K. (2004b). Shaking table tests on model piled rafts in sand considering influence of superstructures. Int. *Journal of Physical Modelling in Geotechnics*, Vol. 4, No. 3, pp 20-37.

Matsumoto, T., Fukumura, K. and Oki, A. (2005). Influence of superstructure on behaviour of model piled rafts in sand under Seismic Loading, *Proc. 16th ICSMFE*, Osaka, pp 2017-2021.

Matsumoto, T., Nemoto, H. Mikami, H., Yaegashi, K., Arai, T. and Kitiyodom, P. (2010). Load tests of piled raft models with different pile head connection conditions and their analyses, *Soils & Foundations*, Vol. 50, No. 1, pp. 63-81.

Plaxis BV Netherlands (2013). User Manuals, Plaxis 3D.

Reul, O. (2004). Numerical study of the bearing behaviour of piled rafts. *International Journal of Geomechanics* 4(2), pp 59-68.

Russo, G. and Viggiani, C. (1998). Factors controlling soil-structure interaction for piled rafts. Proceedings of International Conference on Soil-Structure Interaction in Urban Civil Engineering, Darmstadt, pp 297-322.

Sonoda, R., Matsumoto, T., Kitiyodom, P., Moritaka, H. and Ono, T. (2009). A case study of piled raft foundation using reverse construction method and its post-analysis, *Canadian Geotechnical Journal*, Vol. 46, pp 142-159.

Unsever, Y.S. Matsumoto, T. and Shimono, S. (2014). Static cyclic load tests on model foundations in dry sand Geotechnical Engineering. *Journal of the SEAGS & AGSSEA*, Vol. 45, No. 2, pp 40-51.

Unsever, Y.S., Matsumoto, T. and Ozkan, M. Y. (2015). Numerical analyses of load tests on model foundations in dry sand. *Computers and Geotechnics*, Vol. 63, pp 40-51.

Unsever, Y.S., Matsumoto, T. and Shimono, S. (2015). Shaking table tests of piled raft and pile group foundations in dry sand. *Proc. 6th Int. Conf. on Earthquake Geotech. Engineering* (6ICEGE), Christchurch, New Zealand, Paper No.328, 9p.

Unsever, Y.S., Matsumoto, T., $E_s$ashi, K. and Kobayashi, S. (2017). Behaviour of model pile foundations under dynamic loads in saturated sand, *Bulletin of Earthquake Engineering*, Vol. 15, pp 1355-1373, Springer, Netherlands, DOI 10.1007/s10518-016-0029-y.

Vu, A.T., Matsumoto, T., Kobayashi, S. and Nguyen, T. L. (2016). Model load tests on battered pile foundations and finite-element analysis", Int. *Journal of Physical Modelling in Geotechnics*, published online on 2016 Nov 30th, 22pp.

Vu, A.T., Masumoto, T., Ryo Yoshitani, R. and Nguyen , T.L. (2017): Behaviours of pile group and piled raft foundation models having batter piles, *Journal of Earth Engineering*, accepted for publication, 14 pages.

Yamada, T., Yamashita, K., Kakurai, M. and Tsukatani, H. (2001). Long-term behaviour of tall building on raft foundation constructed by top-down method. *Proc. of the 5th Int. Conf. on Deep Foundation Practice*, Singapore, pp 411-417.

Yamashita, K. and Kakurai, M. (1991). Settlement behavior of raft foundation with friction piles. *Proc. of the 8th Int. Deep Foundation Institute Conference*, Stresa, pp 461-466.

Yamashita, K., Kakurai, M. and Yamada, T. (1994). Investigation of a piled raft foundation on stiff clay. *Proc. of ICSMFE*, New Delhi, Vo. 3, pp 543-546.

Yamashita, K., Yamada, T. and Kakurai, M. (1998). Simplified method for analyzing piled raft foundations. *Proc. of Deep Foundations on Bored and Auger Piles*, Ghent, pp 457-464.

Yamashita, K., Yamada, T. and Hamada, J. (2011a). Investigation of settlement and load sharing on piled rafts by monitoring full-scale structures. *Soils & Foundations*, Vol . 51, No. 3, pp 513–532.

Yamashita, K., Hamada, J. and Yamada, T. (2011b). Field measurements on piled rafts with grid-form deep mixing walls on soft ground. Geotechnical Engineering *Journal of the SEAGS & AGSSEA*, Vol. 42, No. 2, pp 1-10.

Yamashita, K., Hamada, J., Onimaru, S., Higashino, M. (2012). Seismic behavior of piled raft with ground improvement supporting a base-isolated building on soft ground in Tokyo. *Soils & Foundations*, Vol. 52, No. 5, pp 1000–1015.

Yamashita, K., Hamada, J. and Tanikawa, T. (2016). Static and seismic performance of a friction piled combined with grid-form deep mixing walls in soft ground. *Soils & Foundations*, Vol. 56, No. 3, pp 559-573.

CHAPTER 3

PROPOSED 3-D ANALYTICAL METHOD FOR PILED RAFT FOUNDATIONS

Sangseom Jeong*
Hyunsung Lim

Department of Civil and Environmental Engineering, Yonsei University, Seoul, Republic of Korea
*soj9081@yonsei.ac.kr

ABSTRACT : An improved analytical method (YSPR:YonSei Piled raft) considering raft flexibility and soil nonlinearity was developed for analysis of behavior of piled raft foundations. A load transfer approach using p–y, t–z and q–z curves is used for the analysis of piles. A 3-D analytical method of the soil–structure interaction is incorporated by taking into account the soil spring coupling effects based on the Filonenko-Borodich model. The proposed method has been verified by comparing the results with other numerical methods and field case studies on piled raft. Through comparative studies, it is found that the proposed method in the present study is in good agreement with general trend observed by field measurements. It was concluded that YSPR could be effectively used in analysis and design of piled raft foundations.

1. INTRODUCTION

A number of huge construction projects, such as high-rise buildings are being undertaken. The piled raft foundations are recently being recognized as an economical foundation system. Piles as settlement reducers have been discussed for several decades and some significant applications have been reported. An optimized design of a piled raft can be defined as a design with minimum costs for the installation of the foundation and satisfactory bearing behavior for a given geometry and raft loading. The piled raft is a composite foundation system consisting of three bearing elements: raft, piles and subsoil. Therefore, the behavior of a piled raft is affected by the 3D interaction between the soil, piles and raft, thus, a simple and convenient analytical method is needed to evaluate these interactions.

A numerous research work has been carried out to the characteristics of load sharing and behavior of piled raft. Numerical methods have been developed widely in the last two decades. There are three broad classes of numerical analysis methods: (1) simplified calculation methods (Poulos, 1994; Randolph, 1983) (2) approximate computer-based methods (Clancy and Randolph, 1993; Russo, 1998) and (3) more rigorous computer based methods (Katzenbach et al., 1997; Lee et al., 2010). Poulos (2001) noted that the most feasible method of analysis was the three-dimensional linear/nonlinear FE method.

The first type of method is based on the linear elastic analysis of piled raft subjected to axial loading. It is most commonly used procedure for the preliminary design of a piled raft foundation. However, it may not represent the nonlinear behavior of actual piled raft in the field: it does not take into account the actual behavior of finite flexible raft and pile–soil interaction, etc. The second type of method has been used to investigate the piled raft system, which is analyzed as a continuous elastic medium using finite element formulation. It did not predict the membrane behavior of raft because the raft is generally modeled as plate element. Therefore, the raft used in these methods may not reflect the displacement due to membrane action of large size raft foundations for high-rise buildings. The third type of method is based on the three-dimensional finite-element or finite-difference techniques. However, a rigorous numerical approach of the piled raft system is computationally expensive and requires extensive training because of the three dimensional and nonlinear nature of the problem.

In this study, an improved analytical method (YSPR) for the design of piled raft has been proposed to overcome some limitations of the existing methods. It is intermediate in complexity and theoretical accuracy between the second and third type of method. In order to examine the validity of the proposed method, the analysis results are compared with the field case study.

2. Improved analytical method (YSPR)

2.1 Modeling of flexible raft

According to the former methods, the raft can be treated as a plate and the soil can be treated as a series of interactive springs by using a Mindlin's solutions(1936), where the contact pressure at any point on the base of the raft is proportional to the deformation of the soil at that point or as an elastic half-space in which the behavior of the soil can be obtained from a number of closed-form solutions. In the later method, the raft is modeled as thin plates and the piles as elastic beams and the soil is treated as interactive springs. The interactions between structural members are made by the use of Mindlin's solutions. The primary limitation of these methods is that the membrane behavior of the flexible raft cannot be considered because the nodal displacements (in the x- and y-direction) for the membrane action are not included. This limitation can be overcome by using a flat-shell element. An improved four-node flat-shell element proposed by the authors, which combines a

Mindlin's plate element and a membrane element with torsional degrees of freedom, is adopted in this study. The flat-shell element can be subjected to the membrane and bending actions that are shown in Fig. 1. The displacement due to the membrane action is considered independent of the displacement due to the bending action, therefore it can be considered separately. For the bending action, the displacement field for an individual element can be described in terms of the vertical nodal displacement and the rotations about the x and y axes. For the membrane action, the displacement field can be described in terms of the nodal displacements in the x and y directions.

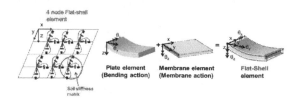

Fig. 1 Flat-shell element

2.2 Modeling of single and pile groups

In this study, piles are treated as beam-column elements. The behavior of soil surrounding the individual piles is represented by load–transfer curves (t–z, q–z, and p–y curves), and the interaction between piles is represented by p-multiplier (f_m) and group efficiency factor (G_e). The load–deformation relationship of individual pile heads may be derived by a single pile analysis based on beam-column method. In this method, a pile member is described as a series of beam column elements with discrete springs to represent the soil support condition as shown in Fig. 2. The governing differential equations for the axially loaded and laterally loaded pile can be expressed as:

Axially loaded pile:

$$EA\frac{d^2w}{dz^2} - C\beta_z w = 0 \tag{1}$$

Laterally loaded pile:

$$EI\frac{d^4y}{dz^4} + Q\frac{d^2y}{dz^2} + q - K_s y = 0 \qquad (2)$$

where EA, EI are the axial stiffness and the flexural rigidity the pile, w is the vertical deflection of the pile at point z, β_z is the stiffness/circumference for the axial reaction represented by the modulus of the soil-response (t–z or q–z or both), which depends on the depth z and pile movement w, *and C* is circumference of the pile at point z. Q is the axial load on the pile, q is the distributed load along the length of the pile, and K_s is the stiffness for the lateral soil reaction represented by the modulus of the soil-response (p–y) curve.

In the next step, finite difference technique is used to solve the differential equations governing the compatibility between the pile displacement and the load transfer along a pile. These techniques are generally based on load tests on full-scale and parametric finite element analyses of pile–soil interactions, which are represented by load–transfer curves (t–z, q–z, and p–y curves).

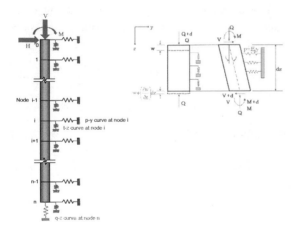

Fig. 2 Modeling of pile element

2.3 Soil-structure interaction

The load-bearing behavior of a piled raft is characterized by complex soil–structure interaction between the piles, raft and the subsoil, as shown in Fig. 3. The present method makes use of pile–soil–pile and raft–soil–pile interaction to simulate

the real piled raft–soil response under lateral and vertical loadings. Additionally, for the raft–soil–raft interaction, this study uses a semi empirical parameters proposed by many researcher as the modulus of soil reaction below the raft. The use of these parameters as assumed in the derivation procedure, may be a limitation. However, these interactions are incorporated in a calculation

Piles in such groups interact with one another through the surrounding soil, resulting in the pile–soil–pile interactions. In this study, a set of nonlinear p–y curves which can be modified by reducing all of the p-values on each curve by a p-multiplier (f_m) are used as input to study the behavior of the laterally loaded piles. The p-multiplier can be calculated for each pile in the group. For each pile i in the group, the p-multiplier can be expressed as:

$$f_{mi} = \beta_{1i}\beta_{2i}\beta_{3i}\ldots\beta_{ji} \qquad (3)$$

where β_{ji} is the p-reduction factor due to the effect of pile *j* on pile *i*.

In a group of closely-spaced piles, the axial capacity of group is also dominated by variation in settlement behavior of individual piles due to pile–soil–pile interaction. The most reliable data concerning the efficiency of the piles in a group is derived by many researchers. In this study, load–transfer curves in side resistance (t–z curve) and in end bearing resistance (q–w curve) which can be modified by reducing all of the t- and q-values on each curve by a group efficiency factor (G_e) are used as input to study the behavior of the vertically loaded piles.

For the raft–soil–pile interaction, in this study a membrane-spring system originally proposed by Filonenko-Borodich was incorporated to involve the soil spring-coupling effects. This system can provide a mechanical interaction between the individual soil spring and pile elements by using the flat-shell element. As shown in Fig. 4, the present method proposed an improved raft–soil–

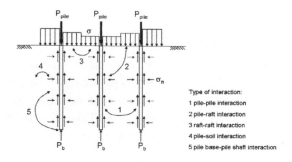

Fig. 3 Soil-structure interactions in piled raft foundation

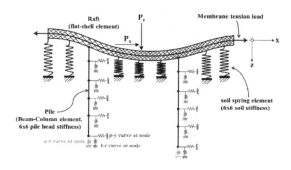

Fig. 4 Interactions between raft, piles, subsoil in present method

pile system by connecting the top ends of soil springs and pile elements with an elastic flat-shell element including membrane action. By using flat-shell element, a realistic representation of the subgrade reaction can be established directly in terms of coupled soil resistance in which the response at any point on the interface affects other points. The authors believe that a combination of the soil spring and the elastic flat-shell element may be used to overcome the restrictions associated with conventional methods, and thereby also used to analyze appropriately axially loaded piled raft, in soil deposits. Consequently, the proposed analytical method should be based on the concept of soil–structure interaction under the lateral and vertical loadings.

2.4 Global stiffness matrix

The stiffness matrix of a flat-shell element

($K_{flat\text{-}shell=raft}$) in local coordinate system was constructed through combining separately the stiffness matrix of a plate element (K_{plate}) and that of a membrane element ($K_{membrane}$) as followings:

$$K_{flat-shell} = \begin{bmatrix} K_{plate} & 0 \\ 0 & K_{membrane} \end{bmatrix} \quad (4)$$

The stiffness matrix of a plate element K_{plate} is represented in the following form:

$$K_{plate} = \int_V B_b^t D_b B_b dV + \int_V B_s^T D_s B_s dV \quad (5)$$

where B_b is the bending strain matrix and B_s is the shear strain matrix. For an isotropic material, D_b and D_s are given as follows:

$$D_b = \frac{Et^3}{12(1-v^2)} \begin{bmatrix} 1 & v & 0 \\ v & 1 & 0 \\ 0 & 0 & (1-v)/2 \end{bmatrix} \quad (6a)$$

$$D_s = \frac{\psi Et}{2(1+v)} \begin{bmatrix} 1 & 0 \\ 0 & 1 \end{bmatrix}; \; \psi = \frac{5}{6} \quad (6b)$$

where E is Young's modulus, v is Poisson's ratio, and t is constant thickness of the plate. On the other hand, the stiffness matrix of a membrane element Kmembrane is represented in the following form:

$$K_{membrane} = \int_v [B_m GR]^T \cdot C \cdot [B_m \overline{GR}]dV + \frac{1}{\gamma V} hh^T \quad (7a)$$

$$h = \int_v [bg\overline{b}\overline{g}]^T dV \quad (7b)$$

$$\gamma = \frac{E}{2(1+v)} \quad (7c)$$

where C is the constitutive modulus, γ is taken as the shear modulus. B_m, $\overline{G}$, $\overline{R}$ are the strain matrices representing the relationship between the displacements (the membrane displacement, the rotation, and midside incompatible displacement respectively) and the strains. b, g, $\overline{b}$ and $\overline{g}$ are also the strain matrices for the infinitesimal rotation fields.

The pile head stiffness ($K_{11} \sim K_{66}$) is assumed to be constant within each load increment and each iteration and then superposition can be applied in order to develop a pile head stiffness matrix (Eq. (8)) in individual piles. Using load–displacement relationships representing pile behaviors according to pile head movements, the relationship between the nodal force and nodal displacements can be expressed in Eq. (9). In addition, the stiffness matrix for pile groups can be formed by sum of n single pile stiffness matrix (Eq. (10)).

$$K_{pile} = \begin{bmatrix} K_{11} & 0 & 0 & 0 & -K_{15} & 0 \\ 0 & K_{22} & 0 & K_{24} & 0 & 0 \\ 0 & 0 & K_{33} & 0 & 0 & 0 \\ 0 & K_{42} & 0 & K_{44} & 0 & 0 \\ -K_{51} & 0 & 0 & 0 & K_{55} & 0 \\ 0 & 0 & 0 & 0 & 0 & K_{66} \end{bmatrix}_i \quad (8)$$

$$[K]_{pile(i)}\{\delta\}_i = \{F_i\} \quad (9)$$

$$K_{pilegroups} = \sum_{i=1}^{n}[K_{pile_{(i)}}] \quad (10)$$

where $[K]_{pile(i)}$ is an individual pile head stiffness matrix, $\{\delta_i\}$ a displacement or rotation, and $\{F_i\}$ force or moment at the ith pile head.

A component ($K_{11} \sim K_{66}$) of pile head stiffness matrix is changed at each load increment and iteration stage.

The soil support at various nodes of raft foundation is simulated by a series of equivalent and independent springs in three directions (x, y and z directions). The spring behavior can be linear or nonlinear. In linear case, soil behavior is defined by soil stiffness ($K_{11} \sim K_{33}$) which is assumed to be constant within each load increment and each iteration. The soil reactions at any point can be expressed as

$$\begin{bmatrix} k_{11} & 0 & 0 & 0 & 0 & 0 \\ 0 & k_{22} & 0 & 0 & 0 & 0 \\ 0 & 0 & k_{33} & 0 & 0 & 0 \\ 0 & 0 & 0 & 0 & 0 & 0 \\ 0 & 0 & 0 & 0 & 0 & 0 \\ 0 & 0 & 0 & 0 & 0 & 0 \end{bmatrix}_i \begin{Bmatrix} \delta_u \\ \delta_v \\ \delta_w \\ \alpha_u \\ \alpha_v \\ \alpha_w \end{Bmatrix}_i = \begin{Bmatrix} F_u \\ F_v \\ F_w \\ M_u \\ M_v \\ M_w \end{Bmatrix}_i \quad (11)$$

$$[K]_{soil(i)}\{\delta\}_i = \{F_i\} \quad (12)$$

where $[K]_{soil(i)}$ = individual soil stiffness matrix, $\{\delta_i\}$ = displacement or rotation, and $\{F_i\}$ = force of soil at point i. In nonlinear case, spring behavior is defined by giving pairs of load–relative displacement values. At this point, soil stiffness is calculated by nonlinear solution procedure.

Finally, the stiffness matrix of a piled raft can be defined by the combination of the foundation system and the supporting soil. Therefore, the stiffness matrix formulations of a piled raft system can be written as the following:

$$[K_{piled\,raft}] = [K_{raft}] + [K_{soil}] + [K_{pilegroups}] \quad (13)$$

2.5 Nonlinear solution procedure

To consider the nonlinear load–displacement relationship at each pile head and soil (below the raft), an incremental secant modulus method developed by Won et al. (2006) is used. When this incremental secant modulus method" is used, the displacement u_2 corresponding to load P_2 is increased to u'_2 as shown in Fig. 5(a), so that point (P_2, u'_2) will be located on the curve and consequently the displacement will be close to the exact solutions. The procedure for nonlinear solution in this study includes the following step. In total, 10 (ten) load–displacement curves (axial 1; lateral 8; torsional 1) are estimated per each pile head. Fig. 5(b) shows the estimation method of stiffness at an ith load increment. In this method, external forces are first divided by N (number of load increment). The stiffness at ith load increment and jth iteration is represented $(k_i)_j$. In each load increment, tangential slope is adopted at first iteration ($j = 1$) and the secant modulus at $j > 1$ for the stiffness of pile head, which is expressed as Eqs. (14) and (15), respectively.

$$(k_i)_j = \left(\frac{df(u)}{du}\right)_{u=(u)_{i-1}} (j = 1) \quad (14)$$

$$(k_i)_j = \frac{f((u_i)_j) - f((u)_{i-1})}{(u_i)_j - (u)_{i-1}} \ (j > 1) \qquad (15)$$

$$(u_i)_j = (u)_{i-1} + \Delta u_j \qquad (16)$$

where $(u)_{i-1}$ is an accumulated final displacement at a previous load increment and $(u_i)_j$ is an accumulated displacement at the ith load increment and jth iteration.

At each load increment, displacements (Δu_j) are calculated through structural analysis and then accumulated displacements ($u_i)_j$ are estimated using Eq. (16). If the convergence criteria, $\Delta u_j - \Delta u_{i-1}$ < e is satisfied, the accumulated final displacements $(u)_i$ are calculated and continue to the next load increment. This process iterates until the load increment number reaches N. In the structure analyses, the tangential slope ($df(u)/du$) and load ($f(u)$) of individual piles are estimated using cubic spline method. The procedure described above is iterated until the error between the assumed and calculated displacements falls within a tolerance limit.

As a final outcome, an improved numerical method (YSPR) was proposed to analyze the response of a raft and a piled raft considering raft flexibility and soil nonlinearity (Fig. 6). Fig. 7 shows the flow chart of present method.

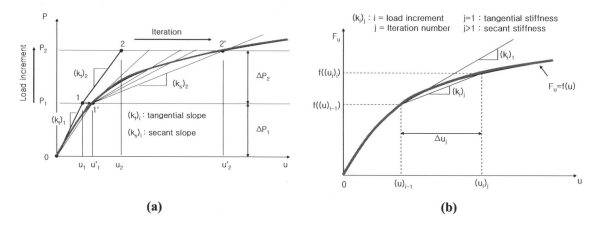

(a)   (b)

Fig. 5 Increment secant modulus method. (a) concept of increment secant modulus method (b)estimating stiffness at ith load increment

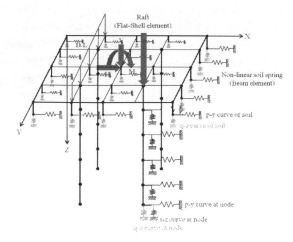

Fig. 6 Modeling of piled raft (YSPR)

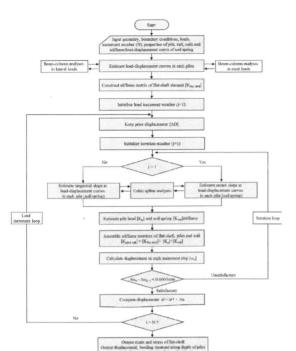

Fig. 7 Flow chart of YSPR

3. Comparison with case histories

The validity of the proposed method was examined by comparing the results from the present approach with some of the field measured results. The pile and soil properties employed with the YSPR and PLAXIS 3D analyses for the case histories were the same properties mentioned in their research. In the field, the soil stiffness significantly depends on the stress level, indicating that the stiffness generally increases with depth. To account for the increase of the stiffness with the depth, the Young's modulus of soil ($E_{increment}$) value which is the increment of stiffness per unit of depth was used in FE analyses. Table 1 summarizes the material properties used in the case studies.

3.1 Japan case

The settlement behavior of axially loaded piled raft reported by Koizumi and Ito(1967) is compared with the predicted values by the proposed method.

Table 1 Material parameters used for this study

Case	Type		Depth (m)	Model
Japan	Pile	Steel pipe	0 ~ −5.5	L.E.
	Raft	Concrete	0 ~ 2.2	L.E.
	Soil	Sandy silt	0 ~ −1.7	M.C.
		Silty clay	−1.7 ~ −13.5	M.C.
Germany	Pile	Concrete	−5.5 ~ −25.5	L.E.
	Raft	Concrete	−3 ~ −5.5	L.E.
	Soil	Sand	−3 ~ −8	M.C.
		Frankfurt clay	−8 ~ −113	M.C.
Korea	Pile	Concrete	0 ~ −30	YSPR
	Raft	Concrete	0 ~ 6	
	Soil	Gneiss	0 ~ 204,250	

Case	Type		E (MPa)	υ
Japan	Pile	Steel pipe	210,000	0.2
	Raft	Concrete	30,000	0.2
	Soil	Sandy silt	13	0.3
		Silty clay	15	0.3
Germany	Pile	Concrete	23,500	0.2
	Raft	Concrete	34,000	0.2
	Soil	Sand	75	0.25
		Frankfurt clay	47	0.15
Korea	Pile	Concrete	28,000	0.2
	Raft	Concrete	33,234	0.15
	Soil	Gneiss		

Case	Type		γ (kN/m³)	ϕ (°)	c (kPa)
Japan	Pile	Steel pipe	75	-	-
	Raft	Concrete	25	-	-
	Soil	Sandy silt	18	0	25
		Silty clay	18	0	29.64
Germany	Pile	Concrete	25	-	-
	Raft	Concrete	25	-	-
	Soil	Sand	18	32.5	0
		Frankfurt clay	19	20	20
Korea	Pile	Concrete	-	-	-
	Raft	Concrete			
	Soil	Gneiss			

L. E : Linear Elastic
M.C : Mohr-Coulomb

This test site was located near the 1-chome, Otemachi in Tokyo. A fully instrumented piled raft was installed in the clay soil, which consists of sandy silt with gravel and organic silty clay. Fig. 8 shows the subsurface profile and pile configurations of the test piled raft. All of the test piles are 300 mm in dia. and 5.5 m in length. The soil and material properties were determined by back-analysis of field load test results using PLAXIS 3D Foundation. From full-scale tests in clay soil presented by O'Neill(1984) and Whitaker(1957), the group efficiency factor, G_e, was set at 0.7 for the reduction of side resistance (t–z curve) and end bearing resistance (q–w curve) of piles. The input parameter of soil used to generate the load transfer curve and soil-spring are summarized in Table 2.

Table 3 shows the estimated stiffness of single pile and piled raft when a vertical load of unity is applied. Compared to the stiffness in which the group efficiency factor was 1.0, the stiffness of piled raft showed a significant decrease in K_{33} of about 28%. This is because the decrease of the pile resistance due to the pile– soil–pile interaction (i.e. group efficiency factor), change the global stiffness of piled raft.

The proposed analysis method (YSPR) and a finite element program analysis (PLAXIS 3D) results were compared with the measured load–settlement curves in Fig. 9. All the methods predicted the general trend of the measured values reasonably well. However, the calculated results by Roberto and Enrico(2006) have a relatively smaller settlement as the applied load increased than the results of the proposed solution. This clearly demonstrates that for analysis result, YSPR gives more flexible results for nonlinear behavior of soil, because the Roberto and Enrico use soil flexibility matrix(based on linear elastic analysis of pile groups) for soil–pile interaction and the proposed method does so using nonlinear load transfer curves and solution algorithm. These discrepancies between predicted and measured behavior at the high load levels are because the assumptions of raft–soil relative stiffness and group efficiency factor are influenced on the settlement behavior of piled raft. In addition, computational time to run this case saves 57 min of computer time, and is about 20 times faster than the 3D FE analysis.

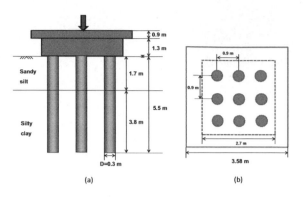

Fig. 8 Field test of piled raft. (a) Plan-view and (b) section-view

Table 2 Properties used for estimating load transfer curves (Japan case)

	Contents	Sandy silt	Silty clay
t-z, q-z curves	Ultimate skin, τ (kPa)	40	40
	Initial shear modulus, G_i (kPa)	5,000	5,769
	Poisson's ratio, υ	0.3	0.3
	Ultimate bearing capacity, Q_f (kN)	-	250
		-	-
p-y curves	Undrained shear strength(kPa)	25	29.64
		-	-
	Unit weights (kN/m³)	18.0	18.0
	p-y modulus, k(kN/m³)	27,150	27,150
Subgrade reaction modulus	K_x, K_y (kN/m³)	27,150	-
	K_z (kN/m³)	5291	-

Table 3 Calculated stiffness of single pile and piled raft(Japan case)

	K_{11}(kN/m)	K_{22}(kN/m)	K_{33}(kN/m)
Single pile	0.4052E+02	0.4052E+02	0.3877E+05
Piled raft (w/o G_e)	0.2735E+05	0.2735E+05	0.3453E+06
Piled raft (w/G_e)	0.2735E+05	0.2735E+05	0.2492E+06
	K_{44}(kN/rad)	K_{55}(kN/rad)	K_{66}(kN/rad)
Single pile	0.3434E+03	0.3434E+03	0
Piled raft (w/o G_e)	0.2730E+06	0.2730E+06	0
Piled raft (w/G_e)	0.2208E+06	0.2208E+06	0

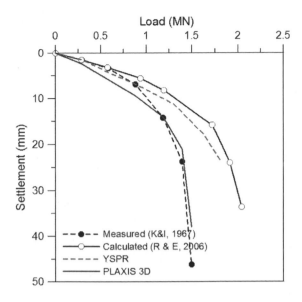

**Fig. 9 Computed and measured response of
piled raft settlement**

3.2 Germany case

The settlement and load sharing behavior of instrumented, large, piled raft installed in stiff clay was compared with the predicted values of the proposed method and the FE analyses. Constructed between 1983 and 1986, the 130 m high Torhaus was the first building in Germany with a foundation designed as a piled raft. A total number of 84 bored piles with a length of 20 m and diameter of 0.9 m are located under two 17.5 × 24.5 m large rafts. The bottom of the 2.5 m thick raft lies just 3 m below ground level (Fig. 10(a)).

The subsoil comprises quaternary sand and gravel up to 2.5 m below the bottom of the rafts, followed by the Frankfurt clay. And a schematic diagram of 7 × 6 piled raft structure is shown in Fig. 10(b). The maximum load of P_{eff} = 200 MN for each raft minus the weight of the raft is successively applied by means of a uniform load over the whole raft area. In the present method (YSPR), the soil around individual pile is modeled with nonlinear load transfer curves. The axial load transfer curves (t–z, q–z curves) are estimated using the equation developed by Wang et al. (1993), the lateral load transfer curve (p–y curve) is used as an API model (O'Neill et al., 1984). The group efficiency factor, G_e, was set at 0.73 for the average value of pile spacing: 3D ~ 4D. The input parameter of soil used to generate the load transfer curve and soil-spring are summarized in Table 4.

Fig. 11 shows a comparison of the measured and calculated pile loads. The prediction of the present method is much more conservative than that of 3D FE analyses and the measured one. However, the proposed method is in good agreement with general trend of pile load which increase from a center pile (pile1) to the edge (piles 2, 4 and 6) and to the corner pile (piles 3 and 5). Fig. 12 shows a settlement behavior of the piled raft. The measured maximum settlement is about 124 mm, YSPR is 106mm and PLAXIS 3D predicted 117mm. All values of the YSPR and 3D FE analyses are smaller than those measured. However, these two

Table 4 Properties used for estimating load transfer curves (Germany case)

	Contents	Quaternary sand	Frankfrurt clay
t-z, q-z curves	Ultimate skin, τ (kPa)	143	91.6
	Initial shear modulus, G_i (kPa)	30,000	20,434
	Poisson's ratio, υ	0.25	0.15
	Ultimate bearing capacity, Q_f (kN)	-	90
		-	-
p-y curves	Internal friction angle (°)	32.5	20
	Unit weights (kN/m³)	18.0	19.0
	p-y modulus, k (kN/m³)	16,300	136,000
Subgrade reaction modulus	K_x, K_y (kN/m³)	16,300	136,000
	K_z (kN/m³)	294,000	-

numerical methods provide an acceptable design prediction. Despite the approximate assumptions involved (i.e., loading condition, construction process, consolidation of clay), the present method when used in nonlinear analysis is useful for predicting the settlement behavior of a piled raft foundation taking account of soil nonlinearity,

the flexibility of the large raft, and the pile arrangement. The time taken for the computer to run this case saves 115 min of computer time, and is about 24 times faster than the 3D FE analysis. For large problems this computational saving can be very significant.

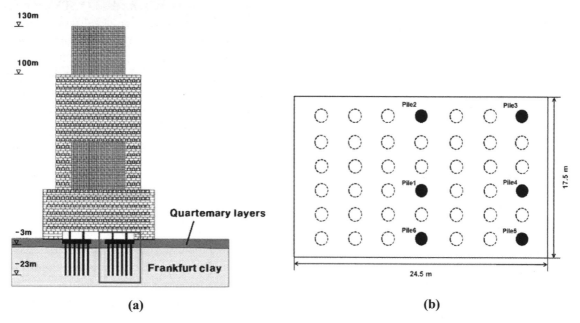

(a)   (b)

Fig. 10 Torhaus Der Messe: (a) profile view and (b) configuration of pile

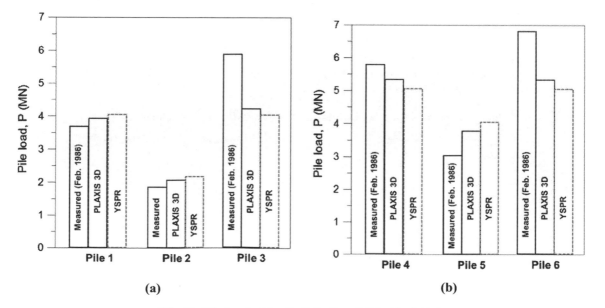

(a)   (b)

Fig. 11 Pile load: (a) pile 1, 2, 3 and (b) pile 4, 5, 6

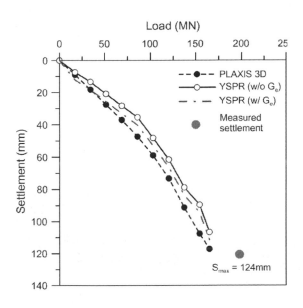

Fig. 12 Settlement behavior of large piled raft foundation

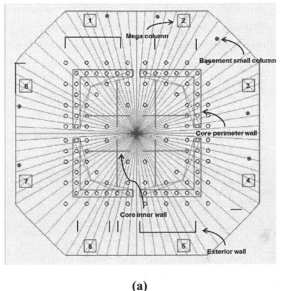

(a)

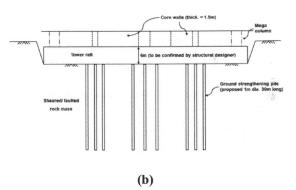

(b)

Fig. 13 Preliminary design case of large piled raft: (a) plan view and (b) profile view

3.3 Korea case

As shown in Fig. 13, preliminary design case of a piled raft (OO super tower) conducted at high-rise building construction sites in Korea were representatively selected for the design application. The construction site is comprised mainly of normally banded gneiss, brecciated gneiss and fault core zones. Based on the results of pressure meter, Goodman Jack and plate load tests carried out in the field, a nonlinear elastic modulus design line is established to represent the stiffness of the ground. A schematic diagram of a raft foundation with piles is shown in Fig. 13(b). This structure consists of a raft, and 112 of ground strengthen piles. The piles have an embedded length of 30 m, a diameter of 1.0 m. A large raft size 71.7 × 71.7 m with a thickness of 6.0 m is resting on a banded gneiss. The raft and ground strengthen piles, with a Young's modulus of 30 GPa and 28 GPa respectively, is subjected to a vertical load (P_{total} = 6,701 MN).

Fig. 14 shows the raft settlement at different sections predicted by RAFT and YSPR. Agreement between the RAFT and YSPR of settlement is generally good; however there is a slight difference in prediction of settlement in the faulting zone where the sudden drop of the magnitudes were occurred. This can be attributed to the inappropriate assumption of material properties due to no accurate ground investigation data on this section. The calculated raft settlement has some difference between the proposed method and the existing solution, based on the same analysis conditions. This is because the conceptual methodology of the present method is completely different from that of general structural models. The raft is modeled as a grillage and the piles are treated as bar element with axial stiffness only in RAFT while YSPR is adopted flat-shell element and 6 × 6 pile head stiffness. Although there are no measured profiles of raft settlement, the proposed analysis method showed reasonably good correspondence with well-known in-house program.

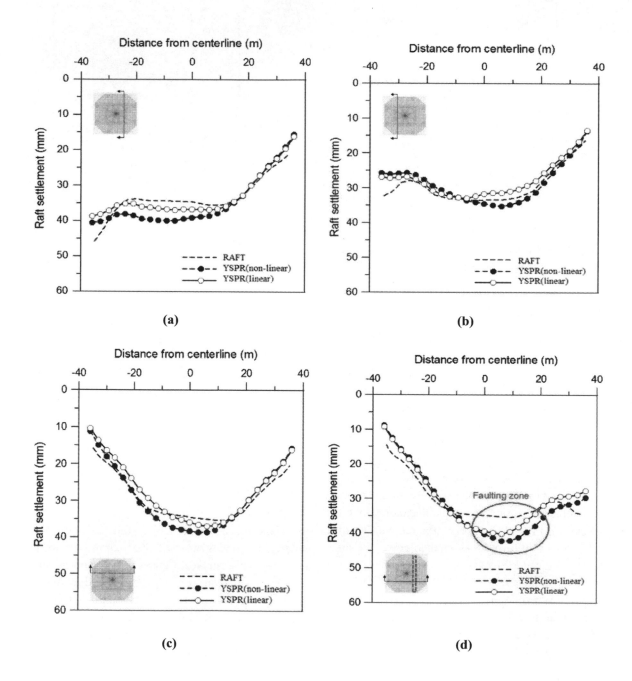

Fig. 14 Raft settlement distribution (a) section 1, (b) section2, (c) section 3, (d) section 4

4. CONCLUSIONS

The primary objective of this study was to propose an improved analytical method for pile raft foundations. The analytical method was proposed to take into account the raft flexibility, soil nonlinearity and raft-soil-pile interaction. Through comparisons with case histories, it is clearly demonstrated that the proposed method was found to be in good agreement with measurement data. From the findings of this study, the following conclusions can be drawn:

1) By taking into account the raft flexibility and soil nonlinearity, the proposed analytical method is an appropriate and realistic representation of the settlement and load sharing behavior of piled raft foundation. It provides results that are in good agreement with the field measurement and numerical analyses.

2) From the example case histories, the proposed method is shown to be capable of predicting the behavior of a large piled raft. Nonlinear load–transfer curve and flat-shell element can overcome the limitations of existing numerical methods, to some extent, by considering the realistic nonlinear behavior of soil and membrane action of flexible raft.

3) Additionally, the comparative studies demonstrated that the present method, when used in analysis of large scale piled raft, is useful for computational saving and improving performance in engineering practice.

ACKNOWLEDGEMENTS

This work was supported by the National Research Foundation of Korea (NRF) grant funded by the Korea government (MSIP) (No.2011-0030040 and NRF-2014R1A2A1A11054606).

REFERENCES

Burland JB, Broms BB, De Mello VFB. (1977). Behaviour of foundations and structures. In: State-of-the-Art Rep., *Proc., IX Int. conf. of soil mechanics and foundation engineering (ICSMFE)*, Rotterdam, The Netherlands: Balkema, pp 495–546.

Brown DA, Reese LC, O'Neill MW. (1987). Cyclic lateral loading of a large-scale pile group. *J Geotech Eng, ASCE*, Vol: 113, No.11., pp 1326–43.

Clancy P, Randolph MF. (1993). An approximate analysis procedure for piled raft foundations. *Int J Numer Anal Meth Geomech*, Vol: 17, No.12., pp 849–69.

Filonenko-Borodich M. (1940). Some approximate theories of the elastic foundation. *Uchenyie Zapiski Moskovskogo Gosudarstvennoho Universiteta Mekhanica*, Vol: 46, pp. 3–18.

Jeong SS, Kim SI, Briaud JL. (1997). Analysis of downdrag on pile groups by finite element method. *Computer and Geotechnics* Vol: 21, No.2., pp 143–61.

Katzenbach R, Arslan U, Gutwald J, Holzhauser J, Quick H. (1997). Soil–structure interaction of the 300-m-high Commerzbank Tower in Frankfurt am Main. Measurements and numerical studies. In: *Proc, 14th ICSMFE*, Vol: 2., pp 1081–4.

Kitiyodom P, Matsumoto T. (2003). A simplified analysis method for piled raft foundations in non-homogeneous soils. *Int J Numer Anal Meth Geomech*, Vol: 27, pp 85–109.

Hain SJ, Lee IK. (1978). The analysis of flexible raft–pile systems. *Geotechnique*, Vol: 28, No.1., pp 65–83.

Lee JH, Kim YH, Jeong SS. (2010). Three-dimensional analysis of bearing behavior of piled raft on soft clay. *Computer and Geotechnics*, Vol: 37., pp 103–14.

O'Neill MW, Dunnavant TW. (1984). A study of effect of scale, velocity, and cyclic degradability on laterally loaded single piles in overconsolidated clay. *Rep. No. UHCE 84-7, Dept of Civil Engineering*, Univ of Houston, Houston, TX.

Poulos HG. (1994). An approximate numerical analysis of pile–raft interaction. *Int J Numer Anal Meth Geomech*, London, Vol: 18, No.2., pp 73–92.

Poulos HG. (2001). Piled raft foundations: design and applications. *Geotechnique*, Vol: 51, No.2., pp 95–113.

Randolph MF. (1983). Design of piled foundations. Research Report Soils TR143, Cambridge: Cambridge University Engineering Department.

Reese LC, O'Neill MW, Smith RE. (1970). Generalized analysis of pile foundations. *J Soil Mech Found Div, ASCE*, Vol: 96, No.1., pp 235–50.

Roberto C, Enrico C. (2006). Settlement analysis of pile groups in layered soils. *Can Geotech J*, Vol: 43, pp 788–801.

Russo G. (1998). Numerical analysis of piled rafts. *Int J Numer Anal Meth Geomech*, Vol: 22, No.6., pp 477–93.

Wang ST, Reese LC. COM624P. (1993). Laterally loaded pile analysis for the microcomputer.ver. 2.0, *FHWA-SA-91-048*, Springfield, VA

Wang A. (1996). Three dimensional finite element analysis of pile groups and piled-raft, Ph.D. dissertation, University of Manchester, U.K.

Whitaker T. (1957). Experiments with model piles in groups. *Geotechnique*, Vol: 7, No.4., pp 147–67.

Won JO, Jeong SS, Lee JH, Jang SY. (2006). Nonlinear three-dimensional analysis of pile group supported columns considering pile cap flexibility. *Computer and Geotechnics*, Vol: 33, pp 355–70.

CHAPTER 4

SEISMIC RESPONSE OF COMBINED PILE-RAFT FOUNDATION - THE STATE OF THE ART REVIEW

Deepankar Choudhury*
Ashutosh Kumar
Department of Civil Engineering, Indian Institute of Technology Bombay, Powai, Mumbai 400076, India.
*dc@civil.iitb.ac.in

ABSTRACT: This chapter presents a state of the art review of the research work carried out by various researchers for analyzing the behavior of combined pile-raft foundation (CPRF) under seismic loading conditions. It emphasizes on the load sharing mechanism of the CPRF components which indicated better performance of this foundation system over conventional group pile foundation during seismic loading. The study shows that lateral loads are resisted by passive resistance provided by the surrounding soil media and explicitly depends on the magnitude of lateral displacement. The input motion characteristics, the natural frequency of the CPRF and surrounding soil media dictate the response of CPRF under seismic loading. The connection rigidity between piles and raft components affects the load-displacement characteristics, bending moment and shear force response of piles. A brief insight on field measurements and a case study on CPRF are highlighted. Finally, key aspects of the design of CPRF subjected to seismic loading are discussed.

1. INTRODUCTION

Combined pile-raft foundation system has been identified as one of the economic and sustainable foundation for high-rise buildings which results into smaller settlements with a lesser number of piles compared to pile group. This approach is adopted due to its effectiveness in load sharing between its pile and raft components. The successful use of CPRF having 64 piles under 256 m high Messeturm Tower of Germany proved it as most economical foundation system. This foundation concept saved approximately 5.9 million USD as if only pile foundation having 316 piles were used (Katzenbach et al. 2005 & 2016) and many such applications are available worldwide. However, the traditional design of pile foundation is still dominant in the engineering practice due to the guidelines and provisions suggested by design codes. These codes are strictly followed for the conventional design in many countries which may be due to the lack of confidence among the designers for incorporating load sharing advantage between raft and piles to avoid conservatism through capacity based design. To boost up the confidence among the geotechnical practitioners and to promote the performance-based design, Architectural Institute of Japan (AIJ, 2001) and International Society of Soil Mechanics and Geotechnical Engineering published the international guideline for the design, construction, and practice of CPRF (Katzenbach and Choudhury 2013). Burland et al. (1977) first introduced an efficient designed philosophy to introduce few piles below the raft foundation where unserviceability in the foundation design exist. Figure 1 shows the basic pile-soil-raft interaction mechanism in CPRF as given in ISSMGE guideline by Katzenbach and Choudhury (2013).

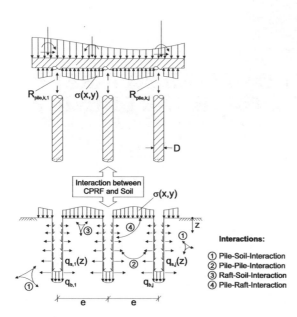

Fig. 1 Soil-structure interaction in CPRF under static conditions (Katzenbach and Choudhury, 2013)

Their design approach pushes designer towards serviceability based design criteria and was strongly put in evidence by Randolph (1994) which increases the research on this improved and economical foundation. Since then, it is widely recognized as economical and rational foundation under the application of vertical load considering load sharing by raft and pile with reduced number of piles as compared to conventional pile foundation (Poulos and Davis 1980, Clancy and Randolph 1993, Horikoshi and Randolph 1998, Poulos 2001, Katzenbach et al. 2005, 2016 & Kumar et al. 2017). The above-mentioned works are related to CPRF subjected to vertical load alone.

In addition, high-rise buildings are usually subjected to vertical load due to the superstructure, horizontal load and overturning moment due to wind and earthquake forces. Pile foundation is a most preferred choice in such loading considerations. In conventional design, the contribution of raft is usually ignored even if they rest on competent soil strata. This approach is usually adopted due to limited understanding

of pile-soil-raft interaction and unavailability of a validated method of analysis which results in the installation of more piles than required. For the optimization of the design, the lateral displacement, moment and axial load distribution should be controlled to an acceptable level rather than suppressed to a lower level than that a structure can withstand. In highly seismic areas such as Asia which contribute 85.5% of the total share of earthquakes around the globe (Walling and Mohanty, 2009), the performance-based design of CPRF subjected to horizontal, moment and seismic loading should be given prime importance. In this chapter, the state of the art review has been presented for CPRF subjected to pseudo-static and seismic loading conditions. It also explains the response of CPRF under different connections rigidity and highlights practical implications of CPRF with few case studies.

2. RESPONSE UNDER LATERAL LOAD

The lateral loads, overturning moments or both may get induced to the foundation components especially in the case of high-rise buildings and bridge abutments where the center of gravity of the system lies above the foundation level. In the case of the seismic event also, lateral forces act on the foundation system in terms of inertial loading which can be calculated as seismic coefficient times the vertical load, named as pseudo-static load by few researchers. The lateral load sharing mechanism in CPRF where both the foundation components share the load depending on their individual stiffnesses differs from pile group foundation where only piles carry the entire load. This phenomenon can be clearly seen in Fig. 2. Such behavior of the foundation system where the contribution of raft can also be taken interests several researchers and forces them towards the use of this improved and economical foundation. Several researchers have used different techniques to investigate the response of CPRF and compared with pile group foundation.

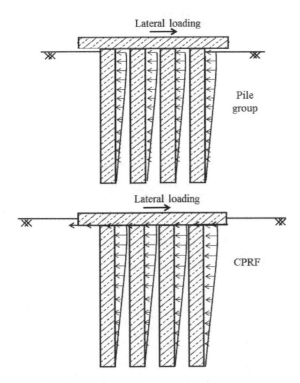

Fig. 2 Schematic representation of load bearing in pile group and CPRF under lateral loading

2.1 Experimental Study using Centrifuge Modelling

Horikoshi et al. (2003a) performed a series of vertical and horizontal loading tests on CPRF and group piles embedded in Toyoura sand by using geotechnical centrifuge (50g). They reported that the response of individual pile differs from that of the pile in CPRF due to the presence of confining stress around the piles. There was hardly any effect on the proportion of vertical load sharing by foundation components with an increase in lateral loading. Raft took a larger proportion of lateral load at the initial stage of loading but it mobilized its strength gradually as loading progresses and reached its limiting value. Thereafter, any further increase in lateral load was borne entirely by piles.

Sawada and Takemura (2014) performed a series of static horizontal loading tests on CPRF, group pile and unpiled raft foundation by using centrifuge

modeling technique (50g). Figure 3 illustrates the schematic representation of centrifuge test set up for CPRF. They investigated the effect of large moment load and rotation on piled raft, pile group and raft foundation behavior in dry Toyoura sand. The horizontal loads were applied at two different heights from the level of raft (h/s=1 and 1.8), where s is pile spacing. They observed that shaft friction in the piled raft was more than pile group but similar end bearing resistance for both the cases. The load proportion by raft was dependent on an increase in settlement of the system which helped them to fix the load sharing to 27% prior to the application of horizontal load. An alternate horizontal and moment load caused a large amount of settlement in pile group foundation but piled raft was able to reduce settlements. The moment resistance of push-in piles in CPRF was larger than pile group foundation which makes the significance of raft stiffness in reducing rotation.

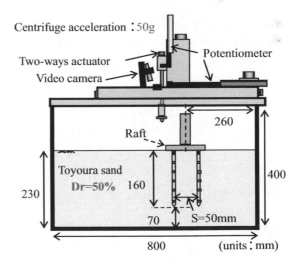

Fig. 3 Test Setup for CPRF in Geotechnical Centrifuge (Sawada and Takemura, 2014)

2.2 Experimental Study by using 1-g Tests

Matsumoto et al. (2004a) performed a 1g experiment on CPRF embedded in dry Toyoura sand by varying height of force and rigidity in the connection conditions. They observed that the horizontal displacement, bending moment in piles and inclination in raft increases with increase in height of horizontal load from the raft base. They also clarified that the 1-g model was unrealistic because the bending rigidity of the prototype pile was much higher than that of the model pile. So, the reported bending moment values cannot be adopted in actual practice. However, the interaction mechanism will not change even if the model is compared to prototype scale.

Unsever et al. (2015) examined the response of CPRF subjected to vertical and cyclic horizontal load embedded in dry silica sand. The test setup is shown in Figure 4. They reported that the vertical settlement and displacement response of CPRF are largely dependent on the soil-pile-raft interaction. The proportion of vertical load sharing by raft component of CPRF does not change considerably during lateral load application. Front facing piles subjected to lateral loads induces to higher bending moment as compared to rear facing piles. Results obtained in the experimental study were validated by using three-dimensional finite element software, PLAXIS3D.

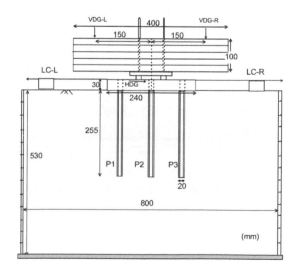

Fig. 4 Experimental test setup for horizontal load tests on CPRF (Unsever et al. 2015)

2.3 Numerical Study

Comodromos et al. (2015) studied the response of CPRF under combined loading conditions by using numerical modeling software, FLAC3D. They proposed simplified design methodology by using p-y and t-z curve incorporating soil-pile-raft interaction to evaluate the foundation response. The validity of the proposed method was assessed by employing it on Torhaus de Messe building of Frankfurt and bridge foundation of Greece.

Kumar et al. (2016) reported the behavior of CPRF under pseudo-static loading conditions which is one of the practical conventions to replace the seismically induced horizontal load which is seismic coefficient times the vertical load. Figure 5 shows discretized three-dimensional view of CPRF model subjected to a vertical and pseudo-static load. CPRF was subjected to different earthquake loads viz. 1979 El-Centro (0.43g), 1989 Loma Prieta (0.279g), 2011 Sikkim (0.201g) and 2001 Bhuj (0.106g). The modeling details of soil, pile and raft system are given in Kumar et al. (2016). Figure 6 shows horizontal displacement contour under various pseudo-static loading conditions. The maximum horizontal displacement was observed in the case of 1979 El-Centro earthquake due to the greater magnitude of the pseudo-static load. Figure 7 represents the shear force profile under different earthquake conditions for both front and rear piles and it increased with increase in the magnitude of earthquake loads. It can be observed that shear force in rear piles is more as compared to front piles due to additional load of soil acting on the rear pile. Similar behavior of pile under pseudo-static load was also reported by Poulos and Davis (1980) and Phanikanth et al. (2013).

2.4 Analytical Approach

Kitiyodom and Matsumoto (2002) proposed a simplified numerical analysis for estimation of the response of CPRF subjected to combined loading. They modeled raft as thin plates, piles with elastic beams and soil with linear springs. Both vertical

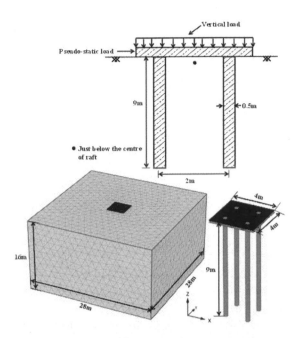

Fig. 5 Schematic representation and discretized
mesh of CPRF (Kumar et al. 2016)

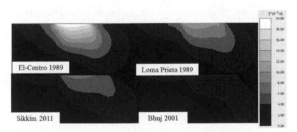

**Fig. 6 Horizontal displacement contour under
various pseudo-static loads**

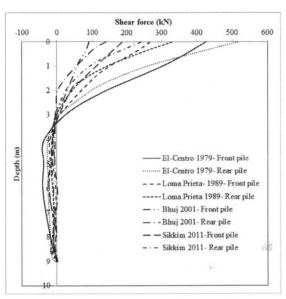

**Fig. 7 Shear force profile in front and rear pile
under different pseudo-static conditions**

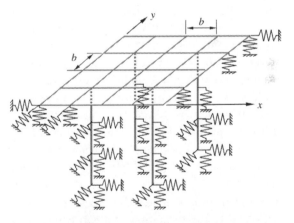

**Fig. 8 Representation of pile-raft-soil as beam-
plate-spring model**

and lateral resistance of piles and raft base were incorporated in the model by using the stiffness equation provided by different researchers. Pile-soil-raft interaction is considered using Mindlin's solutions. Figure 8 shows mainly three types of arrangement of springs in piles and raft. The obtained results were compared with the available literature. They also investigated the response of batter piles subjected to a lateral load.

Kitiyodom and Matsumoto (2003) proposed a simplified method of numerical analysis for CPRF embedded in non-homogeneous soil deposits. The modeling approach was based on elasticity theory

for axially and laterally loaded CPRF. Here, the raft was modeled with thin plate element, pile with elastic beam element and soil with spring. The pile-soil-raft interaction was established via Mindlin's solutions. Linear stiffness expressions were used to model the stiffnesses of the pile, soil, and raft. They validated the proposed methodology with three-dimensional finite element method. The simplified methodology predicted the response of single pile, group pile, and CPRF with reasonable accuracy.

Mu et al. (2016) proposed an efficient hybrid approach for the analyzing the response of CPRF subjected to coupled load in layered soils. Shear displacement and elastic foundation methods were applied to calculate vertical and horizontal responses of single piles. Piles were divided into two categories viz. active piles (establishment of interaction is by movement of piles) and passive piles (establishment of interaction by movement of soils). Pile-pile, pile-soil and soil-pile interactions were considered in the study. They validated their proposed methodology with finite element method.

From the above discussion, it can be concluded that the load sharing and displacement response of CPRF are largely dependent upon the stiffness of soil, foundation pile, and raft. Lateral loads are resisted by foundation components due to the passive resistance provided by surrounding soil media. Therefore, it can be asserted that load sharing is explicitly dependent upon lateral displacement. There is the negligible influence of the proportion of vertical load sharing by foundation components with increment in lateral loading as reported by Horikoshi et al. (2003a) and confirmed by Matsumoto et al. (2004a). However, push-in pile (Pile moving inward due to the application of lateral load) carry more axial load than pull-out pile (Pile moving outward due to the application of lateral load) with an increase in lateral load. This behavior may be attributed to the formation of a gap between the pile surface and surrounding soil leading to a reduction in passive resistance. Raft contact with the ground surface contributed in positive raft-soil interaction thereby densifying the soil below raft which resulted in larger shaft resistance in the piles. This phenomenon may also be postulated as the probable reason for the increase in the lateral load carrying capacity of piles. The variation in the position of lateral load application may induce overturning moment to the foundation system in addition to the lateral load which results in sliding and rotation of the raft. A similar response was reported by Matsumoto et al. (2004a) and Sawada and Takemura (2014). It was also reported that

rotation in the raft is proportional to the lateral displacement in the system and it also depends upon the stiffness of raft. The load sharing by push-in and pull-out pile changes with a change in the height of application of lateral load from raft base. This occurs mainly because of a decrease in the resistance of pull out pile under such loading consideration.

3. RESPONSE UNDER REAL SEISMIC LOADING CONDITIONS

Seismic events are critical to every geotechnical structure because of its redundancy in the duration, frequency content, and magnitudes. Piles are usually designed to withstand the lateral load but the performance of pile in several devastating earthquakes still remains a concern to the designers. Several researchers investigated the load sharing mechanism and response of CPRF under earthquake by using various available methodologies.

3.1 Experimental Study using Centrifuge Modelling

Horikoshi et al. (2003b) examined the behavior of group pile and CPRF subjected to sinusoidal motion at 50g. Figure 9 illustrates the schematic representation of the centrifuge setup. They reported that CPRF showed better performance in comparison to group piles due to the contribution of the raft in providing lateral soil resistance.

The proportion of horizontal load carried by each foundation component was dependent up on the horizontal displacement of the foundation system, hence, evaluation of horizontal displacement holds prime importance in the seismic design of the CPRF.

Banerjee et al. (2007) did an experimental and numerical investigation on piled raft foundation with the solid pile, hollow pile and pile filled-in with cement under three different earthquake

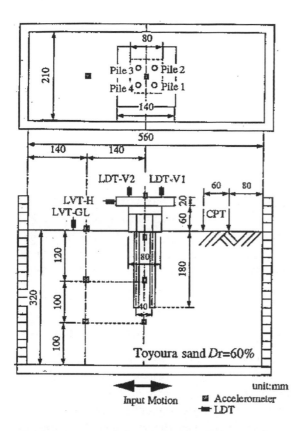

Fig. 9 Schematic representation of the centrifuge setup (Horikoshi et al. 2003b)

excitations. Piles were embedded in kaolin clay to capture response under seismic shaking. Steel plates were used to apply superstructure load onto the raft. Three types of earthquakes large (0.065g), medium (0.03g) and small (0.015g) were fired having same duration and frequency. Under earthquake excitation, remolding in clay was observed. The surroundings soil imposed an inertial loading onto the piles leading to an increase in the natural frequency of the system. The movement of soil just below the raft was completely different from the far field. Lengthening in resonance period was observed due to combined movement of the soil-pile-raft system. The observed results using centrifuge technique were back analyzed with finite element based software ABAQUS and a similar response was observed. They did not examine loading sharing by foundation component and stress resultant in the foundation components

like bending moment, shear and axial force.

Kang et al. (2012) studied the response of CPRF with flexible and stiff piles embedded in kaolin clay using geotechnical centrifuge test at 50g and numerical studies. In centrifuge test studies, four piles were connected to the rigid raft and were embedded in clay and superstructure load on the top of the raft modeled by fastening steel plates of varying thicknesses on the top of the raft having prototype loads 368ton, 605ton, 863ton respectively. Model dimensions were taken as per Banerjee et al. (2007). Three scaled earthquakes were fired having an acceleration of 0.022g, 0.052g and 0.13g respectively. The nearly same response was observed for both flexible and stiff pile-raft system. They reported that soft clay act as an inertial loading in stiff pile system rather than providing support but in a flexible pile, clay contributed in load sharing. For rigid pile, bending moment transition from positive on the top and negative on the bottom was observed however for flexible pile negligible bending moment below certain length observed. A significant difference in resonance period was observed between stiff and flexible pile raft system as soil applies inertial loading onto the rigid pile raft system. The Same trend was observed when modeling was done using ABAQUS computer program.

Banerjee et al. (2014) examined the seismic effect on fixed headed piles embedded in soft clay by using centrifuge (50g) and numerical modeling procedure. Based on the analysis, they derived a dimensionless expression to obtain maximum bending moment in stiff as well as flexible piles considering inertial effects of loading, ground motion parameters, a variation of soil modulus with depth and soil non-linearity.

For stiff pile:

$$\frac{M_{max}r}{(EI)_p} = 0.007 \left(\frac{E_{ep}}{c_2 r^n}\right)^{-0.54} \left(\frac{a_b}{g}\right)^{0.91} \left(\frac{m}{\rho r^3}\right)^{0.4} \left(\frac{l_p}{r}\right)^{1.031}$$

(1)

For flexible pile:

$$\frac{M_{max}r}{(EI)_p} = 3 \times 10^{-5} \left(\frac{E_{ep}}{c_2 r^n}\right)^{-0.7} \left(\frac{a_b}{g}\right)^{0.65} \left(\frac{m}{\rho r^3}\right)^{0.85} \left(\frac{l_a}{r}\right)^{1.005}$$

$$(2)$$

where Mmax is the maximum bending moment in pile, r is the radius of pile, $(EI)_p$ is the flexural rigidity of pile, E_{ep} is Young's modulus of equivalent solid cylinder pile, c_2 is $1005.33\{(1+2Ko)\gamma'\}n$, a_b is base acceleration, g is acceleration due to gravity, m is the mass of raft along with additional plate, ρ is the density of soil, l_a is the active length of pile and l_p is the full length of pile. The above expression indicates that the stiff pile experiences maximum bending moment as compared to the flexible pile. The slenderness ratio has little influence but the mass ratio and ground acceleration has a significant influence on the bending moment for both piles.

Zhang et al. (2017a) performed a series of dynamic centrifuge test (50g) on 4x3 CPRF embedded in kaolin clay to investigate the bending moment and raft acceleration response. Two types of free-field motion viz. short (25 sec) and long (800 sec) durations having different peak base accelerations were applied at the base of centrifuge model, as shown in schematically represented Figure 10. They reported two dimensionless expressions to evaluate peak acceleration at the raft and peak bending moment in piles.

Zhang et al. (2017b) performed series of dynamic centrifuge tests (50g) and numerical modeling on 2×1 and 4×3 CPRF embedded in soft kaolin clay. Long duration motion of 200 sec was chosen to simulate long duration earthquake arising from Sunda Subduction Trench. They reported that both acceleration and bending moment in CPRF was greatly influenced by pile-soil stiffness ratio. The bending moment response of pile in 4×3 CPRF system depends mainly on the location of the pile. Three-dimensional finite element model by using ABAQUS simulated the centrifuge modeling results both qualitatively and quantitatively.

3.2 Experimental Study by using 1-g Tests

Matsumoto et al. (2004b) performed shaking table tests to investigate the response of CPRF embedded in dry Toyoura sand by varying height of the center of gravity of superstructure and frequency of input accelerations. They reported that the resonance period of the foundation increases with increase in height of center of gravity of the vertical loading mass. The increase in height increased the bending moment, shear forces in piles and inclination in raft may be due to inertial effect of the loading. However, the pile resistance decreased due to differences in the load reversal for push-in and pull-out piles. This may due to simultaneous change in the stiffness of soil around push-in and pull-out side, respectively during shaking event. CPRF displacement, inclination, horizontal load, bending moment and shear forces in piles increases with increases in height of center of gravity of structure at low frequency but, at resonance frequency they observed larger displacement in case of lower height structure and they mentioned the magnitude of motion as the only probable reason. However, in addition to the magnitude of the input motion, the frequency of the input motion and natural frequency of CPRF system also played a significant role in attaining resonance condition. The response of CPRF was also dependent

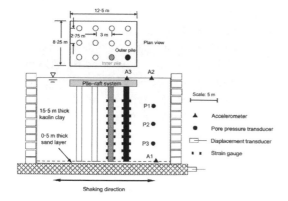

Fig. 10 Test setup of soil-pile-raft system in centrifuge model (Zhang et al. 2017a)

upon the closeness of natural frequency of the foundation and input frequency of seismic shaking. Such behavior of CPRF was also explained by Kumar et al. (2016).

Unsever et al. (2016) performed 1g shaking table tests on 3 pile- CPRF and group piles embedded in the saturated sand under the combination of vertical and seismic loads. The input motion was having a frequency of 20 Hz and amplitude of 1.5 m/s^2 and 6 m/s^2, respectively. The spacing to diameter (S/d) ratio was kept as 4. They observed that group pile foundation underwent more vertical settlement than CPRF due to the presence of raft in providing lateral resistance. Group pile foundation undergone lesser displacement as compared to CRPF at the expense of higher bending moment. The contact between raft and soil in CPRF caused an increase in effective stress at a shallow depth which terminated liquefaction phenomenon at those levels during lower shaking intensity. In the case of liquefaction, the horizontal resistance provided by raft reduced drastically due to loss of contact between the raft and underlying soil.

3.3 Numerical Study

Kumar et al. (2016) analyzed the response of CPRF under real earthquake acceleration-time histories. Figure 11 illustrates a bending moment in pile during real earthquake motion which shows the maximum bending moment of 78kN. m, 186kN.m, 75kN.m and 67kN.m under 1979 El-Centro, 1989 Loma Prieta, 2001 Bhuj and 2011 Sikkim earthquake, respectively. It is to be noted that the bending moment response obtained under 1989 Loma Prieta earthquake motion is more as compared to all other bending moments values observed under other different earthquake input motions. The probable reason such behavior may be attributed to the attainment of a condition of resonance occurred which is unlike in all other cases. It is also observed that bending moment is more in the case of 2001 Bhuj earthquake input motion as compared to 2011 Sikkim earthquake input motion though 2011 Sikkim motion has

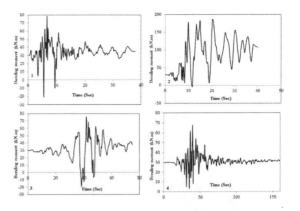

Fig. 11 Variation of bending moment in pile with dynamic time under different earthquake input motions (1- 1979 El-Centro, 2- 1989 Loma Prieta, 3- 2001 Bhuj, 4- 2011 Sikkim)

higher PGA. It can be concluded that input motion characteristics and condition of resonance played a significant role in the overall response of foundation system.

Kumar and Choudhury (2016) reported dynamic soil-structure interaction (DSSI) analysis for the design of an oil tank foundation in Iraq by using finite difference based commercial software, FLAC3D. Piles were passing through soft clayey soil strata. Based on the obtained result of probabilistic seismic hazard analysis, acceleration-time history was chosen for the site and was applied to the base of the numerical model. Figure 12 illustrates the three-dimensional view of the numerical model showing oil tank foundation and free field boundary condition generated to stop any seismic wave reflection from the boundaries.

The variation of excess pore water pressure ratio with dynamic time was obtained, as shown in Figure 13. It was observed that the soils were undergoing partial cyclic mobility under the applied acceleration-time history. In comparison to a static load, axial load on piles increased by 142% during seismic loading.

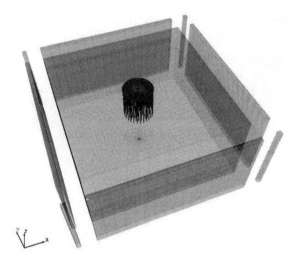

Fig. 12 Three-dimensional views of numerical model developed in FLAC3D

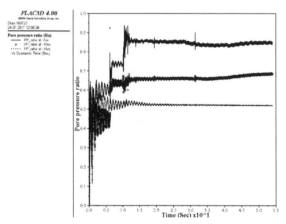

Fig. 13 Pore pressure ratio at different depth obtained in FLAC3D

The above discussion indicates that the displacement of CPRF dictate the load sharing response and hence should be given prime importance in the design. The flexibility of piles in CPRF dominates the overall behavior and may lead to change in the condition of resonance. Lateral load sharing or imposing an inertial load of soil onto the pile is dependent on pile rigidity. The length of influence i.e. called active length of pile actively contributing in the flexure is directly proportional to the flexural stiffness of the pile. The lateral displacement, shear force and bending

moment in pile are largely dependent on the flexural stiffness of pile. Poulos and Davis (1980), Gazetas (1984) and Nikolaou et al. (2001) also obtained similar behavior. Pile shares a maximum percentage of the lateral load which is unlike the case of a vertical load. The natural frequency of soil media, input motion characteristics and natural frequency of the foundation system dictate the overall foundation response and these are the main reason behind the variation in the results obtained through pseudo-static analysis and real acceleration-time history analysis. There is hardly any impact on vertical load sharing by the foundation components during the entire process of shaking and is same as obtained in static lateral loading case also. The observation is similar even in the resonance conditions

4. EFFECT OF CONNECTION RIGIDITY

The response of CPRF is greatly influenced by changing the connection condition of piles with the raft. The connection of piles with raft varies from fully rigid to fully hinged. Researchers who study the influence of connection rigidity onto the behavior of CPRF are Horikoshi et al. (2003a,b), Matsumoto et al. (2004a) and Matsumoto et al. (2010) and Kumar et al. (2015b). Their major findings are summarized below:

Connection rigidity has negligible influence on vertical load sharing by raft but it depends greatly on the mobilization of foundation displacement. The magnitude of bending moment, shear forces and lateral displacement in pile increases with increase in connection rigidity. Figure 14 illustrates the bending moment and lateral load distribution along pile length for fully rigid and hinged connection condition, respectively under different earthquake horizontal load. It can be observed that the magnitude and profile of bending moment are largely dependent on connection rigidity. The magnitude of bending moment decreases with a decrease in connection rigidity whereas the lateral displacement decreases with increase in connection rigidity. The bending moment at pile head decreases with decrease in connection rigidity and finally becomes zero for fully hinged connection condition. Crossover point i.e. change of sign of bending moment can also be observed in fully rigid connection condition unlike the case of the fully hinged condition.

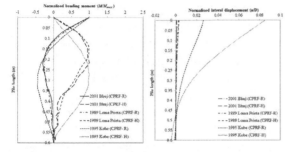

Fig. 14 Normalized bending moment and lateral distribution along pile length in fully rigid and fully hinged conditions (Kumar et al. 2015,b)

Horikoshi et al. (2003a,b) mentioned that inclination of raft decreases with increase in connection rigidity, however, Matsumoto et al. (2004) and Matsumoto et al. (2010) observed a decrease in inclination with a decrease in connection rigidity. The later observation seems realistic because lateral loads are resisted by passive resistance provided by surrounding soil in addition to the stiffness of connection. Rigid connection condition having more stiffness than hinged tries to offer more resistance towards lateral load and hence undergoes more rotation at the connection point along with displacement which is unlike the case of hinged connection where lateral displacement is predominant than rotation due to lesser stiffness. Horikoshi et al. (2003b) observed that the residual displacement under seismic shaking in CPRF was independent of connection rigidity. However, findings in static horizontal loading tests as reported by Matsumoto et al. (2004), Matsumoto et al. (2010), Matsumoto (2014) and Kumar et al. (2015b) stated dependency of lateral displacement on connection rigidity. The probable reason for this postulation may be due to

the increase in the overall stiffness of the system with an increase in connection rigidity.

5. CASE STUDIES

The utilization of raft in load sharing under horizontal and seismic loading makes CRPF more sustainable and economical foundation for highly seismic areas. Many researchers have reported the behavior of CPRF during huge devastating earthquakes like 1995 Hyogoken-Nambu earthquake (Yamada et al. 2001), 2001 Bhuj earthquake (Dash et al. 2009), 2011 Tohoku Pacific earthquake (Yamashita et al. 2012).

An earthquake event results into the development of an excess pore water pressure in the soil mass which reduces the effective stress beneath the raft and surrounding piles leads to loss in the contact pressure beneath the raft and shaft resistance in piles. The above phenomenon may lead to the failure of foundation components. Such case was reported by Dash et al. (2009) in 2001 Bhuj earthquake of moment magnitude (Mw) 7.8. They reported that 22m tall building (Custom Tower) as shown in Figure 15, resting on soft clay underlain by sand underwent tilt due to the lateral spreading and excessive settlements due to loss of strength of soil mass, this phenomenon is called liquefaction. The liquefaction in the sandy strata caused an excessive increase in axial load on pile leading to failure. They back analyzed the building foundation by employing p-y, t-z, q-z, and q-u curve to model CPRF. The above-mentioned building did not undergo complete collapse because of resistance of raft supported on soft clay strata. The stiffness degradation in clay was also observed but the remolded clay after the earthquake was able to provide sufficient contact pressure to raft which avoided a complete collapse of the building.

They also modeled the similar condition by using SAP computer program to capture possible failure mechanism and result obtained indicated reasonable agreement with field measurements.

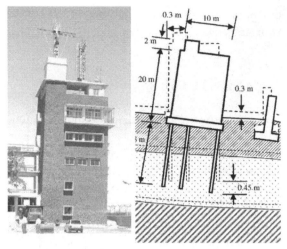

Fig. 15 Tilting of 12 stories Custom Tower in 2001 Bhuj earthquake in the Kandla port region, Gujrat, India (Dash et al. 2009)

The successful use of ground improvement technique like deep cement mixing wall for 22 stories base isolated building, as shown in Figure 16 reported by Yamashita et al. (2012) increased the confinement in the soil surrounding the foundation footprint.

Fig. 16 Twelve stories base isolated building survived in 2011 Tohuku earthquake (Yamashita et al. 2012)

Foundation monitoring indicated that the development of excess pore water pressure was negligible during 2011 Tohuku earthquake of moment magnitude (Mw) 9.0 which lead to a marginal decrease in effective shear strength of soil mass. Such response of a soil induced marginal increase in axial forces, the bending moment in piles and contact pressure beneath the raft causing a negligible effect on existing building. They also reported the advantage of using base isolation technique which cutoff the direct contact of superstructure and substructure. This technique reduced the acceleration amplification from foundation level to the floor level and also it helped in reducing the rotation of entire system allowing a structure to sway only during the earthquake. This caused negligible variation in the rotation, bending moment and axial forces in the foundation components. The coupled use of ground improvement and base isolation technique contributed in successfully withstanding the devastating 2011 Tohuku earthquake.

6. DESIGN IMPLICATIONS

Based on current design practice, following points can be noted while designing CPRF under seismic conditions:

• The evaluation of displacements like settlements, horizontal displacement, inclination, load sharing by each foundation components and stress resultants like bending moments, shear forces, and axial forces are highly important factors.

• The factor of safety, defined as the ratio of the ultimate bearing capacity of CPRF to vertical load together with lateral load should be more than 1.5 (Yamashita et al. 2011).

• The factor of safety expressed as the ratio of the ultimate bearing capacity of piles to maximum axial load obtained in load sharing should be more than 1.5 (Yamashita et al. 2011).

• The connection rigidity between raft and piles should be chosen based on allowable rotation in raft. The permissible angular rotation under static load is 1/1000 to 1/500 (AIJ, 2001). The influence of lateral loading on shear force and bending moment response in piles should be evaluated and it must be less than the permissible structural strength of piles.

• Soil-raft interaction dominates the design at the initial stage of loading but at later stage, pile-soil interaction plays an important role. This peculiar behavior of CPRF can be utilized in the actual design depending up on the tolerable lateral displacement. JRA (2002) recommends the allowable lateral displacement of pile as 1% of pile diameter.

• For the seismic design of CPRF, the condition of resonance must be checked for the soil media and the foundation itself. The condition of resonance can be avoided by varying the stiffness of pile as per the equation is given below:

$$w_{piled\ raft} = \sqrt{\frac{z(EI)_p}{l^3 m_{raft}}} \qquad (3)$$

where $w_{piled\ raft}$ is the natural frequency of piled raft, z is the constant depending upon connection condition, $(EI)_p$ is the flexural stiffness of pile, m_{raft} is the mass of raft. The natural frequency of soil can be found out from the equation given as per Kramer (1996):

$$w_{Soil} = \frac{V_s}{4H} \qquad (4)$$

where V_s is shear wave velocity and H is the thickness of soil mass.

7. CONCLUSIONS

In this chapter, the state of the art review of the behavior of combined pile-raft foundation under seismic condition are presented. Various researchers have used different methodologies

viz. experimental methods at normal gravity and enhanced gravity level, analytical and numeral modeling approach to investigate the response of CPRF embedded in different subsoil conditions. The major findings of their research works are as follows:

• The stiffness of soil and foundation components plays very important role in lateral load sharing between pile and raft. Initially, raft shares the more load than piles but as the displacement progresses, raft reaches to its limiting value. Thereafter, any further increase in lateral load is borne entirely by piles.

• The proportion of vertical load sharing remains unchanged during the application of a horizontal load which indicates that soil-pile-raft interaction mechanism developed during vertical load remains unaltered throughout the course of lateral load application. Such behavior is obtained in the case of the real seismic load as well.

• The push-in piles carry the more axial load as compared to pull-out piles due to the formation of a gap between the raft and underlying soil which causes negative raft-soil interaction and decreases the confining stress. The phenomenon also decreases the lateral load carrying capacity of the pile in CPRF. Such behavior is very likely when the height of application of lateral load lies above the level of raft.

• Under lateral loading, pile flexibility in CPRF may change the condition of attainment of resonance and decides the development of bending moment and shear forces in piles. This behavior directly affects the magnitude of inertial and kinematic interaction in CPRF.

• The response of CPRF under real seismic loading conditions depends on the input motion characteristics and natural frequency of soil media, the natural frequency of the combined pile-raft system.

• The contact at the raft base helps in reducing the horizontal displacement, acceleration and bending moment in piles which are unlike the case of group piles. The proportion of horizontal load carried by each foundation components is non-linear and is dependent on the relative displacement between soil and CPRF.

• The acceleration response of soil just below the CPRF and far-field differs widely due to strong pile-soil-raft interaction. Therefore, the near-field and far-field soil movements are not in tandem.

• The connection rigidity plays an important role in deciding the magnitude of maximum displacements and stress resultants like bending moment, shear force in piles. These stress resultants decrease with a decrease in connection rigidity. It also dictates the overall inclination of the foundation system where fully rigid connected raft undergoes more inclination as compared to fully hinged connected raft.

• In the case of liquefaction, the horizontal load carried by raft drops suddenly due to loss of base resistance. Hence, it may be critical for the design. However, if CPRF is founded in layered soil deposits then raft may provide buckling stability to the piles in case piles are subjected to an excessive axial load. The possible ground improvement technique can be adopted for implying such foundation in liquefiable soil deposits.

This study indicated that CPRF is a cost effective and safer foundation as compared to conventional group pile foundation. In a reality where foundation subsoil is highly non-homogeneous, hence, the behavior of CPRF in non-homogeneous soil deposit should be investigated to get confidence in the design which is not available till date. The response of CPRF passing through liquefiable soil deposits should be examined and proper quantification of both inertial and kinematic interactions should be obtained.

REFERENCES

Architectural Institute of Japan (2001). Recommendation for Design of Building Foundation. (In Japanese).

Banerjee, S., Goh, S. H. and Lee, F. H. (2007). The response of soft clay strata and clay-pile-raft systems to seismic shaking. *Journal of Earthquake and Tsunami*, Vol: 1, No.3., pp 233–255.

Banerjee, S., Goh, S. H. and Lee, F. H. (2014). Earthquake induced bending moment in fixed head piles in soft clay. *Geotechnique*, Vol: 64, No. 6., pp. 431-446.

Burland, J. B., Broms, B. B. and De Mello, V.F.B. (1977). Behaviour of foundation and structures. *Proceedings of 9th ICSMFE*, Tokyo, Vol: 2, pp. 495-546.

Clancy, P. and Randolph, M. (1993). An approximate analysis procedure for piled raft foundation. *International Journal for Numerical and Analytical Methods in Geomechanics*, Vol: 17, pp 849–869.

Comodromos, E. M., Papadopoulou, M. C., and Laloui, L. (2015). Contribution to the design methodologies of piled raft foundations under combined loadings. *Canadian Geotechnical Journal*, Vol: 53, pp. 559-577.

Dash, S., Govindaraju, L. and Bhattacharya, S. (2009). A case study of damages of the Kandla Port and Customs Office tower supported on a mat–pile foundation in liquefied soils under the 2001 Bhuj earthquake. *Soil Dynamics and Earthquake Engineering*, Vol: 29, No.2., pp 333–346.

Gazetas G. (1984). Seismic response of end-bearing single piles. *Soil Dynamics and Earthquake Engineering*, Vol: 3, No.2., pp 82–93.

Horikoshi, K., Matsumoto, T., Hashizume, Y., Watanabe, T. and Fukuyama H. (2003a). Performance of Piled raft subjected to static horizontal load. *International Journal of Physical Modeling*, Vol: 2, pp 37-50.

Horikoshi, K., Matsumoto, T., Hashizume, Y., Watanabe, T. and Fukuyama, H. (2003b). Performance of Piled raft subjected to dynamic loading. *International Journal of Physical Modelling*, Vol: 2, pp. 51-62.

Horikoshi, K. and Randolph, M. F. (1998). A contribution of optimum design of piled rafts. *Geotechnique*, Vol: 48, No.3., pp 301-317.

JRA (Japan Road Association). (2002). Specification for highway bridges: Seismic design, Part V, Tokyo.

Kang, M. A., Banerjee, S., Lee, F. H. and Xie, H. P. (2012). Dynamic soil-pile-raft interaction in normally consolidated soft clay during earthquakes. *Journal of Earthquake and Tsunami*, Vol: 6, No.4., pp 1250031-1 - 1250031-12.

Katzenbach, R., Bachmann, G., Boled- Mekasha, G. and Ramm, H. (2005). Combined Pile- Raft Foundation (CPRF): An approximate solution for the foundation of high rise buildings. *Slovak Journal of Civil Engineering*, Vol: 3, pp 19-29.

Katzenbach, K. and Choudhury, D. (2013). ISSMGE Combined Pile-Raft Foundation Guideline. *International Society for Soil Mechanics and Geotechnical Engineering (ISSMGE)*, Deep Foundations, pp 1-28.

Katzenbach, R., Leppla, S and Choudhury, D. (2016). *Foundation Systems for High-Rise Structures*, CRC Press, Taylor and Francis Group, UK (ISBN: 978-1-4978-4477-5), 2016, pp. 1-298.

Kitiyodom, P. and Matsumoto, T. (2002). A simplified analysis method for piled raft and pile group foundations with batter piles. *International Journal for Numerical and Analytical Methods in Geomechanics*, Vol: 26, pp 1349–1369.

Kitiyodom, P. and Matsumoto, T. (2003). A simplified analysis method for piled raft foundations in non-homogeneous soils. *International Journal for Numerical and Analytical Methods in Geomechanics*, Vol: 27, pp 85–109.

Kumar, A., Choudhury, D. and Katzenbach, R. (2015a). Behaviour of Combined Pile-Raft Foundation (CPRF) under Static and Pseudo-static Conditions using PLAXIS3D. *6th International Conference on Earthquake Geotechnical Engineering (6ICEGE)*, Christchurch, New Zealand, pp 1-8.

Kumar, A., Choudhury D, Shukla, J. and Shah, D.L. (2015b). Seismic Design of Pile Foundation for Oil Tank by using PLAXIS3D. *Disaster Advances*, Vol: 8, No. 6., pp 33–42.

Kumar A, Choudhury, D. and Katzenbach, R. (2016). Effect of earthquake on combined pile-raft foundation. *International Journal of Geomechanics, ASCE*, Vol: 16, No.5., pp 04016013: 1-16.

Kumar, A. and Choudhury, D. (2016). DSSI analysis of pile foundations for an oil tank in Iraq. *Proceedings of Institution of Civil Engineers-Geotechnical Engineering*, Vol: 169, No.2., pp 129-138.

Kumar, A., Patil, M. and Choudhury, D. (2017). Soil–structure interaction in a combined pile–raft foundation – a case study. *Proceedings of Institution of Civil Engineers-Geotechnical Engineering*, Vol: 170, No.2., pp 117-128.

Matsumoto, T., Fukumura, K., Horikoshi, K., Oki, A. (2004a). Shaking table test on model piled rafts in considering influence of superstructures. *International Journal of Physical Modelling* in Geotechnics, Vol: 31, pp 21–38.

Matsumoto, T., Fukumara K., Kitiyodom, P., Horikoshi, K. and Oki, A. (2004b). Experimental and analytical modelling study on behavior of model piled raft in sand subjected to horizontal and moment loading. *International Journal of Physical Modelling* in Geotechnics, Vol: 4, No.3., pp 1-19.

Matsumoto, T., Fujita, M., Mikami, H., Yaegashi, K., Arai, T. and Kitiyodom, P. (2010). Load tests of piled raft models with different pile head connection conditions and their analyses. *Soils and Foundations*, Vol: 50, No.1., pp 63–81.

Matsumoto, T. (2014). Implication for Design of Piled Raft Foundations subjected to Lateral Loading. *Advances in Foundation Engineering*, ISBN: 978-981-07-4623: doi: 10.3850/978-981-07-4623-0_KN-08.

Mu, L., Chen, Q., Huang, M. and Basack, S. (2016). Hybrid Approach for Rigid Piled-Raft Foundations Subjected to Coupled Loads in Layered Soils. *International Journal of Geomechanics*, Vol: 16, pp 04016122: 1–15. doi:10.1061/(ASCE)GM.1943-5622.0000825.

Nikolaou, A. S., Mylonakis, G. & Gazetas, G. (1995). Kinematic bending moments in seismically stressed piles. Report NCEER-95–0022. Buffalo, NY, USA: *National Center for Earthquake Engineering Research, State University of New York*.

Poulos, H.G. and Davis, E.H. *Pile Foundation Analysis and Design*. John Wiley and Sons, New York, 1980.

Poulos, H. G. (2001). Piled raft foundations: design and applications. *Géotechnique*, Vol: 51, No.2., pp 95–113.

Phanikanth, V. S., Choudhury, D., and Reddy, G. R. (2013). Behavior of single pile in liquefied deposits during earthquakes. *International Journal of Geomechanics*, Vol: 13, No.4., pp 454-462.

Randolph, M. F. (1994). Design methods for pile groups and piled rafts. *Proceedings of 13th ICSMFE*, New Delhi, 5, 61-82.

Sawada, K. and Takemura, J. (2014). Centrifuge model tests on the piled raft foundation in sand subjected to lateral and moment load. *Soils and Foundations*, Vol: 54, No.2., pp 126-140.

Unsever, Y.S., Matsumoto. T. and Özkan, M.Y. (2015). Numerical analyses of load tests on model foundations in dry sand. *Computer and Geotechics*, Vol: 63, pp. 255–66.

Unsever, Y. S., Matsumoto, T., Eshashi, K. and Kobayashi S. (2016). Behaviour of model pile foundations under dynamic loads in saturated sand. *Bulletin of Earthquake Engineering*, doi:10.1007/s10518-016-0029-y.

Walling, M. and Mohanty, W. (2009). An overview on the seismic zonation and microzonation studies in India. *Earthquake Science Reviews*, Vol: 96, pp 67-91.

Yamada, T., Yamashita, K., Kakurai, M. and Tsukatani, H. (2001). Long- term behaviour of tall building on raft foundation constructed by top- down method. *Proc., 5th Int. Conf. on Deep Foundation Practice*, CI- Premier Pte Ltd., Singapore, pp 411–417.

Yamashita, K., Yamada, T. and Hamada, J. (2011). Investigation of settlement and load sharing on piled rafts by monitoring full-scale structures. *Soils and Foundations*, Vol: 51, No.3., pp 513–532.

Yamashita, K., Hamada, J., Onimaru, S. and Higashino, M. (2012). Seismic behaviour of piled raft with ground improvement supporting a base-isolated building on soft ground in Tokyo. *Soils and Foundations*, Vol: 52, pp 1000-1015.

Zhang, L.Ã., Goh, S.H. and Yi, J. A. (2017). Centrifuge study of the seismic response of pile – raft systems embedded in soft clay.

Geotechnique, in press with doi: dx.doi.org/10.1680/jgeot.15.P.099.

Zhang, L., Goh, S.H. and Liu, H. (2017). Seismic response of pile-raft-clay system subjected to a long-duration earthquake: centrifuge test and finite element analysis. *Soil Dynamics and Earthquake Engineering*, Vol: 92, pp 488–502.

CHAPTER 5

ANALYSIS OF A LATERALLY LOADED CAPPED BORED PILE GROUP USING 3D FINITE ELEMENT METHOD

San-Shyan Lin*
Department of Harbor and River Engineering, National Taiwan Ocean University, Keelung, Taiwan
Swinburne University of Technology, Sarawak Campus
**sslin@mail.ntou.edu.tw*

Chao-Kuang Hsueh
Department of Merchant Marine, National Taiwan Ocean University, Keelung, Taiwan

Dominic E. L. Ong
Swinburne University of Technology, Sarawak Campus

ABSTRACT: Finite element simulation for analysis of a capped pile group was conducted to investigate the interaction among piles, soil and pile cap, especially the effects resulted from concrete damaging. The simulation was to develop a calibrated model using the test data and to apply that model for conditions not present during the test. In addition to consider pile/soil and cap/pile interaction in the numerical simulation, interaction between steel reinforcement and concrete was also modelled in the analysis. Each steel reinforcement installed in the tested piles and the pile cap was modelled as an individual element at its installed position in the numerical analysis. The simulation results showed that the leading and the middle row piles in the group carried the highest and the lowest fraction of pile head loads when concrete around the pile cap/soil contact area remained its integrity. Increasing loading level, the pile head load carried by the middle row increased due to constraint of the pile cap affected by the concrete damage at the pile cap/soil contact zone.

1. INTRODUCTION

To provide enough capacity for lateral loading, a pile foundation is often designed in groups with a cap providing the connection between the structure and each single pile under the cap. Depending on the pile-to-cap embedment length and the amount of the provided reinforcement, the pile cap induces some degree of horizontal restraint at the top of the pile. Studies have found that resistance to a lateral loading is then provided by pile-soil-pile interaction, base and/or side friction along the concrete-soil interface (Rollins and Cole 2006). Several studies on pile group performance have provided important insight into the behavior of pile-soil-pile interaction because of the stress overlapping caused reduction of overall capacity relative to that of a single pile (Muqtadir and Desai 1986; Brown and Shie 1990; Bhowmik 1992; Yang and Jeremic 2003; Comodromosa et al. 2009, and Lin et al. 2005 etc.). Previous works either neglected the nonlinear flexural behavior of pile or simplified the connection between pile head and cap as a fixed or a free boundary condition. The works by Mokwa and Duncan (2003), Rollins and Cole (2006) and Lin and Liao (2013) were available on cap-pile head interaction. Lemnitzer et al. (2010) focused on the nonlinear efficiency of bored pile group under lateral load. Relatively little information on effect of concrete damaging evaluated for large scale concrete pile group is reported in the literature.

A large-scale lateral loading test was conducted on two capped pile groups in Chiayi, Taiwan in 1997. The bored pile group consisted of six drilled shafts with diameter 1.5m, which was installed to a depth of 34.9m. The ratio of center to center spacing between piles over pile diameter was 3. The reinforced concrete pile cap was rectangular: 12m in length (L), 8.5m in width (W) and a thickness (D) of 2m. To have more understanding on the effect on concrete cracking on performance of a capped bored pile group subjected to lateral loading, the purpose of the study is to calibrate a model to the test data obtained from the pile group tested in Chiayi and to use the model to evaluate the interaction among pile, soil and pile cap. A model calibrated using the Chiayi test data for the free head single pile was studied by Hsueh et al. (2004). In this study, the 3D finite element software ABAQUS (Hibbit et al. 2002) is used for pile group simulation. The properties of soil, concrete and steel reinforcement are all modelled using nonlinear constitutive law. The installed steel reinforcement is modelled using a special individual element which can anchor at the interface node of the concrete element at exact the same location of the tested pile group.

2. BRIEF OF THE PILE GROUP TEST (CHEN 1997; BROWN ET AL. 2001 AND LIN AND LIAO 2006)

A large scale lateral loading test of two pile groups were conducted at Chiayi, Taiwan. The arrangement of the test set up of the pile groups is shown in Fig. 1. One of the pile groups consisted of six drilled shafts and the other group consisted of twelve driven precast concrete (PC) piles. The pre-stressed PC piles were circular and hollow cast in 17m long segments in the manufacture factory.

In this paper, the study is only focusing on the drilled shaft group. The drilled shafts were installed by reverse circulation method. Reinforcing cage consists of fifty-two 32mm longitudinal reinforcement placed in a circular arrangement within each pile, with 16mm hoop steel bars used as circular ties.

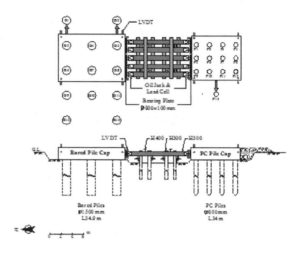

Fig. 1 Arrangement of the test setup (Chen 1997)

The bars extended 1.65m into each pile, leaving 1.35m bond length within the pile cap. Detail of the connection between pile head and pile cap is shown in Fig. 2. The reinforced concrete cap was sitting on the excavated level ground surface. Inclinometer casings were attached to the longitudinal bars of the reinforcement cage. The inclinometer casings were extending to the full thickness of the pile cap. The ratio of center to center spacing between piles over pile diameter was 3 for both groups. Structural properties of the tested piles and typical soil properties of the testing site are given in Tables 1 and 2, respectively. Lateral loading tests on the two groups were conducted by push the two pile caps away from each other (Fig. 1). Ten pairs of 5MN hydraulic jacks and load cells were used for lateral force application. Detail information regarding testing of the pile group can be referred to Chen (1997), Brown et al. (2001), or Lin and Liao (2006).

Table 1 Structural properties of test piles (Chen 1997)

	Cross-Section (m²)	Concrete				Steel		
		f_c' (MPa)	f_t' (MPa)	E_c (GPa)	v_c	f_y (MPa)	E_{st} (GPa)	v_{st}
B3~B8	1.767	27.47	3.28	24.62	0.18	412.02	200.12	0.29
Cap	102							

Table 2 Site stratigraphy and soil conditions at the test site (Chen 1997)

Depth(m)	SPT-N	Classification	γ_t (kN/m³)	E_s (kPa)	c (kPa)	ϕ (°)	S_u (kPa)	ϕ' (°)	v_s	K_o
0-3	1~5	ML/SM	18.64	44584	1.0	13.5	—	31.7	0.4	0.63
3-8	8~19	SM	18.64	49407	1.0	12	—	33.4	0.3	0.72
8-12	4~12	CL	18.69	81935	14.81	10.8	45.38	—	0.45	0.78
12-16	15~29	SM	18.84	96605	1.0	18.2	—	35	0.3	0.76
16-22	11~23	CL/SM	18.84	122379	1.0	16.8	—	33.3	0.4	0.68
22-32	9~27	CL	18.76	242855	19.6	21	64.41	—	0.45	0.6
32-40	14~45	SM	19.07	282625	1.0	25	—	41.5	0.3	0.55

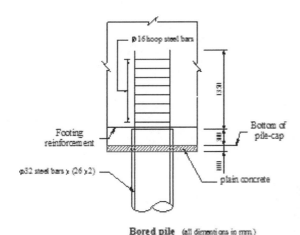

Fig. 2 Detail of the reinforcement connection between pile head and cap (Chen 1997)

3. FINITE ELEMENT ANALYSIS

3.1 Finite Element Modelling

A 3D finite element model created in ABAQUS (Hibbit et al. 2002) is used to simulate the tested pile group (see Fig. 1) given in Fig. 3 to 5. The shaft cross-section and the pile cap is modelled with 8-node solid element (C3D8). The longitudinal and hoop steel reinforcement are modelled using REBAR element in the software library. These elements in the software are anchored at the interface nodes of the concrete element. Each steel reinforcement is arranged at the exact location of the tested pile group. Plan and elevation view of the finite element mesh including soil boundary are shown in Fig. 4 and 5, respectively. In the figures, the dark dash line is the boundary of the near and the far field soil. The infinite element (CIN3D8) was used in the far field to simulate the semi-infinite boundary. The soil domain in the near field is also modelled with 8-node solid element. The distance of the near field is assumed as ten times of the pile diameter. In addition, the dark solid line represents the interface between pile structure and soil. The function "CONTACT PAIR" in the software library is used to model the frictional contact for the shaft-soil interaction by assuming the master and slave surface as the shaft surface and soil, respectively.

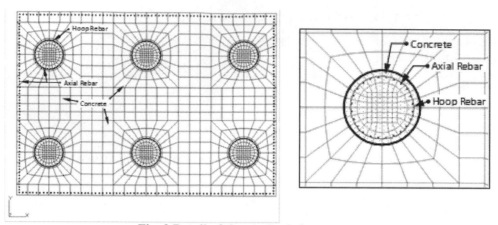

Fig. 3 Detail of the steel reinforcement

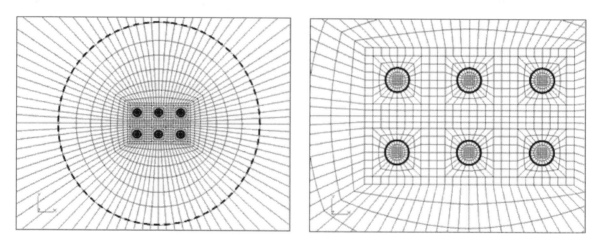

Fig. 4 Plane view of the finite element mesh

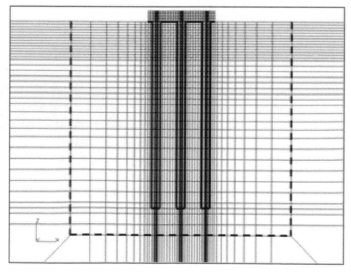

Fig. 5 Elevation view of the finite element mesh

3.2   Material Modelling

The uniaxial compressive stress-strain relationship
given in Fig. 6 is assumed to represent the behavior
of concrete. Strain hardening is considered in the steel
reinforcement as shown Fig. 7. The Mohr-Coulomb
constitutive law with elastic-perfectly plastic
behavior is used to model soil behavior. The required
parameters are Mohr-Coulomb strength parameters
for shear strength (i.e. cohesion c and friction angle ϕ)
and elastic moduli as given in Table 2.

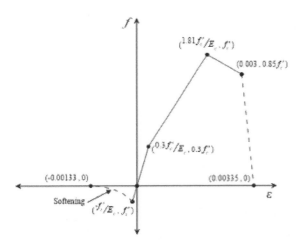

**Fig. 6 Uniaxial compressive stress-strain
relationship of concrete (Hsueh et al. 2004)**

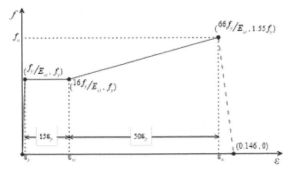

**Fig. 7 Stress-strain relationship of steel
reinforcement**

3.3   Single Pile Analysis

Lateral test was firstly conducted on the B2 pile
given in Fig. 1. The cap of pile group was served as
a reaction system. The calculated and the measured

load deflection relationship at the pile head are
shown in Fig. 8 for comparison. Good agreement
is obtained because nonlinear flexural stiffness of
the piles was considered in the numerical analysis.
The calculated deflection and the soil plastic strain
zones around the shaft under maximum applied
loading are shown in Fig. 9. It also indicates the
ground displacement at distance of 15m (about 10
times of shaft diameter) away from the shaft center,
which is less than 1.5mm and its corresponding
strain is only about 0.018%. In addition, the
contour diagram of the soil plastic strain zone
shows the soil yields within the distance of six
times of shaft diameter. Since ground displacement
at location of fifteen times of the shaft diameter
from the shaft center approaches zero, hence the
assumed boundary between near and far field is
appropriate.

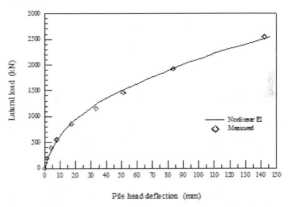

Fig. 8 Load deflection curve at pile head

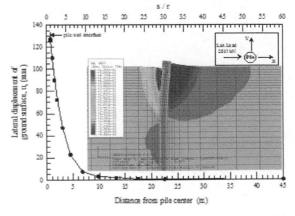

**Fig. 9 Calculated lateral displacement of ground
and pile (Hsueh et al. 2004)**

The calculated and the measured slope and rebar stress along shaft are given in Fig. 10 and 11, respectively. When the applied loading level reaches 2,541kN, the rebar stress at the tension side has reached its yield strength of the reinforcement. The maximum rebar stress occurred at 7m below the ground surface. In addition, effect of concrete crack pattern on the moment-curvature relationship is given in Fig. 12. Based on these calculated results, we can see that pile shaft rigidity is significantly affected by the concrete cracking pattern along shaft. The calculated shaft cracking moment is about 1,700kN-m, which matches the tested shaft material and geometric properties. When lateral load increased to 854kN, the bending moments of the shaft at depth 3m to 9m exceeded their cracking moment, resulting in some local concrete cracking in the shaft. The concrete cracking effect is more severe and spread up- and downward when the applied lateral loading increased, as shown in Fig. 12.

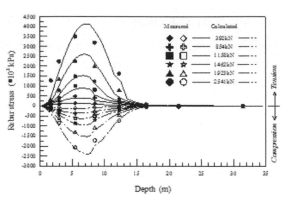

Fig. 11 Comparison between calculated and measured rebar stress (Hsueh et al. 2004)

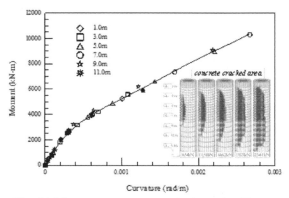

Fig. 12 Moment curvature relationship (Hsueh et al. 2004)

3.4 Pile Group Analysis

The load-deflection response at the pile cap is nonlinear as shown in Fig. 13, in which the measured results based on two different tests are also given for comparison. Reasonable agreement is observed between the calculated and measured results. The first test for this case was a virgin loading, which was stopped when the PC-pile group was observed too weak when applied lateral load reached the level of 6,000kN. The second test was carried out with lateral load increased to 10,948kN, after placement of backfill behind the PC-pile group.

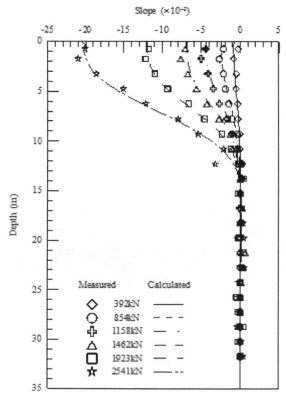

Fig. 10 Comparison between calculated and measured slope (Hsueh et al. 2004)

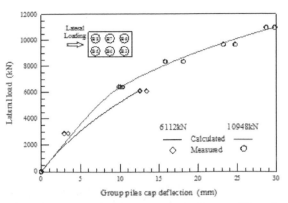

Fig. 13 Load deflection curve at pile cap (Hsueh et al. 2004)

Fig. 14 and 15 present the simulated displacement of the pile cap, piles and ground under maximum applied loading. As shown in the figures, the pile cap appears to have a clockwise rotation of degree 0.03°, which caused 36.9mm uplifting of the ground in front of the pile cap. These calculated values coincide with the observed results during the test.

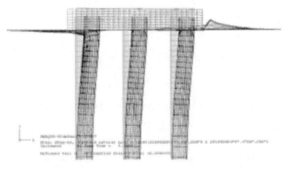

Fig. 14 Simulated lateral displacement of the pile group and ground surface

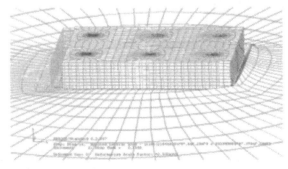

Fig. 15 Simulated lateral displacement at the pile cap/soil contact area

The simulated lateral displacement of the ground surface at the pile cap/soil contact area under maximum applied loading is shown in Fig. 16, it showed that the ground surface affected by the lateral load reached out to the far field either in front of the pile cap or behind the pile cap.

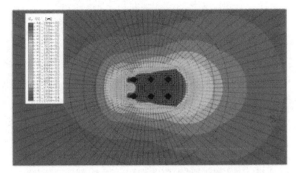

Fig. 16 Plan view of simulated lateral displacement

Elevation view of the simulated ground lateral displacement given in Fig. 17 showed the disturbed area is deeper than that of a single pile with free head given in Fig. 9. Separation between the pile cap and the ground behind the trailing row piles was also observed as shown in the figure.

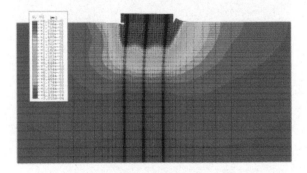

Fig. 17 Elevation view of simulated lateral displacement

Fig. 18 and 19 showed the plan view and elevation view of the simulated plastic strain distribution under the maximum applied loading. The yield zone at the ground surface in front of the pile cap was extended to a distance four times the shaft diameter. In addition, localized plastic strain zone was also observed behind the trailing row piles as shown in these figures. Behind the trailing row piles, it was observed that the plastic strain extended down to a depth about 7m below the pile cap.

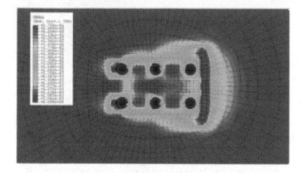

Fig. 18 Plan view of simulated plastic strain under maximum applied loading

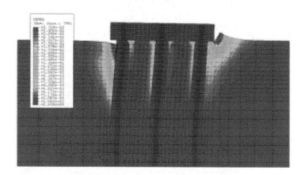

Fig. 19 Elevation view of simulated plastic strain under the maximum applied load

Table 3 gives the calculated values of the load carried at the pile head of the piles on each row

and the base shear below the pile cap. In the table, Stol represents the level of total lateral load applied at the pile cap. Based on the table, the contribution of the pile cap base shear frictional resistance was 3.5%. In addition, the leading, middle and trailing row piles carried 34.4%, 30.6% and 31.4%, respectively, of the total applied load at the pile cap. The data given in Table 3 can be re-drawn in Fig. 20, in which the Savg is the applied lateral forced at the pile cap divided by the total numbers of pile. In general, the load carried by the leading row and the middle row increases with increasing of applied lateral load. On the contrary, the trailing row and the pile cap base friction decreases with increasing of applied load. In addition, it was also shown that the load carried by the leading row piles was higher than that of the Savg.

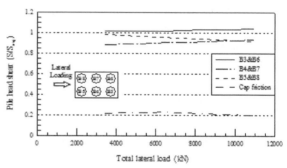

Fig. 20 Ratio of shear force carried by each row of piles

Fig. 21 presents the profiles of deflection, moment, shear force and soil lateral resistance of the piles B3 to B8 under the maximum applied loading.

Table 3 Ratio of load carried by each row of piles

Load (Stol, kN)	B5&B8 Avg. (S58, kN)	B5&B8 S58 / Stol	B4&B7 Avg. (S47, kN)	B4&B7 S47 / Stol	B3&B6 Avg. (S36, kN)	B3&B6 S36 / Stol	Cap Friction (F, kN)	Cap F / Stol
2894	465.1	0.161	438.5	0.152	492.1	0.170	102.6	0.035
6112	966.6	0.158	940.9	0.154	1063.6	0.174	169.4	0.028
6416	1022.7	0.159	968.6	0.151	1092.1	0.170	249.0	0.039
8348	1310.0	0.157	1273.7	0.153	1438.1	0.172	304.7	0.037
9643	1498.5	0.155	1486.0	0.154	1669.3	0.173	335.7	0.035
10948	1676.5	0.153	1705.5	0.156	1907.6	0.174	386.7	0.034
Avg.	—	0.157	—	0.153	—	0.172	—	0.035

The measured inclinometer data is also provided for comparison. The maximum moment occurs at a depth of 8m below ground surface. In addition, as shown in the figure, the piles in the leading row and the middle row have the lowest and the highest lateral deflection below the pile cap. The soil resistance profile showed that the highest resistance occurred near the maximum moment location. The maximum and the minimum soil resistance also occurs at leading row and middle row, respectively. At top 4m below pile head, the highest soil resistance was observed at the leading row piles.

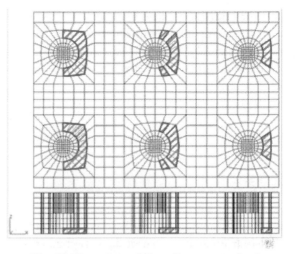

Fig. 22 Plan view of the pile cap cracked concrete pattern

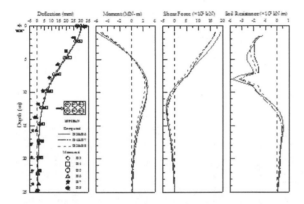

Fig. 21 Deflection, moment, shear, and soil resistance profile

Predicted pile cap concrete crack pattern under the maximum applied lateral loading level is shown in Fig. 22. It's shown concrete cracking was severe in trailing row piles but moderate in leading rows. As shown in Fig. 13, the first step loading level of the second test was 6,112kN, which already caused the moment in the pile section higher than that of the crack moment of 1,554kN-m.

The predicted concrete crack pattern along shaft is shown in Fig. 23, in which the most severe condition occurred at the trailing row piles. Based on the calculated shear force profile, the maximum and the minimum shear force occurs at the leading row and the middle row before concrete cracked. However, after the pile cap concrete began cracking around the base of the trailing row, the

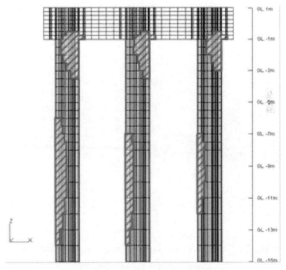

Fig. 23 Elevation view of the cracked concrete pattern

middle row and the leading row started taking more load because the constraint at the pile head of the trailing rows was affected by the concrete cracking. Subsequently, the load carried by the middle row increases due to the force transferred from the trailing rows after concrete cracked.

Fig. 24 gives the comparison between the calculated and the measured rebar stress distribution profile of pile B6. Similar results are also found for the rest of other piles. As shown in the figure, the maximum rebar stress locations coincide with the cracked concrete location given in Fig. 23. Unlike the B2 single pile with free head condition shown in Fig. 11, the calculated and measured rebar stress is smaller than the yield strength of reinforcement. In addition, the rebar stress profile given in Fig. 24 is also different from that of the B2 pile of Fig. 11.

Calculated effects of linear and nonlinear flexural stiffness assumption of pile section on variation of the shear force at pile head, the deflection profile, and the moment curvature relationship are shown in Fig. 25, 26 and 27, respectively. As shown in Fig. 25 and 26, calculation based on a constant flexural stiffness assumption tends to under predict

the calculated values. On the contrary, a constant pile section flexural stiffness assumption will over predict the moment versus curvature relationship as shown in Fig. 27.

In Table 4 and Fig. 28, under the same displacement, it's defined that the pile group efficiency is the ratio of the average load carried at pile head on each row of pile group to the load at pile head of the B2 single pile, with fixed head

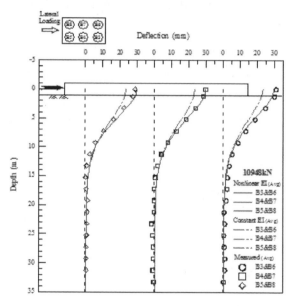

Fig. 26 Effect of nonlinear flexural rigidity on calculated results of the tested pile group

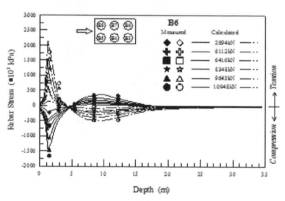

Fig. 24 Comparison between the calculated and measured rebar stress

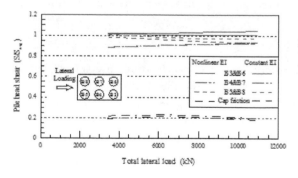

Fig. 25 Effect of nonlinear flexural rigidity on the shear forces at group pile head

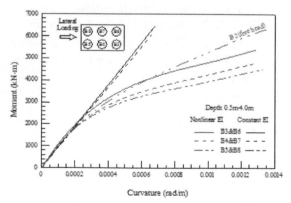

Fig. 27 Effect of nonlinear flexural rigidity on the moment-curvature relationship

condition. In Table 4, SB2F is the load carried at
head of the B2 pile with the fixed head condition.
Based on the calculation, the leading row and the
middle row showed the highest and the lowest
efficiency. However, when the applied loading
level was higher than 10,000kN, the middle row
showed higher efficiency than that of the trailing
row piles, possibly resulted from the effect of
cracked concrete. To enable comparisons between
the test results of the pile group, a calibrated model
of the single pile, B2 was developed and used to
simulate the response of a single shaft with fixed
head condition. The calculated lateral load versus
displacement at pile head and the p-y curves along
shaft of the B2 pile is shown in Fig. 29 and 30,
respectively. Significant increasing of the lateral
bearing capacity was observed for the fixed head
than that of free head condition. The reduced initial
modulus of the p-y curves with free head at depth
shallower than 7m was observed in Fig. 30.

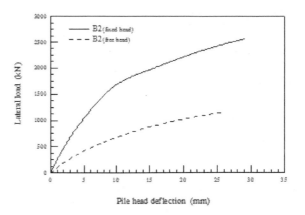

**Fig. 29 Comparison of load-deflection curves
under different head conditions**

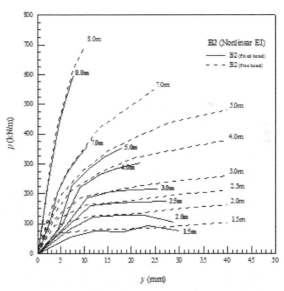

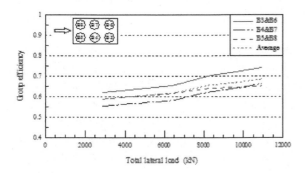

**Fig. 28 Simulated group efficiency versus total
lateral load**

**Fig. 30 Effect of free and fixed head conditions
on the p-y curves of B2 pile**

Table 4 Ratio of load carried at each row of piles / single pile with fixed head condition

Load (kN)	B2 (fixed) (S_{B2F}, kN)	B5&B8 Avg. (S_{58}, kN)	B5&B8 S_{58} / S_{B2F}	B4&B7 Avg. (S_{47}, kN)	B4&B7 S_{47} / S_{B2F}	B3&B6 Avg. (S_{36}, kN)	B3&B6 S_{36} / S_{B2F}
6416	1662.7	1022.7	0.616	968.6	0.583	1092.1	0.657
8348	2039.2	1310.0	0.642	1273.7	0.625	1438.1	0.706
9643	2317.0	1498.5	0.647	1486.0	0.641	1669.3	0.720
10948	2567.4	1676.5	0.653	1705.5	0.664	1907.6	0.743
Avg.	—	—	0.640	—	0.628	—	0.707

The p-y curves of the pile group are shown in Fig. 31, in which the simulated p-y curves of the B2 single pile with fixed head condition are also given for comparison. Based on Fig. 31, the p-multiplier of the leading, middle and trailing row piles are 0.867, 0.655 and 0.688, respectively. Study of the same case example using pressuremeter investigation results by Huang et al. (2001) suggested that the p-multiplier of the leading, middle and trailing row piles are 0.93, 0.70 and 0.74, respectively.

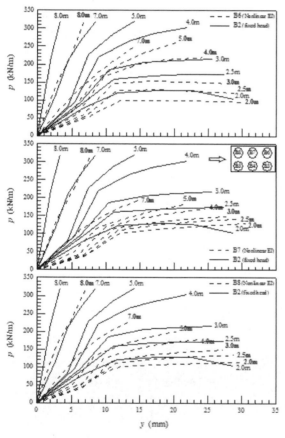

Fig. 31 p-y curves of leading, middle and trailing row piles

4. CONCLUSIONS

Finite element analyses of a pile group were carried out to calibrate a model to the test data and to use the model to evaluate the effects of concrete cracking. Based on the numerical simulation results, the following conclusions can be drawn:

1) The free head B2 pile was cracked at the loading level of 630kN and at the respective deflection of 10.1mm. The nonlinear moment curvature relationship of the pile section was highly dependent on distribution of the extensiveness of the cracked concrete area. In addition, calculated results revealed significant differences in the load-deflection response between the fixed and the free head conditions.

2) Both calculated and measured rebar stress profile of the free head B2 pile showed the maximum tension occurred at depth of 7m. Unlike free head single pile which had only one maximum tension along depth, calculated and measured rebar stress profile of the piles below cap showed the larger tension occurred at depth of 1.25m and the second larger tension at depth of 9.5m. It helped to explain why the disturbed area of the soil surround a pile in a capped pile group was deeper than that of a single pile with free head.

3) The leading and the middle row piles in the group carried the highest and the lowest load when the concrete at the pile cap/soil contact area remained its integrity. Increasing the applied loading until concrete cracked, the release of cap constraint due to cracked concrete caused increasing of load carried by the middle row. In general, the load carried by the leading row and the middle row increased with increasing of applied lateral load. On the contrary, the load carried at the trailing row and the frictional resistance at pile cap and ground contact surface decreased with increasing of applied load.

ACKNOWLEDGEMENTS

The presented study was carried out as part of a research project funded by the Ministry of Science and Technology (102-2221-E-019 -028 -MY3), Taiwan ROC. The second author is grateful for the financial support.

REFERENCES

Bhowmik, S. K., (1992). *Three-dimensional nonlinear finite element analysis of laterally loaded piles in clay*, Ph.D. Thesis, University of Illinois at Urbana-Champaign.

Brown, D. A., O'Nerill, M. W., Hoit, M., McVay, M., El Naggar, M. H., and Chakraborty, S. (2001). *Static and dynamic lateral loading of pile groups*, NCHRP Report No. 461, Transportation Research Board, Washington D.C., USA.

Brown, D. A., and Shie, C.-F., (1990). "Three-dimensional finite element model of laterally loaded piles", Computers and Geotechnics, Vol: 10, No.1, pp 59-79.

Chen, C. H. (1997). *Data for planned pile groups tests at Chiayi test site: Workshop report*, Department of Civil Engineering, National Taiwan University, Taipei, Taiwan.

Comodromosa, E. M., Papadopouloub, M. C., and Rentzeperis, I. K. (2009). Pile foundation analysis and design using experimental data and 3-D numerical analysis, *Computers and Geotechnics*, Vol: 36, No.5, pp 819-836

Hibbit, H. D., Karlsson, B. I., and Sorensen, P., (2002). *ABAQUS Theory and User's Manual*, Version 6.2, Hibbit, Karlsson & Sorensen, Inc., U.S.A.

Hsueh, C. K., Lin, S. S., and Chern, S. G. (2004). Lateral performance of drilled shaft considering nonlinear soil and structure material behavior, *Journal of Marine Science and Technology*, Vol: 12, No.1, pp 62-70.

Huang, A. B., Hsueh, C. K., O'Neill, M. W., Chern, S., and Chen, C. (2001). Effects of construction on laterally loaded pile groups, *Journal of Geotechnical and Geoenviroenemntal Engineering*, ASCE, Vol: 127, No.5, pp 385-397.

Lemnitzer, A., Khalili-Tehrani, P., Ahlberg, E. R., Rha, C., Taciroglu, E., Wallace, J. W., and Stewart, J. P. (2010). Nonlinear efficiency of bored pile group under lateral loading, *Journal of Geotechnical and Geoenvironmental Engineering*, Vol: 136, No.12, pp 1673-1685.

Lin, S. S., and Liao, J. C., (2013). Lateral Load Resistance between Pile-Group and Cap, *International Symposium on Advances in Foundation Engineering*, Singapore, pp 205-210.

Lin, S. S., and Liao, J. C. (2006). Lateral Response Evaluation of Single Piles Using Inclinometer Data, *Journal of Geotechnical and Geoenvironmental Engineering, ASCE*, Vol: 132, No.12, pp 1566-1573.

Lin, S. S., Liao, J. C., Chen, J. T., and Chen, L. (2005). Lateral Performance of Piles Evaluated via Inclinometer Data, *Computers and Geotechnics*, Vol: 32, No.6, pp 411-421.

Mokwa, R. L., and Duncan, J. M. (2003). Rotational resistance of pile caps during lateral loading, *Journal of Geotechnical and Geoenvironmental Engineering*, Vol: 129, No.9, pp 829-837.

Muqtadir, A., and Desai, C. S., (1986). Three-dimensional analysis of a pile-group foundation, *International Journal for Numerical and Analytical Methods in Geomechanics*, Vol: 10, pp 41-58.

Rollins, K. M., and Cole, R. T. (2006). Cyclic lateral load behavior of a pile cap and backfill, *Journal of Geotechnical and Geoenvironmental Engineering, ASCE*, Vol: 132, No.9, pp 1143-1153.

Yang, Z. and Jeremic, B. (2003). Numerical study of group effects for pile groups in sands, *International Journal for Numerical and Analytical Methods in Geomechanics*, Vol: 27, No.15, pp 1255-1276.

CHAPTER 6

EXAMPLE OF SEISMIC DESIGN OF PILED RAFT FOUNDATION USING FINITE ELMENT METHOD AND SIMPLIFIED METHOD

Junjj Hamada*

*Research and Development Institute, Takenaka Corporation, Chiba, Japan, *hamada.junji@takenaka.co.jp*

ABSTRACT: This article presents an example of seismic design of piled raft. First, proposed simplified analytical method and proposed theoretical equations capable for estimation of lateral load sharing ratio and sectional forces of piles on piled raft foundation are introduced. Secondary, a case history of seismic design of piled raft foundation supporting eleven-story office building with base isolated system is presented by using finite element method and these proposed methods. By comparing these analyses, the proposed theoretical equations are recognized to be effective tool for seismic design of piled raft foundation because of saving of calculation time and its function to check some insecure ground conditions.

1. INTRODUCTION

There has been increasing recognition that the use of piles to reduce raft settlement can lead to considerable economy without compromising foundation safety and performance (Poulos, 2001; Mandolini et al., 2005). A lot of experimental and analytical studies and field measurements on piled raft foundations have been conducted to investigate their settlement behavior and the load-sharing between raft and piles for vertical loading (Katzenbach et al., 2000; Yamashita et al., 2011a; Yamashita et al., 2011b). However, much less research has been done on the lateral resistance of piled rafts to seismic loads.

A seismic design concept needs to be developed for piled rafts, especially in highly active seismic areas such as Japan and Taiwan. In the conventional design concept for pile groups, all lateral loads are assumed to be carried by the piles only, despite the fact that some of the load is transferred to the soil through the raft by friction. Hence, the required pile diameter and the number of piles are generally large. In the rational design concept for piled rafts, the lateral load is carried by both the piles and by raft friction. In this case, the bending moment in the piles is caused not only by shear force at pile heads but also by ground displacement caused by raft friction as shown in Figure 1.

In the last decade or so, shaking table tests (Horikoshi et al., 2003a), static lateral loading tests using centrifuge models (Horikoshi et al., 2003b; Katzenbach & Turek, 2005) and shaking table tests in 1 g fields (Watanabe et al., 2001; Matsumoto et al., 2004a, b; Matsumoto et al., 2010; Unsever et al., 2014, 2015; Vu et al., 2016, 2017) have been carried out. Recently, a seismic response

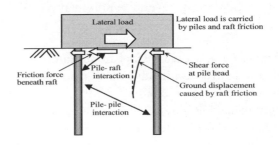

Fig. 1 Lateral load distribution within piled raft foundations under lateral load for rational design concept

of a piled raft foundation was successfully recorded during the 2011 off the Pacific Coast of Tohoku Earthquake (Yamashita et al., 2012) and the simulation analysis was conducted using a detailed three-dimensional finite-element model (Hamada et al., 2014). Sawada & Takemura (2014) carried out horizontal loading tests subjected to relatively large moment load and rotation using a geotechnical centrifuge.

This paper shows an example of seismic design of a piled raft foundation conducted by simplified analytical method, simple theoretical method and finite element method. The most important issues in developing a seismic design concept for piled rafts are evaluating the sectional force on the piles and the load sharing ratio between the piles and the raft. These analytical method and theoretical method can estimate both the sectional force and the load sharing.

In Section 2, simplified analytical method based on Mindlin's solution for piled rafts subjected to lateral load is prescribed. The analytical method is able to be considered full interactions among the raft, piles and subsoil, so the method is still a little bit complicated. If the interaction effects from pile to pile or pile to raft are ignored, the calculation procedure becomes simpler.

In Section 3, theoretical equations for piled rafts subjected to lateral load are described. The theoretical equations were derived for making rough evaluations of the lateral resistance of piled rafts while using several approximations and assumptions.

In Section 4, a case history of seismic design of piled rafts is introduced. Seismic design of piled rafts was conducted for the eleven-story office building of 60.8 m in height above ground surface located in Japan. Finite element method, the proposed simplified analysis and the derived theoretical equations were applied for the foundation design.

2. SIMPIFIED ANALYTICAL METHOD BASED ON MINDLIN'S SOLUTION FOR PILED RAFTS SUBJECTED TO LATERAL LOAD

Most of the lateral load for the piled raft foundations was transferred to the soil through the raft by friction. Bending moments in the piles were caused not only by shear force at the piles' heads but also by ground displacement through raft friction. A simplified analytical method that considers these phenomena would be useful for seismic design. Analytical methods using computer programs for piled rafts based on Mindlin's solution (Mindlin, 1936) have been developed by Kitiyodom and Matsumoto (2002, 2003), Mano and Nakai (2000, 2001) and Tsuchiya et al. (2002). In their programs, a hybrid model was employed in which the flexible raft was modeled as a thin plate, the piles as elastic beams, and the soil as interactive springs.

Kitiyodom and Matsumoto (2003) used a weighted average modulus to compute the responses of piled rafts in multi-layered soils although the theory of the method assumed an elastic linear homogeneous half space based on Mindlin's solution. Mano and Nakai (2001) applied Mindlin's solution for non-linear soils by estimating each layer's shear deformation.

The model the authors have developed (Figure 2) expands on the response to nonlinear fields and adds features as follows.

1. Pile-soil-pile and pile-soil-raft interactions are incorporated into the model. Ground deformations caused by the lateral ground reaction on an arbitrarily pile and friction between the raft and subsoil are taken into account based on Mindlin's solution. The lateral resistance of piles is calculated using the elastic beam equation for ground deformations.

2. Multi-layered soil deposits are incorporated into the model. The model for the ground is divided

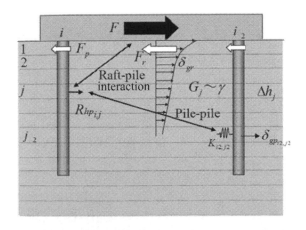

Fig.2 Developed analytical model for piled rafts subjected to lateral load

into many layers. The shear modulus G_j is set for each layer j. The ground displacement of the bottom layer is calculated using the semi-infinite elastic theory (Mindlin's solution), and that of an arbitrarily layer is calculated starting from the bottom and moving upward, integrating the relative displacement on each divided layer.

3. The model incorporates nonlinear soil deposits. The relationship between the shear modulus and shear strain G-γ is set for each layer. The shear strain γ of an arbitrary layer is calculated by the relative displacement between the layers just above and below it divided by the thickness of the layer (Δh_j). The equivalent shear modulus of an arbitrary layer is used to estimate the effect of pile-soil-pile and pile-soil-raft interactions. The thickness of Δh_j is usually employed from 0.5 m to 2 m in practical design, it is considered to be not so sensitive for evaluation of the ground deformation caused by raft friction.

4. The model incorporates nonlinearity of the coefficient of lateral subgrade reaction of piles (k_h). The stiffness of the reaction between a pile and soil at an arbitrary depth decreases as their relative displacement. The decrease in stiffness is considered to occur only around piles.

5. Pile material nonlinearity is incorporated into the model. The relationship between bending moment and curvature (M-ϕ) is considered, depending on the axial load on the piles.

The procedure of the analysis is shown in Figure 3. i) First, the lateral temporary loads for the piles and the raft are set as F_p and F_r respectively. ii) The ground displacement δ_{rp} and the displacement of the raft (footing) δ_{rr} caused by F_r are calculated based on Mindlin's solution, taking the nonlinearity of the soil deposits into consideration. iii) Next, the lateral displacement δ_{hp} and subgrade reaction Rhp of each pile are estimated using the elastic beam method based on the values δ_{rp} and F_p. iv) Then, the ground displacement at other piles' positions δ_{pp} and the displacement of the raft δ_{pr} induced by R_{hp} are calculated based on Mindlin's solution. v) The total displacement of the raft δ_r ($=\delta_{gr(0)} = \delta_{rr} + \delta_{pr}$) should be the same as the displacement at the piles' heads δhp at z = 0. If δ_r differs from δ_{hp}, then the above calculations are repeated by resetting F_p and F_r.

Equation (1) shows the lateral displacement of each component with a flexibility matrix where α_{pipj}, α_{rirj}, α_{pirj} and α_{ripj} are interaction factors, and K_{pi}, and K_{ri} are the stiffness of the pile and the raft. The flexibility matrix follows Randolph (1994). Each flexibility component ($1/K_p$, etc) isn't calculated in our procedure. In step iii), the displacement of the pile heads, δ_{hp} is calculated directly considering pile head shear forces, ground displacements induced by raft friction and ground displacements induced by other piles' reaction forces.

$$\begin{pmatrix}\delta_{hp1}\\\delta_{hp2}\\\delta_{hp3}\\\vdots\\\delta_{hpn}\\\delta_{r1}\\\delta_{r2}\\\delta_{r3}\\\vdots\\\delta_{rm}\end{pmatrix}=\begin{pmatrix}1/K_{p1}&\alpha_{p1p2}/K_{p2}&\cdots&\alpha_{p1r1}/K_{r1}&\alpha_{p1r2}/K_{r2}&\cdots&\alpha_{p1rm}/K_{rm}\\\alpha_{p2p1}/K_{p1}&1/K_{p1}&\cdots&\alpha_{p2r1}/K_{r1}&\alpha_{p2r2}/K_{r2}&\cdots&\alpha_{p2rm}/K_{rm}\\\alpha_{p3p1}/K_{p1}&\alpha_{p3p2}/K_{p2}&\cdots&\alpha_{p3r1}/K_{r1}&\alpha_{p3r2}/K_{r2}&\cdots&\alpha_{p3rm}/K_{rm}\\\vdots&&&&&&\\\alpha_{pnp1}/K_{p1}&\alpha_{pnp2}/K_{p2}&\cdots&\alpha_{pnr1}/K_{r1}&\alpha_{pnr2}/K_{r2}&\cdots&\alpha_{pnrm}/K_{rm}\\\alpha_{r1p1}/K_{p1}&\alpha_{r1p2}/K_{p2}&\cdots&1/K_{r1}&\alpha_{r1r2}/K_{r2}&\cdots&\alpha_{r1rm}/K_{rm}\\\alpha_{r2p1}/K_{p1}&\alpha_{r2p2}/K_{p2}&\cdots&\alpha_{r2r1}/K_{r1}&1/K_{r1}&\cdots&\alpha_{r2rm}/K_{rm}\\\alpha_{r3p1}/K_{p1}&\alpha_{r3p2}/K_{p2}&\cdots&\alpha_{r3r1}/K_{r1}&\alpha_{r3r2}/K_{r2}&\cdots&\alpha_{r3rm}/K_{rm}\\\vdots&&&&&&\\\alpha_{rmp1}/K_{p1}&\alpha_{rmp2}/K_{p2}&\cdots&\alpha_{rmr1}/K_{r1}&\alpha_{rmr2}/K_{r2}&\cdots&1/K_{rm}\end{pmatrix}\begin{pmatrix}F_{p1}\\F_{p2}\\F_{p3}\\\vdots\\F_{pn}\\F_{r1}\\F_{r2}\\F_{r3}\\\vdots\\F_{rm}\end{pmatrix}\tag{1}$$

iii), iv) δ_{pp} ii) δ_{rp}

$$=\begin{pmatrix}F_{p1}/K_{p1}+&F_{p2}\alpha_{p1p2}/K_{p2}+&\cdots&F_{r1}\alpha_{p1r1}/K_{r1}&+F_{r2}\alpha_{p1r2}/K_{r2}+&\cdots&+F_{rm}\alpha_{p1rm}/K_{rm}\\F_{p1}\alpha_{p2p1}/K_{p1}+&F_{p2}/K_{p2}+&\cdots&F_{r1}\alpha_{p2r1}/K_{r1}&+F_{r2}\alpha_{p2r2}/K_{r2}+&\cdots&+F_{rm}\alpha_{p2rm}/K_{rm}\\F_{p1}\alpha_{p3p1}/K_{p1}+&F_{p2}\alpha_{p3p2}/K_{p2}+&\cdots&F_{r1}\alpha_{p3r1}/K_{r1}&+F_{r2}\alpha_{p3r2}/K_{r2}+&\cdots&+F_{rm}\alpha_{p3rm}/K_{rm}\\\vdots&&&\vdots&&&\\F_{p1}\alpha_{r1p1}/K_{p1}+&F_{p2}\alpha_{r1p2}/K_{p2}+&\cdots&+F_{r1}\alpha_{r1r1}/K_{r1}&+F_{r2}\alpha_{r1r2}/K_{r2}+&\cdots&+F_{rm}\alpha_{r1rm}/K_{rm}\\F_{p1}\alpha_{r2p1}/K_{p1}+&F_{p2}\alpha_{r2p2}/K_{p2}+&\cdots&+F_{r1}\alpha_{r2r1}/K_{r1}&+F_{r2}/K_{r2}+&\cdots&+F_{rm}\alpha_{r2rm}/K_{rm}\\F_{p1}\alpha_{r3p1}/K_{p1}+&F_{p2}\alpha_{r3p2}/K_{p2}+&\cdots&+F_{r1}\alpha_{r3r1}/K_{r1}&+F_{r2}\alpha_{r3r2}/K_{r2}+&\cdots&+F_{rm}\alpha_{r3rm}/K_{rm}\\\vdots&&&&&&\\F_{p1}\alpha_{rmp1}/K_{p1}+&F_{p2}\alpha_{rmp2}/K_{p2}+&\cdots&+F_{r1}\alpha_{rmr1}/K_{r1}&+F_{r2}\alpha_{rmr2}/K_{r2}+&\cdots&+F_{rm}/K_{rm}\end{pmatrix}$$

iv) δ_{pr} ii) δ_{rr}

Mano et al. (2000) analyzed bending moment of pile caused by raft friction is 1/3 to 1/4 of that by its own shear force at the pile head, however that caused by other piles reactions is very small, and it is acceptable for large pile spacing ratios. When the interaction from piles to raft and piles to piles are ignored, the analytical procedure becomes considerably simpler than the above mentioned procedure, namely the procedure iv) in Figure 3(a) can be skipped to become Figure 3(b). This simple procedure was applied to the latter case history.

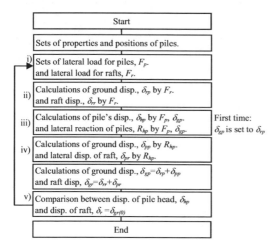

(a) Considering fully interaction

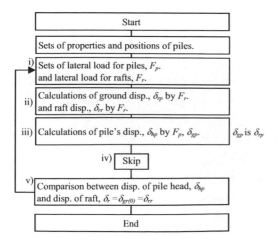

(b) Simpler procedure (ignoring interaction from pile to pile and from pile to raft)

Fig. 3 Procedure of developed analysis

3. THEORETICAL EQUATIONS FOR PILED RAFTS SUBJECTED TO LATERAL LOAD

While various experiments and numerical analyses of piled raft foundations subjected to seismic loads have been conducted, simplified theoretical equations for quickly and appropriately estimating the stresses on piles and the lateral load sharing ratios between piles and rafts have not been proposed for seismic design. The first attempt should be attributed to Hamada et al. (2009, 2011). Part of these results has been presented in previous works (Hamada et al., 2012, 2015).

3.1 Approximations and assumptions for proposed theoretical equations

As illustrated in Figure 4, the lateral load F is distributed over the piles (load F_p) and the raft (load F_r) and bending moment M is caused by the shear force at piles' heads (inducing a moment M_i) and by ground displacement (inducing a moment M_g). The theoretical equations to estimate the stress of piles for seismic design of piled rafts were derived based on the model shown in Figure 5, assuming a building area basement A_r of a circular foundation with an equivalent radius $r = \sqrt{A_r / \pi}$ and making the following approximations and assumptions.

(1) The soil deposits are homogeneous. Ground displacement is derived theoretically by integration using Cerruti's solution.

(2) As to the interaction piles-soil-raft, influences related to pile-to-pile and pile-to-raft interactions are ignored. This assumption is based on the analytical results of Mano et al. (2000) and are acceptable for large pile spacing ratios.

(3) The ground displacement caused by raft friction is expressed as an exponential or polynomial function to solve the differential equation for pile deflections taking ground displacement into consideration.

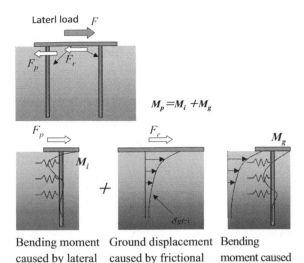

Fig. 4 Mechanism of bending moments of pile in
piled rafts subjected to lateral load

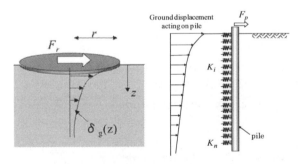

Fig. 5 Simplified evaluation model for piled rafts
subjected to lateral load

Equation (2) shows the lateral displacement of
each component with a flexibility matrix based
on the approximations and assumptions noted
above. Compare this to Eq. (1), which takes all
the interactions between the piles and raft into
consideration.

$$
\begin{pmatrix} \delta_{hp1} \\ \delta_{hp2} \\ \delta_{hp3} \\ \vdots \\ \delta_{hpm} \\ \delta_{r1} \\ \delta_{r2} \\ \delta_{r3} \\ \vdots \\ \delta_{rm} \end{pmatrix} = \begin{pmatrix} 1/K_{p1} & 0 & \vdots & \vdots & \vdots & \alpha_{p1r1}/K_{r1} & \alpha_{p1r2}/K_{r2} & \vdots & \vdots & \alpha_{p1rm}/K_{rm} \\ 0 & 1/K_{p2} & \vdots & \vdots & \vdots & \alpha_{p2r1}/K_{r1} & \alpha_{p2r2}/K_{r2} & \vdots & \vdots & \alpha_{p2rm}/K_{rm} \\ 0 & 0 & \vdots & \vdots & \vdots & \alpha_{p3r1}/K_{r1} & \alpha_{p3r2}/K_{r2} & \vdots & \vdots & \alpha_{p3rm}/K_{rm} \\ \vdots & \vdots & \vdots & \vdots & \vdots & \vdots & \vdots & \vdots & \vdots & \vdots \\ 0 & 0 & \vdots & \vdots & \vdots & \alpha_{pmr1}/K_{r1} & \alpha_{pmr2}/K_{r2} & \vdots & \vdots & \alpha_{pmrm}/K_{rm} \\ 0 & 0 & \vdots & \vdots & \vdots & 1/K_{r1} & \alpha_{r1r2}/K_{r2} & \vdots & \vdots & \alpha_{r1rm}/K_{rm} \\ 0 & 0 & \vdots & \vdots & \vdots & \alpha_{r2r1}/K_{r1} & 1/K_{r2} & \vdots & \vdots & \alpha_{r2rm}/K_{rm} \\ 0 & 0 & \vdots & \vdots & \vdots & \alpha_{r3r1}/K_{r1} & \alpha_{r3r2}/K_{r2} & \vdots & \vdots & \alpha_{r3rm}/K_{rm} \\ \vdots & \vdots & \vdots & \vdots & \vdots & \vdots & \vdots & \vdots & \vdots & \vdots \\ 0 & 0 & \vdots & \vdots & \vdots & \alpha_{rmr1}/K_{r1} & \alpha_{rmr2}/K_{r2} & \vdots & \vdots & 1/K_{rm} \end{pmatrix} \begin{pmatrix} F_{p1} \\ F_{p2} \\ \vdots \\ F_{pm} \\ F_{r1} \\ F_{r2} \\ \vdots \\ F_{rm} \end{pmatrix}
$$

(2)

3.2 Ground displacement caused by frictional force between raft and subsoil

Ground displacements caused by raft friction at a
given depth and at ground level are estimated by,
respectively, the non-dimensional Eqs. (3) and (4)
(Kanai et al. 1968). Equation (5) is an exponential
function that can approximate the ground
displacement. Here, δg is the ground displacement,
$\varsigma = z/r$ is the non-dimensional depth, z is the depth,
r is the equivalent radius of the building basement
area, v is Poisson's ratio, F_r is the lateral sharing
load carried by the raft, G is the shear stiffness of
the soil and e is the natural exponential number.
Constant coefficients "a" and "b" are estimated
by the least square method as 1.49 and 0.8845,
respectively, having a Poisson's ratio of 0.49 and
$0 < \zeta < 3$. Parameter "b" is expressed by $2/a(2-v)$
when the shear strain of the soil beneath the raft is
given by τ/G. Equation (6) is another polynomial
function that can also approximate the ground
displacement. Coefficients "a_1", "b_1" and "c_1" are
estimated by the least square method.

Figure 6 compares Eqs. (3), (5) and (6) in terms
of non-dimensional depth and non-dimensional
ground displacement. Equations (5) and (6) can
accurately approximate Eq. (3).

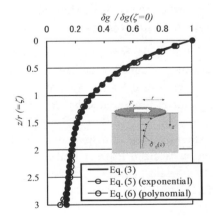

Fig. 6 Relationship between non-dimensional
depth and non-dimensional ground
displacement

The ground displacement at the corner of building foundation can be expressed by Eqs. (5) and (6) using different coefficients (a, b or a_1, b_1, c_1).

$$\frac{\delta g(\varsigma)}{\delta g(\varsigma=0)} = \frac{1}{(2-v)}\left[\frac{1}{2}\frac{3+4\varsigma^2}{\sqrt{1+\varsigma^2}} - 2\varsigma + \frac{1-2v}{2}\left(\sqrt{1+\varsigma^2}-\varsigma\right)\right]$$

(3)

$$\delta g(\varsigma=0) = \frac{F_r}{2\pi Gr}(2-v)$$

(4)

$$\frac{\delta g(\varsigma)}{\delta g(\varsigma=0)} = be^{-a\varsigma} + 1 - b$$

(5)

where $v = 0.49$ $0 \le z/r \le 3$

$a = 1.490$

$b = 0.8845$

$$\frac{\delta g(\varsigma)}{\delta g(\varsigma=0)} = 1 - a_1\varsigma - b_1\varsigma^2 - c_1\varsigma^3$$

(6)

where $v = 0.49$ $0 \le z/r \le 3$

$a_1 = 1.141572$

$b_2 = 0.53329039$

$c_3 = 0.08496990$

3.3 Sectional force on piles considering ground displacement

The deflection of piles considering ground displacement is obtained by solving the differential equation expressed by Eq. (7). When ground displacement is represented by the exponential function of Eq. (5), the differential Eq. (7) is easily solved. The piles' lateral displacement is obtained mathematically from Eq. (8). The constant A_5 is obtained using Eqs. (4), (5), (7) and (8), as in Eq. (9). Constants A_1, A_2, A_3 and A_4 are determined as given in Eqs. (10), (11) and (12), respectively, based on the following assumed boundary conditions. The piles are sufficiently long, the coefficient of subgrade reaction for the piles, k_h is

constant, the pile heads do not rotate, and piles and ground displacements are equal at piles' heads as well as at large depths.

$$EI\frac{d^4\delta(z)}{dz^4} = dk_h(\delta g(z) - \delta(z))$$

(7)

$$\delta(z) = A_1 e^{\beta(1+i)z} + A_2 e^{\beta(1-i)z} + A_3 e^{\beta(-1+i)z} + A_4 e^{-\beta(1+i)z}$$

(8)

$$+ A_5 e^{-\frac{a}{r}z} + \frac{F_r}{2\pi Gr}(2-v)(1-b)$$

$$A_5 = \frac{4\beta^4}{4\beta^4 + a'^4} \times b'$$

(9)

$$A_1 = A_2 = 0$$

(10)

$$A_3 = \frac{A_5}{2}\left\{\frac{a'^4}{4\beta^4} - i\left(\frac{a'}{\beta} + \frac{a'^4}{4\beta^4}\right)\right\}$$

(11)

$$A_4 = \frac{A_5}{2}\left\{\frac{a'^4}{4\beta^4} + i\left(\frac{a'}{\beta} + \frac{a'^4}{4\beta^4}\right)\right\}$$

(12)

Here, $a' = \dfrac{a}{r}$, $b' = \dfrac{F_r}{2\pi Gr}(2-v)b = \delta g(0) \times b$

EI: bending stiffness of pile, $\delta(z)$: horizontal displacement of pile, d: pile diameter, k_h: coefficient of subgrade reaction, $\beta = \sqrt[4]{dk_h/4EI}$, $i = \sqrt{-1}$.

$$Q(z) = a'b'\left[e^{-\beta z}\left\{(-\frac{a'^3}{\beta} - 2\beta^2)\cos\beta z - 2\beta^2\sin\beta z\right\} + a'^2 e^{-a'z}\right]\left(\frac{4\beta^4}{4\beta^4 + a'^4}\right)\times EI$$

(13)

$$M(z) = a'b'\left[e^{-\beta z}\left\{(\frac{a'^3}{2\beta^2} + 2\beta)\cos\beta z - \frac{a'^3}{2\beta^2}\sin\beta z\right\} - a'e^{-a'z}\right]\left(\frac{4\beta^4}{4\beta^4 + a'^4}\right)\times EI$$

(14)

The shear force and bending moment in a pile are evaluated by Eqs. (13) and (14), respectively. These equations were derived by differentiating equation (8). The sectional shear force and bending moment in a pile head depend on the value $a'b'$ which is the ground shear strain beneath the raft, as shown schematically in Figure 7, approximating ground displacement and pile displacements. If the sectional forces of piles should be estimated accurately considering pile position, center pile or corner pile, appropriate values of a' and b' at

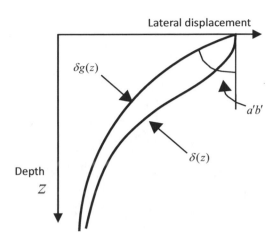

Fig. 7 Schematic figure of approximate ground displacement and pile displacement

$$\alpha_p = \frac{F_p}{F} = \frac{K_p}{K_r + K_P}$$

$$= \frac{-n\frac{a}{r}b\left(-\frac{(a/r)^3}{\beta} - 2\beta^2 + \left(\frac{a}{r}\right)^2\right)\left(\frac{4\beta^4}{4\beta^4 + \left(\frac{a}{r}\right)^4}\right)EI}{\frac{2\pi Gr}{2-v} - n\frac{a}{r}b\left(-\frac{(a/r)^3}{\beta} - 2\beta^2 + \left(\frac{a}{r}\right)^2\right)\left(\frac{4\beta^4}{4\beta^4 + \left(\frac{a}{r}\right)^4}\right)EI}$$

$$= \frac{4nEI\beta^3 ab\left(\frac{a^3 + 2(r\beta)^3 - a^2 r\beta}{4(r\beta)^4 + a^4}\right)}{\frac{2\pi Gr}{2-v} + 4nEI\beta^3 ab\left(\frac{a^3 + 2(r\beta)^3 - a^2 r\beta}{4(r\beta)^4 + a^4}\right)}$$

$$= \frac{\frac{K_{gp}}{K_r} ab\left(\frac{a^3 + 2(r\beta)^3 - a^2 r\beta}{4(r\beta)^4 + a^4}\right)}{1 + \frac{K_{gp}}{K_r} ab\left(\frac{a^3 + 2(r\beta)^3 - a^2 r\beta}{4(r\beta)^4 + a^4}\right)}$$

$$(15)$$

equations (13) and (14) are used by fitting to the each center/corner ground displacements caused by raft friction. This technique was applied in the latter case history.

The proposed equations do not account for the vertical load. Therefore the method cannot be used in the case of second order phenomena (moment arising from the eccentricity of the vertical loading).

3.4 Lateral load sharing ratios of piles and raft

Piles lateral resistances vary depending on the piles' positions because of the difference in earth pressure beneath the raft and/or group pile effects. However, it is assumed that the sum of the shear forces at the piles' heads is obtained by counting Eq. (13) n times for $z = 0$, where n is the number of piles. The piles' load sharing ratio α_p, which is the ratio of the pile's sharing lateral load to the total lateral load can be expressed by Eq. (15).

K_p is the lateral stiffness of the total of all the piles in a piled raft. K_r is the lateral stiffness of the raft expressed as $2\pi Gr/(2-v)$, derived from Eq. (4). "$K_p + K_r$" is used as the total lateral stiffness because "pile to raft" interactions are ignored. This equation consists of two independent parameters K_{gp}/K_r and $r\beta$. K_{gp} is n times the lateral stiffness of a single pile expressed as $4nEI\beta^3$. The parameter $r\beta$ is a non-dimensional parameter.

When the lateral loading ratio of piles should be estimated considering pile position and each pile's bending modulus, the appropriate values of a' and b' depending on the each position and each EI and β are used for equation (16).

$$\alpha_p = \frac{-\sum_{i=1}^{n} a_i' b_i'\left(-\frac{a_i'^3}{\beta_i} - 2\beta^2 + a_i'^2\right)\left(\frac{4\beta_i^4}{4\beta_i^4 + a_i'^4}\right)EI_i}{F_r - \sum_{i=1}^{n} a_i' b_i'\left(-\frac{a_i'^3}{\beta_i} - 2\beta^2 + a_i'^2\right)\left(\frac{4\beta_i^4}{4\beta_i^4 + a_i'^4}\right)EI_i} \quad (16)$$

Here, n is a total number of pile, i is a pile number.

4. EXAMPLE OF SEISMIC DESIGN

4.1 Model case (building and soil conditions)

Seismic design of piled raft foundation was

conducted for the eleven-story office building of 60.8 m in height above ground surface located in Japan (Yamashita et al., 2011a). Figure 8 shows a schematic view of the building and foundation with soil profile. The building is a steel-frame structure with a base isolated system of laminated rubber bearings and its plan measures 80 m by 43.5 m. The foundation level is a depth of 3.0 m from the ground surface. The subsoil consists of a diluvial loose to medium sand with SPT N-values of 10 to 25 to a depth of 12 m, underlain by clayey soil, medium sand-and-gravel and dense sand with SPT N-values of 10 to 50 to a depth of 28 m, there lie dense to very dense sand-and-gravel layers where a hard sandy-silt layer is inserted. The ground water table appears about 17 m below the ground surface. The shear wave velocity derived from P-S logging carried out in the neighboring site were 220 to 260 m/s at the foundation levels and 420 to 520 m/s in the dense gravel layers below the depth of 28 m.

The average contact pressure over the raft is 145 kPa. The reinforced concrete raft is founded on loose sand with SPT N-values of about 10. Because the building has the base isolation system, differential settlement is rigorously restricted: the maximum angular rotation of the raft should be less than 1/2000 radian at working load conditions. To reduce the differential settlement to an acceptable level, piled raft foundation consisting of 40 piles was proposed. The cast-in-place underreamed concrete piles are 27.5 m in length, partly 26.9 m in length, having a diameter varying from 1.1 to 1.5 m and a 1.4 to 1.8 m enlarged bell at the pile bottom. The pile toes were embedded in the dense sand-and-gravel layer below the depth of 28 m. Figure 9 shows the foundation plan with a layout of the piles.

In this paper, several estimation methods are described, (1) elastic finite element method, (2) proposed simplified analytical method based on Mindlin's solution, (3) proposed theoretical method.

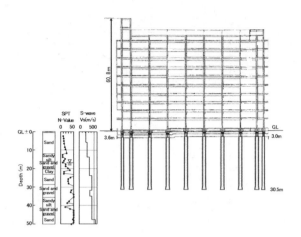

Fig. 8 Schematic view of the building and foundation with soil profile

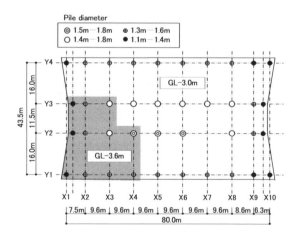

Fig. 9 Foundation plan with a layout of piles

4.2 Seismic load versus raft frictional resistance

The design lateral load is set to 10,400 kN for the foundation under an extremely large earthquake. The value corresponds to equivalent lateral seismic intensity (lateral load / dead load) of 0.181 (= 104,000 kN/573,678 kN).

The frictional resistance between raft and subsoil, R_{bf}, can be estimated by equation (17).

$$R_{bf} = \sigma_v' \times \mu \times A \qquad (17)$$

Here,

σ_v': effective contact pressure between raft and subsoil (can be estimated by equation (18))

μ: coefficient of friction (ordinary to be 0.4 to 0.6)

A: area of raft

$$\sigma_v' = w \times (1 - \alpha_{pv}) - w_w \qquad (18)$$

Here ,

w: average contact pressure of building dead load

α_{pv}: vertical load sharing ratio of piles

w_w: contact water pressure beneath raft

In this case,

$w = 145 \text{ kN/m}^2$

$A = 84\text{m} \times 47.1\text{m} = 3956.4 \text{ m}^2$

$\alpha_{pv} = 0.60$ (calculated by vertical load sharing analysis)

$\mu = 0.5$

$w_w = 0.0$

$R_{bf} = 145\text{kN/m}^2 \times (1-0.60) \times 0.5 \times 3956.4 \text{ m}^2$
$\quad = 114,736 \text{ kN}$

The frictional resistance of 114,736 kN is enough larger than lateral external design load of 104,000 kN.

When the frictional resistance is smaller than the lateral design load of raft, the slip mode of the raft should be consider for the seismic design of piles.

4.3 Finite element analysis

Static elastic finite element (FE) method was conducted to verify the simplified analytical design and the theoretical equations.

Figure 10 shows the configuration of a case history of piled rafts by modeling a quarter of the whole raft and piles. The model used for calculations is slightly different from the actual building as shown in figures 8 and 9. The raft shape was modeled as a rectangular shape: the inner four piles' diameters were the same as those of piles with which they were symmetric, and the depth of the raft bottom was uniformly set to 3.0 m. In this analysis, the embedment was not modeled.

To consider the shape and volume of the piles, cavities in the shape of the piles were made in the FE model. The nodes of the piles and the adjacent ground nodes at the same depth were bound by rigid bar elements.

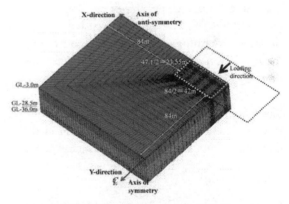

(a) Finite element mesh of soil

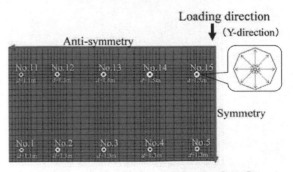

(b) Plan view of FE mesh beneath raft

Fig. 10 Finite element model of piled raft foundation

The lateral boundaries consist of symmetry boundaries in the parallel loading direction and anti-symmetry boundaries in the perpendicular loading direction. The lateral boundaries far from the building are free boundaries which are positioned 84 m outside of the building to minimize the boundary effect. The bottom is a fixed boundary. The building and the raft were not modeled. The raft was modeled by setting the nodes below the raft to be a displacement constraint, fixed in the vertical direction and perpendicular loading direction, with the same displacements in the loading direction.

The soil properties are shown in Table 1. The initial shear modulus is set to from 87.6 MPa ($\rho = 1.81$ t/m^3, $V_S = 220$ m/s) to 366.1MPa ($\rho = 1.81$ t/m^3, $V_S = 450$ m/s). To simulate the actual phenomenon, reduction of the soil modulus, G/G_0 should be accurately estimated. In the design, however, the soil modulus should be considered with a margin of safety. Therefore the G/G_0 of 0.3 according to the whole soil depth was employed for the seismic design.

Table 2 shows the properties of the piles and raft. Piles are modeled as elastic beams in this analysis. 40 piles are modeled using the symmetric and anti-symmetric boundary conditions.

Table 3 shows the calculated results of the lateral stiffness and lateral load sharing ratio of piles. The calculation parameters are the ground stiffness, loading directions and foundation types. The lateral force of 104,000 kN is loaded as an inertia force from the superstructure. The lateral stiffness ratios of the piles and the raft are the values as compared to that of the piled raft foundation. The lateral loading stiffness of raft is only decreased by 3-8 % compared with that of piled raft. The lateral load sharing ratio of piles for a piled raft is about 16 % on the condition of ground stiffness of G0, whereas about 27 % on the condition of 0.3 G0. For the safety design of piles, an appropriate reduction from the initial shear modulus should be considered for the ground stiffness. The calculated bending moments of piles are described in the next section in comparison to those given by a simplified method.

4.4 Simplified analytical method

The simplified analytical method described in Section 2 was used for seismic design of the foundation. In this design, the simpler procedure in Figure 3 (b) was applied. Here again the pile

Table 1 Soil modulus according to depth

Depth (m)	Shear wave velocity V_s (m/s)	Unit weight γ (kN/m^3)	Shear modulus G_0 (kN/m^2)	$0.3 \times G_0$ (kN/m^2)
GL $-3 \sim -6$	220	18	87604	26281
GL $-6 \sim -16$	260	18	122356	36707
GL $-16 \sim -29$	340	18	206910	62073
GL $-29 \sim$	450	18	366102	109831

Poisson ratio 0.49

Table 2 Properties of piles and raft

Pile

Young's modulus	2.5×10^7 kN/m^2
Pile length	27.5m
Pile diameter	1.1~1.5m
Number of piles	40 piles

Raft

Young's modulus	Infinity
Width of foundation	84.0×47.1m

Table 3 Lateral stiffness and load sharing ratio of piles

Loading direction and ground stiffness		Foundation type	Lateral disp. at pile head (m)	Lateral stiffness (kN/m)	Lateral stiffness ratio	Lateral load sharing ratio of piles
Y direction	G_0	Pild raft	2.214E-03	4.697E+07	1.00	15.6%
		Raft	2.282E-03	4.557E+07	0.97	—
		Piles	3.388E-03	3.070E+07	0.65	—
	$0.3 \times G_0$	Pild raft	7.118E-03	1.461E+07	1.00	26.3%
		Raft	7.607E-03	1.367E+07	0.94	—
		Piles	9.639E-03	1.079E+07	0.74	—
X direction	G_0	Pild raft	2.542E-03	4.091E+07	1.00	16.2%
		Raft	2.650E-03	3.924E+07	0.96	—
		Piles	3.992E-03	2.605E+07	0.64	—
	$0.3 \times G_0$	Pild raft	8.172E-03	1.273E+07	1.00	26.9%
		Raft	8.835E-03	1.177E+07	0.92	—
		Piles	1.140E-02	9.123E+06	0.72	—

modulus was defined as an elastic beam, and the ground modulus was as elastic as 0.3 times of G0 considering the reduction from the initial shear modulus. The loading direction is the Y-direction as a short side direction. The procedures are as follows.

i) First, the temporary lateral loads for the piles and the raft are set as F_p and F_r respectively. However, in case of elastic analysis, the lateral loads of F_p and F_r do not need to be set.

ii) The ground displacement δ_{rp} and the displacement of the raft (footing) δ_{rr} caused by F_r are calculated based on Mindlin's solution. Figure 11 shows the lateral ground displacements at the positions of the pile numbers from 1 to 15. No.1 and No.15 correspond to the corner pile and the center pile respectively, as shown in Figure 10 (b). Here, the lateral load of raft F_r is set to the total external load of 104,000 kN. The lateral displacement at the footing level is 9.72 mm and the relative displacement is about 7.7 mm (9.72 mm –about 2.0 mm) from GL-36 m which corresponds to the relative displacement of 7.607 mm evaluated by the FEM shown in Table 3.

iii) Next, the lateral displacement δ_{hp} of each pile is estimated by using the elastic beam method based on the values δ_{rp} and F_p. In an alternative method, the lateral shear forces at pile heads were estimated automatically by forcing each pile head's displacement, δ_{hp}, to be the same as the raft displacement, δ_{rr}. Figure 12 shows the relationship between the lateral displacement at each pile head and the lateral load on each pile. The lateral loads on the

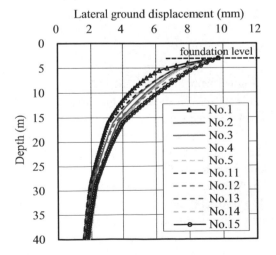

Fig. 11 Lateral ground displacements

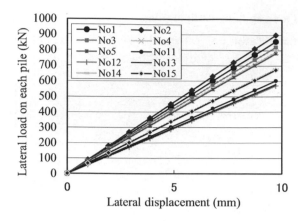

Fig. 12 Lateral pile head displacements versus lateral loads on pile heads

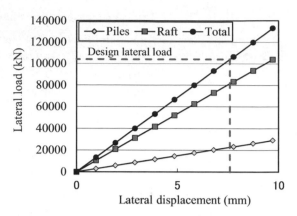

Fig. 13 Lateral pile head displacements versus total lateral load

corner piles were relatively larger than those on the center piles. The lateral load acting on the pile No.2 was the largest because the pile diameter of No.2 is larger than that of No.1. The employed coefficient of lateral subgrade reaction of piles k_h was estimated by Equation (19). This equation is familiar to the Japanese geotechnical designers, as it is presented in the Specifications for Highway Bridges in Japan (Japan Road Association, 2002). Here, d represents the pile diameter, and the equivalent Young's modulus, E_s, was estimated using the modulus of $0.3G_0$ and the Poisson ratio of 0.49.

$$k_h = 80 \times E_s \times d^{-3/4} \qquad (19)$$

iv) Skip

v) In non-linear analysis, the raft displacement, $\delta_r (=\delta_{gr}(0) = \delta_{rr})$ should be the same as the pile head displacements δ_{hp}. The above calculations should be repeated by resetting F_p and F_r. In this design, by comparing the summation of the pile head shear forces and the raft's frictional resistance with the design lateral load of 104,000 kN, the lateral displacement of pile head (raft) and lateral load sharing of piles are evaluated. Figure 13 shows relationship between the lateral displacements at pile heads and the total lateral load compared to the

design load. The lateral load sharing ratio of piles is 21.8 % which corresponds to 26.3 % in an FEM. The sectional forces of piles, the corner pile (No.1) and the center pile (No.15) are shown in Figure 14 compared with those given by an FEM. They are found to be in quite good agreement with the FEM results. The lateral displacement by FEM indicated herein is underestimated because of fixed at GL-36 m.

4.5 Theoretical equations

The theoretical equations described in Section 3 were also applied to the seismic design of the foundation.

If the sectional forces of piles should be estimated accurately considering pile positions, whether they are center piles or corner piles, appropriate values are used for a' and b' in the equations (13) and (14) by inputting the center/corner ground displacements caused by raft friction.

By applying the value of a' and b' used in the equation (5) to the center/corner ground displacements shown in Figure 15, the values of $a' = 0.1876$ (1/m), $b' = 5.88$ mm and $a'b' = 0.0011$ were approximated for the corner pile (No.1), and $a' = 0.0815$ (1/m), $b' = 6.62$ mm and $a'b' = 0.00054$ were approximated for the center pile (No.15). The

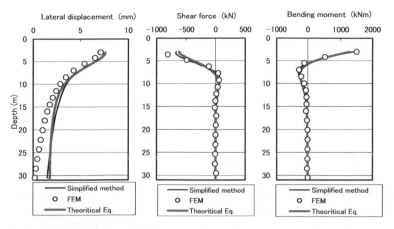

(a) Corner pile (No.1, pile diameter of 1.1m)

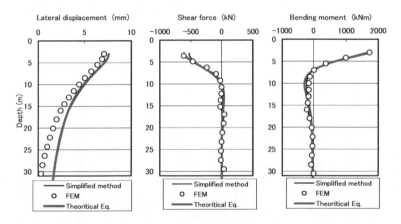

(b) Center pile (No.15, pile diameter of 1.5m)

Fig. 14 Sectional forces of piles by simplified analytical method, in comparison with the results of FEM and theoretical equations

ground displacements shown in Figure 15 are the values when the lateral load of raft, F_r is 81,328kN (lateral displacement at the ground surface of 7.6 mm) as shown in Figure 13.

The shear forces and bending moments of piles were calculated by using equations (13) and (14). To utilize these equations, the coefficient of subgrade reaction, k_h, should be set to one value despite the multi-layered ground. In this design, the values near the surface was employed for k_h as follows.

Corner pile:

$d = 1.1$m, $EI = 1,796,721$kNm^2, $k_h = 184,462$kN/m^3

Center pile:

$d = 1.5$m, $EI = 6,212,622$kNm^2, $k_h = 146,178$kN/m^3

The results given by theoretical equations were overlaid in Figure 14. Those results agreed well with those given by an FEM and a simplified analytical method.

Figure 16 shows the data in case of using $a = 1.490$,

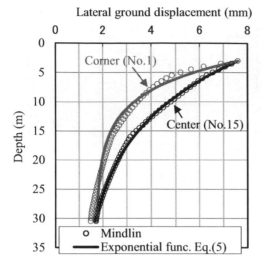

Fig. 15 Lateral ground displacements

$b = 0.8845$ and $r = 35.5$ m without consideration of pile positions. They correspond to $a' = a/r = 0.042$, $b' = 23.7$ mm and $a'b' = 0.0010$ respectively. The ground shear modulus was set to one value near the ground surface. The proposed simplified equations underestimate the bending moment and shear force at corner piles because the gradient of ground displacement at a corner position, $a'b'$ is underestimated. However, the lateral load sharing ratio of piles is 25.2 % which agrees well with the ratio in case of the FEM analysis.

Table 4 shows the case studies conducted by varying the ground stiffness G_0 or $0.3G_0$, and k_h. The coefficients of lateral subgrade reaction on pile k_h given by Eq.(20) are employed in the cases (b)

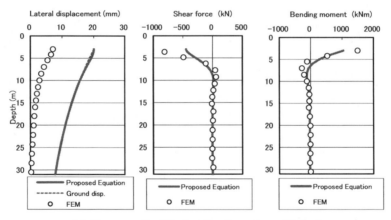

(a) Corner pile (No.1, pile diameter of 1.1m)

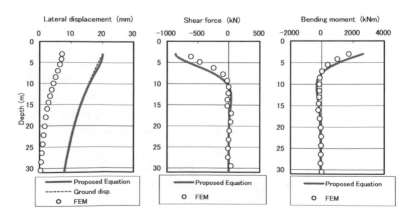

(b) Center pile (No.15, pile diameter of 1.5m)

Fig. 16 Sectional forces of piles given by theoretical equations

Table 4 Case studies by varying ground modulus and coefficient of subgrade reaction on pile

(a) $G = 0.3Gd$, k_h : Eq.(19), $Es = 0.3Ed$

	$d = 1.5$m	$d = 1.4$m	$d = 1.3$m	$d = 1.1$m
Bending moment at pile head (kNm)	2643	2149	1720	1041
Shear force at pile head (kNm)	862	745	637	447
Lateral load sharing ratio of pile	25.2%			

(b) $G = 0.3Gd$, k_h : Eq.(20), $Es = 0.3Ed$

	$d = 1.5$m	$d = 1.4$m	$d = 1.3$m	$d = 1.1$m
Bending moment at pile head (kNm)	2349	1921	1547	948
Shear force at pile head (kNm)	647	564	487	350
Lateral load sharing ratio of pile	19.2%			

(c) $G = 1.0Gd$, k_h : Eq.(19), $Es = 1.0Ed$

	$d = 1.5$m	$d = 1.4$m	$d = 1.3$m	$d = 1.1$m
Bending moment at pile head (kNm)	1231	1000	800	483
Shear force at pile head (kNm)	534	462	395	277
Lateral load sharing ratio of pile	15.6%			

(d) $G = 1.0Gd$, k_h : Eq.(20), $Es = 1.0Ed$

	$d = 1.5$m	$d = 1.4$m	$d = 1.3$m	$d = 1.1$m
Bending moment at pile head (kNm)	1088	888	714	436
Shear force at pile head (kNm)	407	355	306	220
Lateral load sharing ratio of pile	12.1%			

(e) $G = 0.3Gd$, k_h : Eq.(19), $Es = Ed/30$

	$d = 1.5$m	$d = 1.4$m	$d = 1.3$m	$d = 1.1$m
Bending moment at pile head (kNm)	1741	1421	1141	695
Shear force at pile head (kNm)	341	295	253	178
Lateral load sharing ratio of pile	10.0%			

and (d). For the safety design of piles, a sufficient reduction in the ground shear modulus should be considered and it is recommended to use larger coefficients of subgrade reaction on pile for piled rafts subjected to the inertial force of the structure in order to estimate the larger lateral load sharing ratio of piles.

$$k_h = \frac{1.3}{d} \frac{E_s}{1-v^2} \sqrt[12]{\frac{E_s d^4}{EI}} \qquad (20)$$

In addition to the inertial force of the structure, the ground displacements caused by oscillation of the ground should be also taken into account for estimation of pile sectional forces (Hamada et al., 2015) as shown in Figure 17.

Generally, for the pile foundation without base

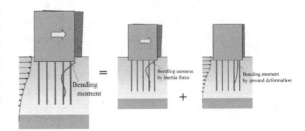

Fig. 17 Bending moment on pile induced by inertial force and ground oscillation

isolation, the bending moment on pile is mainly caused by the inertial force of the structure. However, for the piled raft foundation especially with base isolation, the inertial force had relatively a little effect on the bending moment on pile, which is mainly caused by ground deformation.

It is important to consider appropriate ground deformation effects on the piled rafts in design process.

And also, axial loads of piles and contact pressures beneath a raft vary with rocking motion of a building, and pulling axial loads of piles and no-contact pressure will occur in a tall building without base isolation during large earthquake. It is necessary to consider the effect of the rocking behavior of a building for seismic design of piled rafts for a tall building.

5. CONCLUSIONS

One example of seismic design of a piled raft foundation supporting an isolated building was introduced in this paper. The seismic design of the piled rafts subjected to inertial force of the building was conducted by three types of methods: simplified analytical, simple theoretical and finite element methods.

In the simplified analytical method based on Mindlin's solution, we are able to consider full interactions among raft, the piles and subsoil. If the interaction effects from pile to pile or pile to raft are ignored, the calculation procedure becomes simpler, which is sufficiently effective for the seismic design, compared to a finite element method.

The theoretical equations for piled rafts subjected to lateral load were derived for making rough evaluations of the lateral resistance of piled rafts while using several approximations and assumptions. If compared with a finite element method and simplified analyses, the proposed theoretical equations are recognized to be an effective tool for an early stage of seismic design of piled raft foundation because of saving of calculation time and its function to check some insecure ground conditions.

For the safety design of piles, a sufficient

reduction in the ground shear modulus should be considered, and it is recommended to use larger coefficients of subgrade reaction on pile for piled rafts subjected to the inertial force of the structure in order to estimate larger lateral load sharing ratio of the piles. In addition to the inertial force of the structure, the ground displacements caused by oscillation of ground should be also taken into account for estimation of pile sectional forces.

REFERENCES

Hamada, J., Tsuchiya, T. and Yamashita, K. (2009). Theoretical equations to evaluate the stress of piles on piled raft foundation during earthquake, *Journal of Structural Construction Eng.* (Transactions of AIJ), Vol. 74, No. 644, 1759-1767 (in Japanese).

Hamada, J., Tsuchiya, T. and Yamashita, K. (2011). Theoretical equations to evaluate the stress of piles on piled raft foundation during earthquake considering nonlinearity of soil, *Journal of Structural Construction Eng.* (Transactions of AIJ), Vol. 76, No. 660, 301-310 (in Japanese).

Hamada, J., Tsuchiya, T., Tanikawa, T. and Yamashita, K. (2012). Lateral loading model tests on piled rafts and their evaluation with simplified theoretical equations, *IS-Kanazawa*, 467-476.

Hamada, J., Shigeno, Y., Onimaru, S., Tanikawa, T., Nakamura, N. and Yamashita, K. (2014). Numerical analysis on seismic response of piled raft foundation with ground improvement based on seismic observation records, *14th International Association Computer Methods and Recent Advances in Geomechanics*, 719-724.

Hamada, J., Tsuchiya, T., Tanikawa, T. and Yamashita, K. (2015). Lateral Loading Tests on Piled Rafts and Simplified Method to Evaluate Sectional Forces of Piles, *Geotechnical*

Engineering Journal of the SEAGS & AGSSEA, Vol.46, No.2, pp.29-42.

Hamada, J. (2015). Bending moment of piles on piled raft foundation subjected to ground deformation during earthquake in centrifuge model test, *Proc. of the 15th Asia Regional Conf. on SMGE*, Fukuoka, Japan.

Horikoshi, K., Matsumoto, T., Hashizume, Y. and Watanabe, T. (2003a). Performance of piled raft foundations subjected to dynamic loading, *International Journal of Physical Modelling in Geotechnics*, 3(2), 51-62.

Horikoshi, K., Matsumoto, T., Hashizume, Y., Watanabe, T. and Fukuyama, H. (2003b). Performance of piled raft foundations subjected to static horizontal loads, *International Journal of Physical Modelling in Geotechnics*, 3(2), 37-50.

Japan Road Association (2002). Specifications for Highway Bridges - Part V. Seismic Design, 210-221 (in Japanese).

Kanai, K., Tajimi, H., Osawa, Y. and Kobayashi, H. (1968). Kenchiku-Kouzougaku-Taikei Jishin Kougaku, *SYOUKOKUSYA*, p.75 (in Japanese).

Katzenbach, R., Arslan, U. and Moormann, C. (2000). Piled raft foundation projects in Germany, Design applications of raft foundations, *Hemsley J.A. Editor, Thomas Telford*, 323-392.

Katzenbach, R. and Turek, J. (2005). Combined pile-raft foundation subjected to lateral loads, *Proc. 16th Int. Conf. On Soil Mechanics and Geotechnical Engineering*, 2001-2004.

Kitiyodom, P. and Matsumoto, T. (2002). A simplified analysis method for piled raft and pile group foundations with batter piles, *International Journal for Numerical and Analytical Methods in Geomechanics*, 26,
1349-1369.

Kitiyodom, P. and Matsumoto, T. (2003). A simplified analysis method for piled raft foundations in non-homogeneous soils, *International Journal for Numerical and Analytical Methods in Geomechanics*, 27, 85-109.

Mandolini, A., Russo, G. and Viggiani, C. (2005). Pile foundations: experimental investigations, analysis and design, *Proc. 16th ICSMGE*, Vol.1, 177-213.

Mano, H. and Nakai, S. (2000). An Approximate Analysis for Stress of Piles in a Laterally Loaded Piled Raft Foundation, *Journal of Structural Engineering*, 46B, 43-50 (in Japanese).

Mano, H. and Nakai, S. (2001). A New Simplified Nonlinear Analysis for Evaluating Stress of Piles in a Laterally Loaded Piled Raft Foundation, *Journal of Structural Engineering*, 47B, 427-434 (in Japanese).

Matsumoto, T., Fukumura, K., Kitiyodom,P., Horikoshi, K. and Oki, A. (2004a). Experimental and analytical study on behaviour of model piled rafts in sand subjected to horizontal and moment loading, *International Journal of Physical Modeling in Geotechnics*, 4(3), 1-19.

Matsumoto, T., Fukumura, K., Horikoshi, K. and Oki, A. (2004b). Shaking Table tests on model piled rafts in sand considering influence of superstructures, *International Journal of Physical Modeling in Geotechnics*, 4(3), 21-38.

Matsumoto, T., Nemoto, H., Mikami, H., Yaegashi, K., $A_r$ai, T. and Kitiyodom, P. (2010). Load tests of piled raft models with different pile head connection conditions and their analyses, *Soils and Foundations*, Vol.50, No.50, 63-81.

Mindlin, R. D. (1936). Force at a point interior of a semi-infinite solid, *Physics,* 7, 195-202.

Poulos, H.G. (2001). Piled raft foundations: design and applications, *Geotechnique* 51, No.2, 95-113.

Randlph, M.F. (1994). Design methods for pile groups and piled rafts, *Proc. 13th ICSMFE,* 61-82.

Sawada, K., Takemura, J. (2014). Centrifuge tests on piled raft foundation in sand subjected to lateral and moment loads, *Soils & Foundations,* Vol.52, No.2, 126-140.

Tsuchiya, T., Nagai, H. and Ikeda, A. (2002). Analytical study on behavior of piled raft subjected to seismic load, *Journal of Structural Engineering,* 48B, 343-350 (in Japanese).

Unsever, Y.S. Matsumoto, T. and Shimono, S. (2014). Static cyclic load tests on model foundations in dry sand Geotechnical Engineering. *Journal of the SEAGS & AGSSEA,* Vol. 45, No. 2, pp 40-51.

Unsever, Y.S., Matsumoto, T. and Shimono, S. (2015). Shaking table tests of piled raft and pile group foundations in dry sand. *Proc. 6th Int. Conf. on Earthquake Geotech. Engineering* (6ICEGE), Christchurch, New Zealand, Paper No.328, 9p.

Vu, A.T., Matsumoto, T., Kobayashi, S. and Nguyen, T. L. (2016). Model load tests on battered pile foundations and finite-element analysis", Int. *Journal of Physical Modelling in Geotechnics,* published online on 2016 Nov 30th, 22pp.

Vu, A.T., Masumoto, T., Ryo Yoshitani, R. and Nguyen, T.L. (2017): Behaviours of pile group and piled raft foundation models having batter piles, *Journal of Earth Engineering,* accepted for publication, 14 pages.

Watanabe,T., Fukuyama,H., Horikoshi,K. and Matsumoto,T (2001). Centrifuge modeling of piled raft foundations subjected to horizontal loads, *Proc. 5th Int. Conf. On Deep Foundation Practice incorporating Piletalk Int.,* 371-378.

Yamashita, K., Yamada, T. and Hamada, J. (2011a). Investigation of settlement and load sharing on piled rafts by monitoring full-scale structures, *Soils & Foundations,* Vol.51, No.3, 513-532.

Yamashita, K., Hamada, J. and Yamada, T. (2011b). Field measurements on piled rafts with grid-form deep mixing walls on soft ground, *Geotechnical Engineering Journal of the SEAGS & AGSSEA,* Vol.42, No.2, 1-10.

Yamashita, K., Hamada, J., Onimaru, S. and Higashino, M. (2012). Seismic behavior of piled raft with ground improvement supporting a base-isolated building on soft ground in Tokyo, *Soils & Foundations,* Vol.52, No.5, Special issue on Geotechnical Aspects of the 2011 off the Pacific coast of Tohoku Earthquake, 1000-1015.

CHAPTER 7

PILE BEHAVIOR IN LIQUEFIABLE SEABED SAND SUBJECTED TO LATERAL LOADING

Sheng-Huoo Ni*

Professor, Department of Civil Engineering, National Cheng Kung University, ROC
*tonyni@mail.ncku.edu.tw

Zong-Wei Feng

Projects engineering manager, ODE Ltd., Taiwan, ROC
will.feng@ode-ltd.co.uk

Shu-Yu Chang

Graduate Student, Department of Civil Engineering, National Cheng Kung University, ROC
n68981107@mail.ncku.edu.tw

ABSTRACT: External forces such as the wind, wave, and ocean current are factors to be considered during the installation of offshore wind turbine foundation. Limited by the weak soil layer of Taiwan offshore region and the lack of monopole construction capability, plus the consideration of typhoon, earthquake, and potential of soil liquefaction, submerged group pile foundation is believed to be the most suitable option. This study analyzed the change of pile body displacement, moment, and the maximum angle of rotation with depth by using GROUP software to simulate the interaction between seabed sand and pile foundation using data obtained from soil layer under one turbine in Changhua offshore wind farm in Taiwan. Fully and partially liquefied p-y curves were established by analyzing offshore group pile installed in liquefiable soil. By using excess pore water pressure ratio as a reference, two excess pore water pressure modifying methods, Liu and Dobry (1995) and Chang and Hutchinson (2013), were selected to correct the p-y curve after the excess pore water pressure built up during an earthquake. The two modifying methods were combined to provide a complete method to describe the process from sand non-liquefied to completely sand liquefied. The analyzing result shows that p-y curves modified by this method are able to simulate the interaction between soil and pile body more reasonably. Keywords: Pile, soil liquefaction, p-y curve, excess pore water pressure.

1. INTRODUCTION

In recent years, energy conservation, carbon emission reduction, and the development of renewable energy have been the focuses of our government, and wind power is considered to be one of the most important sources of renewable energy. Currently, all the wind energy is generated from onshore wind farms. However, due to the limited terrain of Taiwan, the government had planned a precursor offshore wind farm at the western sea of Taiwan, e.g. Fang-Yuan County, Chang-Hua, etc.

The force conditions of an offshore wind turbine are different from that of on-shore wind turbines; the lateral force of an offshore wind turbine is usually greater than its axial force. Typically, pile structure is selected for offshore wind farms with water depth less than 30 meters. Western offshore wind turbine design regulations, such as DNV-OS-J101 (2013) from Det Norske Veritas, IEC61400-3 (2009) from International Electro Technical Commission, and API RP 2A-WSD (2005) from American Petroleum Institute, are major regulations used to design wind turbine pile foundations. P-y curve approach is the most often used method for analyzing bearing capacity and deformation of pile foundations under lateral external loads.

This study analyzed the effect of soil liquefaction on pile foundations in seabed sand, in order to gain more understanding of the seabed sand layer and to provide a guideline for the design of offshore wind turbines.

Offshore wind turbine pile foundations are installed mostly in saturated loose sand layers, which have the potential of suffering from earthquake-induced soil liquefaction (Ni, et al. 2014, 2017). Taiwan is located on tectonic plate boundary earthquake zone, they lack the consideration of the effects of soil liquefaction on pile foundation in the above regulations. Japan Road Association (JRA, 1996) considers the effect of soil liquefaction on ultimate strength reduction factor with liquefaction potential index (LPI). However, the LPI is calculated by the zone of soil liquefied only. This study analyzed the effect of soil liquefaction on pile foundations in seabed sand, in order to gain more understanding of the seabed sand layer and to provide a guideline for the design of offshore wind turbines. The relationship between p-y curves under different excess pore water pressure ratio ru and pile lateral deformation is also discussed.

2. API p-y Curve of Sand

P-y curve method is an analytical mode that analyzes a pile under lateral loading and is also the most popular method used in practical practice. The concept of Winkler model is applied in this method, which simulates the surrounding soil with numbers of springs. These springs in different depths are isolated and possess their own load-deformation curves or so-called p-y curves.

In the case of this study, the uppermost sand layer controls the whole pile behavior. The p-y curve of sand and the liquefiable sand layer is described in details below.

Currently, the most popular p-y curve of sand is the hyperbolic tangent model purposed by Murchison and O' Neill (1984) and suggested by American Petroleum Institute (API, 2005). The following two equations can be used to determine the maximum soil reaction force per unit length. Equation (1) determines the maximum lateral resistance of the shallower soil, and Equation (2) for the deeper soil. The smaller of the two is then the ultimate resistance pu for the conservative consideration.

$$p_{us} = (C_1 z + C_2 D)\gamma' z \qquad (1)$$

$$p_{ud} = C_3 D\gamma' z \qquad (2)$$

Where D is pile diameter (m),

γ' is effective unit weight of soil (kN/m³),

z is the depth (m),

C_1, C_2, C_3 are dimensionless coefficients.

Finally, the relationship between soil reaction force p and deformation y at a specific depth can be represented by Equation (3):

$$p = Ap_u \tanh\left(\frac{kz}{Ap_u}y\right) \qquad (3)$$

Where k is the subgrade reaction coefficient,

A is the ultimate bearing capacity adjustment coefficient. It is obtained from the testing results of pile load tests with different pile head loading conditions.

Considering statistic loading condition:

$$A = \left(3.0 - 0.8\frac{z}{D}\right) \geq 0.9$$

Considering cyclic loading condition:

$$A = 0.9$$

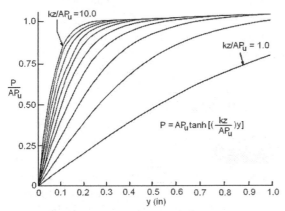

Fig. 1 API's p-y curve of sand

3. Modification of p-y curve for Liquefiable sand

3.1 Rollins' p-y Curve of Liquefied Sand

A full-scale pile test was performed by Rollins et al. (2005) at Treasure Island, California, USA. By detonating dynamites, excess pore water pressure was excited and soil was liquefied. A concave-up p-y curve was then back-calculated from data obtained from strain gages installed on pile body.

This concave-up p-y curve was the hysteresis loop resulted from the force applied by brakes and pile head deflection. It can be seen that in the beginning of cyclic loading, as numbers of cycles increased, the hysteresis loops gradually flatten. It means that the stiffness of soil was gradually decreased until it stabilized at the 10th cycle. The residual strength was reached at this 10th cycle and was considered

completely liquefied. The p-y curve of this 10th cycle was then back-calculated. The relationship between soil reaction force p and deformation y is shown below.

$$p = P_d A(By)^C \tag{4}$$

Among them,

$$A = 3 \times 10^{-7}(z + 1)^{6.05}$$

$$B = 2.80(z + 1)^{0.11}$$

$$C = 2.85(z + 1)^{-0.41}$$

$$P_d = 3.81 \ln|D| + 5.6$$

z is the depth (m),

P_d is unit less pile diameter affection coefficient.

Since this function was derived from the in-situ test performed by Rollins et al., there are limitations to equation (4) above:

(1) The relative density of soil has to be between 40% ~ 55%.

(2) Soil lateral resistance must be less than 15 kN/m.

(3) The lateral deformation pile must be less than 150 mm.

(4) Water level must be higher, or close to, ground level.

(5) Soil depth must be less than 6 m.

3.2 Liu & Dobry Modified Method

Different from using the traditional method of determining the relationship between (N1)60 of soil sample and soil strength reduction after liquefaction, Liu and Dobry (1995) performed a series of centrifuge tests to determine the trend of soil strength reduction under a different level of soil liquefaction. It is done by excited different excess pore water pressure in the sand soil samples. A linear decreasing relationship was found between excess pore water pressure ratio ru and soil strength reduction factor Cu by regression analysis from a large amount of test data:

$$C_u = 1 - r_u \qquad (5)$$

Liu and Dobry (1995) suggested that, in order to simulate sand soil strength reduction after liquefaction, traditional non-liquefied p-y curve, for example, sand p-y curves proposed by Reese et al. (1974), can be selected as the base. Cu factors under different excess pore water pressure ratio calculated using equation (10) and reduced ultimate soil resistance were also taking into account:

$$p = p_y \times C_u \qquad (6)$$

Where p_y is the ultimate soil resistance of the non-liquefied sand p-y curve.

When $r_u = 1.0$, the Cu calculated from equation (6) is zero. However, in practical practice, it is believed that residual strength still exists after the soil was liquefied, the value $C_u = 0.1$ is given in

such cases. Liu and Dobry modifying method is just to multiply the p-y curves of non-liquefied sand by a reduction coefficient to reduce ultimate soil resistance to represent p-y curves under different levels of liquefaction, as shown in Fig. 3.

3.3 Chang and Hutchinson Modified Method

Chang and Hutchinson (2013) studied the p-y curves under different excess pore water pressure ratios using modeled tests with layered soil box of length 3.9 m, width 1.8 m, and height 1.9 m. A shaking table was used to generate different earthquake signals to excite different excess pore water pressure.

Chang and Hutchinson (2013) discovered that p-y curves concave up as excess pore water pressure increased, which matches the full-scaled testing results of Rollins et al. (2005). Therefore, the p-y curve of Rollins et al. (2005), which is equation (4), was used as the base equation. Along with equation (7), the soil resistance was multiplied by the reciprocal of Cru to enlarge the strength p of completely liquefied sand:

$$p = p_R \times \frac{1}{C_{ru}} \qquad (7)$$

$$y = y_R \times C_{ru} \qquad (8)$$

Where

C_{ru} is the excess pore water pressure ratio in decimal form,

p_R is the soil resistance in Rollins liquefied sand model,

y_R is the pile body deflection in Rollins liquefied sand model,

Chang and Hutchinson (2013) modifying method is just using the p-y curve of Rollins et al. (2005) as bases, and the pore water pressure as a

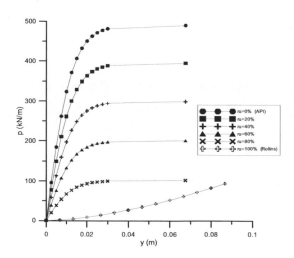

Fig. 3 p-y curves before and after correction

correction coefficient, to correct the ultimate soil resistance and lateral displacement to represent p-y curves under different levels of liquefaction, as shown in Figure 4. When using equation (7), as ru approaches 0, the calculated soil resistance will be infinitely large. Therefore, this modification method does not apply to soil layers with small ru.

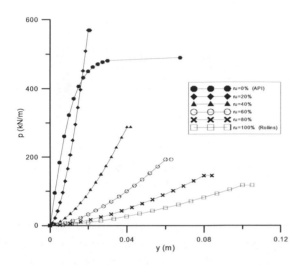

Fig. 4 p-y curves before and after correction

3.4 Hybrid Modified Method

Dash (2008)'s proposed that p-y curves change from concave-down shape to concave-up shape, as shown in Figure 5 below. He combined the two modifying methods described in Sec 3.1 and sec.3.2 to obtain a complete modifying method for better describing the process from non-liquefied to completely liquefied. It can be seen in Fig. 5 that the p-y curve is difficult to use for ru ranged from 0.3 to 0.85.

Previous studies suggested that the Chang and Hutchinson (2013) modifying method is applicable when ruis greater than 10% to 15%. However, from the analytical results of this study, Chang and Hutchinson (2013) modifying method is applicable when ru is greater than 20%, and Liu and Dobry (1995) modifying method can be used when ru is less than or equal to 20%. Therefore, assumed that, as excess pore water pressure ratio change, p-y

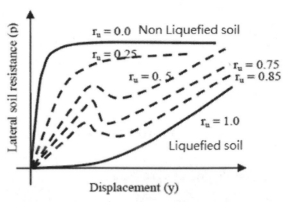

Fig. 5 Trends of p-y curves under different excess pore water pressure ratio (Dash, et al., 2008)

curves change from concave-up shape to concave-down shape when soil goes from non-liquefied to completely liquefied, the concepts of Liu and Dobry (1995) and Chang and Hutchinson (2013) modifying methods can be combined to establish a new hybrid modifying method. The base of the p-y curve:

$$P_q = UP_P + (1 - U)P_r \qquad (9)$$

The relationship formula of liquefied correction:

$$P = P_q \times C_{up} \qquad (10)$$

$$y = y_q \times C_{uy} \qquad (11)$$

Where P_q and y_q is the ultimate soil resistance and displacement of the base p-y curve, respectively. They are established based on API (2005) and Rollins (2005) p-y curves of sand. U is related to r_u, $U = 0$ when $r_u > 20\%$, $U = 1$ when r_u less than or equal to 20%. P_P is the ultimate soil resistance obtained from API sand p-y curve. P_r is the ultimate soil resistance obtained from Rollins liquefied sand p-y curve. C_{up} is the pore water reduction factor for the P_q while C_{uy} is the pore water reduction factor for the y_q. They are:

$$C_{up} = U\left(1 - r_u - \frac{1}{r_u}\right) + \frac{1}{r_u} \qquad (12)$$

$$C_{uy} = U(1 - r_u) + r_u \qquad (13)$$

The typical of p-y curves in various depths with this hybrid modified method are shown in Fig. 7 and Fig. 8 in Section 4.2.

4. Case Study and Results Discussion

4.1 Soil Profile of Case Site

The analysis of this study focuses on the four-pile group. Analytical software GROUP 2013 was used to discuss p-y curves before and after soil liquefaction, pile lateral displacement, moment, and the maximum rotational angle. The modified p-y curve method was also used to determine the difference of p-y curves under different levels of soil liquefaction. The simulations include the distribution of shear force, moment, soil reaction force, and pile body deflection.

Chang-Hua precursor offshore wind-farm is selected to perform case study (Chien et al. 2015). The simplified soil profile of this site is shown in Fig. 6(a). The soil parameters of this simplified soil profile are listed in Table 1. The layout of the four-pile group is shown in Fig. 6(b). The following pile cap loads, transferring from upper structures, were assumed: axial force 95200 kN, shear force 15640 kN, and moment 85440 kN-m. A steel pile with the following parameters was installed: pile diameter D = 1.8 m, wall thickness t = 0.08 m, and length L = 70 m. The yield strength of pile is 345 MPa.

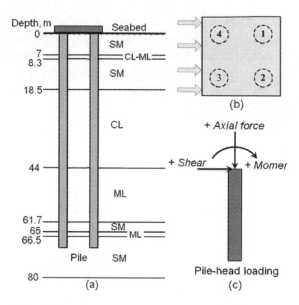

Fig. 6 Simplified soil profile and four-pile group layout

Note - N= SPT-N value, N_{60} = SPT-N value with 60%energy correction, e = void ratio, ω = water content, γ_t = unit weight, Cc = compression index, Cs = swelling index, c = cohesion, ϕ = friction angle, c' = effective cohesion, ϕ' = effective friction angle.

4.2 Modification of p-y Curve with Excess Pore Water Pressure Ratio

The soil liquefaction study showed that the soil will be liquefied for the depth less than 7.5 m. The soil resistance of the upper two meters depth is neglected due to the souring effect of the pile.

Table 1 Soil parameters of simplified soil profile

Depth m	Soil type	N	N_{60}	e	$\omega\%$	γ_t kN/m³	Cc/Cs	c kP	ϕ deg	c' kPa	ϕ' deg.
0.0~7.0	SM	2.8	2.7	0.78	25.00	19.1	–	–	–	0.00	31.5
7.0~8.3	CL-ML	5.0	6.0	0.89	21.00	17.6	–	20.5	0.00	–	–
8.3~18.5	SM	24.2	30.3	0.62	18.20	19.8	–	–	–	0.00	34.70
18.5~44.0	CL	10.6	15.4	0.78	27.59	19.4	0.32/0.034	5.7	20.65	0.00	33.53
44.0~61.7	ML	18.9	25.2	0.97	34.92	18.8	–	–	–	0.00	35.6
61.7~65.0	SM	34.5	46.0	0.49	16.00	21.1	–	–	–	0.00	37.4
65.0~66.5	ML	34.0	45.3	0.52	18.00	20.5	–	–	–	0.00	39.2
66.5~80.0	SM	30.6	40.7	0.52	17.22	21.0	–	–	–	0.00	36.9

As described Sec. 3.4, a new hybrid modifying p-y curve with excess pore water pressure ratio is established. The typical of p-y curves varied with excess pore water pressure ratio for the depth at 3 to 6 meter with this hybrid modified method are shown from Fig. 7 to Fig. 10.

There is generally group effect (e.g. shadowing) of closely-spaced piles. A p-factor is usually applied to modify the p-y curve to reflect this group effect. The p-factors were calculated for the pile layout as shown in Fig. 6(b) (Cox et al., 1974, Reese and Wang, 2000). The result is listed in Table 2. AS shown in Table 2, the group effect can be neglected as the pile spacing is greater than 3.5.

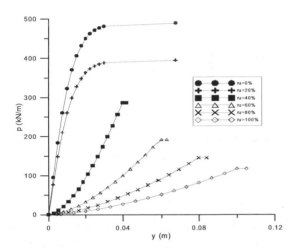

**Fig. 7 Trend of p-y curves with new modified
method at depth of 3 m**

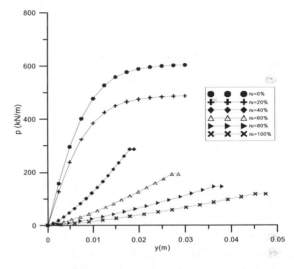

**Fig. 9 Trend of p-y curves with new modified
method at depth of 5 m**

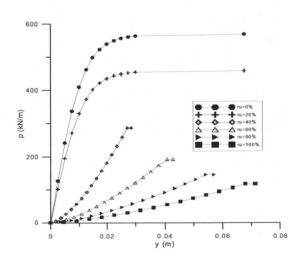

**Fig. 8 Trend of p-y curves with new modified
method at depth of 4 m**

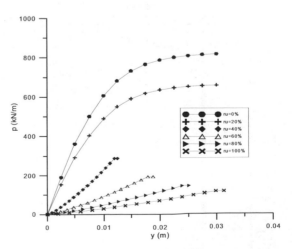

**Fig. 10 Trend of p-y curves with new modified
method at depth of 6 m**

Table 2 P-factor for pile spacing and pile number

Pile spacing	1.5D	2D	2.5D	3D	3.5D
Pile no	P-factor	P-factor	P-factor	P-factor	P-factor
1	0.46	0.65	0.86	0.96	1.0
2	0.46	0.65	0.86	0.96	1.0
3	0.34	0.5	0.65	0.79	0.86
4	0.34	0.5	0.65	0.79	0.86

4.3 Effect of Pile Head Condition

Jacket type with four piles foundation will be used for the offshore wind turbine in this case. There are generally three pile head boundary conditions for the connection between jacket frame and pile head. They are pinned, fixed, and elastically restrained connection. The loadings for the single pile are axial force 23800 kN, shear force 3910 kN, and moment 21360 kN-m. The variation of pile deflection and bending moment with depth for the three boundary conditions for pile no. 1 are shown in Fig. 11 and Fig. 12, respectively. As shown in the two figures, the maximum deflection and moment happen at the pinned head while fixed end has minimum deflection and moment.

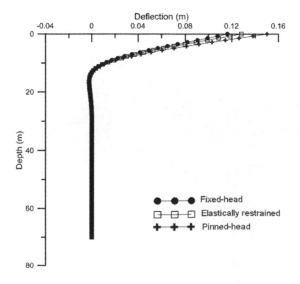

Fig.11 Variation of pile deflection with depth for three boundary conditions

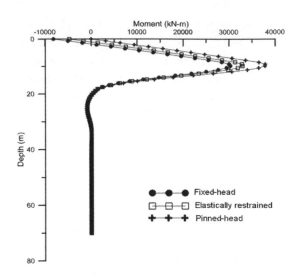

Fig.12 Variation of pile deflection with depth for three boundary conditions

4.4 Performance-Based Curves

The soil profile and pile properties used in this design case are described in Sec. 4.1. Engineer is interested in the performance curve of the pile subjected to external loading, especially the lateral deflection and rotation of pile top. The criterion in the design case is to limit the rotation at the foundation to a value of -0.0017 radians or less in order to limit the movement at the turbine. Also, the displacement of pile top is limited to 10% of pile diameter, i.e. 0.18 m for 1.8 m diameter of the pile. The full loadings for the four-pile group are 95200 kN axial force, 15640 kN shear force, and 85440 kN-m moments. The spacing of pile is three-fold of pile diameter. The connection between pile top and pile cap was assumed to be fixed. The typical performance curve for the pile cap deflection and rotation subjected to lateral loading only is shown in Fig. 13 and Fig. 14, respectively. As shown in these figures, the dashed line is for soil non-liquefied (API, $r_u = 0$) while the solid line is for soil is liquefied (Rollins, $r_u = 100\%$). The curve will be located at between these two curve as the r_u ranged from 0% to 100%. Table 3 shows that the variations of deflection with different kind of combined loadings. The deflection and rotation of pile cap for API ($r_u = 0$) are 8.22 cm and -9.18E-

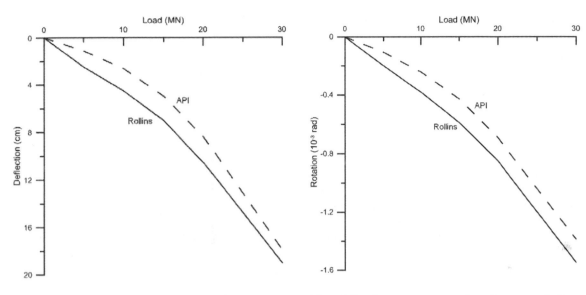

**Fig. 13 Performance curve for pile cap
deflection subjected lateral loading**

**Fig. 14 Performance curve for pile cap rotation
subjected lateral loading**

Table 3 Variations of deflection with loadings

	Lateral load		Lateral load + axial load		Full loads	
	deflection(cm)	rotation(rad)	deflection(cm)	rotation(rad)	deflection(cm)	rotation(rad)
API	5.33	-4.56E-04	6.05	-1.91E-03	8.22	-9.18E-03
Rollins	8.85	-7.46E-04	9.9	-2.63E-03	12.2	-9.92E-03

	Moment		Moment + axial load		Full loads	
	deflection(cm)	rotation(rad)	deflection(cm)	rotation(rad)	deflection(cm)	rotation(rad)
API	0.2	-1.52E-03	0.704	-5.05E-03	8.22	-9.18E-03
Rollins	0.39	-1.60E-03	1.29	-5.15E-03	12.2	-9.92E-03

03 rad, respectively. The deflection and rotation of pile cap for Rollins ($r_u = 100\%$) are 12.2 cm and --9.92E-03 rad, respectively. It is obviously the rotation is over the criterion required. The modification of design is needed.

4.5 Modification of Design Parameter

As described in above section, the rotation of pile cap is over the criterion required. The modification of the original design parameters is needed. There are two ways to increase the stiffness of this pile group. One is to use the bigger diameter of the pile, the other is to increase the spacing of pile. The result of increasing the diameter but

maintaining the 3D spacing is shown in Fig. 15. As shown in the figure, the rotation is decreasing with a diameter of the pile. Fig. 16 shows the result of increasing the spacing but maintain the pile diameter in spite of soil liquefied or not. As shown in the figure, the rotation is also decreasing with the spacing of pile. As shown in the two figures, increasing diameter or spacing of pile can improve the pile cap rotation. In the offshore engineering to increase the spacing of pile is more economic comparing with to increase the diameter of the pile. Therefore, the four-pile group with a diameter of 1.8 m and 7D (12.6 m) spacing is considered. The result of reanalysis the pile group under the full loading with the soil liquefied is shown in Table 4.

The variation of depth with pile cap deflection and moment of the pile for the soil liquefied is shown in Fig. 17 and Fig. 18, respectively. As shown in Table 4, the deflection of the pile is satisfied with the criterion required.

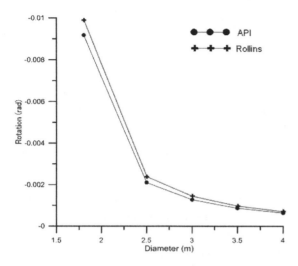

Fig. 15 Variation of pile cap rotation with pile diameter

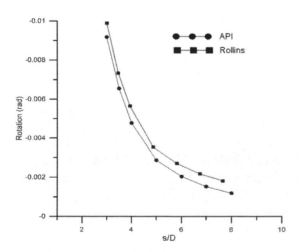

Fig. 16 Variation of pile cap rotation with pile spacing

Table 4 Variation of deflections with spacing for 1.8 m pile diameter

Spacing (m)	Rotation (rad)	Displacement (m)	Max. moment (kN-m)
12.6 (7D)	-1.64E-03	0.096	2.60E+04
5.4 (3D)	-9.92E-03	0.122	3.30E+04

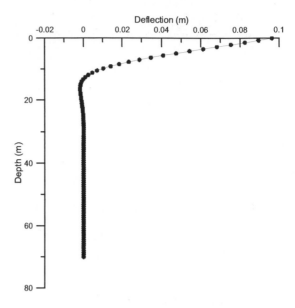

Fig. 17 Variation of deflection of pile with depth

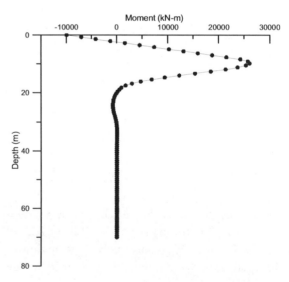

Fig. 18 Variation of moment of pile with depth

5. CONCLUSIONS

The following conclusions from this study can be drawn.

1. Select Chang and Hutchinson modifying method when $r\_u > 20\%$. Select Liu and Dobry modifying method when $r\_u \leq 20\%$.

2. The new pore water pressure ratio modifying method suggested in this study is limited to small scale model test. The applicability of this approach in full-scale cases requires further study.

3. The rotation angle obtained from completely liquefied sand is greater than non-liquefied sand despite changes in pile diameter and spacing between piles.

4. The group effect decreased with the pile spacing increased. Therefore, the change of pile body displacement, moment, and the maximum angle of rotation with depth was decreased. However, the ultimate soil resistance increased with the same lateral displacement, so the p-y curve upward.

5. Using four-pile group with 1.8-meter diameter and 7D spacing of pile can satisfy the requirement of criterion of the case project.

ACKNOWLEDGEMENTS

The study on which this paper is based was supported in part by the Ministry of Science and Technology, Taiwan, R.O.C. under the grant number MOST 104- 3113-E-006- 015-CC2. Grateful appreciation is expressed for this support.

REFERENCES

American Petroleum Institute (API) (2005). "Recommended practice for planning designing, and constructing fixed offshore platforms." *API Report No.2A-WSD*, Houston.

Chang, B.. J. and Hutchinson, T. .C. (2013). "Experimental evaluation of p-y curves considering development of liquefaction." *Journal of Geotechnical and Geoenvironmental Engineering*, ASCE, 139(4), 577-586.

Chien, L.K., Chiu, S.Y., Feng, Z.W., and Lin, C.K. (2015). "The geotechnical investigation of offshore wind farm for Fuhai development zone." *Sino-Geotechnics*, 142, 59-68. (in Chinese)

Cox, W.R., Reese, L.C., and Grubbs, B.R. (1974), "Field testing of laterally loaded piles in sand," *Proceeding of 6th Annual Offshore Technology Conference*, Houston, Texas, Vol. 2, pp. 459-472.

Dash, S.R., Bhattacharya, S., Blakeborough, A., and Hyodo, M. (2008), "p-y curve to model lateral response of pile foundation in liquefied soils." *The 14th World Conference on Earthquake Engineering*, October 12-17, Beijing, China.

Det Norske Veritas (DNV) (2013). *Design of Offshore Wind Turbine Structures, Offshore Standard* DNV-OS-J101, DNV, Norway.

Ensoft (2013). *Computer Program LPILE v2013 – A Program to Analyze Deep Foundations under Lateral Loading*, Austin, Texas.

International Electrotechnical Commission (IEC) (2009). "Design requirements for offshore wind turbines." *IEC61400-3*, Switzerland.

Japan Road Association (1996), *Design Specifications of Highway Bridges, Part V Seismic Design*, JRA, Japan.

Liu, L. and Dobry, R. (1995). "Effect of liquefaction on lateral response of piles by centrifuge model tests," *NCEER Bulletin*, 9(1), 7-11.

Murchinson, J.M. and O'Neill, M.W. (1984). "Evaluation of p-y relationships in cohesionless soils." *Analysis and Design of Pile Foundations. Proceedings of a Symposium in conjunction with the ASCE National Convention*, 174-191.

Ni, S.H., Xiao, X., and Yang, Y.Z. (2014). "A p-y curve-based approach to analyze pile behavior for liquefied sand under different stress states." *Journal of GeoEngineering*, 9(3), 85-94.

Ni, S.H., Huang, K.C., Feng, Z.W., Fan, C.H., and Su, S.P. (2017), "Analysis of Pile Behavior in Liquefiable Seabed Sand with p-y Curve Approach," *Journal of GeoEngineering*, Vol.12, No. 1, pp. 151-159

Reese, L.C., Cox, W.R., and Koop, F.D. (1974). "Analysis of laterally loaded piles in sand," *Proceedings* of the Sixth Annual Offshore Technology Conference, Houston, Texas, OTC 2080, 473-483.

Reese, L.C., and Wang, S.T. (2000), *Documentation of Computer Program GROUP 5.0, Ensoft, Inc.*, Austin, Texas.

Reese, L.C. and Wang, S.T. (2008). "Design of foundations for a wind turbine employing modern principles." *ASCE Geotechnical Special Publication No. 180 – From Research to Practice in Geotechnical Engineering*, edited by Laier J., Crapps D., and Hussein, M., 351-365.

Rollins, K.M., Gerber, T.M., Dusty, L.J., and Ashford, S.A. (2005). "Lateral resistance of a full-scale pile group in liquefied sand." *Journal of Geotechnical and Geoenvironmental Engineering*, ASCE, 131(1), 115-125.

Wang, S.T., and Reese, L.C. (1998), Design of pile foundation in liquefied soils." *Geotechnical Earthquake Engineering and Soil Dynamics III*, pp. 1331-1343.

CHAPTER 8

NUMERICAL EVALUATION OF SEISMIC PERFORMANCE OF PILED RAFT WITH GRID-FORM DMWS UNDER LARGE EARTHQUAKE LOADS

Yoshimasa Shigeno*
Kiyoshi Yamashita
Junji Hamada
Research & Development Institute, Takenaka Corporation, Chiba, Japan
**shigeno.yoshimasa@takenaka.co.jp*

Naohiro Nakamura
Department of Architecture, Hiroshima University, Hiroshima, Japan

ABSTRACT : The seismic performance of a piled raft foundation with grid-form deep mixing walls (DMWs) in soft ground under strong earthquake loads is numerically evaluated in this study. A base-isolated building located in Tokyo is modeled as a detailed three-dimensional finite element soil structure interaction model. First the model is adjusted using the records of the 2011 off the Pacific coast of Tohoku Earthquake, and seismic response analyses under strong earthquake loads are then conducted. Artificial earthquakes that are officially notified for performance design in Japanese building design codes are used in the analysis. The case without grid-form DMWs is also analyzed to elucidate the effect of the DMWs on the seismic performance. Based on the analysis results, the maximum bending moment of the piles in the cases with the DMWs is found to be markedly smaller than that without the DMWs, and it is within the allowable structural capacity of the pile. It is also found that the induced stress in the DMWs reaches the tensile strength in limited parts. Consequently, the grid-form DMWs are found to be quite effective at reducing the bending moment of the piles to an acceptable level, even if partial failure occurs in the DMWs under strong earthquake loads.

1. INTRODUCTION

In recent years, the effectiveness of piled rafts at reducing average and differential settlements has been confirmed on soft clay and even on liquefiable sand by adding grid-form cement deep mixing walls (DMWs) (Yamashita et al., 2011, 2013, 2016). Grid-form DMWs work not only as a countermeasure against liquefaction by increasing the resistance of unstabilized soil but also as a component providing resistance against the horizontal load. However, when grid-form DMWs are added to a piled raft as a new component,

the seismic behavior becomes more complex, and the necessity for detailed seismic evaluation is increasing to develop more reliable design methods, particularly in highly active seismic areas such as Japan.

To investigate the seismic response of a piled raft foundation with grid-form DMWs, the field monitoring has been performed on the piled raft system in soft ground supporting the 12-story building, and the seismic response of the soil-foundation system was successfully recorded at the time of the 2011 off the Pacific coast of Tohoku

Earthquake (Yamashita et al., 2012). Targeting these observation records, seismic response analysis using a detailed three-dimensional finite element (FE) model with equivalent linear moduli was conducted, and the analytical results agreed well with the observation records (Hamada et al., 2014).

However the soil and the DMWs must be modeled nonlinearly under strong earthquakes, and the properties of the DMWs must to be considered in more detail to improve the accuracy of the sectional force of the piles. Thus in this study, nonlinear analysis is conducted using the data of the 2011 off the Pacific coast of Tohoku Earthquake, and suitable parameters are obtained to improve the simulation accuracy. Then seismic response analysis using two strong artificial earthquake motions are conducted. The effectiveness of the grid-form DMWs at reducing the sectional force on the piles is discussed according to the design concept of performance-based design (PBD).

2. BUILDING, GROUND CONDITION AND NUMERICAL MODEL

Figure 1 shows a schematic view of the building and its foundation with the soil profile. The building analyzed is the 12-story residential building located in Tokyo. The soil down to a depth of 44m is alluvial stratum. The soil profile down to a depth of 7m is composed of fill, soft silt and loose silty sand, and the ground water table appears approximately 1.8 m below the ground surface. The piled raft with grid-form DMWs has been employed to prevent liquefaction of the silty sand from GL -3 to -7 m and to improve the bearing capacity of the foundation. The foundation design and the monitoring instrumentation have been reported in detail by Yamashita et al. (2012).

2.1 Finite Element Model

Figure 2 shows the FE mesh of the model used in this study. The number of elements is

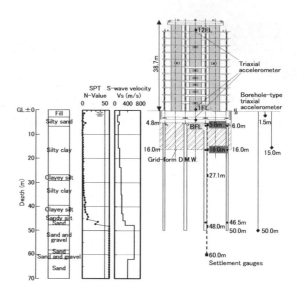

Fig.1 Schematic view of building foundation with soil profile

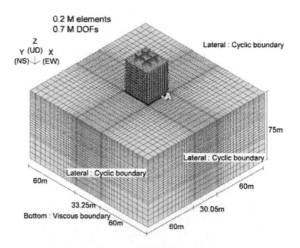

Fig.2 FE mesh of soil structure interaction model

213,622, and the number of degrees-of-freedom (DOFs) is 656,543. The lateral boundaries are periodic boundaries, positioned 60 m outside of the building to reduce the boundary effect. The bottom is a viscous boundary at a depth of 75 m from the ground surface. The columns of the superstructure are modeled using an elastic bar, and the earthquake-resistant walls and the floors are modeled using an elastic shell. The raft is modeled using elastic solid elements with the modulus of concrete. Rayleigh damping is applied to these components with a damping ratio of 2%. The base isolation system is modeled using the tri-linear spring (Hamada et al., 2014). Figure 3 shows the skeleton curve of the tri-linear spring model. The bilinear spring model that was used in the structural design is also shown in this figure. The first break point of the tri-linear model is added to the bilinear model to fit the vibration characteristic before the seismic motion of the superstructure becomes large in the analysis of the 2011 off the Pacific coast of Tohoku Earthquake.

Figure 4 shows a top-down view of the FE mesh beneath the raft and the foundation plan. The spacing between the DMWs ranges from approximately 6 to 9 m. The DMWs are modeled using solid elements and divided into 4-quarters in the thickness direction to ensure sufficient accuracy. The piles are modeled using an elastic bar. To consider the shape and volume of the piles, cavities in the shape of the piles are made in the FE model. The nodes of the piles and the adjacent ground nodes at the same depth are bound by a rigid bar. Figure 5 shows how the piles are modeled. Table 1 shows the dimensions and material properties of the piles.

The software is an in-house program called MuDIAN (Shiomi et al., 1993). It is parallelized using the hybrid parallel method and is able to rapidly analyze a large-DOF model (Shigeno et al., 2014)

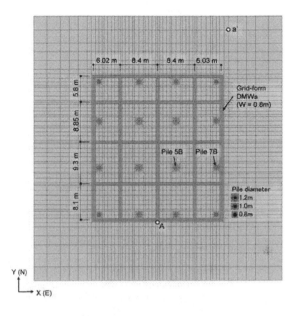

Fig.4 Top-down view of FE mesh for piles and grid-form DMWs

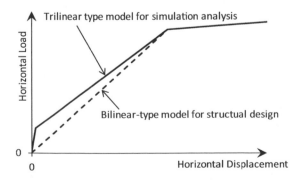

Fig.3 Schematic of lateral load vs. displacement relation of base isolator used in analysis

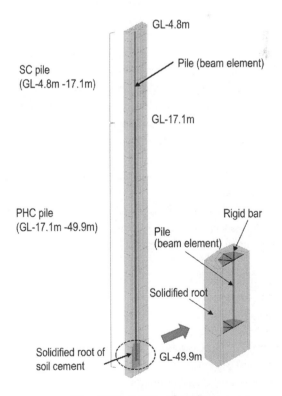

Fig. 5 Modeling of a pile

Table 1 Pile properties

Pile diameter	(mm)	800	1000	1200
Young's modulus	(MN/m^2)	40000	40000	40000
Damping	(%)	2	2	2
Ae[*1] of SC pile[*3]	(m^2)	0.3268	0.4649	0.6714
Ie[*2] of SC pile	(m^4)	0.02199	0.04899	0.10316
Ae of PHC pile[*4]	(m^2)	0.2441	0.3633	0.5054
Ie of PHC pile	(m^4)	0.01455	0.03437	0.06958

*1 Ae : Equivalent cross-sectional area   *2 Ie : Equivalent moment of inertia of area
*3 SC pile : steel pipe–concrete composite pile   *4 PHC pile : prestressed high-strength concrete pile

2.2 Modeling of Soil

The shear wave velocity profile is based on the P–S logging results obtained at the building site, which is located at the eastern edge of the building. The optimized *Vs* profile was obtained by matching the vibrational characteristics of the soil deposit for the theoretical transfer function with that for the ground surface records in the H/V form. The ground surface records were obtained from the three small earthquakes prior to the 2011 off the Pacific coast of the Tohoku Earthquake of which the maximum accelerations at GL-1.5 m are 3.6, 8.0, 18.2 gals. Considering these values, the final optimized *Vs* profile can be corresponded to the initial shear modulus. Layer 3 in Figure 6 is declined, and the layer boundary between layers 3 and 4 is 10 m higher at the western edge than at the eastern edge. However the ground is assumed to be horizontally layered for the sake of convenience in modeling. Then the *Vs* of layer 3 is changed to be gradually increased value from the original optimized value. The *Vs* profile used in the present analysis is shown in Figure 6.

As the three–dimensional constitutive model of the soil, the Yoshida model for multi-dimensional analysis (Tsujino et al., 1994) is used. The Yoshida model is a two –surface model that uses a yielding surface and a loading surface that describes the state of the current stress. The Mohr–Coulomb model is used as the yielding surface that provides the strength of the soil. In this model, the stress–strain relationship is based on a nonlinear elastic model then the yielding function is only used as a

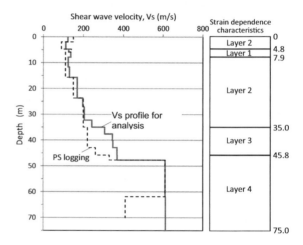

Fig. 6 Profiles of logged initial shear wave velocity and that used in the model

strength criterion. The skeleton curve of this model is derived discretely using the normalized shear modulus–shear strain ($G/G_0-\gamma$) characteristic. The damping characteristic is obtained by combining the Masing's rule and the hyperbolic function. The parameters of the function are determined from the damping ratio–shear strain ($h-\gamma$) characteristic. This model is characterized by directly using the $G/G_0-\gamma$ and $h-\gamma$ characteristics as input data. However, the $G/G_0-\gamma$ curve must be modeled such that the shear stress–shear strain curve obtained from the $G/G_0-\gamma$ relation does not exceed the strength given by the Mohr–Coulomb criteria at a large shear strain.

The $G/G_0-\gamma$ and $h-\gamma$ characteristics of each soil layer are obtained from dynamic triaxial tests of in-situ samples and are shown in Figure 7. The dependence of the confined stress on the strength is not considered here, and the strength is given by the cohesion c. The cohesion of layers below GL-35 m is determined from $G_0 \gamma_{50}$, where γ_{50} is the shear strain at which $G/G_0 = 0.5$. And in the layers above GL-35 m, the cohesion is determined such that the shear stress–strain curve agrees well up to 4% of the shear strain between the curves given by the original $G/G_0 - \gamma$ curve and modeled $G/G_0 - \gamma$ curve. Initial damping other than the damping induced by the constitutive model is assumed to be 1%, and is given by Rayleigh damping. The soil properties are listed in Table 2.

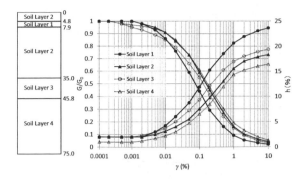

Fig. 7 Strain dependent characteristics of soil

Table 2 Soil properties

Layer upper depth (m)	Layer bottom depth (m)	Stratum	Density (t/m³)	Initial shear modulus (kPa)	Poisson's ratio	Cohesion (kPa)
0.0	2.0	Fill	1.70	25,442	0.467	60.0
2.0	4.8	Silty clay	1.60	19,948	0.496	60.0
4.8	5.9	Silty sand	1.80	28,945	0.490	60.0
5.9	7.9	Silty sand	1.60	29,987	0.495	100.0
7.9	11.7	Silty clay	1.60	24,522	0.495	100.0
11.7	15.7	Silty clay	1.60	27,198	0.496	120.0
15.7	19.7	Silty clay	1.60	45,610	0.495	180.0
19.7	23.7	Silty clay	1.60	45,959	0.495	180.0
23.7	27.1	Silty clay	1.60	62,637	0.491	240.0
27.1	32.3	Silty clay	1.60	67,240	0.491	260.0
32.3	35.0	Silty clay	1.60	93,912	0.491	260.0
35.0	37.6	Silty clay	1.70	159,801	0.490	223.7
37.6	40.2	Silty clay	1.70	202,821	0.490	283.9
40.2	42.9	Silty clay	1.70	205,883	0.490	288.2
42.9	45.8	Clayey silt	1.70	230,470	0.487	414.8
45.8	47.7	Sand	1.80	245,197	0.479	441.4
47.7	49.9	Sand and gravel	1.80	671,011	0.458	1207.8
49.9	61.9	Sand and gravel	2.00	745,621	0.458	1342.1
61.9	75.0	Sand	2.00	749,513	0.471	1349.1

2.3 Modeling of Stabilized Soil

The DMWs are composed of a mixture of cement milk and soil. The failure of the DMWs is characterized by their tensile, compressive, and shear strengths. The compressive strength of stabilized soil is very high, and thus failure due to the ground motion is caused by tension or shear. The Mohr–Coulomb and Drucker–Prager yield criteria are often applied for stabilized soil. These

models give the shear strength that depends on confining pressure. They are also able to give the tensile strength if the friction angle is not zero. However, the tensile strength of these models is generally larger than the actual value. The tensile criterion must be used to evaluate the correct tensile strength.

The maximum principal stress σ_1 corresponds to the maximum tensile stress (note that tension is positive) is expressed using the stress variants J'_2 and σ_m by applying the Lode angle $\theta(-\pi/6 < \theta < \pi/6)$ as

$$\sigma_t = \sigma_1 = \frac{2(J'_2)^{\frac{1}{2}}}{\sqrt{3}}\sin\left(\theta + \frac{2\pi}{3}\right) + \sigma_m \qquad (1)$$

where J'_2 is the second invariant of the deviatoric stress, and σ_m is the mean stress. Additionally, the Mohr–Coulomb criterion for shear failure is expressed using stress invariants as

$$\sigma_m \sin\phi + (J'_2)^{\frac{1}{2}}\left(\cos\theta - \frac{1}{\sqrt{3}}\sin\theta\sin\phi\right) = c\cos\phi \qquad (2)$$

where ϕ is the friction angle and c is the cohesion. These criteria are shown in Figure 8. The tensile strength is evaluated correctly by taking the lower strength between the two criteria.

The Hayashi–Hibino model (Motojima et al., 1978) is used as a two criteria model in this study. The Hayashi–Hibino model is a nonlinear elastic model that is able to evaluate tensile and shear failure, and the elastic modulus is reduced to a user specified value at failure. This model is also able to express nonlinearity before failure using the proximity ratio to the criteria R. The elastic modulus is reduced with decreasing R in the following equations using the nonlinear parameter a.

$$E = R^{1/a}E_0, \ 0.45 - v = R^{1/2a}(0.45 - v_0) \qquad (3)$$

where E is the Young's modulus, v is the Poisson's ratio, and the subscript 0 is indicates an initial value.

The design standard compressive strength F_c is used as the compressive strength of the stabilized soil. The value of F_c is calculated using the average compressive strength of in-situ core samples q_{uf} and its variation V_{quf} referred to the Building Center of Japan (BJC) (2002) as follows.

$$F_c = (1 - 1.3V_{quf})q_{uf} \qquad (4)$$

The values of q_{uf} and V_{quf} are 3.8 MPa and 0.25, respectively, corresponding to the average and variance of 36 core samples aged for 28 days (Yamashita et al., 2015), The value of Fc is thus 2.6 MPa. The tensile strength and the cohesion are 0.2 times (520 kPa) and 0.3 times (720 kPa) the compressive strength respectively, and the friction angle and the Poisson's ratio are assumed to be 30° and 0.26 also referred to the BCJ (2002).

The exponent a is obtained by simulating a simple shear test to fit the G–γ curve reported by Kuroda et al. (2001), as shown in Figure 9. In the Hayashi–Hibino model, only the skeleton curve is modeled, and the hysteresis is not included in the model. Then the damping is given by Rayleigh damping, and the damping ratio is assumed to be 5% referred to Kuroda et al. (2001) as shown in Figure 10.

As for the initial stress in the DMWs, an isotropic stress of 170 kPa is assumed by considering the measured vertical pressure of 300 kPa between the raft and the DMWs (Yamashita et al., 2015) and the horizontal stress calculated using the coefficient of earth pressure at rest.

3. SEISMIC RESPONSE ANALYSIS

The analysis is conducted with the input motion based on the records obtained during the 2011 off the Pacific coast of Tohoku Earthquake at first. Through the analysis, the initial shear modulus of the DMWs is determined to fit the observed record of the bending moment of the piles. Then, further analysis under the artificial strong earthquakes are conducted to evaluate the seismic performance of

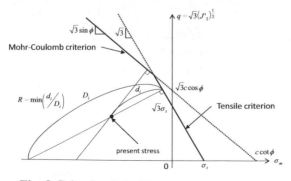

Fig. 8 Criteria of the Hayashi–Hibino model

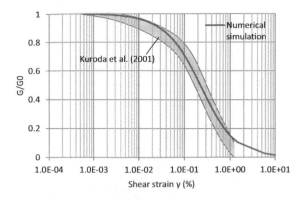

Fig. 9 Strain dependence characteristics on rigidity of stabilized soil

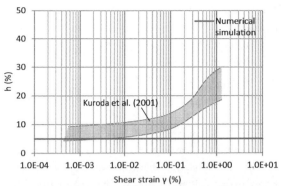

Fig. 10 Strain dependence characteristics on damping ratio of stabilized soil

the foundation.

3.1 Seismic Response Analysis of the 2011 Off the Pacific Coast of Tohoku Earthquake

3.1.1 Input Motion

Prior to the three-dimensional analysis, one-dimensional wave propagation analysis was conducted using the equivalent linear modulus based on the strain characteristics of the ground shown in Figure 7. The observation records of the deepest observation point, at GL -50 m (Fig. 2), were used as the input motion. The peak values of the calculated results are shown in Figure 11 and the observed acceleration results were successfully simulated. Based on the calculation results, the maximum ground shear strain was 0.2% and the overall distribution was almost 0.1%. In consideration of the ground strain level, the reduction in ground stiffness was relatively small. The upward transmitting wave at the depth of 75m, which is set as the bottom depth of the three-dimensional FEM model, was calculated in this analysis, and it is input as the motion of the bottom of the three-dimensional model. Figure 12 shows the input motion in each direction. These input motions are categorized as a moderate earthquake based on the recorded peak ground acceleration of 174.8 cm/s^2 at the depth of -1.5 m in Figure 11.

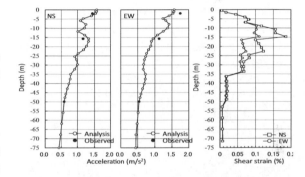

(a) Acceleration   **(b) Shear strain**

Fig. 11 Maximum response obtained from one-dimensional wave propagation analysis of soil column

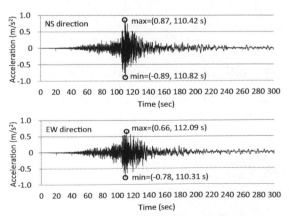

Fig. 12 Input motion of the2011 off the Pacific coast of Tohoku Earthquake at GL -75 m (2E)

3.1.2 Analysis Results

In the three dimensional analysis under the 2011 off the Pacific coast of Tohoku Earthquake, the initial shear modulus of the DMWs is determined to enable the accurate estimation of the observed records, especially those of the bending moment of the piles. It is reasonable to estimate the initial shear modulus from the simulation because it is difficult to know the rigidity of the DMWs on the actual scale, though some formulas have been proposed to estimate the value form the core sample tests. The exponent a of Eq. (4) is simulated according to the initial shear modulus of the DMWs referring to the data in Figure 9. The $G-\gamma$ characteristic of the soil is also adjusted to accurately simulate the bending moment. The $G-\gamma$ curve of layer 2 (Fig. 7) is modified to take into account the increase in stiffness with the effective mean stress as

$$\gamma_i' = \gamma_i \left(\frac{\sigma'_m}{\sigma'_{m\,\text{ref}}} \right)^{0.5} \tag{5}$$

where γ_i' is the corrected shear strain, γ_i is the original shear strain, σ'_m is the effective mean stress, and $\sigma'_{m\,\text{ref}}$ is the effective mean stress at GL -12.2 m. Layer 2 is 27.1 m thick, and it is thus appropriate to consider the confined pressure instead of using one $G-\gamma$ curve.

From the fitting of the analytical peak bending moment of the piles to the observed data, the initial shear modulus of the DMWs and the exponent a are determined to be 500 MPa and 1.0. Figure 13 shows the profiles of the peak acceleration and relative displacement to the point at GL-50 m below the center of the superstructure and the ground at the observation point shown as a' in Figure 4. The profiles are in the EW direction. The results of the analysis agree well with the observations. Figure 14 shows the profiles of the peak bending moment of the piles that monitoring devices are set. The observed peak profiles of the bending moment are reproduced well by the simulation.

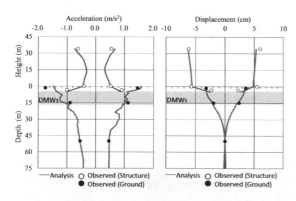

(a) Acceleration   (b) Displacement

Fig. 13 Profiles of peak responses of the ground (point a' in Fig. 4) and the structure (EW direction)

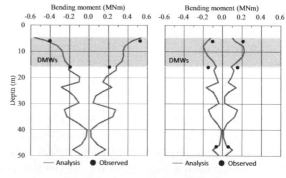

(a) Pile 5B   (b) Pile 7B

Fig. 14 Profiles of peak bending moment of the piles (EW direction)

Figure 15 shows the time history of the acceleration from 100 to 140 s when the response is large in each direction. The accelerations at 12F and the pit are at the center of the superstructure, and the acceleration at GL -1.5 m is at the ground observation point a'. The results also agree well with the observations in the time domain, especially in the EW direction. Figure 16 shows the time history of the relative displacement to GL -50 m. At the pit and the ground at GL -1.5 m, the results agree fairly well with the observations. At 12F, the maximum and minimum accelerations and phase are simulated well, but some of the peaks differ slightly from those in the simulation. Figure 17 shows the response spectra of the acceleration.

The analytical spectra of the superstructure coincide well with those of the observations, but in the spectrum of the ground at GL -1.5m, they differ slightly in the short period region from 0.3 to 0.6 s. Figure 18 shows the time history of the pile head of pile 5B in each direction. The observed bending moment is simulated well using the modeled properties. These results indicate that this numerical model accurately simulates the seismic response under a moderate earthquake. Additionally, the stress in the DMWs is much less than the tensile strength (520 kPa), as shown in the contour of the maximum principal stress obtained during the analysis presented in Figure 19.

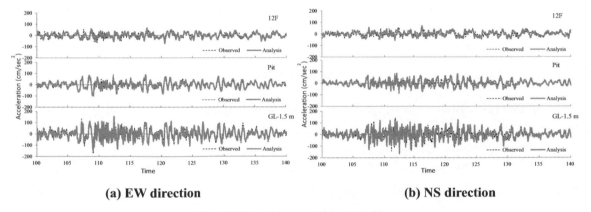

(a) EW direction   (b) NS direction

Fig. 15 Time history of acceleration

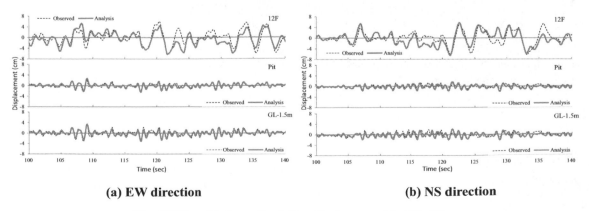

(a) EW direction   (b) NS direction

Fig. 16 Time history of relative displacement to GL -50 m

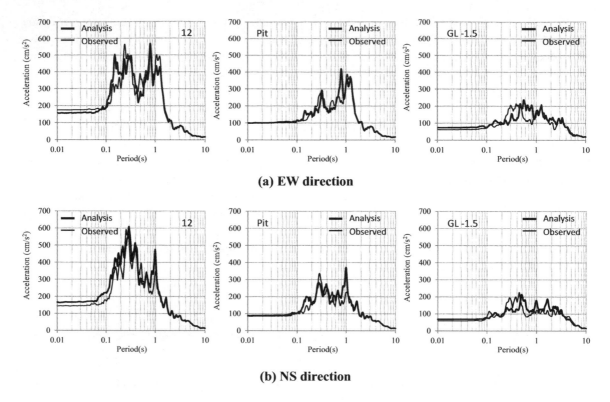

(a) EW direction

(b) NS direction

Fig. 17 Acceleration response spectra of superstructure and ground near surface (h = 5%)

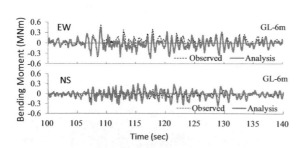

Fig. 18 Time history of bending moment at the pile head of pile 5B

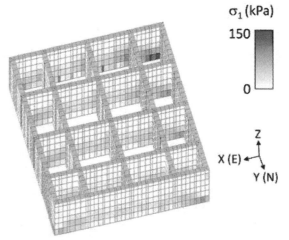

Fig. 19 Contour map of maximum tensile stress in grid-form DMWs

3.2 Seismic Response Analyses under Strong Earthquake Loads

3.2.1 Input Motion

Strong earthquakes are chosen from level 2 waves that have been officially notified in Japanese design code. Level 2 wave was determined considering the past earthquake damages in 2000, and it is used for the performance design of a building. The wave is defined as the response spectrum as shown in Fig. 21, and the waves are generated using phase data. In this paper, two sets of phase data are used; the Kobe and the Hachinohe phase data. The Kobe phase data was obtained at the Kobe Marine Observatory during the 1995 Hyogoken-

Nambu earthquake (referred as the Kobe phase hereafter). The Hachinohe phase data was obtained at Tokachi-Oki Earthquake (1968) at Hachinohe Bay (referred as the Hachinohe phase hereafter). Figure 20 shows the input accelerations in the NS direction at the bedrock (the waves are 2E). The time interval is 0.005 s and the analysis time is 120 s. Figure 21 shows the acceleration response spectrum for the given input waves.

3.2.2 Analysis Cases

The cases without DMWs are also analyzed to clarify the effect of them under each input motion. Table 3 lists the four cases that are considered in this analysis.

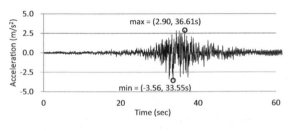

(a) Kobe phase

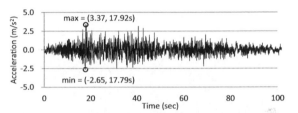

(b) Hachinohe phase

Fig. 20 Input acceleration waveforms at a depth of 75 m (2E) in the NS direction

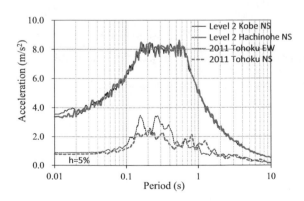

Fig. 21 Acceleration response spectra of level 2 waves and the 2011 Tohoku earthquake (GL -75 m)

Table 3 Analysis Cases

Case	Input motion	DMWs
K1	Kobe phase	Yes
K2	Kobe phase	No
H1	Hachinohe phase	Yes
H2	Hachinohe phase	No

3.2.3 Response of Ground and Structure

Figure 22 shows the profiles of the peak horizontal acceleration at the center of the superstructure and the raft in the NS direction together with those of the ground at point A (Fig. 2). The response of the soil column model is also shown denoted as "Free Field".

The maximum ground surface acceleration at the free field is 3.33 and 2.95 m/s2 under Kobe and Hachinohe phase motion, respectively. The responses at the raft top (GL-4.8 m) are slightly smaller than the free field in all cases due to the input loss.

In Case K1 (with DMWs), the acceleration peaks are 2.57 m/s^2 at the raft and 1.46 m/s^2 on the first floor,

and the reduction rate by the base isolation system is 57%. In Case K2 (without DMWs), the corresponding peaks are 2.87 and 1.31 m/s^2, respectively. The peak acceleration at the raft in Case K1 is smaller than that in Case K2. This may be attributable to the input loss due to presence of the DMWs.

In Case H1 (with DMWs), the peaks are 2.65 m/s2 at the raft and 1.31 m/s^2 on the first floor, and the reduction rate is 49%. In Case H2 (without DMWs), the peaks are 2.79 and 1.10 m/s^2, respectively. Input loss by the DMWs is also observed between these two cases.

Figure 23 shows the profiles of the peak horizontal displacement relative to the depth of 49.9 m at

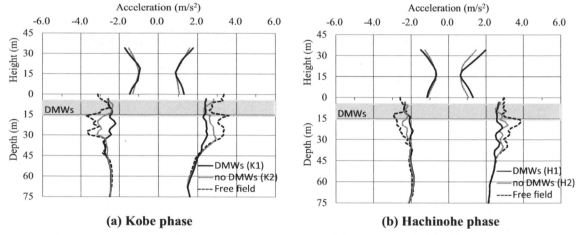

(a) Kobe phase   **(b) Hachinohe phase**

Fig. 22 Peak acceleration profiles of superstructure at center, ground at point A and free field

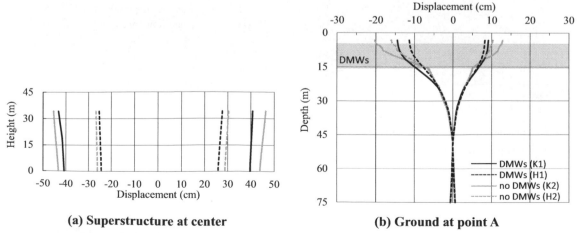

(a) Superstructure at center   **(b) Ground at point A**

Fig. 23 Peak displacement profiles of superstructure at center and ground at point

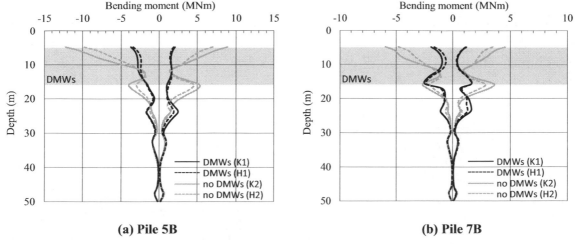

(a) Pile 5B **(b) Pile 7B**

Fig. 24 Profiles of peak bending moment in Piles 5B and 7B

the center of the superstructure and the ground at point A in the NS direction. This figure shows that the ground displacements above the bottom of the DMWs in the cases with DMWs are considerably smaller than those in the cases without DMWs. The maximum displacements are reduced by the presence of the DMWs approximately 70% of those without DMWs. This indicates that the ground deformation is significantly reduced by the DMWs.

Figure 24 shows the profiles of the peak bending moment in piles 5B and 7B (Fig. 4) in the NS direction. The peak bending moments near the pile heads in the cases with DMWs are remarkably smaller than those in the cases without DMWs. Additionally, the bending moments near the pile head in Case K2 are somewhat larger than those in Case H2, whereas those in Case K1 are similar to those in Case H1, which suggests that the bending moments near the pile head in the cases with DMWs would be less affected by the input motions. Figures 23 and 24 show that the deformation of the soil enclosed by the grid-form DMWs is reduced, resulting in the decrease of the bending moment near the pile head.

3.2.4 Lateral Resistance of Piled Raft System against Strong Earthquake Loads

The mechanism of the lateral resistance of the

piled raft system against strong earthquake is investigated using the results of Case K1 (with DMWs) and K2 (without DMWs). Figure 25(a) shows the time histories of the lateral external forces acting on the bottom surface of the raft during the time interval of 32–39 s when the response of the building is large. The external forces consist of the inertial forces from the superstructure and the raft and the earth pressure induced by ground movements acting on the sides of the buried raft. In both the cases, the peak value of the earth pressure is significantly large than the other two forces. The peak value of the earth pressure in Case K1 is also observed to be larger than that in Case K2.

Figure 25(b) shows the time histories of the lateral resistance forces of the foundation acting on the bottom surface of the raft. The resistance forces are the shear force of the piles at the pile head, that of the soil beneath the raft, and that of the grid-form DMWs. In Case K1 (with DMWs), it is seen that the shear force of the grid-form DMWs is significantly larger than those of the piles and soil, and the shear force of the piles is quite small. However, the shear force of the piles is similar to that of the soil in Case K2 (without DMWs).

Figure 26 illustrates the lateral force equilibrium at the level of the raft bottom in the shaking direction

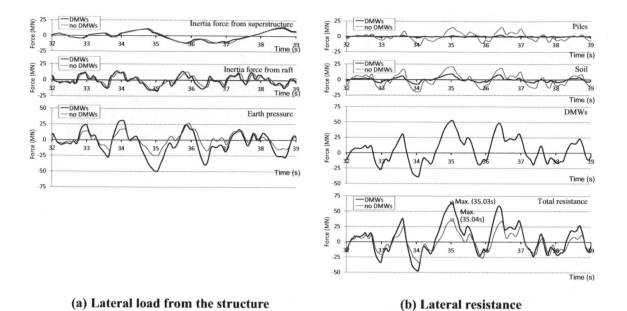

(a) Lateral load from the structure   (b) Lateral resistance

Fig. 25 Time histories of lateral load and resistance at the raft bottom, Kobe phase

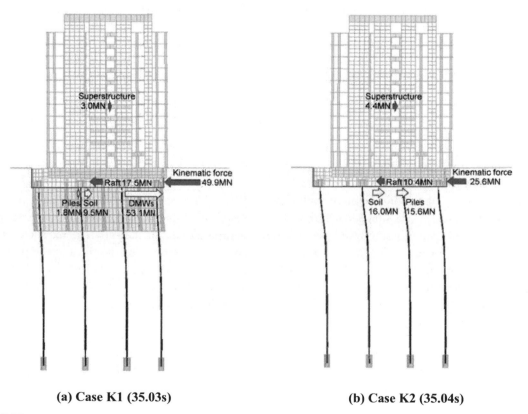

(a) Case K1 (35.03s)   (b) Case K2 (35.04s)

Fig. 26 Lateral force equilibrium at the raft bottom, Kobe phase (deformation is magnified 10 times)

when the total external force in Case K1 reaches its peak value. In Case K1, the dynamic earth pressure corresponded to approximately 78% of the total external force. The dynamic earth pressure is canceled entirely by the shear force of the DMWs which carries 83% of the lateral load. In contrast, the shear force of the piles is very small, and the 15% of the lateral load is carried by the soil. In Case K2, the dynamic earth pressure corresponded to 81% of the lateral load, and is carried equally by the piles and the soil. Under the Hachinohe wave, the lateral load and the ratio of load sharing among the foundation elements show the same tendencies.

3.2.5 Deformation and Partial Failure in DMWs

As shown in Figures 25 and 26, a significant part of the lateral load is carried by the grid-form DMWs,

and the induced internal stresses in the DMWs should thus be examined against their ultimate capacity for the PBD of this combined piled raft system. Figure 27 illustrates the deformation mode of the grid-form DMWs in Cases K1 and H1 at the time when the peak lateral load from the structure occurred. The shear deformation of the longitudinal walls in Case K1 is larger than that in Case H1. In addition, the displacements in both cases showed significant flexure due to bending, at the midpoint along the length of the transverse walls, but little flexure near the top of the walls.

Figure 28 illustrates the extent of tensile failure in the grid-form DMWs in Cases K1 and H1 during the earthquake. The elements are colored according to the number of Gauss points at which tensile failure occurs. The total number of Gauss

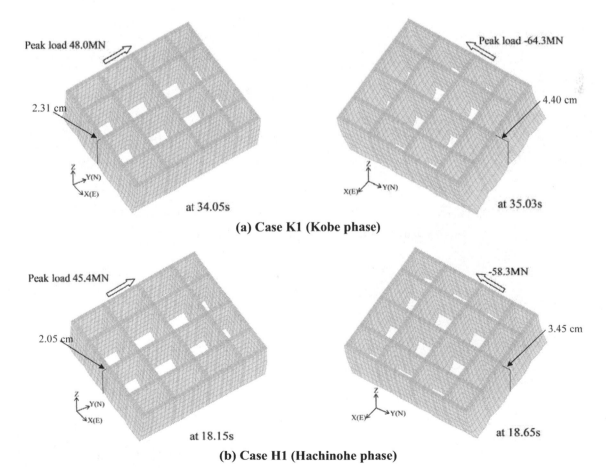

(a) Case K1 (Kobe phase)

(b) Case H1 (Hachinohe phase)

Fig. 27 Deformation of DMWs at the time of the peak external force occurred

points in each element is eight. The tensile failure is very limited, and the degree of tensile failure is larger in Case H1 than in Case K1. Thus, the failure behavior is clearly affected by the input motion. The tensile failure occurred mostly in the longitudinal walls, and this is thus due to shear. In the transverse walls, a few elements fail at the bottom of grid crossing corners as a result of bending, though there are few elements in which all the Gauss points fail.

Figure 29 shows the extent of shear failure in the grid-form DMWs. The maximum number of shear failure Gauss points in a single element is four in Case H1. The degree of shear failure is much smaller than that of tensile failure. This shows that the DMWs fail mainly by tension. The degree of shear failure is also larger in Case H1 than in Case

K1, and no shear failure elements are observed in Case K1. The shear failure is also affected by the input motion. Figure 29 also shows that top surface of the DMWs does not fail by shear. This means that no sliding occurs between the top surface of the DMWs and the bottom surface of the raft.

Although the constitutive model for the DMWs used in this study does not consider the softening of the stabilized soil after failure (Namikawa et al., 2007), the analysis results are acceptable from an engineering viewpoint because the extent of failure in the DMWs is very limited as shown in Figures 28 and 29.

Figure 30 shows the energy spectrum for each input wave. The equivalent pseudo-velocity V_E of the total input energy is defined as

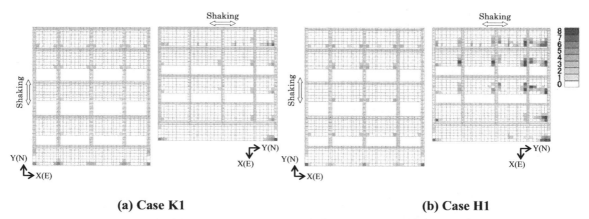

(a) Case K1   (b) Case H1

Fig. 28 Tensile failure Gauss points in grid-form DMWs

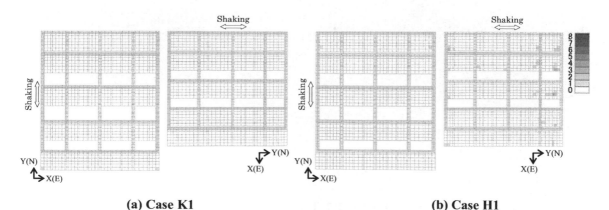

(a) Case K1   (b) Case H1

Fig. 29 Shear failure Gauss points in grid-form DMWs

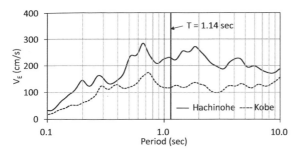

Fig. 30 Energy spectra of input waves ($h = 10\%$)

$$V_E = \sqrt{\frac{2E}{M}} \qquad (6)$$

where E is relative input energy of the earthquake and M is the mass of the viscous damped single–mass elastic oscillatory system. The input energy is directly related to the cumulative plastic deformation of the structure. As shown in the figure, the input energy of the Hachinohe phase is larger than that of the Kobe phase over a specified period, including at 1.14 s which is the initial first natural period of the ground and the foundation system. This is considered to be the reason for the larger extension of the failure in the DMWs that occurs under the Hachinohe phase wave.

3.2.6 Bending Moment of Piles

Figure 31 shows the relationship between the axial force and the bending moment of piles 5B and 7B, together with the design interaction curves of the steel pipe–concrete composite (SC) pile (which is used in the top portion at 12 m) (Japan pile corporation 2011). Here, the axial force represents the sum of the statically measured pile head load and the maximum and minimum dynamic incremental force in the analysis, and the bending moment represents the maximum value along the SC pile in the shaking direction. In the case without DMWs (K2 and H2), it is noted that the axial forces are equal to the observed static values of the building with DMWs plus the analytical dynamic increment of the case without DMWs. The analysis results show that the maximum bending moments of piles 5B and 7B in Case K1 and H1 are well below the allowable criterion (the unit stress at the edge of the concrete is in the elastic condition). In contrast, the maximum bending moments in Case K2 and H2 are fairly beyond the allowable criterion. In particular, in Case K2, the bending moments are nearly equal to the ultimate criterion (the unit stress at the edge of the concrete reaches the compressive strength). Hence, the grid-form DMWs are quite effective at reducing the pile bending moment to an acceptable level, although the induced stress in the stabilized soil partially reached the tensile strength under level 2 earthquake motions. This indicates that the grid-

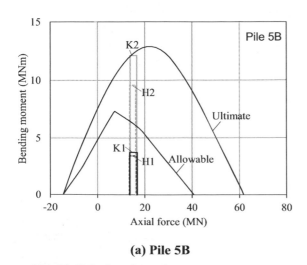

(a) Pile 5B

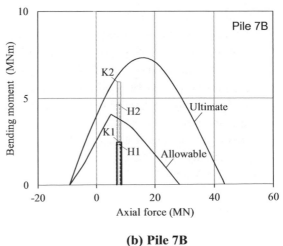

(b) Pile 7B

Fig. 31 Calculated maximum moment along pile and design N–M interaction curves of SC piles

form DMWs can be designed more rationally using the PBD method, in which the partial failure of the DMWs is accepted, as pointed out by Namikawa et al. (2007). The analysis results also suggest that the three dimensional FE simulation method employed in this study can provide adequate solutions for the PBD of piled rafts with grid-form DMWs.

4. CONCLUSION

The following conclusions can be drawn from the results of the present dynamic simulation analyses.

(1) The peak ground displacements near the surface in the cases with DMWs are reduced considerably from those without DMWs, and the peak bending moments of the piles near the pile head in the cases with DMWs are significantly smaller than those without DMWs.

(2) Tensile failure occurred in the DMWs but only to a very limited degree. Tensile failure is observed mostly in the longitudinal walls. This suggests that the lateral load from the structure is carried mainly by the longitudinal walls. The extent of the failure in Case H1 is larger than in Case K1. This shows the failure behavior is affected by the input motion. However, almost no shear failure occurs in the DMWs.

(3) The maximum bending moments along the pile in the cases with DMWs are considerably below the allowable criterion of the design N–M relation of the piles, whereas those in the case without DMWs are markedly large. This is because the lateral ground movements below the raft are significantly reduced by the DMWs and the lateral load from the structure is carried mostly by the DMWs. Thus, the grid-form DMWs are found to be quite effective at reducing the sectional force of piles to an acceptable level, even if partial failure of the DMWs occurs.

(4) DMWs can be regarded as supplementary

structural elements in the foundation. Therefore, minor damage to the DMWs can be tolerated under strong earthquake loads providing that the required foundation performance is satisfied. Consequently, piled rafts with grid-form DMWs could be designed more rationally following the principles of PBD, in which the partial failure of the DMWs is accepted under the performance level required.

ACKNOWLEDGEMENTS

This work was supported by JSPS KAKENHI Grant Number JP26289197.

REFERENCES

Building Center of Japan, (2002). *Specification for design and quality control of cement treated soil* (in Japanese).

Hamada, J., Shigeno, Y., Onimaru, S., Tanikawa, T., Nakamura, N. and Yamashita, K. (2014). Numerical analysis on seismic response of piled raft foundation with ground improvement based on seismic observation records, *Proc. of the 14th IACMAG*, Kyoto, Japan.

Kuroda, T., Tanaka, H., Tomii, Y. and Suzuki, Y. (2001). Evaluation of characteristics of improved soil by deep mixing method of soil stabilization, *2001 Summaries of Technical Papers of Annual Meeting of AIJ (Kanto)*, Tokyo, Japan, 699-700 (in Japanese).

Japan pile corporation, (2011). *Pile foundation design materials* (in Japanese)

Motojima, M., Hibino S. and Hayashi, M. (1978). Development of computer program for stability analysis of excavation, *Central Research Institute of Electric Power Industry Report*, 377012 (in Japanese).

Namikawa, T., Koseki, J. and Suzuki, Y. (2007). Finite element analysis of lattice-shaped ground improvement by cement-mixing for liquefaction mitigation, *Soils & Foundations*, Vol.47, 559-576.

Shigeno, Y., Hamada, J. and Nakamura, N. (2014). Hybrid parallelization of earthquake response analysis using K computer, *Proc. of the 14th IACMAG*. Kyoto, Japan

Shiomi, T., Shigeno, Y. and Zienkiewicz, O. C., (1993). Numerical prediction for model No. 1., *Verification of Numerical Procedures for the Analysis of Soil Liquefaction Problems*, Balkema, 213-219.

Tsujino, S., Yoshida, N. and Yasuda, S. (1994). A simplified practical stress-strain model in multi-dimensional analysis, *Proc. of International Symposium on Pre-failure Deformation Characteristics of Geomaterials*, Sapporo, Japan, 463-468.

Yamashita, K., Yamada, T., and Hamada, J. (2011). Investigation of settlement and load sharing on piled rafts by monitoring full-scale structures, *Soils & Foundations*, Vol. 51 (3), 513–532.

Yamashita, K., Hamada, J., Onimaru, S. and Higashino, M. (2012). Seismic behavior of piled raft with ground improvement supporting a base-isolated building on soft ground in Tokyo, *Soils & Foundations*, Vol. 52, 1000–1015.

Yamashita, K., Wakai, S. and Hamada, J. (2013). Large-scale piled raft with grid-form deep mixing walls on soft ground, *Proc. of the 18th Int. Conference on SMGE*, Paris, France, 2637-2640.

Yamashita, K., Tanikawa, T., Shigeno, Y. and Hamada, J. (2015). Vertical load sharing of piled raft with grid-form deep mixing walls, *Conference on Deep Mixing 2015*, San Francisco, USA, 437-446.

Yamashita, K., Hamada, J. and Tanikawa, T. (2016). Static and seismic performance of a friction piled combined with grid-form deep mixing walls in soft ground, *Soils & Foundations*, Vol. 56, 559-573.

CHAPTER 9

NUMERICAL STUDY FOR AN OFFSHORE WIND TURBINE MODAL TEST USING EFFECTIVE STRESS ANALYSIS

Chih-Wei Lu*

Department of Construction Engineering, National Kaohsiung First University of Science and Technology, Kaohsiung City, Taiwan
*cwlu@nkfust.edu.tw

Yi-Shun Chou
Jian-Hong Wu
Der-Her Lee
Jing-Wen Chen
Department of Civil Engineering, National Cheng Kung University, Tainan City, Taiwan

ABSTRACT: Offshore wind turbine gives a great hope to green energy, however, a great demand on the foundation design is generated when the planned offshore wind farms are built in seismic active regions. Earthquakes can cause significant damage to both foundations and wind towers depending on the performance of the integrated system of turbines, superstructures, foundations, and grounds. In the offshore environment, soils can be significantly softened by the increased pore water pressure under earthquake loading that is called soil liquefaction. In this research, the authors applied a three dimensional effective stress analysis on studying the mechanism of an offshore wind turbine structure carried out in a centrifuge test by Yu et al. Not only comparing the analyzed and experiment results, the authors probed into more details that are the advantages provided by the numerical analysis.

1. INTRODUCTION

After a long planning, Taiwan reached a major milestone when the first two offshore wind turbines were installed at the Formosa 1 wind farm offshore Miaoli County. The two 4MW turbines are the first phase in setting up the Formosa 1 offshore wind farm. The installation of turbines was completed in October in 2016 with the wind farm expected to be commissioned in early 2017. The entire project consists of 32 turbines, with the second phase planned to be constructed in 2018/2019. And many are still under planning.

It also goes without reminding that Taiwan is located in an earthquake region, all the foundation design shall be taken into consideration the seismic effect. Especially, Taiwanese people were aware of the impact of soil liquefaction after the 0206 Meinung earthquake, of which, many residential buildings suffered a great settlement and inclination because of the earthquake. Shi- Din area which implies the top of river area in Taiwanese has experienced excessive soil liquefaction ever in the history due to the 2016 Meinung earthquake. The earthquake was in 6.4 Magnitude with epicenter in Meinung at 23 Km depth revealed by USGS. Most damages were found in Tainan because geological condition and strike direction of the earthquake, in which the major seismic direction is east- west. Tainan city is located at west side of Meinung and the maximum value was recorded as 0.23g PGA in the Tainan seismic station. The $(Vs)_{30}$ of Tainan is 198 m/sec studied by NCREE showing that the ground condition in Tainan belongs to relative soft soils. Many liquefaction induced phenomena was found in Shi- Din area such as sand boils, ground settlement, settlement and tilt of shallow founded houses, lateral displacement, and some foundation failures at the tallest building, of which, many cracks on diaphragm wall and columns and boiled soils were observed in the basement after the earthquake.

In the literatures, the damages caused by the soil liquefaction including surface damages, settlement damages, and underground structures damages were observed in around the world as well. 1964 Nigata (Japanese Society of Soil Mechanics and Foundation Engineering, 1986), 1983 Chubu-Nihonkai (Japan Society of Civil Engineers 1993), 1990 Luzon (Khoshnoudian, 2002), 1995 Kobe earthquake (Shibata et al. 1996), the 1999 Chi-Chi earthquake (Chu et al. 2004), the 2008 Wenchuan earthquake (Huang and Jiang 2010), the 2011 Christchurch earthquake (Bray et al. 2014), and the 2011 Tohoku earthquake (Ishihara 2012) are other examples for geotechnical damages on buildings due to soil liquefaction.

Countermeasures for soil liquefaction and seismic design become a very important issue for the civil engineering design since then.

Therefore, the seismic performance of the wind turbine system considering the impact of soil liquefaction is the main key for the offshore wind turbine design incorporating with the construction method. The effective stress analysis goes without saying that plays an important role on devoting a more appropriate design and research related to the topics.

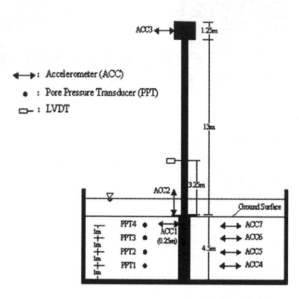

Figure 1 Centrifuge model of a wind turbine on mono- pile foundation in 50g scale [1]

2. METHODOLOGY

2.1 Experiment work

In Yu et al. (2015), a group of earthquake centrifuge tests was performed on wind turbine models with mono-pile foundations to examine their seismic response. They found that the seismic behavior of models was quite different in the dry or saturated conditions and again pointed out the consideration of soil liquefaction is very critical for an offshore foundation design. They furthermore carried out the centrifuge tests using the geotechnical centrifuge at Case Western Reserve University. The centrifuge arm has an effective radius of 1.37 m. The payload capacity is 20 g ton with a maximum acceleration of 200 g for static tests and 100 g for dynamic tests. The centrifuge is equipped with a hydraulic shaker and with a rigid container employed in the tests was of internal dimensions 53.3cm (length), 24.1cm (width) and 17.7cm (height). They employed well graded Toyoura sand. Toyoura sand is a uniform sand with angular particles with the following physical properties: $e_{max} = 0{:}98$; $e_{min} = 0.6$; $Gs = 2.65$; and

$D_{50} = 0.17$ mm. The general properties and many other characters of its dynamic/ static behaviors of Toyoura sand were carried out abundantly in Japan. In this research, all the parameters used for the soil model in the analysis were adopted from the previous researches. The model container was to keep the relative density at about 68%. The thickness of the soil layer was 4.5 m and the water table was maintained at 1.5m above the ground surface for an offshore location. They monitored accelerations, excess pore water pressures, deformations of the ground and structures by means of corresponding sensors.

3. NUMERICAL ANALYSIS

In the present study, the governing equations for the coupling problems of soil skeleton and pore water pressure are obtained based on the two-phase mixture theory (Biot 1962), using a u-p (u: displacement of soil; p: pore water pressure) formulation (Zienkiewicz and Bettes 1982). The finite element method (FEM) is used for the spatial discretization of the equilibrium equation, while the finite difference method (FDM) is used for the spatial discretization of the excess pore water pressure in the continuity equation (Oka et al. 1994). Oka et al. (1994) numerically studied the accuracy through a comparison between the numerical results and the analytical results by Simon et al. (1984) for the compressive wave propagation problem. They found that the proposed numerical algorithm has sufficient accuracy.

3.1 Constitutive models

In order to study the influence of soil characteristics, four different sandy materials are considered for upper sandy ground, that is, dense sand, medium dense sand, loose sand, and reclaimed soil. The lower layer is composed of clayey soils. For sandy soils, a cyclic elasto-plastic model (Oka et al. 1999) for sandy soils is used which has been developed based on non-linear kinematical hardening rule with generalized

non-associated flow rule. The model has been successfully applied to loose, medium and dense sands (Oka et al., 2004). For clayey soils, a cyclic elasto-viscoplastic model (Oka 1992) for clayey soils is used which is based on overstress type viscoplasticity with kinematic hardening theory. The parameters of the soil model was given as Dr = 70% Toyura sand in the previous researches, it again shows that the importance of the determination of a standard sand for data base accumulation.

3.2 Governing equations

Oka et al. (1994) proposed the FEM-FDM coupled analysis which succeeded in reducing the degree of freedom in the descretized equations and the accuracy of the model is verified. Lu et al. (2007) and the others (Lu and Lai (2008), Lu (2007), Lu et al. (2013), Lu and Gui. (2013), Lu and Chang (2015) and Lu (2017) employed the formulas and validated this practice.

The following items were assumed for formulating the governing equations.

(i) The infinitesimal strain is used; (ii) The distribution of porosity in the soil is sufficiently smooth; (iii) The relative acceleration of the fluid phase to that of the solid phase is much smaller than the acceleration of the solid phase; (iv) Grain particles in the soil are incompressible.

The equilibrium equation for the mixture is given as follows:

$$\rho \ddot{u}^s_i = \sigma_{ij,j} + \rho b_i \tag{1}$$

in which ρ is the total density, $\ddot{u}^s_i$ is the acceleration of the solid phase, σ_{ij} is the total stress tensor and b_i is the body force vector. Terzaghi's effective stress concept is used without notice as $\sigma'_{ij} = \sigma_{ij} - p\delta_{ij}$; σ'_{ij}: effective stress tensor, p: pore water pressure.

The continuity equation is written as

$$\rho^f \ddot{u}^s_{i,i} - p_{,ii} - \frac{\gamma_w}{k}\dot{\varepsilon}^s_{ii} + \frac{n\gamma_w}{kK^f}\dot{p} = 0 \qquad (2)$$

where ρ^f is the density of fluid, p is the pore water pressure, γ_w is the unit weight of the fluid, k is the coefficient of permeability, ε^s_{ii} is the volumetric strain of the solid phase, n is porosity and K^f is he bulk modulus of the fluid phase.

Equations (1) and (2) are discretized spatially by FEM and FDM, respectively in the following sections.

3.3 Spatial and time discretization

Denoting $\{u_N\}$ as the displacement vector at node N, the displacement vector for the soil skeleton in the element, $\{u^s\}$, is defined with the shape function matrix, $[N]$, as

$$\{u^s\} = [N]\{u_N\} \qquad (3)$$

in which the symbol $\{\ \}$ indicates that the variable is a vector.

The strain vector of the soil skeleton in the element, $\{\varepsilon^s\}$, is given

$$\{\varepsilon^s\} = [L]\{u^s\} \qquad (4)$$

where $[L]$ is the matrix which transforms the displacement into strain.

Substituting Eq.(3) into Eq.(4) produces

$$\{\varepsilon^s\} = [L][N]\{u_N\} = [B]\{u_N\} \qquad (5)$$

The volumetric strain in element ε^s_v is calculated by the displacement vector at nodal point $\{u_N\}$ as:

$$\varepsilon^s_v = \nabla[N]\{u_N\} = [B_v]^T\{u_N\} = \{u_N\}^T\{B_v\} \qquad (6)$$

where $\{B_v\}$ is the vector which transforms the nodal displacement vector into the volumetric strain in the element and ∇ is the gradient operator. The constitutive equation for the solid phase is expressed as

$$\Delta\sigma' = [D]\Delta\varepsilon^s \qquad (7)$$

where $[D]$ is the matrix of the elasto-plastic modulus, and $\{\Delta\sigma'\}$ is the effective stress increment vector.

The current effective stress vector at time $t + \Delta t$ is defined as

$$\{\sigma_{t+\Delta t}'\} = \{\Delta\sigma'\} + \{\Delta\sigma_t'\} \qquad (8)$$

Where $\{\Delta\sigma_t'\}$ is the effective stress vector at the previous time t.

Using the virtual work theorem, Eq.(1) is rewritten as follows:

$$\int_V \rho\{\delta u^S\}^T\{\ddot{u}^S\}dV + \int_V \{\delta\varepsilon^S\}^T(\{\Delta\sigma'\} + \{\Delta\sigma_t'\})dV$$
$$+ \int_V P_E \delta\varepsilon^s_v dV = \int_{S_1}\{\delta u^S\}^T d\{T^*\}dS + \int_V \rho\{\delta u^S\}^T\{b\}dV \qquad (9)$$

in which δ means the virtual value of the variables, P_E is the pore water pressure at the center in the element and $\{T^*\}$ is the surface traction vector, and $\{b\}$ is the body force vector.

Substituting Eqs.(5), (6), (7), (8) into Eq.(9) yields

$$\{\rho\int_v\{\delta u_N\}^T[N]^T[N]dV\}\{\ddot{u}_N\}$$
$$+ \{\int_v\{\delta u_N\}^T[B]^T[D][B]dV\}\{\Delta u_N\}^T$$
$$+ \{\int_v\{\delta u_N\}^T\{B_v\}dV\}P_E$$
$$= \int_S\{\delta u_N\}^T[N]^T\{T^*\}dS + \rho\int_v\{\delta u_N\}^T[N]^T\{b\}dV$$
$$- \int_v\{\delta u_N\}^T[B]^T\{\sigma_t'\}dV \qquad (10)$$

in which $\{\Delta u_N\}$ is the displacement increment vector at the node N. Since $\{\delta u_N\}$ is individually discretized at the unconstrained boundary,

$$\rho\int_V[N]^T[N]dV\{\ddot{u}_N\} + \int_V[B]^T[D][B]dV\{\Delta u_N\}$$
$$+ \int_V[B_v]dVp_E$$
$$= \int_S[N]^T\{T^*\}dS + \rho\int_v[N]^T\{b\}dV - \int_V[B]^T\{\sigma_t'\}dV \qquad (11)$$

From Eq.(11), the equations of motion discretized spatially by the finite element method are obtained as

$$[M]\{\ddot{u}_N\} + [C]\{\dot{u}_N\} + [K]\{\Delta u_N\} + [K_v]p_E = \{F\} - \{R_t\} \tag{12}$$

Where the Rayleigh damping term, $[C]\{\dot{u}^S\}$, is added to Eq.(11).

The matrices and the vectors in Eq.(12) are denoted as follows:

$$[M] = \rho \int_V [N]^T[N]dV \tag{13}$$

$$[K] = \int_V [B]^T[D][B]dV \tag{14}$$

$$[K_v] = \int_V \{B_v\}dV \tag{15}$$

$$\{F\} = \int_S [N]^T\{T^*\}dS + \rho \int_V [N]^T\{B\}dV \tag{16}$$

$$\{R_t\} = \int_V [B]^T\{\sigma_t'\}dV \tag{17}$$

The matrix of Rayleigh damping is given by

$$[C] = a_0[M] + a_1[K] \tag{18}$$

where a_0 and a_1 are constants. In the present study, the Rayleigh damping proportional to $[K]$ and $[M]$ is considered through a series of numerical tests including mode analysis and back analysis, and decided as 0.712 and 0.6 respectively.

The continuity equation can be discretized spatially by the finite difference method.

By applying the same manner to Eq.(6), the following are given by

$$\rho^f \ddot{u}_{i,i}^s - p_{,ii} - \frac{\gamma_w}{k}\dot{\varepsilon}_{ii}^s + \frac{n\gamma_w}{kK^f}\dot{p} = 0 \tag{19}$$

When the soil particle is incompressible and the pore fluid is compressible, it can be rewritten by Gauss's theorem after integrating Eqs.(2) with Eq.(15), as follows:

$$\rho^F[K_v]^T\{\ddot{u}_N\} - \frac{\gamma_w}{k}[K_v]^T\{\dot{u}_N\} + Ap_E - \int_V \frac{\partial^2 p_E}{\partial x_i^2}dV$$

$$= \rho^F[K_v]^T\{\ddot{u}_N\} - \frac{\gamma_w}{k}[K_v]^T\{\dot{u}_N\} + Ap_E - \int_S \frac{\partial p_E}{\partial x_i}n_i dS = 0 \tag{20}$$

in which

$$A = \int_V \frac{n\gamma_w}{kK^f}dV \tag{21}$$

Herein, we will take the finite difference approximation to the fourth term on the left hand side of Eq.(20). A rectangular parallel element is considered in the three dimensional case. P_E is the pore water pressure at the central point of the subject element and P_{e1} to P_{e6} denote those of the neighboring elements. Moreover, A_1 to A_6 denote each area of the hexahedron and S_1 to S_6 denote the distance of the central point between the subject element and the neighboring elements. Furthermore, S_{1i} to S_{6i} denote that of the projection to X_i in the direction; it can be derived by the following approximation.

$$\int_S \frac{\partial p_E}{\partial x_i}n_i dS = \sum_{k=1}^6 \left\{ (p_E - p_{ek})(\frac{A_k n_1}{s_{k1}} + \frac{A_k n_2}{s_{k2}} + \frac{A_k n_3}{s_{k3}}) \right\} \tag{22}$$

Since it is possible to take the finite difference approximation for the two-dimensional case in the same manner "k" denotes the number of side lines for the two-dimensional case or the area for the three-dimensional case,

$$\int_S \frac{\partial p_E}{\partial x_i}n_i dS = p_E \sum_{k=1}^k (\sum_{i=1}^N \frac{A_k n_i}{s_{ki}}) - \sum_{k=1}^k p_{ek}(\sum_{i=1}^N \frac{A_k n_i}{s_{ki}}) \tag{23}$$

where $N = 3$ for the three-dimensional case and $N = 2$ for the two-dimensional case. In the two-dimensional case, A_k denotes the length of side b_k

$$\alpha = \sum_{k=1}^k (\sum_{i=1}^N \frac{A_k n_i}{s_{ki}}); \tag{24}$$

$$\alpha_k = \sum_{i=1}^N \frac{A_k n_i}{s_{ki}} \tag{25}$$

Finally, when the soil particle is incompressible

and the pore fluid is compressible, the law of mass conservation discretized spatially by the finite difference method is as follows.

$$\rho^F [K_v]^T \{\ddot{u}_N\} - \frac{\gamma_w}{k}[K_v]^T \{\dot{u}_N\} - \alpha p_E + \sum_{k=1}^{k} \alpha_k p_{ek} + A\dot{p}_E = 0 \quad (26)$$

The method adopted above can be easily applied to the non-rectangular element based on the finite volume method.

Both Eqs.(12) and (26) are also discretized in the time domain by Newmark's β method. The following discretized equations were obtained as

$$\left[\begin{bmatrix} [M] + \gamma\Delta t[C] + \beta(\Delta t)^2 [K]_{|t+\Delta t} & \{K_v\} & 0 \\ \{K_v\} & A - \alpha' & \{\alpha'_i\}^{\mathrm{T}} \end{bmatrix}\right] \begin{Bmatrix} \{\ddot{u}_N\}_{|t+\Delta t} \\ p_{dEt+\Delta t} \\ \{p_{dEit+\Delta t}\} \end{Bmatrix}$$

$$= \left[\begin{matrix} [F]_{|t+\Delta t} - \{R_d\}_{|t+\Delta t} - [C]_{|t+\Delta t}\left\{\{\dot{u}_N\}_{|t} + (1-\gamma)\Delta t\{\ddot{u}_N\}_{|t}\right\} \\ -\{K\}_{|t+\Delta t}(\Delta t)\{\dot{u}_N\}_{|t} + \left(\frac{1}{2}-\beta\right)(\Delta t)^2 \{\ddot{u}_N\}_{|t} \\ K\dfrac{1}{\left(\left(\dfrac{k}{g}-\gamma\Delta t\right)\right)}\{K_v\}^T \left(\{\dot{u}_N\}_{|t} + (1-\gamma)\Delta t\{\ddot{u}_N\}_{|t}\right) + A'p_{dE|t} \end{matrix}\right]$$

$$(27)$$

Where

$$\alpha' = \frac{1}{\left(\left(\dfrac{k}{g}-\gamma\Delta t\right)\right)}\alpha \quad (28)$$

$$\alpha'_i = \frac{1}{\dfrac{k}{g}-\gamma\Delta t}\alpha_i \quad (29)$$

$$A' = \frac{1}{\left(\Delta t\left(\dfrac{k}{g}-\gamma\Delta t\right)\right)}A \quad (30)$$

4. NUMERICAL MODELS AND ANALYZED RESULTS

According to the physical model, the numerical configuration is set up to be as Figure 2, of which the tower is of 15m height and the pier is of 4.5m depth in the numerical model corresponding to the physical model in 50g acceleration. The corresponding locations of all the accelerations, movements, excess pore water pressure are established in the numerical model the as the physical model.

As to the boundary condition, the side boundaries of the domain considered is assumed to be equal-displacement boundaries at the same depth so that it is easy to get rid of echo vibration possibly produced by the introduction of artificial boundary in FEM. The displacement of the bottom of the domain, which is regarded as a base ground where the earthquake wave is installed, is fixed. For the drainage boundary condition, only the ground surface is assumed to be permeable and the rest of the boundaries are impermeable. The ground water table is at GL-1.5 m above the ground surface according to the physical model.

The major constitutive parameters for different soils are the void ratio = 0.68, unit weight of soil = 1.8t/m³, Mm = 0.707, Mf = 0.99, and the parameter of the pile are determined as E = 200Gpa, and possion's ratio = 0.3. The diameters of the pile and tower are 0.9m and 0.5m, respectively, which are all determined following the physical model.

The numerically analyzed results in Figure 3 showed that the horizontal acceleration responses and development of excess pore water pressure fit the experiment well. Not only the analyzed peak acceleration but the frequency fit to the experiment results. But the vertical acceleration (ACC2) in the numerical model is not as big as in the experiment work, probably because the bottom boundary condition of the wind tower in the numerical model is perfectly attached with the ground. The excess pore water pressure from the numerical model developed with the excitement of the seismic movement in the most PTT, and raised to 0.5 excess pore water pressure / original effective stress from the beginning to 5th second. The initial liquefaction was triggered at 10 second in the

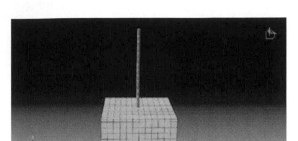

Figure 2 Numerical model of the wind turbine tower in Figure 1.

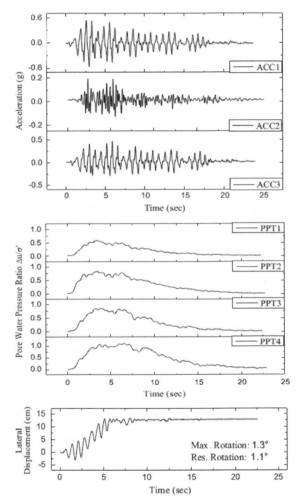

Figure 3(a) Physical model test for the wind tower in Figure 1 [1]

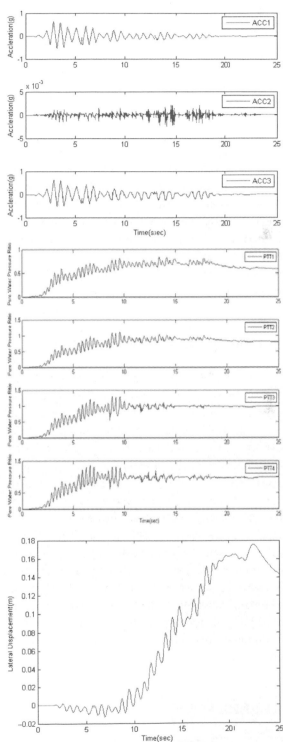

Figure 3(b) Numerically analyzed results for the wind tower in Figure 2.

prediction, however, much faster in the physical model. Only PTT1 in both the numerical model and physical model did not reach the criterion of liquefaction state. After 10 second, the ground in the numerical model reached complete soil liquefaction state and, therefore, the movement of the tower started to increase. The lateral movement of wind tower in model test started significantly as soon as the seismic activity reached the peak in less than 10 second. The peak value of the movement in both models was close. And the excess pore water transducer in the physical model decreased when the ground liquefied, which does occur in the numerical model. Which is considered to be an up-float movement of the transducer occurs during the great access pore water pressure and therefore the measured pore water pressure decreases.

5. DISCUSSIONS AND SUMMARY

The numerical model employed herein performs well on predicting the seismic performance of an offshore wind turbine structures in a centrifugal test. The 1.5 m water depth produces a damping effect on the wind tower more than the air, therefore, the Rayleigh damping shall be adopted appropriately. Unlike the experiment result, the analyzed excess pore water pressure in this numerical analysis was developed more stably and would not decrease dramatically that is considered more realistic. And the peak of the deformation occurred at the moment when the soil liquefaction occurrence shown both in numerical study and experiment study. This again shows that the major key factor to protect the wind tower from deformation is to countermeasure soil liquefaction occurrence.

REFERENCES

H. Yu , X. W. Zeng , B. Li , and J. J. Lian (2015). " Centrifuge modeling of offshore wind foundations under earthquake loading," *Soil Dyn. Earthquake Eng.* 77, 402–415.

Bray J, Cubrinovski M, Zupan J, Taylor M (2014). Liquefaction effects on buildings in the Central Business District of Christchurch, Earthquake Spectra. *EERI*, Volume 30(1):85–110

Chu DB, Stewart JP, Lee S, Tsai JS, Lin PS, Chu BL, Seed RB, Hsu SC, Yu MS, Wang MCH (2004). Documentation of soil conditions at liquefaction and non- liquefaction sites from 1999 Chi- Chi (Taiwan) earthquake. *Soil Dyn Earthq Eng* 24 (9-10):647–657

Hamada M, Yasuda S, Isoyama R, Emoto K (1986). Study on liquefaction-induced permanent ground displacement. Report for the Association for the Development of Earthquake Prediction

Huang Y, Jiang XM (2010). Field-observed phenomena of seismic liquefaction and subsidence during the 2008 Wenchuan earthquake. *Natural Hazards* 54(3):839-850

Ishihara K (2012). Liquefaction in Tokyo Bay and Kanto Regions in the 2011 Great East Japan Earthquake. In: Proceedings of the International Symposium on Engineering Lessons Learned from the 2011 Great East Japan Earthquake, March 1-4, 2012, Tokyo, Japan, 63–81

Acacio, A., Kobayashi, Y., Towhata, I., Bautista, R.T. & Ishihara, K. (2001). "Subsidence of building foundation resting upon liquefied subsoil: case studies and assessment" , *Soils and Foundations*, Vol. 41, No. 6, pp.111–128.

Marques, A.S., Coelho, P.A.L.F., Cilingir, U., Haigh, S.K., & Madabhushi, S.P.G. (2013). "Centrifuge modelling of liquefaction-induced effects on shallow foundations with different bearing pressures", 2nd Eurofuge conference on physical modelling in geotechnics, delft.

Marasini, N. & Okamura, M. (2014). "Numerical simulation of centrifuge tests on seismic behavior of residential building on liquefiable foundation soil", Computer Methods and Recent Advances in Geomechanics, pp.847-852.

Oka, F., Yashima, A., Taguchi, Y. & Yamashita, S. (1999). "A cyclic-plastic constitutive model for sand considering a plastic-strain dependence of the shear modulus", *Geotechnique*, Vol. 49, No. 5, pp.661-680.

Oka, F., Furuya, K. & Uzuoka, R. (2004). "Numerical simulation of cyclic behavior of dense sand using a cyclic elasto-plastic model", *Cyclic Behaviour of Soils and Liquefaction Phenomena*, Triantafyllidis(ed), Taylor & Francis Group, London, ISBN 90 5809 620 3.

Dashti, S., Bray, J.D., Pestana, J. M., Riemer, M., & Wilson, D. (2010). "Mechanisms of seismically induced settlement of buildings with shallow foundations on liquefiable soil", *Journal of Geotechnical and Geoenvironmental Engineering, ASCE*, Vol. 136, No. 1, pp.151-164.

Dashti, S., Bray, J.D., Pestana, J.M., Riemer, M., & Wilson, D. (2010). "Centrifuge Testing to Evaluate and Mitigate Liquefaction-Induced Building Settlement Mechanisms", *Journal of Geotechnical and Geoenvironmental Engineering, ASCE*, Vol. 136, No. 7, pp.918-929.

Dashti, S. & Bray, J.D. (2013). "Numerical Simulation of Building Response on Liquefiable Sand", *Journal of Geotechnical and Geoenvironmental Engineering, ASCE*, Vol. 139, No. 8, pp.1235-1249.

Lu, C.W., Zhang F., Kimura M. (2001). "A study on seismic behavior of jacket- type foundation using numerical simulation (II)", *Proceeding of 26th Earthquake Engineering Symposium* (in Japanese title), pp. 62-68.

Lu, C.W. and Chang, D.W. (2015). Case study of dynamic responses of a single pile foundation installed in coal ash landfills using effective stress analysis and EQWEAP. *Journal of SEAGS-AGSSEA* 46(2), pp.77-81.

Lu, C.W. and Gui, M.W. (2013). Three-dimensional dynamic soil-structure interaction analysis of a bridge-pier pile foundation. *Journal of Earthquake and Tsunami Engineering*.

Lu, C.W., Gui, M.W. and Chang, B.Y. (2013). Numerical Analysis for earth structure sitting on liquefiable soils in roller boundary. *Advanced Materials Research*, Vol. 287-290, pp. 1911-1914.

Lu, C.W. and Lai, S.C. (2008). Evaluation of Side Boundary Effects on Dynamic Numerical Modeling for Centrifugal Model Tests. *Journal of Earthquake Engineering*, Vol. 12, Issue 5, pp. 760-778.

Lu, C.W. (2007). Numerical study for centrifugal model tests of a single pile foundation installed in sandy deposits. *Journal of Mechanics*, 23, 389-397.

Lu, C.W., Oka, F., Zhang, F.(2007). Analysis of soil–pile–structure interaction in a two-layer ground during earthquakes considering liquefaction. *International Journal for Numerical and Analytical Methods in Geomechanics*, 863-895

Lu, C.W. (2017). A simplified calculation method for liquefaction- induced settlement of shallow foundation, *Journal of earthquake engineering* (to be published).

CHAPTER 10

ANALYSIS OF AN IN-SITU PILE GROUP UNDER LATERAL LOADING

Jiunn-Shyang Chiou*

Department of Civil Engineering, National Taiwan University, Taipei City, Taiwan
*jschiou@ntu.edu.tw

ABSTRACT: This paper introduces an analysis of an in-situ lateral load test of PC pile group by p-y curve approach. The location of the test site was at Taipo, Chiayi, Taiwan. The p-y curves used for group pile analysis are deduced by modifying experimental single-pile p-y curve to consider group pile effects. The modification procedure has two stages: (1) at the small displacement where the elastic interaction among piles is significant y modification is applied to enlarge the displacement y of the single-pile p-y curve and (2) at the larger lateral displacement, p modification is applied to reduce the soil reaction p of the single-pile p-y curve to consider the overlap of the passive wedges among piles. Once all the p-y curves of the group piles are deduced, Winkler analysis can be performed. From the analysis results, the load-deflection curve of piles as well as the deflection and moment profiles with depth is in good agreement with the measured values.

1. INTRODUCTION

The p-y curve method is commonly used in practice for analyzing the response of a laterally loaded single pile. When this method is applied to group piles, it needs to modify the single-pile p-y curve to consider group pile effects. The simplest way of modification is to multiply the p-y curves directly by a modification factor which can account for the group pile effects.

In literature, there are two major modification methods proposed, including y- and p- modification methods (Scott, 1981; Brown and Shie, 1990; Brown et al, 1988; McVay, et al., 1995). These methods modify the whole single-pile p-y curve using single modification factor, but do not consider the variation of group effects at different displacement stages.

To consider group effects at different displacement stages, this study introduces a two-stage modification method (Chiou and Chen, 2006) to modify single pile p-y curves for retrieving group-pile p-y curves. The first stage is referred to as y modification, which is to enlarge the elastic displacement of the single-pile p-y curve for accounting for the increase of elastic displacement of pile due to the influence of the stress zone of neighboring piles. With increasing displacement, the influence of elastic interaction will decay. The second stage of modification is referred to as p modification, which is to modify the soil reaction of single-pile curve to account for the reduction of pile resistance due to the overlap of passive wedges of piles.

We apply this approach to analyze an in-situ group PC pile test.

2. GROUP PILE LOAD TEST PROGRAM

The test site was located at Taipo, Chiayi, Taiwan. The group pile test program contained a PC pile group and a bored pile group, as displayed in Figure 1. For the PC pile group, the size of the pile cap was 9m×8m×2m, including 12 PC piles with diameter 0.8m. For the bored pile group, the dimension of the pile cap was 12m×8.5m×2m, including 6 reverse circulation piles with diameter 1.5 m. During the test, actuators were placed between the two pile caps. The lateral load was applied on the pile caps to have them produce lateral movement. In this paper, the PC pile test was adopted for analysis.

The site was on a very flat alluvial plain, where the alluvial deposits are generally interbedded layers of silty clays and clayey sands. Near the ground surface, the soils are clays at depths 0 to 3 m, fine sands at depths 3 to 7 m, and soft clays at depths 7 to 12 m. The SPT-N values of the shallow soils are generally quite low.

3. ANALYSIS METHOD

3.1 Simplified Single-Pile *p-y* Curve

According to a single PC pile load test at the same site, inclinometer slope data were analyzed to deduce the single-pile *p-y* curves (Chiou et al., 2008) and further simplified as shown in Figure 2. This simplified curve is defined by the yield and ultimate points. The *p* on the figure represents a line soil reaction acting on the pile and has a unit of force/length. Before the yield point (yield stress p_y was about 80 kN/m), the *p-y* response is linear with slope of 44637 kN/m² (initial modulus). After the yield point, the *p-y* response becomes nonlinear and is described as an exponential function with an exponent *n* of 0.37. The nonlinear portion terminates at the ultimate stress p_u of about 302 kN/m.

3.3 Modifications for Group Pile Effects

In a pile group, the interaction within the piles varies for different locations of the piles. Therefore, the *p-y* curve for each pile will be

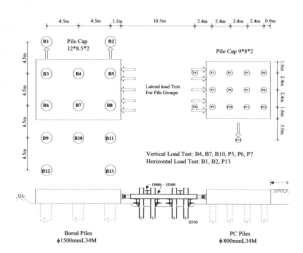

Fig. 1 In-situ group pile test configuration (Chen, 1997)

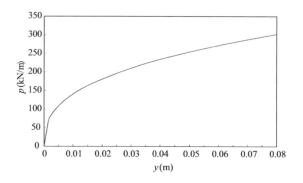

Fig. 2 Simplified single-pile *p-y* curve

different. The modification method for group effects is shown as in Figure 3. There are two stages: *y* and *p* modification. The purpose of *y* modification is to consider an additional increase in lateral displacement due to the stress influence of neighboring piles. In this stage, we do not directly apply a modification factor to enlarge the displacement of the single-pile *p-y* curve. First, the displacement influence factors f_{ij} for different distances of pile *i* to pile *j* based on the Mindlin solution (Mindlin, 1936) is built, as shown in Figure 4. Then, as shown in Figure 5, at the same action of soil reaction the group displacement Y_G of pile *i* considering the contribution of neighboring piles is to sum up its own displacement y_i and the displacement contribution of neighboring piles

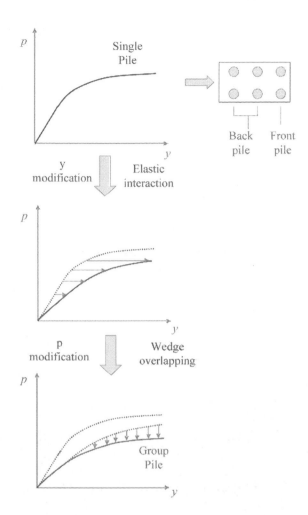

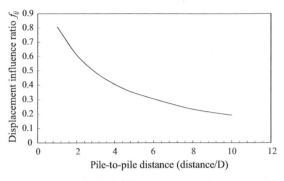

Fig. 4 Displacement influence factor f_{ij}

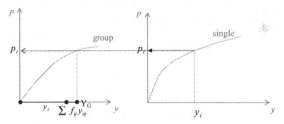

Fig. 5 Enlargement of y **for pile** i **influenced by pile** j

Fig. 3 Modification method of group pile effects

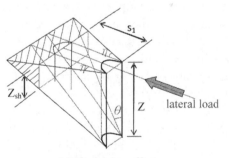

(a) Shadowing effect

$\sum f_{ij}y_{ej}$ by multiplying the lateral elastic displacement of neighboring piles y_{ej} by the displacement influence factor f_{ij}. The second stage is p modification, which is to consider a reduction of soil resistance due to overlap of passive wedges of piles. The wedge model is applied to compute the ultimate resistance. Then the group effects such as shadowing effects and side-by-side (or edge pile) effects are considered, as shown in Figure 6. This p modification factor applies to the ultimate state only, and therefore, for other displacement stage, the linear interpolation is applied for the displacement range between the yield and ultimate displacement.

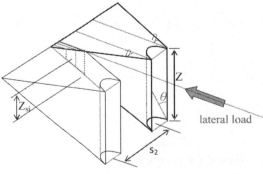

(b) Side by side effect

Fig. 6 Wedge models for shadowing and side-by-side effects

3.3 *p-y* curves after *y* modification

In performing *y* modification, we separate the displacement on the *p-y* curve into two parts: elastic and plastic, as shown in Figure 7. Considering the elastic interaction effect, *y* modification factors apply to the elastic displacement.

Figure 8 shows the *p-y* curves after *y* modification. Due to the symmetric arrangement of the PC group, the figure only shows the modified *p-y* curves of P1, P2, P5 and P6. It can be seen that the modified curves are on the right side of the single *p-y* curve, implying the enlargement of displacement. At the small displacement, the elastic interaction effect is significant, especially for P6 and P7, and decays with increasing plastic displacement.

3.5 *p-y* curves after *p* modification

With increasing plastic displacement, the elastic interaction effect will decay; on the other hand, the passive wedges of the piles will develop and overlap with other neighbor piles, which will cause a reduction in soil resistance. Consider the shadowing and side-by-side effects, the *p* modification factor is 0.9 for P4 and P12; 0.8 for P8, and 0.55 for the back piles. P4 and P12 are the front piles, and thus they only consider the side-by-side effect, whereas the P8 is in row with P4 and P12 and thus the reduction is twice of that in P4 or P12. For the back piles, they consider the shadowing effect only.

Figure 9 shows the *p-y* curves after *p* modification. It can be seen that the soil reactions are significantly reduced. The influence of shadowing effect is largest, which leads to a large reduction on soil resistance for the P1-P3, P5-P7 and P9-P11 piles.

4. WINKLER ANALYSIS

In this section, we adopt the obtained group *p-y* curves for Winkler analysis. According to the

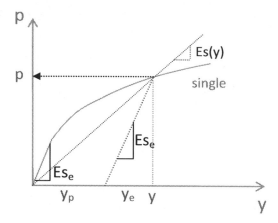

Fig. 7 Separation of elastic and plastic displacement for single-pile *p-y* curve

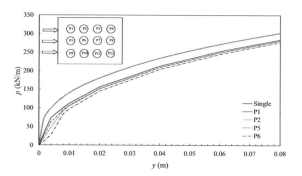

Fig. 8 Group-pile *p-y* curve after *y* modification

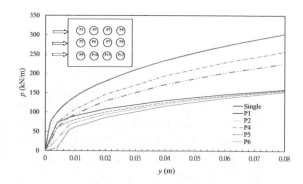

Fig. 9 Group-pile *p-y* curve after *p* modification

inclinometer data, the pile-cap connection of the PC pile group was close to hinged connection (Chen, 1997). Therefore, in this analysis, we assume the hinged pile-head condition (free rotation at the pile head) and apply the displacement controlled approach to analyze the load-deflection curve of the pile group. Besides, considering the nonlinear flexural response of pile section, we build the moment-curvature curve of pile section as shown in Figure 10 for analysis.

Figure 11 displays the simulated load-deflection curve of the pile cap, which summing up the load-deflection curves of all the piles in the group under the free head condition. Compared with the measured data, the overall trends of both are in good agreement; however, at very small loading, the calculated displacement is more than double of the measured values. This may be due to the densification effect due to pile driving, frictional resistance at the bottom the pile cap, and that the pile-head condition is not fully hinged. At larger displacement, the analyzed and measured responses are very close.

Figure 12 further displays the pile-head shear ratio

of each pile in the group. The shear ratio represents the ratio of shear sustained by each pile to the average lateral load at specific displacements. It can be seen that at the beginning of loading, the corner piles (P1, P4, P9 and P12) have largest contribution and the middle piles (P4 and P7) provides the minimum lateral resistance; with increasing loading, due to soil plasticity, the middle piles gradually sustain lager lateral load, but the lateral load sustained by the corner piles P1 and P9 gradually decreases.

For example, Figure 13 shows the pile deflection curves of P1 pile at lateral loads of 2.94, 5.89, 7.85, 9.12, and 9.81 MN. It can be seen that the deflection profiles are in good agreement with the measured. Figure 14 further displays the moment profiles of P1 pile. Based on the moment-curvature curve as shown in Figure 10, the pile experiences cracking, yielding and eventually almost reaches the ultimate state during the whole loading process.

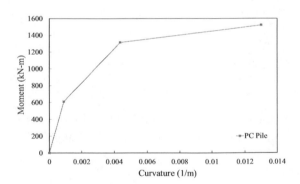

Fig. 10 Moment-curvature relationship of PC pile

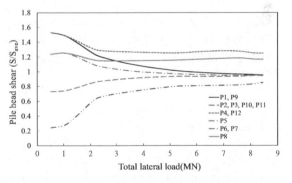

Fig. 12 Distribution of pile-head shear

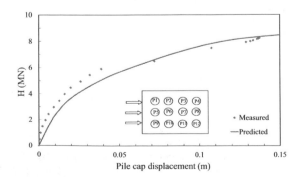

Fig. 11 Load-deflection of PC group

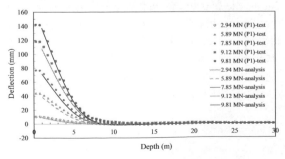

Fig. 13 Deflection profile of P1 pile

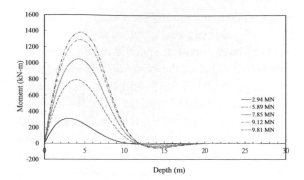

Fig. 14 Moment profile of P1 pile

5. GROUP EFFICIENCY

Figure 15 displays the average load-deflection curve of the PC group. Compared to the single-pile load-deflection curve, it can be seen that the lateral capacity of the pile group is reduced due to the group effects. Define group efficiency Rd as below,

$$R_d = \frac{\overline{H_G}}{H_S} \qquad (1)$$

where $\overline{H_G}$ is the average lateral load at specific lateral displacement and H_s is the lateral load on the free-head single pile to have the same lateral displacement as the pile group.

Figure 16 displays the variation of group efficiency with lateral displacement. It can be seen that at the beginning of loading, the group efficiency is about 0.3-0.4; when the displacement increases to 8 mm, the group efficiency increases and reaches at a constant value of about 0.6 to 0.7. At the small displacement, the group pile effect is significant due to the elastic interaction effect; however, with increasing displacement, the elastic interaction effect gradually decreases so that the group efficiency increases. Finally, the group efficiency is governed by the overlap of the failure wedges of the group piles.

6. CONCLUSIONS

This study adopts *p-y* approach to analyze an in-situ PC group pile lateral load test. The approach considers two-stage modification for the group pile effects to obtain the group-pile *p-y* curves based on experimental single-pile *p-y* curves. The simulated load-deflection curve as well as the profiles of pile deflection and moment with depth agrees well with the measured. From the analysis results, it can be seen that group pile effects are more significant at small displacements due to elastic interaction. Therefore, it should be noted that when the allowable lateral displacement is considered in design, the elastic interaction effect cannot be ignored.

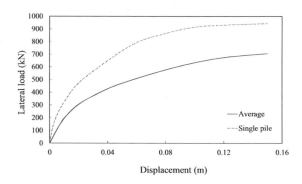

Fig. 15 Comparison of equivalent capacity curve of PC group and capacity curve of single PC pile

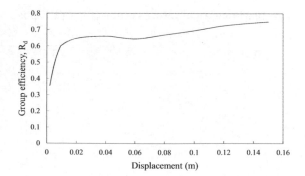

Fig. 16 Group efficiency of PC pile group

REFERENCES

Brown, D.A., and Shie, C.F. (1990). Numerical experiments into group effects on the response of piles to lateral loading. *Computers and Geotechnics*, Vol: 10., pp 221-230.

Brown, D.A., Morrison, C., and Reese, L.C. (1988). Lateral load behavior of pile group in sand. *Journal of Geotechnical Engineering, ASCE*, Vol: 114, No.11., pp 1261-1276.

Chen, C. H. (1997). *Optimal design for bridge foundation of HSR project*, Report Prepared for Bureau of Taiwan High Speed Rail, Taiwan, Construction Research Institute, Taiwan.

Chiou, J.S., and Chen, C.H. (2006). Modification of P-y curves for group piles. *Journal of the Chinese Institute of Civil and Hydraulic Engineering*, Vol: 18, No.3., pp 325-335.

Chiou, J.S., Chen, C.H., and Chen, Y.C. (2008). Deducing pile responses and soil reactions from inclinometer data of a lateral load test. *Soils and Foundations*, Vol: 48, No.5., pp 609–620.

McVay, M., Casper, R. and Shang, T.I. (1995). Lateral response of three-row group in loose to dense sand at 3D and 5D pile spacing. *Journal of Geotechnical Engineering, ASCE*, Vol: 121, No.5., pp 436-441.

Mindlin, R.D. (1936). Forces at a point in the interior of a semi-infinite solid. *Physics*, Vol: 7, pp 195-202.

Scott, R.F. (1981). *Foundation Analysis*, Prentice-Hall International, Inc., London.

CHAPTER 11

PERFORMANCE BASED SEISMIC DESIGN OF PILED RAFT FOUNDATIONS – ALTERNATE APPROACHES USING APPROXIMATE COMPUTER BASED ANALYSES

Der-Wen Chang*

Professor, Department of Civil Engineering, Tamkang University, New Taipei City, Taiwan
*dwchang@mail.tku.edu.tw

Tatsunori Matsumoto

Professor, Department of Civil Engineering, Kanazawa University, Kanazawa, Japan

ABSTRACT: Performance-Based Seismic Design (PBSD) of the geotechnical engineering structures can be evaluated by a number of methods taking into account the uncertainties of the influence factors. Structural analysis such as the three dimensional finite element and finite difference methods as well as the approximate computer based methods can be used to analyse the foundation behaviours at various design stages. This paper intends to discuss alternate methods with the emphasis on deformations of piled raft foundations using possible static and dynamic solutions. A number of case studies are presented. For horizontal seismic motions, the PBSD could be conducted with the emphasis on piles comparing the resulted bending moment, shear, and axial force with the designed pile capacities. For vertical seismic motions, the safeties of the piles and the raft must be examined especially for relatively large piled raft foundations. The effects of seismic forces from superstructure and ground soils during earthquake should be analysed. Variability of the seismic forces requires the use of numerous seismic records modified at different seismic levels when dynamic analysis was conducted. If pseudo static analysis was used, variability of the seismic forces can be approximated using only the seismic intensity. Both serviceability and capacities of the foundation need to be examined to avoid the damages and distress caused by the earthquake.

1. INTRODUCTION

Piled raft foundation is commonly used to overcome the problems of large and differential settlements of the massive structure located in soft soils. Additionally, it can provide sufficient lateral capacities which can minimize the foundation's movements due to the lateral and overturning loads. The design philosophy of the piled raft foundation according to Randolph (1994) can be suggested as, 1. Grouped piles, in which the raft is able to ignore, only the piles are carrying the loads. 2. Creep piles, in which a certain amount of the pile capacities are mobilized. The piles will settle as the loads increased. Allowable capacity of the piles needs to be controlled by adjusting the number of piles while the contact pressures between the raft and the underneath soils are limited within the pre-consolidation pressure of the soils. 3. Oriented piles, in which the settlements and differential settlements are controlled by allocating the piles in proper positions. It will need detailed information of the site geological condition.

The grouped piles design concept has been adopted for years for simplicity in conventional design procedures. It is applicable if a relatively smaller piled raft foundation is encountered. However for relatively large piled raft foundation, the raft should be carefully taken into account to satisfy the economic and eco-energy concerns. According to De Sanctis *et al.* (2001) and Viggiani (2001), for any piled raft foundation whose width is less than 15m, it can be regarded as a small piled raft foundation. For large piled raft foundation, the width of the raft should be larger than the length of the piles.

The mechanism of the grouped piles has been studied comprehensively in the past years and it needs typically the pile load test to ensure and/or to calibrate the design. The creep piles design on the other hand reveals the importance of knowing the load-displacement relationships of the piles in soft soil sites. The raft must be carefully designed since the underneath soils are kept within their limited resistances. The piles will settle while the applied loads are increased. Figure 1 illustrates the load-displacement relationships of the piles and the piled raft foundation in soft soils. The difference between the lines of the whole piled raft foundation and the piles is attributed to the raft. Conventional design excluding the raft can be governed by calculating the ultimate capacity of the piles and reducing it to allowable capacity. If the raft is included, to keep the loads equally carried by the piles and the raft would be desired. Such mechanism and adjusting the pile locations to reduce differential settlements need adequate tools. It is obvious that to control the displacement/ deformation of the foundation is the key in the design. Mobilizing the full capacity of foundation is not expected unless the load is applied at the extreme conditions.

Another significant feature of the piled raft foundation is its high resistance against the seismic forces during the earthquake. The design methods, particularly the Performance-Based Seismic Design (PBSD) procedures applicable will be discussed in next section.

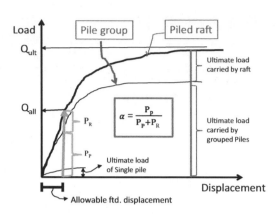

Fig. 1 Load and displacement relationship of piled raft foundation in soft soils

2. PERFORMACE BASED SEISMIC DESIGN

2.1 General Design Methods

Performance-Based Design (PBD) has been introduced to geotechnical engineering society for nearly two decades (ISO, 1998; Honjo *et al.*, 2002; Fajfar and Kawinkler, 2004; Frank, 2007; Kokusho *et al.*, 2009; PEER, 2010; Bolton, 2012). The principle of PBD is that the uncertainties involved in the design must be taken into account. The uncertainties involved in the design of any geotechnical structure can be classified as aleatoric uncertainties and epistemic uncertainties. The former could be introduced statistically by natural changing and/or engineering measurements, whereas the latter could be systematically produced by man-made errors and/or limits of the methods. In geotechnical engineering, the influence factors of the design are mostly focusing on ground conditions (*e.g.*, geometry and geology of the site), physical properties and engineering parameters of the soils, and loads and/or prescribed displacements of the structure, etc. The uncertainties of these influence factors must be computed and/ or considered in a scientific manner whereas the probability of their occurrence and/or the reliabilities of their quantities should be analysed and incorporated into the design. Consequently, the design could be assured by quality controlled procedures. Performance functions of the structure must be known prior to the design. Requirements and design conditions shall be combined in order to satisfy the design.

The Limit State Design (LSD) often used in geotechnical engineering are categorized by, 1. Ultimate Limit State (ULS) Design, and 2. Serviceability Limit State (SLS) Design. The former is mainly conducted on factored soil resistances and factored loads, while the stress and capacity of the foundation are examined carefully. For example, load and Resistance Factor Design (LRFD) method suggested by AASHTO in 1990s is representable for ULS. The latter is made on evaluations of the displacement and/ or deformations in which the structure and its elements must be kept within the elastic regions and/or underneath the yielding point. To do so, it requires the applications of sophisticated numerical tools such as Finite Element Method (FEM) and/ or Finite Difference Method (FDM). With the above design methods, the assessments of the foundation safety can be carefully conducted using more systematic and scientific methods rather than using an empirical factor of safety such as the one suggested in Working Stress Design (WSD) method. Figure 2 illustrates the design methods in geotechnical engineering. In general, external and internal capacities (or resistances) and serviceability (or displacements) of the foundation should be examined. Additionally it should be noted that any method can be applied as long as it can satisfy the required design specifications.

2.2 Static and Seismic Concerns of PBD

For PBD of the piled raft foundation, if the foundation is treated as a grouped pile foundation, the major concerns would be performance of the piles. The raft must be designed rigid enough to behave elastically. Vertical and lateral capacities, uplifting and down-drag resistances and settlements/deformations of the piles should be examined. Variability of the uncertainties will be mainly from the soil parameters and geological conditions. The examples of conducting the PBD analysis on grouped pile foundation could be found in Phoon (2008). The performance functions of the grouped piles can be established upon the overall load-displacement relationships of the foundation and/or the internal capacities of the piles (*e.g.*, the nonlinear moment-curvature relations, the shearing and the compressional/tensile capacities). For example, the approximate Bouc-Wen model (Kunnath and Reinhom, 1989) of the nonlinear moment-curvature relationships could be adopted to evaluate the performance of the concrete piles under lateral loadings. Figure 3 depicts the approximate tri-linear relationships for moment and curvature of concrete pile often used in design practice.

On the other hand, if the interactions between piles and raft with the soils became more important (the raft behaves more like a flexible structure), then the

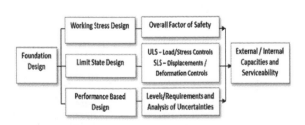

Fig. 2 Design methods used in foundation engr.

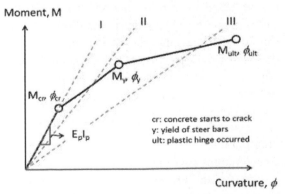

Fig. 3 Approximate tri-linear moment-curvature relationships of concrete piles

Table 1 Seismic performance requirements of transportation structures at various design levels (Chen *et al.*, 2009)

Hazard Level	Embank ment	Bridge Pile Foundation		Underground Structures	
		Ordinary	Important	Ordinary	Important
Moderate EQ	Level I	Level I		Level I	
Design EQ	Level III	Level III	Level II	Level III	Level II
MCE	N/A	N/A	Level III	N/A	Level III
NOTE:	EQ: earthquake; MCE: maximum consideration earthquake; Level I: structure remains elastic; Level II: restricted local damage, damages recoverable; Level III: superstructure and main body collapse prohibited.				

performance of raft foundation should be taken into account. Not only the overall foundation and piles should be examined, the internal stresses exerted in the raft must be evaluated. The bending moment, shear force and normal stresses acting on various cross sections of the raft should be carefully checked to ensure that the raft can satisfy the performance requirements. Table 1 lists the seismic performance requirements at various seismic levels for the transportation structures (Chen *et al.*, 2009). Figure 4 summarizes the performance functions that should be considered for PBD of the combined pile raft foundation (CPRF).

For piled raft foundations located in seismic regions, the PBSD procedures must be taken. The influences of the seismic forces from both the superstructure and the ground to the foundation should be considered. For simplicity, the horizontal and vertical vibrations of the foundation caused by the earthquake could be analysed independently. The seismic design of the foundation needs to follow either the applicable seismic hazard curves obtained from the Probabilistic Seismic Hazard Analysis (PSHA) or the seismic design code in order to find out the target PGAs at various design levels. Figure 5 shows the seismic hazard curves suggested for major cities in Taiwan (Cheng, 2002). Table 2 presents the Target Peak Ground Accelerations (PGAT) obtained from the hazard curves for the cities of Taipei, Taichung and Kaohsiung. Note that the ones obtained from the local seismic design code were found smaller than the ones suggested by Cheng (2002). The

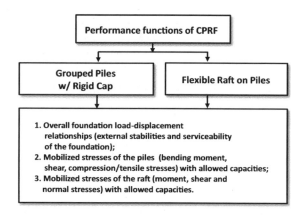

Fig. 4 Performance functions considered for PBD of combined piled raft foundation

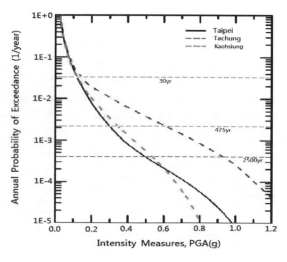

Fig. 5 Seismic hazard curves for major cities in Taiwan (after Cheng, 2002)

major difference between them is mainly due to the blind fault influences involved in the statistics. In Taiwan, the seismic design code requires three seismic levels at the return periods of 30, 475 and 2500 years (annual rates of exceedance are approximately 0.033, 0.0021 and 0.0004). They are denoted respectively as moderate, design and maximum consideration earthquakes.

Table 2 Target peak ground accelerations of metropolitans in Taiwan (after Cheng, 2002)

Metropolitan	Seismic Levels		
	Moderate EQ	Design EQ	MCE
Taipei	0.12g	0.29g	0.51g
Taichung	0.14g	0.60g	0.94g
Kaohsiung	0.12g	0.35g	0.54g

Comparing to other design parameters, the variability of the seismic forces is known to be mostly significant. If the pseudo static analysis was adopted, the target PGA is probably the most important design parameter. The engineer could check the influences of the variability for soil parameters, geological conditions at various target PGAs. Note that pseudo static loads from both the superstructure and the ground soil should be considered. Separated analyses were often conducted to evaluate the pile performance. Push-over types of loading are frequently applied on top of the piles to simulate the horizontal seismic influence of the building to the foundation. On the other hand, the lateral movements of the ground profile and/or the earth pressures under the horizontal earthquake motions were approximately estimated and applied to the piles solving for the flexural deflections. It is important to point out that these approximations may result in over-conservative design and the foundation behaviours may not be interpreted correctly.

If the time-dependent dynamic analysis was used to analyze the foundation behaviours, not only the PGA but also the time history of the seismic record will have significant influences. The design engineer will need to collect and calibrate a set of the seismic records at the vicinity of the

site in order to have adequate artificial seismic inputs for the analysis. Note that the performance functions suggested for PBD of the CPRF can be also applied to PBSD. For horizontal earthquake, the seismic performance of the piles should be assessed carefully.

2.3 Probability- and Reliability-Based Methods

Performance of the geotechnical structures can be categorized as capacity (and/or resistances) and deformation problems. Different techniques have been adopted to solve the problems. For example, analytical formulas for capacities of shallow foundation, slope stability, and retaining structure have been extensively studied. To take into account the uncertainties, Reliability methods such as the First Order Secondary Moment (FOSM) method, the First Order Reliability Method (FORM), and the Monte Carlo Simulation (MCS) method were adopted in various studies. Corresponding performance function needs to be defined first and the reliability index (β) of the function was calculated accordingly. It was reported that the reliability index (β) should be least 2.3 to satisfy the foundation design (Whitman, 1984). For static capacity and deformations of the foundation, some people suggested that the physical modelling could also be used. However, it is always difficult to carry out the experiment to simulate the details of the structural system. Performance functions in this case can be defined by checking either the displacements or the stresses to satisfy the design. Similarly, other types of reliability methods could also be used for the assessment. Details of the applications can be found in Phoon (2008).

Additionally, Honjo *et al.* (2002) suggested that the Probability method and the Load and Resistance Factor Design (LRFD) method are also feasible for PBD analysis. Probability methods can be analysed by estimating the probabilities of failure (or occurrence) by a number of consequent measures. Total Probability Theory can be used in such modelling. For LRFD method, load and

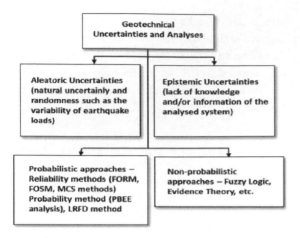

Fig. 6 Geotechnical uncertainties and available analyses

resistance factors are implemented based upon the AASHTO design specifications. These factors were assumed and evaluated incorporating performance function with reliability analysis to validate the design (Paikowski, 2002). It should be noted that the above methods discussed are mostly suggested to count for aleatoric uncertainties. In some references, all the above methods can be referred as the probabilistic approach. For epistemic uncertainties, the efforts should be made to gain better knowledge of the system, process of mechanism, in which the methods such as Fuzzy Logic and Evidence Theory are available. These methods sometimes are called non-probabilistic approach. Figure 6 summarizes the categories of performance of geotechnical structures and the corresponding analytical procedures on design uncertainties.

2.4 PBEE Analysis

For Probability Based method used for PBSD, the so called PBEE (Performance Based Earthquake Engineering) analysis suggested by US Pacific Earthquake Engineering Research Center (PEER) is referable. Such analysis has been conducted by research teams on NEES project with 3D FEM program-OpenSees (2009). Introductions of the PBEE analysis can be found in Kramer (1996, 2008). It suggests that the annual rate of

exceedance (λ) for a decision variable (DV) on any engineering structure can be analyzed as a triple-integral on the products of probabilities of intensity measured (IM), engineering demand parameter (EDP), and the damage measure (DM). For seismic hazard curve in hand, the integral is able to be decomposed in finding the annual rate of exceedance for EDP, DM, and DV, respectively. Based on log-normal distributions, analytical expressions of the rate exceedance for EDP, DM and DV can be found. Simplified methods to compute the statistics of the data were suggested. This approach can ideally include all possible earthquake influences with the uncertainties of soil parameters and spatial variability. For pile foundations, DV, DM, EDP and IM can be defined as cost of the hazard, maximum bending moment of pile, maximum pile displacement and PGA used in the analysis. According to Shin (2007), the effects of the uncertainties of seismic forces are much larger than those from soil parameters and spatial variability. The record-to-record uncertainty was found to be 90%~95% of the total uncertainty involved in the seismic assessment. Such significance could be omitted when using pseudo static analysis to analyze the foundation. The target PGA will become the only representing factor of the seismic force. Using the dynamic analysis, Chang et al. (2009b, 2010) have successfully demonstrated the applications of PBEE analysis to PBSD assessments of bridge pile foundations in Taipei Basin. Figure 7 depicts the relationships for annual rate of exceedance with the maximum pile displacement and the maximum bending moment obtained by Chang et al. (2014b) on a bridge pile foundation using PBEE analysis where the length of the piles are about 60 meters. Figure 8 is the design chart suggested for ordinary seismic design and PBSD with PBEE procedures for pile foundations (Chang et al., 2013).

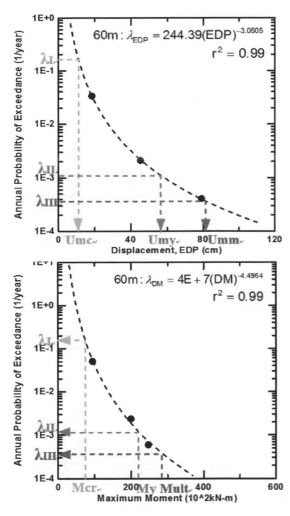

Fig. 7 Annual rate of exceedance for the maximum displacements and bending moments of piles (from Chang *et al.*, 2014b)

3. PILED RAFT FOUNDATION ANALYSES

For piled raft foundation, the combined pile group and raft method, which combines the equivalent pier method for pile group (Poulos and Davis, 1980) and the flexibility matrix method for piled raft (Randolph, 1983), has been proposed by Clancy and Randolph (1993). For non-homogeneous soils, Horikoshi and Randolph (1996) had extended the simplified solution whereas the soil modulus increases linearly

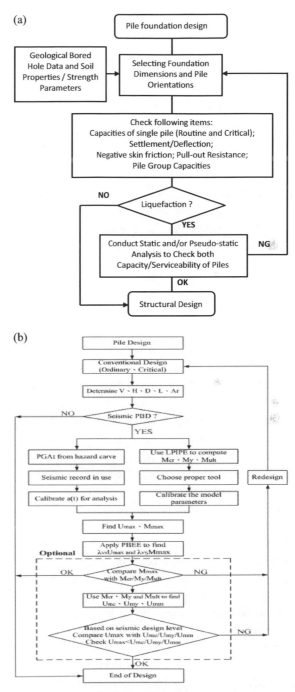

Fig. 8 Pile foundation design steps (a) ordinary design (b) PBSD using PBEE analysis (Chang *et al.*, 2013)

with the depth. The design analyses of piled raft foundation were summarized by Poulos (2001) as: 1. Simplified calculation methods, 2. Approximate computer-based method, and 3. Rigorous computer-based method. A recent study carried by Yamashita *et al.* (2015) on monitoring four case histories in Japan has showed that the simplified calculation method can provide good predictions of the foundation deformations as long as the model and soil parameters were carefully calibrated. Despite that, such method has the disadvantages and limitations for detailed resistance design.

Available approximate computer-based methods such as the so called 3D Hybrid approach (Clancy and Randolph 1993; Kobayashi *et al.* 2009; Kitiyodom and Matsumoto 2002, 2003; Kitiyodom *et al.* 2005) and the rigorous ones based on 3D finite element and/or finite difference analysis had been adopted to model the piled raft foundation behaviors. Unsever *et al.* (2015) has shown that the 3D finite element analysis by PLAXIS can be used to make the comparative studies for model pile behaviors under vertical and horizontal static loads. Applications of the 3D FEM or FDM analyses can be also found in Abderlrazaq *et al.*(2011), Katzenbach *et al.*(2013), Kouroussis *et al.*(2013). While the rigorous methods are helpful at main design and detailed design stages, the approximate computer-based method can provide a fast estimation of the settlement/resistance and load sharing between pile group and raft.

Evaluating the structural deformations and stresses is very important to PBD in geotechnical engineering. For most of the designs, if deformations were limited and the internal safety of the structural elements had been ensued, then external (overall) foundation capacity should be automatically satisfied since the resulting structural displacements are much less than those required to yielding the soils. Although the guideline of Combined Pile-Raft Foundation (CPRF) published by TC212 (Katzenbach and Choudhury, 2013) suggests that both the foundation capacities (ULS) and foundation deformations (SLS) should be proven, it should be noted that deformation of a foundation is the essential key since excessive displacements should be avoided. This is typically

true in the problems of laterally loaded piles and the piled raft foundations appearing to have large differential settlements. The ultimate capacity of the foundation became very important only when foundation capacity was to be fully mobilized in soft soils or when foundation was overstressed in stiff soils under substantial loads.

4. APPROXIMATE COMPUTER METHOD METHODS FOR PBSD

4.1 EQWEAP Analysis on Grouped Piles

The time-dependent wave equation analysis of a single pile subjected to the respective vertical and horizontal earthquake motions has been suggested and studied by Chang since 1990s (Chang *et al.*, 2014a). The simplified one-dimensional analysis is conducted as a decoupled procedure called EQWEAP (Earth-Quake Wave Equation Analysis for Piles). It consists of a lumped-mass analysis to solve for the seismic responses of free-field ground site and a discrete wave equation analysis to solve for pile responses under the resulted ground excitations. Figure 9 shows the layout of the decoupled analysis and the corresponding force equilibrium of the pile segments.

Detailed of this analysis and alternate solution as well as the comparisons with FEM solutions on case histories under the horizontal earthquake motions can be found in Chang *et al.* (2014a). With the nonlinear moment-curvature relationships and the moment capacities from calculations and/or from the experiments, such solution can provide nonlinear pile deflections that can be used to assess the damages of the pile. The superstructure loads applied to the piles can be analyzed based on fundamental mechanics prior to the EQWEAP analysis. Such solution can be treated as an approximate solution for single piles within the group pile foundation under the earthquake loads. The seismic effects of the superstructure can be included by knowing the dynamic forces transmitting to the foundation. This solution is

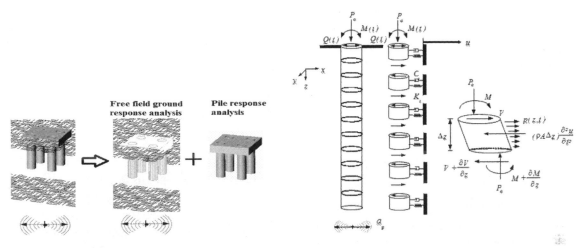

Fig. 9 Schematic layout of the EQWEAP analysis and equilibriums of pile elements (Chang *et al.*, 2014a)

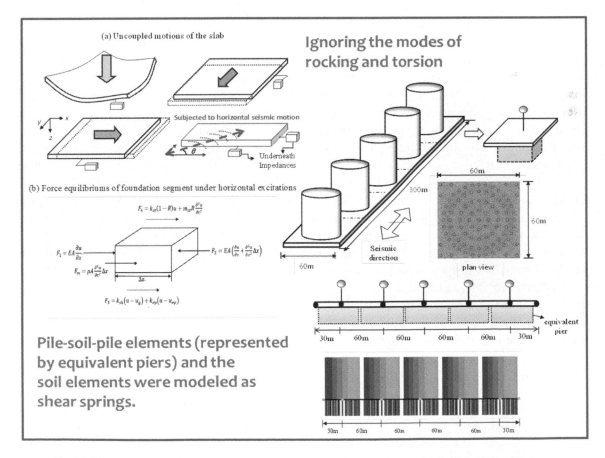

Fig. 10 Numerical model of strip raft on piles and discrete model in EQPR analysis

rational as a preliminary assessment to the piles where the dynamic interactions between the piles can be ignored for transient vibrations (Chang *et al.*, 2009a). This is particularly true if the size of piled raft (or pile cap) is relatively small and the ground impacts will be nearly the same to all the piles.

4.2 EQPR Analysis on Piled Raft Foundation

Based on the EQWEAP analysis, Chang *et al.* (2016) was able to suggest a simplified solution to model the dynamic responses of a rectangular raft foundation on piles subjected to the horizontal earthquake. The finite difference solution was derived to solve for the wave equation of the raft under the horizontals motions. Such analysis was termed as EQPR (Earth-Quake Piled Raft foundation analysis). Seismic forces transmitting through the underneath soils and piles were monitored while the effects of the superstructure were simply simulated though a displacement ratio, R between the superstructure and the foundation. Shear springs were used to model the soils and piles beneath the raft, whereas the equivalent pier model was formed.

Effect of the incidental waves and the influences of structural geometry and soil parameters were discussed. With a case study on silo foundation located in coal-ash pond, the solution was validated with 3D FEM solutions from MIDAS-GTS program (Midas, 2012). It is found that the effects of the superstructure are important, the displacement ratio, R between the structure and the foundation is generally in a range of 0.5~1.2 varying with the time. The observations from the study indicate that the importance of the dynamic influences on the foundation during the earthquake should not be ignored in the design. Figure 10 depicts the model of the case study and Figure 11 shows the variations of the displacement ratio with respect to time obtained from, the back analysis was conducted by treating the raft as a shaking table due to the earthquake.

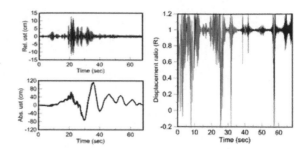

Fig. 11 Motion of the SDOF superstructure subjected to foundation shaking (a) relative displacement time-history (b) absolute displacements time-history (c) displacement ratio R calculated as a time-dependent function (from Chang *et al.*, 2016)

4.3 Analyses on Pseudo Static Loads on CPRF

Both EQWEAP and EQPR analyses were suggested in order to simulate the seismic forces of the ground to the piled raft foundation. Dynamic influences of the superstructure can be taken into account by mounting the dynamic structure loads on top of foundation. However, if the seismic influences onto the foundation are focusing on structural loads only (which is commonly done in design practice), the structural loads can be analyzed by pseudo-static and/or dynamic analysis. The foundation will be enforced to vibrate under the structural loads. Approximate computer-based methods suggested by those methods presented in Section 3 are available for such analysis. The influences of the seismic force of the superstructure can be simply approximated by additional inertia forces caused by the earthquake. Static push-over load is thus applied at top of the foundation to see how the foundation (mainly the piles) will react and how it would be damaged due to the load. Such analysis is aimed to capture the ultimate load induced to the piles. On the other hand, if the model piles are only subjected to the movements or pressures of the surrounding soils, then the lateral resistance of the piles against the ground impacts must be obtained. This approach has been adopted to simulate the soil liquefaction induced lateral spread influences onto the pile foundation. If both solutions were combined, it is obvious that the estimation would be very crucial when structural load and ground movement are in countered directions.

5. CASE STUDIES

5.1 Bridge Pile Foundations

A bridge pile foundation at an expressway located in Sin-Jhuang district at New Taipei City in Taiwan has been studied (Chang *et al.*, 2014b) using EQWEAP analysis with Monte-Carlo Simulation. The past earthquakes causing damages were of interest. For simplicity, seismic records at the stations TAP017 during 1999 Chi-Chi earthquake (in-land/active

faulting triggered quake, M_L = 7.3) and TAP011 during 2002 Yi-Lang earthquake (east coast offshore/subduction plate triggered quake, M_L = 6.8) were selected to generate artificial earthquakes. Figure 12 and Figure 13 show the locations and the acceleration time histories in use. A typical 3×3 pile foundation with piles of 2m diameter (D) and 60m length was investigated. Thickness of the pile cap is 2m and S/D was kept as 2.5 where S is the center-to-center pile spacing. Geological condition of the site is presumed based on in-situ borehole data and representative studies. Table 3 shows the information of the ground site. According to the designer, the maximum vertical loads at the single

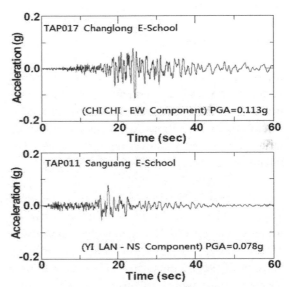

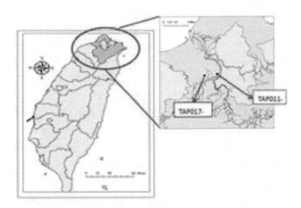

Fig. 12 Locations of seismic stations near to the bridge pile foundation (from Chang *et al.*, 2014b)

Fig. 13 Seismic records used for the study by Chang *et al.* (2014b)

Table 3 Geological condition and soil parameters used in Chang *et al.* (2014b)

Depth(m)	H(m)	Soil Layers	γ(kN/m^3)		SPT-N		ϕ(°)		c(kPa)		Vs
			Avg.	σ	Avg.	σ	Avg.	σ	Avg.	σ	(m/s)
0~4	4	Surface fill	18.0	1.5	3	1	30	1	–	–	115
4~10	6	SS-VI(ML)	18.5	0.7	5	1	6	1	7	1	171
10~20	10	SS-V(SM)	18.9	1.3	14	3	34	2	–	–	192
20~40	20	SS-IV(CL-ML)	18.8	1	11	2	14	1	5	1	222
40~50	10	SS-III(SM)	18.6	0.9	21	4	34	2	–	–	221
50~60	10	SS-II(CL-ML)	19.0	0.7	14	2	21	1	6	1	241
60~70	10	SS-I(SM)	19.3	0.7	30	4	42	1	–	–	248

Note: SS means Songshan formation

piles were designed as 9MN and 18MN for ordinary and seismic cases. Horizontal loads were kept as 15% of the maximum vertical loads.

The moment capacities of M_{cr}, M_y and M_{ult} were able to obtain from LPILE analysis. With 1.94% reinforced bar ratio and 18MN vertical loads, M_{cr}, M_y and M_{ult} were obtained as 7.35, 22.15 and 28.68 MN-m, respectively. Varying the unit weight, SPT-N value, friction angle and cohesion of the layered soils with presumed averages and standard deviations (see Table 3), 5000 combinations of the soil layers were randomly generated. Varying the PGA_T (0.01g~0.51g) with increment of 0.01g with two seismic records, the total number of scenarios is 5.1×10^5. Note that the seismic hazard curve for Taipei (Cheng, 2002) was adopted in this case. For seismic level-I, -II and -III, the performance functions were assumed to be controlled by M_{cr}, M_y and M_{ult} respectively. It should be noted for more conservative requirement, M_y could be used for seismic level-III too. The probability of failure, P_f is defined as the ratio of number for cases at failure divided by the total number of cases. The reliability indexes, β are computed accordingly.

Detailed results for the probabilities of failure at each PGA from EQWEAP analysis can be found in Lin (2013). Calculating the probabilities of failure, P_f at every PGA and multiplying them with the weights, the calibrated P_f can be obtained. Summation of the calibrated P_f up to the target PGA_T will give the total probability of failure, P_{fT} at different seismic levels. It can be seen that the horizontal structural load (F_H) has great influences to the results. If F_H was treated statically, the failures will increase dramatically.

If no static horizontal force considered, then the predictions will become much safe. The effects of soil parameters at each PGA were studied and it was found that the effects of soil parameters are relatively insignificant compared to PGAs.

Following the assumptions of log-normal distribution, the corresponding reliability indexes, β were calculated. Reliability indexes for seismic performance of the numerical piles were found between 2.8~5 under design earthquake and MCE (Maximum Consideration Earthquake) quake. Following the foundation performance and reliability index of 2.3 suggested by Whitman (1984), the piles are acceptable for the seismic design requirements. However for moderate earthquake, the reliability indexes were found less than 2, which is unacceptable to the design. This is attributed to the rigid head assumption to the piles and the static load applied at the pile head.

The factor of safety (FS) for seismic performance of the piles from Reliability analysis was suggested as the ratio of computed reliability index, β divided by the required reliability index, β_R, i.e., β/β_R. FS obtained for the example study are summarized in Table 4. It can be found that the factors of safety calculated from Reliability method using MCS approach showed that the assessment for moderate EQs were too conservative by only checking the damages at the pile head and taking the horizontal structural loads as a static one. The minimum safety factor of the seismic PBD of the piles can be accordingly made at various design levels. In this case, factors of safety on the order of 1.17~2.17 for PBSD of the piles under the design and MCE quakes can be obtained.

Table 4 Factor of safety for seismic performance of the numerical piles

Method	Factor of safety(FS)					
	Moderate EQ		Design EQ		MCE quakes	
MCS w/o F_H	≤ 0.12g	0.12g	≤ .29g	0.29g	≤ 0.51g	0.51g
	0.696	1.08	2.17	2.17	2.17	2.1
MCS w/F_H	0.43	1.08	1.17	1.6	1.79	2.08

Note: F_H is the horizontal load and β_R is kept as 2.3 according to the suggestion of Whitman (1984)

5.2 Mega Raft on Piles

Assessment for the seismic performance of a mega piled raft foundation was shown in this section based on a newly proposed approximate computer-based analysis - EQPR (Chang *et al.*, 2016). The foundation underneath the coal bunkers (silos) is located at a coal-ash pound site around Taipei. Numerical modelling of the structure approximates the foundation underneath a single silo is shown in Figure 10 and Figure 14. 80 piles were oriented in radial directions from the centre pile with four radial distances at 7, 14, 21 and 26 meters. The number of piles from the inner ring to the outer ring is 8, 16, 24 and 32. At each edge of the raft, three single piles were seated in a triangle form.

Table 5 indicates the structural dimensions and

the material properties/parameters used in the modelling. The finite Element analyses using Midas-GTS (Midas, 2012) were conducted to make comparisons. Modified Cam Clay model and Mohr-Coulomb model were simply chosen to model the coal ash and underlaining gravel layers, respectively in FE analysis, where the foundation was assumed linearly elastic. On the other hand, linear solutions of the EQPR analysis were obtained with the solutions resolved from EQWEAP analysis considering both soil and pile nonlinearities. A number of seismic records recorded at the vicinity of the site were used to calibrate the artificial earthquake. The one from 1999 Chi-Chi earthquake at station TAP049 calibrated to 0.24g (following the seismic design code in Taipei) of design earthquake is presented in Figure 15.

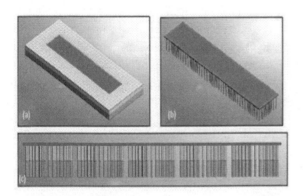

Fig. 14 FEM model used in Midas analysis for mega raft on piles

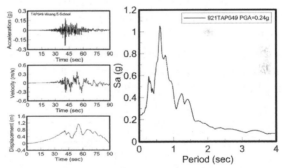

Fig. 15 Seismic response time-history and acceleration spectrum Sa at design earthquake

Table 5 Material properties and model parameters used in EQPR and 3D Midas-GTS analyses (from Chang *et al.*, 2016)

Method	Geometry and Material Parameters	Model and Model Parameters
EQPR analysis	Pile and raft: $E = 3 \times 10^4$MPa; $\gamma = 24$kN/m^3; $\xi = 0.02$; $v = 0.1$;	Pile, raft, soft soil and gravel: linearly elasticity
3D Midas-GTS analysis	Pilelength: 26.5m; Pilediameter: 2m; S/D = 2.5$^+$; Raft length & width: 60m; Raft thickness: 2m Soft soils: $E = 137$MPa; $V_s = 180$m/sec, $\gamma = 14$kN/m^3; $\gamma_{sat} = 16$kN/m^3; $\xi = 0.05$; $v = 0.3$; Gravel: $E = 1760$MPa; $V_s = 560$m/sec, $\gamma = 20$kN/m^3; $\gamma_{sat} = 22$kN/m^3; $\xi = 0.05$; $v = 0.25$;	Pile and raft: Linearly elasticity Soft soils: Modified Cam Clay Model $c = 20$kN/m^2; $\phi = 35°$; OCR = 1.0; $\lambda = 0.087$; $\Gamma = 3.8$; $\kappa = 0.0073$; $e_0 = 1.042$; M = 1.42; k_0(lateral earth pressure coefficient) = 0.38 Gravel: Mohr Coulomb model $c = 0$kPa; $\phi = 36°$; $k_0 = 0.41$

It was found that the solutions from 3D Midas and EQPR analyses are agreeable for raft foundation. However for the piles, the deflections and internal stresses obtained from different solutions have deviations. For example, the deflections, bending moments and shear forces along the centre pile at the design earthquake of one scenario are shown in Figure 16. It indicates that the piles need to be evaluated more carefully when subjected to horizontal earthquake.

With the concern of rigid raft motions under horizontal earthquakes, the PBSD assessment of such foundation was then operated with EQWEAP analysis on single piles. The PBEE approach was adopted. Note that PGA_T at MCE is 0.32g following the seismic design code. Figure 17 depicts the assessments for the maximum pile displacements and maximum bending moments versus the annual probability of exceedance with a set of available seismic records calibrated to the target PGAs. With the possible moment capacities calculated, the factors of safety against seismic failure, FS can be defined as the ratio of moment capacity, M_{cap} and the maximum moment

calculated, M_{max}, *i.e.*, M_{cap}/M_{max}. At different seismic levels in this case, they were reported as 2.7, 4.2 and 2.0 (Lee, 2016). Note that at MCE, the piles are examined by M_y.

5.3 Combined Pile Groups with Raft

The assessment for PBSD of a piled raft foundation under a 70-meter height statue located at the Da-An coast park in Taichung, Taiwan is presented. The foundation was arranged by twenty grouped pile foundations (2×2 piles with pile diameter of 0.7m and pile length of 28m) oriented in a double-ring shape (see Figure 18). The structural dimensions and the material properties/parameters used in the modelling are summarized in Table 6. This foundation is denoted as a combined pile groups connecting by raft.

Again, 3D Midas program was first conducted to solve the foundation responses under a specific earthquake. Mohr Coulomb model herein was used to simulate the site soils of interlayered sand and gravel, the piles are again assumed linearly elastic. Solutions obtained from EQWEAP analysis on single piles were compared with the FE results. Material nonlinearities were again monitored in

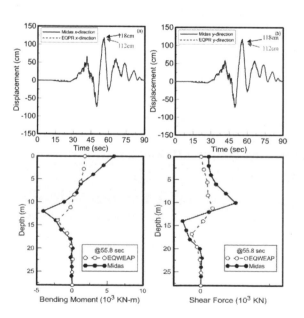

Fig. 16 Comparisons of the solutions from Midas and EQPR analyses

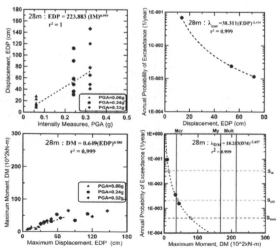

Fig. 17 Results of the PBEE analysis for raft foundation on piles

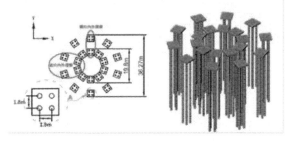

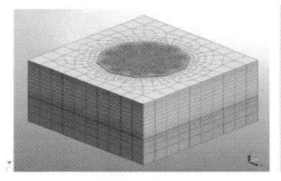

Fig. 18 Numerical model of combined pile groups with raft

Table 6 Structural geometry and material properties of pile groups and soils

Pile Groups Connected by Raft		
Pile fdt	Dimensions	Pile length: 28m; Pile diameter: 0.7m; S/D=2.5; Pile cap length & width: 3.9m; Pile cap thickness: 0.6m
	Material properties	$E = 3\times10^4$ MPa; $v = 0.1$; $\gamma = 24$kN/m^3; $\xi = 0.02$
Sandy gravel	Geometries	Length and width: 100m, Thickness: 50m
	properties/ parameters	Midas analysis: $E = 97$ MPa; $v = 0.3$; $\gamma = 19$ kN/m^3; $\gamma_{sat} = 21$ kN/m^3; $c = 0$ kPa; $\phi = 38°$, $\xi = 0.05$
		EQWEAP analysis: Same as above; SPT-N = 30$^+$

the EQWEAP analysis. Five seismic records from the stations near the site were used to calibrate the scenarios. For example, the EW acceleration time-history recorded in 1999 Chi-Chi earthquake at TCU064 station is shown in Figure 19.

PGA calibrating method was adopted for the artificial earthquakes. Neglecting the loads from the superstructure, Figure 20 shows the corresponding displacement-time histories of the piles at the design earthquake of the site (PGAT=0.32g). It can be found that the solutions obtained from both analyses are in good agreement. The deflections, bending moments and shears along the piles in one of the scenario are plotted in Figure 21 for both

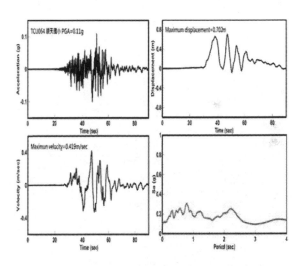

Fig. 19 Seismic response time-history and acceleration spectrum Sa at design earthquake

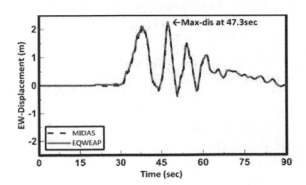

Fig. 20 Comparison of the displacement time history from Midas and EQWEAP analyses

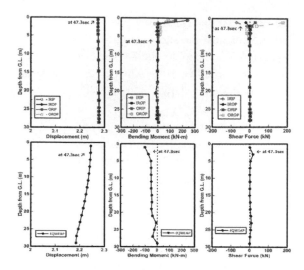

Fig. 21 Deflections, moments and shears along the pile from Midas and EQWEAP analyses

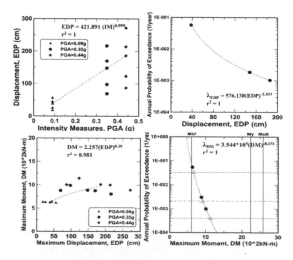

Fig. 22 Results of the PBEE analysis for combined pile groups with raft

analyses, it can be found that the details of the solutions need further attentions (Hong, 2016).

Figure 22 shows the PBSD assessment following the PBEE procedures using EQWEAP analysis. The assessment of the maximum pile displacements and maximum bending moments versus the annual probability of exceedance was conducted with a set of available seismic records calibrated to the target PGAs (PGAT at MCE=0.44g). With the possible

moment capacities calculated, the factors of safety against seismic failure (where FS=M_{cap}/M_{max}) at different seismic levels in this case were reported as 0.9, 2.3 and 2.0 (Hong, 2016). Notice that the slight damages of the piles were only observed at the pile head where the piles are assumed rigid connection to the raft. The piles are relatively safe at the design and maximum consideration earthquakes because the performance requirement under such circumstances is governed by the moment capacity corresponding to the ductility of the pile, i.e., My.

6. CONCLUDING REMARKS

For piled raft foundations located in seismic areas, the performance based seismic design (PBSD) of the foundations should be made in addition to ordinary design. The probabilistic approaches made with the reliability based methods (such as FOSM, FOSM and Monte Carlo Simulation), the probability based method (such as PBEE analysis), and the LRFD procedure can be used to evaluate the design via the variability of loads, soil parameters and geological conditions. Deformations and stresses of the foundation can be analyzed using pseudo static analysis and/or dynamic analysis. Generalized discussion was made in this paper, and a number of case studies were presented using approximate computer based methods which can simulate the dynamic load influences from both of the superstructure and the ground soils. Concluding remarks can be drawn as follows,

1. The knowledge of the performance functions of the structure is important in PBSD. Better controls of the performance functions in use will make the assessments more reliable.

2. Seismic load influences seems to be the most dominant design parameters compared to others such as soil parameters and profile conditions. Both intensity and time-history of the seismic record will affect the predictions.

3. If a pseudo static analysis is adopted, the influences of the superstructure and the ground soils are suggested to be monitored separately. They would result in over-conservative assessments if the ultimate forces were simultaneously assumed in countered directions.

4. If a dynamic analysis is adopted, the interactions between the super-structural load and the ground forces on the foundation can be closely captured and their interactions will be followed naturally according to the mechanism.

5. The rigid connections assumed at the interfaces between the raft and piles will over-predict the internal stresses at the pile head which could cause the concrete to crack even at moderate earthquakes. More details should be studied in defining the required structural behaviors under different seismic levels.

6. The factors of safety defined by β/β_R and M_{cap}/M_{max} seem to be rational considering their order and variations with the required performance. The use of the factor of safety in PBSD should be studied extensively on a much wider spectrum based on all possible performance functions of the foundation.

7. For CPRF subjected to horizontal earthquake, the proposed approximate solutions of the time-dependent foundation responses are agreeable with those from 3D FEM analysis. However the deflections and stresses of the piles at a specific time could have some discrepancies. The deviations should be minimized in PBSD assessments when using approximate computer based analysis.

ACKNOWLEDGEMENTS

The funding supports from Tamkang University and Ministry of Science and Technology on the 2017 International Symposium on Design and Analysis of Pled Raft Foundation are sincerely appreciated by the authors.

REFERENCES

Abderlrazaq, A., Badelow, F., Sung, H.K. and Poulos, H.G. (2011). "Foundation design of the 151 story Incheon Tower in a reclamation area.", *Geotechnical Engineering*, 42(2), 85-93.

Bolton, M., (2012), "Performance-based design in *Geotechnical Engineering*", 52nd Rankine Lecture, 21st March, Imperial College, London.

Chang, D.W., Cheng, S.H. and Wang, Y.L. (2014a). "One-dimensional wave equation analyses for pile responses subjected to seismic horizontal ground motions." *Soils and Foundations*, 54(3), 313-328.

Chang, D.W., Lee, M.R., M.Y. Hong and Y.C. Wang (2016). "A simplified modeling for seismic responses of rectangular foundation on piles subjected to horizontal earthquakes", *J. of GeoEngineering*, 11(3), 109-121.

Chang, D.W., Lin, B.S. and Cheng, S.H. (2009a). "Lateral load distributions on grouped piles from dynamic pile-to-pile interactions factors." *International Journal for Numerical and Analytical Methods in Geomechanics*, 33(2), 173-191.

Chang, D.W., Lin, Y.H., Chao, H.C., Liu, C.H. and Chu, S.C., (2014b). "Seismic Performance of Piles from EQWEAP and Monte Carlo Simulation Analyses", *Procds.*, The 6th Japan-Taiwan Joint Workshop on Geotechnical Hazards from Large Earthquake and Heavy Rainfalls, July 12-14, Kita Kyushu, Fukuoka, Japan.

Chang, D.W., Sung, S.H., Lee, S.M., Zhussupbekov, A. and Saparbek, E. (2013). "On Seismic Performance and Load Capacities for Pile Design", *Procds.*, 18ICSMGE, Paris, France, September 2-6, pp. 1455-1458.

Chang, D.W., Yang, T.Y., Cheng, S.H., Chin, C.T., Su, T.C. and Huang, F.K. (2009b), "Pile Design Practice and Seismic Performance Concerns in Taiwan", *Procds.*, IS-Tokyo 2009-International Conference on Performance-Based Design in Earthquake *Geotechnical Engineering*-from case history to practice, Tsukuba, Japan, June, pp. 1559-1566.

Chang, D.W., Yang, T.Y. and Yang, C.L. (2010), "Seismic Performance of Piles from PBEE and EQWEAP Analysis," *Geotechnical Engineering*, SEAGS & AGSSEA Journal, 41(2), pp. 79-86.

Chen, CH, Hwang, JH and Teng, TJ (2009). Guidelines for Performance Based Design of Public Constructions, Research Report 0970302, Public Construction Commission, Executive Yuan, R.O.C. (in Chinese)

Cheng, C.T. (2002). Uncertainty Analysis and Deaggregation of Seismic Hazard in Taiwan, PhD Thesis, Dept. of Earth Science and Inst. of Geophysics, National Central University, Chung-Li, Taiwan.

Clancy, P. and Randolph, M.F. (1993). "Simple design tests for piled raft foundations." *Geotechnique*, 36(2), 169-203.

De Sanctis, L., Mandolini, A., Russo, G. and Viggiani, C. (2001). Some remarks on the optimum design of piled rafts. personal communication of paper submitted for publication.

Fajfar, P. and Krawinkler, H. (2004), Performance-Based Seismic Design Concepts and Implementation, *Procds.*, International Workshop, Bled Slovenia, June 28-July 1.

Frank, R., (2007), "Basic Principles of Eurocode

7 on Geotechnical Design", 18th EYGEC, Ancona, Italy, June 17-20.

Hong, M.Y. (2016). Studies on static and seismic behaviors of piled raft foundations, Master Thesis, Department of Civil Engineering, Tamkang University, New Taipei City, Taiwan.

Honjo, Y., Kusakabe, O., Matsui, K., Kouda, M. and Pokhard, G. (2002). Foundation Design Codes and Soil Investigation in View of International Harmonization and Performance Based Design, IWS Kamakura, A.A. Balkema Publishers, 457 pp.

Horikoshi, K. and Randolph, M.F. (1996). "Estimation of overall settlement of piled rafts." *Soils and Foundations*, 39(2), 59-68.

ISO, (1998), "International Standard ISO/FDIN 2394, General Principles on Reliability for Structures, International Standardization Organization.

Katzenbach, R. and Choudhury, D. (2013). *ISSMGE Combined Pile-raft Foundation Guideline*, Technische Universitat Darmstadt, Institute and Laboratory of Geotechnics, Darmstadt, Germany.

Katzenbach, R., Choudhury, D. and Chang, D.W. (2013). "General report of TC212 deep foundations.", *Proc.*, *18th ICSMGE*, Paris, France, 2651-2658.

Kitiyodom, P. and Matsumoto, T. (2002). "A simplified analysis method for piled raft and pile group foundations with batter piles." *Int. Journal for Numerical and Analytical Methods in Geomechanics*, 26, 1349-1369.

Kitiyodom, P. and Matsumoto, T. (2003). "A simplified analysis method for piled raft in non-homogeneous soils." *Int. Journal for Numerical and Analytical Methods in Geomechanics*, 27, 85-109.

Kitiyodom, P., Matsumoto, T. and Kawaguchi, K. (2005). "A simplified analysis method for piled raft foundations subjected to ground movements induced by tunneling." *Int. Journal for Numerical and Analytical Methods in Geomechanics*, 29, 1485-1507.

Kobayashi, H., Nishio, H., Nagao, T. Watanabe, T., Horikoshi, K., Matsumoto, T. (2009). "Design and construction practices of piled raft foundations in Japan." *Proc., Int. Conf. on Deep Foundations - CPRF and Energy Piles*, 101-135.

Kokusho, T., Tsukamoto, Y. and Yoshimine, M., (2009). Performance Based Design in Earthquake *Geotechnical Engineering*, From Case History to Practice, Taylor and Francis.

Kouroussis, G., Anastasopoulos, I., Gazetas, G. and Verlinden, O. (2013). "Three-dimensional finite element modeling of dynamic pile-soil-pile interaction in time domain." *Proc., 4th ECCOMAS Thematic Conference on Computational Methods in Structural Dynamics and Earthquake Engineering*, Kos Island, Greece.

Kramer, S.L. (1996). Geotechnical Earthquake Engineering, Prentice Hall.

Kramer, S.L. (2008). Performance-based earthquake engineering: opportunities and implications for geotechnical engineering practice, Geotechnical Earthquake Engineering and Soil Dynamics IV, ASCE GSP 181.

Kunnath, S.K., Reinhorn, A.M., 1989. Inelastic Three-dimensional Response Analysis of Reinforced Concrete Building Structure (IDARC-3D) Part I – Modeling. Technical Report NCEER-89-0011. National Center for Earthquake Engineering Research. State University at New York, Buffalo.

Lee, M.J. (2016). Simplified analysis for piled raft

foundation subjected to horizontal motion of earthquake, Master Theses, Department of Civil Engineering, Tamkang University, New Taipei City, Taiwan.

Lin, Y. H. (2013). Study on reliability based performance of piles under earthquakes, Master Thesis, Department of Civil Engineering, Tamkang University, New Taipei City, Taiwan.

Midas GTS (2012). User Manual, MIDAS Co.

OpenSees (2009). OpenSees 2.4.3, download website: http://opensees.berkeley.edu/.

Paikowski, S.G. (2002). "Load and Resistant Factor Design (LRFD) for Deep Foundations", *Procds.*, International Workshop on Foundation Design Codes and Soil Investigation in view of International Harmonization and Performance Based Design, Tokyo,, pp. 59-94.

PEER (2010), Tall Building Initiative – Guidelines for Performance Based Seismic Design of Tall Buildings, Version 1.0, Report No. 2010/05.

Phoon, K.K. (2008), Reliability-Based Design in *Geotechnical Engineering*: Computations and Applications, Taylor and Francis, 526 pp.

Poulos, H.G. (2001). "Pile-raft foundation: design and applications." *Geotechnique*, 51(2), 95-113

Poulos, H.G. and Davis, E.H. (1980). *Pile Foundation Analysis and Design*, Wiley, New York.

Randolph, M.F. (1983). "Design of Piled Foundations", *Cambridge Univ. Eng. Dept.*, Res. Rep. Soils TR143.

Randolph, M.F. (1994). "Design Methods for Pile Groups and Piled Rafts", *Procds*. XIII ICSMFE, New Delhi, 5. 61-82.

Shin, H.S. (2007). Numerical Modeling of a Bridge

System and Its Application for Performance-Based Earthquake Engineering. PhD Thesis, Dept. of Civil & Environmental Engineering, University of Washington.

Unsever, Y.S., Matsumoto, T. and Özkan, M.Y. (2015). Numerical Analyses of Load Tests on Model Foundations in Dry Sand, *Computers and Geotechnics*, 63, pp. 255-266.

Viggiani, C, (2001). "Analysis and design of piled foundations", 1st Arrigo Croce Lecture, Rivista Italiana de Geot1, 47–75.

Whitman, R.V. (1984). Evaluating Calculated Risk in Geotechnical Engineering, *Journal of Geotechnical Engineering*, ASCE, 110(2), 145-188.

Yamashita, K., Tanikawa, T. and Hamada, J. (2015). "Applicability of simple method to piled raft analysis in comparison with field measurements." *Geotechnical Engineering*, 46(2), 43-53.

Testing, Construction and Monitoring

CHAPTER 12

THE COMPLEXITY OF PILING TESTS IN PROBLEMATICAL SOIL GROUND OF KAZAKHSTAN

Askar Zhussupbekov*
Abdulla Omarov
Department of Civil Engineering, Eurasian National University, Astana, Kazakhstan
**astana-geostroi@mail.ru*

Gennady Sultanov
Corporation Bazis-A, ltd, Almaty, Kazakhstan

ABSTRACT: In this article, loading tests for large diameter and deep drilling piles in Astana, Kazakhstan are introduced. Three bored piles with diameter more than 820 mm and 13.5 m depth have been executed at the construction site of New Monument (The Future of the Free Country) in Astana. Some of the requirements of the designer of piled foundations and to what extent the accessible testing methods comply with these requirements are presented. Static pile load test is used to obtain the load-settlement relation of piles. The number of static load tests in construction site is limited to 3 bored piles in construction site "The Future of the Free Country" of monument in Astana, Kazakhstan.

1. INTRODUCTION

The monument called "The Future of the Free Country" is shown in Figure 1. The project was

Fig. 1 New monument "The Future of the Free Country" in Astana, Kazakhstan

performed in a simple, concise and dynamic format. The total height of the monument is 70 m, symbolizing 25 years of independence of the Republic of Kazakhstan, is located on the square by the cardinal points.

The target of the pile load tests was to obtain bearing capacity of piles on problematical soils ground of construction.

To construct of Megaprojects safety and qualitatively, deep piling foundations with large diameter was selected. Therefore piling foundations must by to design correctly.

Geotechnical condition of construction site and details of piles are shown in Figure 2 and Table 1. A borehole was drilled at the location of the test pile in the case of the site monument is called "The Future of the Free Country" (Zhussupbekov et al., 2016 and Omarov et al., 2016).

Table 1 Physical - mechanical properties of soil ground

Soil#	Soil name	Characteristic of ground						
		ρ, g/sm^3	C, kPa	φ	E, MPa	e	I_L max	S_t
Soil 1	Loam aQ II-IV	1,97	21	31	13	0,60	0,71	0.60
Soil 2	Medium coarse sand aQ II-IV;	1,62	2	35	17,0	-	-	-
Soil 3	Coars sand aQ II-IV	2,00	-	-	23,0	-	-	-
Soil 4	Loam e(C1)	2,00	35	33	16,0	0,66	0,04	0.83

2. THE PROCEDURE OF PILE TESTSING

Static Loading Test (SLT) is one of the more reliable field tests in analyzing pile bearing capacity. SLT should be carried out for driving piles after the "rest" and for bored piles after achievements of the concrete strength, by more than 80%. According to requirements of Kazakhstan Standard - SNiP RK 5.01-03-2002 and SNIP RK 5.01-01-2002, (2002) – ultimate value of settlement of the tested pile is determined as and depending on category of construction is equal to 16 or 24 mm. The last argument shows conditional character of SLT method.

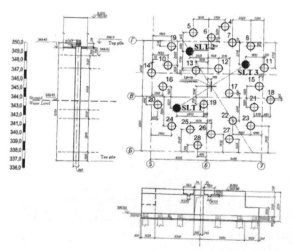

Fig. 2 Testing location in construction site of "The Future of the Free Country" monument

Field test was performed in 21 days after bored pile had been prepared. Static Loading Test was carried out in accordance with requirements of GOST 5686-94 "Soils. Field testing methods by piles".

A device for loading piles must provide coaxial and central transfer loads to the pile, the possibility of transferring loads to feet, the constancy of pressure at each loading step. The distance from the axis, the full-scale pile test to anchor the pile must be at least 3d, but not less than one and a half meters. Instruments for measuring deformation (displacement) of piles (deflectometer) should ensure the measurement accuracy of 0.1 mm. The number of devices installed symmetrically at equal (no more than two meters) distance from the pile under test must be at least 2 units. During use of the deflectometer is used a steel wire of 0.3 mm diameter. Before beginning the test wire must be pre-stretched two days with load of at least four kilograms. During the test, the load on the wire should not be more than one and a half kilograms. Range measurement gauges and division value used to determine the load on the pile during the tests, depending on the chosen maximum load on the pile is provided for testing the program, with a margin of at least 20 percent. The loading of test piles produce uniformly without shocks with load a step, which value is established by the test program, but is taken no more than 1/10 of the programmed maximum load on the pile. At the lower ends f the full-scale burial piles in coarse soils, gravelly and dense sands and clay soils of hard consistency allowed the first three stages of the load is taken equal to 1/5 of the maximum load specified in the program. On each foot loading full-scale pile remove reports from all devices for measuring deformation as follows: zero report - before loading the pile, the first report immediately after application of the load, the field of this series of four reports at intervals of thirty minutes and then every hour until the conditional deformation stabilization.

For criterion conditional deformation stabilization tests of full-scale pile takes speed sediment piles on a given loading level not exceeding 0.1 mm in the last 60 minutes of observation, if at the lower end of the pile lie sandy soil or clay soils from hard consistency to low-plastic consistency, as if under the lower end of the pile lie clay soils from high-plastic to fluid consistency, then two o'clock observation. Test load full-scale pile should be brought to the point where the total sediment pile is not less than forty mm. At the lower ends of the full-scale burial piles in coarse dense sand and clay soils of hard consistency load must be reduced to the value provided by the test program, but not less than one and a half the value of pile carrying capacity determined by calculation or calculated resistance of the pile on the material.

Unloading piles produce stepwise after reaching maximum load equal to twice (in one step) values of the steps of loading each stage delayed at least 15 minutes. Reports for measuring deformation are removed immediately after each stage of discharge and within fifteen minutes of observation. After complete discharge (zero) observations of elastic displacement piles should be done within 30 minutes at the sandy soils lying below the lower end of the pile, and sixty minutes with clay soils. Results of soil test with pile is made in the form of plots of "load - settlement" and strain measurement in time on the steps of loading and unloading (Zhussupbekov and Omarov, 2016 and Zhussupbekov et al., 2016).

2.1 Top down Load Test

Experienced bored piles are with a length of 13.5 m, diameter 820 mm. Static load test carried out in accordance with GOST 5686-94, (1994). Load test on pile amounted to 1477 kN. Tests carried out after reaching the strength of the concrete piles more than 80%.

Layout and design considerations of the bored piles are presented in Figure 3. The load test set up and the platform pile layout are shown in Figure 3.

The results are presented in Figure 4. Bearing capacity F_d on result of field static load test is determined by formulation (1):

$$F_d = \gamma_c \frac{F_{u.n}}{\gamma_g} \qquad (1)$$

where,

γ_c – coefficient of working condition, which received during the load activity equal $\gamma_c = 1$;

$F_{u.n}$ – guideline value of pile limited resistance;

γ_g – safety factor on ground, which equal 1.2;

Fig. 3 Static load tests in site of "The Future of the Free Country" monument

As a result of static load test, bearing capacity of bored pile is 1477 kN corresponding to SLT-1 2.5 mm settlement, SLT - 2 and SLT - 3 (See Figure 4);

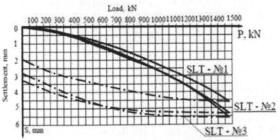

Fig. 4 Results of vertical top down load test from SLT -1 to SLT -3

Allowable bearing capacity of the piles with an

allowance for safety factor (FS = 1.2) equal to 1231 kN.

2.2 Testing Problematic Soils with Static Tensile Load

Static tensile load test do not apply concrete and composite piles, prestressed reinforced concrete piles without transverse reinforcement bored piles with enlarged base and screw piles. It is allowed to use the piles with the help of which the soil test was tested with static top down load. The depth of the pile subsidence during test conducted for the purpose of determination of the negative friction in subsiding soils, apply equal to the distance from the surface of the soil to the depth where the soil additive from its own weight during soaking equal the maximum permissible draft for the planned building or structure. For the criterion of conditional stabilization deformation take the exit velocity of the pile from soil on each stage of the application tensile load must be no more than 0.1 mm in the last 2 hours of observation or pile foundations of buildings and structures (except bridges), and pile foundations for bridge piers - no more than 0.1 mm in the last hour of observation. Load at the control pile test with tensile load during construction should not exceed the design tensile load on pile indicated in calculation of the pile foundation. One pile number №3* tested static, stepwise increasing pulling loads; in steps of 52.75 ÷ 105.5 kN (the first three stages on 105.5 kN and further by 52.75 kN). Maximum load was increased to 686 kN, and the piles of settlement soil was 2.98 mm. The load test set up and the platform pile layout are shown in Figure 5. Result of vertical tensile load test shown in Figure 6 (Zhussupbekov et al., 2015 and Zhussupbekov and Omarov, 2016).

2.3 Results of the Pile Tests Top down and Tensile load tests

The maximum load applied on the pile was equal to 1477 kN and the corresponding settlement of the pile was 4.62, 5.53 and 5.59 mm (See Figure 7).

Fig. 5 Vertical tensile load test in construction site of "The Future of the Free Country" monument

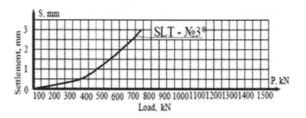

Fig. 6 Results of vertical tensile load test SLT -3

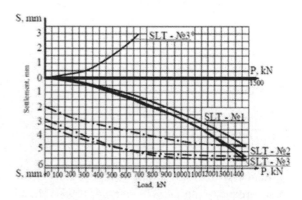

SLT-3* - Static load test (Vertical tensile load test)
SLT-1,2,3 – Static load tests (Top down)

Fig. 7 Results of static load testing.

3. Vibration measurements at Monument in Astana for the determination of the natural frequencies and installation supervising

MAURER SE performed vibration measurements on the Monument Astana from the 7th to 11th November 2016. The natural frequencies are determined according to the measured accelerations.

3.1 Vibration Measurements for the Determination of the Dynamic Properties of the Structure

While there is a safe side when estimating the structural behavior at static loading conditions, an accurate design is difficult at dynamic loading conditions because of the scattering of material properties, the inaccuracies in the foundation and soil conditions and the dispersion of the applied loads. Therefore, the dynamic properties and the structural behavior can only be completely determined by measurements after completion of the construction.

3.1.1 Ambient vibration measurements

Vibration subjected on the building structure the mechanical effects that generate a change its state. The stress of the structure is directly related to the deformations; it can be expressed through the vibration parameters. In this case, peak stress values are associated with peak velocities. Based on the results of vibration measurements is possible to determine the mechanical stress and compare it with the acceptable values for the structural element depending on the type and duration of the dynamic load effect, the properties of the building material and the type of structure.

The state of the structure depends on the peak stresses and also the accumulated fatigue changes of the material that cannot be determined from the results of vibration measurements. Usually fatigue effects are ignored if the dynamic stress is less than 10% of the acceptable static stress. However, in some cases, it may be necessary to measure mechanical stresses to assess the effect of dynamic loads (vibration).

3.1.2 Influence of vibration to the soil ground under the building

Vibration changes the soil properties and the state of the structures of the buildings. One of them is local soil compaction, which can lead to structural damage due to relative settlement of the foundation. If the vibration is a long-term, so the soil compaction can occur at a long distance from the vibration source.

Even more dangerous is the soil liquefaction which is loss of bearing capacity of the soil under the influence of vibration. This is important for the loose saturated soils.

These phenomena are indirect effects of vibration on the structure of the building, which cannot be determined from the results of measurements of structural vibrations. Therefore, to carry out a comprehensive assessment of the impact of vibration, it is recommended to involve geotechnical specialists, especially in cases where buildings are erected on the soft soils.

The geological soil structure affects to the vibration frequency component that transmitted from the source. In addition, the values of natural frequencies of the building structures depend on the dynamic soil-foundation interaction. In general, the higher a rigidity of the foundation and the greater a soil density, the higher the values of the natural frequencies of the soil-foundation-building.

3.2 Description of the Ambient Vibration Measurements

The basic assumption for the determination of modal parameters on the basis of ambient vibrations is that the ambient energy input can be idealized as white noise in the relevant frequency range. This means that all mode shapes within this frequency range are excited with a constant amplitude and phase. However, when ambient vibration measurements are carried out on a construction site, harmonic excitations by non-interrupted construction activities can be inside the signal. In this case the excitation is not perfect white noise.

The object of the ambient vibration measurements at the tower is to determine the natural frequencies of the structure. Based on the evaluated natural frequencies the pendulum damping system can be adjusted/designed if necessary.

An ambient vibration measurement is very useful for the determination of natural frequencies, mode shapes and damping, because

- the procedure is simple and not time-consuming,
- an artificial excitation does not need to be applied.

Measurement equipment:

- 1x Two axial Force Balance Accelerometer BMC, type ACS1002-USB (measurement range: ±1m/s²)
- 1x data logger Software Dasylab 2013 on Notebook

The ambient vibrations of the bridge were measured several times for 15 minutes with a sampling rate of 200 Hz. The data were post-processed with the software DIAdem (See Figure 8).

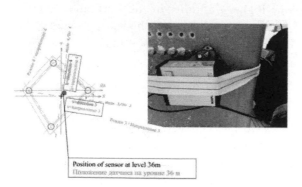

Fig. 8 Location of the accelerometers

3.2.1 Results of the ambient vibration measurements

Figure 9 shows the averaged results of the ambient vibration measurement after FFT analysis of the x- and y- sensor signals. The following natural frequencies are found in the relevant range:

f1 = 0,70 Hz;
f2 = 0,82 Hz;
f3 = 2,39 Hz;
f4 = 2,63 Hz.

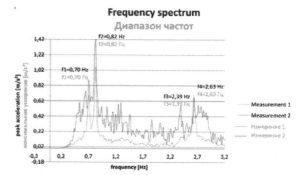

Fig. 9 Frequency spectrum

3.2.2 Interpretation of the results

As the modal mass of the structure was not finalized during the measurement (structure stiffness could be affected by the temporary outside elevators present on site, the tower was not completely achieved), the measured natural frequency are not the final ones. Prof. Capsoni did a rough extrapolation to estimate the final frequency taking into account these elements:

$f1_{final,est}$: 0,56 Hz;
$f2_{final,est}$: 0,64 Hz;
$f3_{final,est}$: 2,01 Hz;
$f4_{final,est}$: 2,24 Hz.

Please note, that this results are only theoretically values and must be verified by a measurement (Peeters, 2000).

4. Damper adjustment

The delivered dampers have the possibility of a frequency- and damping refinement. As far as the site manager informed us, that the accessibility of the damper is later nearly impossible, we agreed to tune the dampers already now as precise as possible at this stage. Eventually, the dampers were adjusted as follows (see Table 2):

Table 2 TMD 1 – final settings

	Direction 1	Direction 2
No of tuning springs	0	18
Frequency [Hz]	0.57	0.63
Damping within SLS range [kNs/m]	1,26	

The damping adjustment shims were set to nominal configuration. (One shim per friction plate)

Fig. 10 TMD 1 – final settings

Measurements were carried out to determine the natural frequencies of monument Astana. Since the structure was not finished at the moment of the measurement, the measurement results present the basis for the calculation for the real frequencies in the finished condition of the structure when the final mass is realized.

The preliminary measured frequencies of mode 3 and 4 are a little bit higher than the expected ones. Consequently they are out of the tuning range from TMD 2 up to now. We suggest to perform a verification measurement as soon as the structure is finalized.

Table 3 TMD 2 – final settings

	Direction 3	Direction 4
No of tuning springs	11	28
Frequency [Hz]	1,92	2,00
Damping within SLS range [kNs/m]	2,87	

Fig. 11 TMD 2 – final settings

The wind speed is possible once in five years -31 m/sec. Once in ten years - 33 m/sec, once in a hundred years - about 40 m/sec. The average annual wind speed is 5.2 m/ sec. The number of days with wind in the year is 280-300.

5 CONCLUSIONS

In construction site monument "The Future of the Free Country" Station the static loading tests of piles No. 1, 2 and 3 were conducted.

Test bored pile diameter 820 mm was constructed up to 348,56 ÷ 348,68 m level, with a depth of 13.5 m.

The vertical static loading (top down) test was successfully employed to proof load on the pile up to 1477 kN, with a maximum displacement of 4.62, 5.53 and 5.59 mm and vertical static loading (vertical pulling load).

Allowable bearing capacity of the piles with an allowance for safety factor (FS = 1.2) equal to 1253 kN and vertical pulling load test 572 kN.

These investigations are important for

understanding of soil-structure interaction especially of behavior of boring piles with 820 mm diameter on soil ground conditions of "The Future of the Free Country" in Astana.

Measurements were carried out to determine the natural frequencies of monument Astana. Since the structure was not finished at the moment of the measurement, the measurement results present the basis for the calculation for the real frequencies in the finished condition of the structure when the final mass is realized.

The preliminary measured frequencies of mode 3 and 4 are a little bit higher than the expected ones. Consequently they are out of the tuning range from TMD 2 up to now. We suggest to perform a verification measurement as soon as the structure is finalized.

During our stay on site, the stiff connection from structure to TMD-top plate was not performed. Since this is a very important precondition for the proper function of the TMDs, the stiff connection has to be implemented in self-responsibility by company Bazis-A, Ltd.

REFERENCES

Zhussupbekov, A., Lukpanov, R.E. and Omarov, A.R. (2016). "Experience in Applying Pile Static Testing Methods at the Expo 2017 Construction Site". *Journal of Soil Mechanics and Foundation Engineering*. Vol: 53, Issue 4, pp 251-256.

Omarov, A.R., Zhussupbekov, A.Z., Tulegulov, A.D., Zhukenova, G.A. and Tanyrbergenova, G.K. (2016). "The analysis of the piling tests on construction site "The future of the free country"" *Proc. of the 8th Asian Young Geotechnical Engineers Conference*, Astana, pp 127-130.

SNiP RK 5.01-03-2002, (2002). Pile foundations.

SNiP RK 5.01-01-2002, (2002). Buildings and structures base.

GOST 5686-94 "Soils. Field test methods by piles"

Zhussupbekov, A. and Omarov A. (2016). "Geotechnical and construction considerations of pile foundations in problematical soils". *Proc. of the 8th Asian Young Geotechnical Engineers Conference*. Astana, pp 27-32.

Zhussupbekov, A., Lukpanov R. and Omarov A. (2016). "The Results of Dynamic (Pile Driving Analysis) and Traditional Static Piling Tests in Capital of Kazakhstan". Proc. of the 13th Baltic Sea Region Geotechnical Conference. Vilnius. pp 201-205.

Zhussupbekov, A., Syrlybaev, M.K., Lukpanov, R.E. and Omarov, A.R. (2015). "The applications of dynamic and static piling tests of Astana". *15th Asian Regional Conference on Soil Mechanics and Geotechnical Engineering*, pp 2726-2729.

Zhussupbekov, A. and Omarov, A. (2016). "Modern Advances in the Field Geotechnical Testing Investigations of Pile Foundations". *Procedia Engineering*. Vol: 165, pp 88-95.

Peeters, B. (2000). *System Identification and Damage Detection in Civil Engineering*; PhD Thesis, Katholieke Universiteit Leuven.

CHAPTER 13

BEARING CAPACITY AND DEFORMATION OF RAFT-PILE FOUNDATIONS WITH A JOINT NONLINEAR DEFORMATION OF PILES AND A GROUND UNDER CYCLIC LOADING

Ilizar T. Mirsayapov*
Irina V. Koroleva

Department of bases, foundations, dynamics of buildings and engineering geology, Kazan State University of Architecture and Engineering, Kazan, Russia
*mirsayapov1@mail.ru

ABSTRACT: Under current conditions in the construction of buildings and structures trend of increasing loads on the foundation ground and the use of weak grounds as a foundation contributed to the fact that one of the common ways to increase the load-carrying capacity and reduce sediment, is the use of plate-pile foundations. These foundations are exposed to both static and cyclic loads. The question of influence of cyclic loads on the behavior of combined plate-pile foundations is studied not enough. In connection with this carried out studies of plate-pile foundations under cyclic loading. Developed calculating method of the plate-pile foundation under cyclic loading, considering joint deformation of ground base, piles and plate grillage. Depending on the loading cycle, cyclic loading leads to a redistribution of load between the elements of plate-pile foundation, the ground base at different levels of the plate grillage and the ground massive at space between piles.

1. INTRODUCTION

The search for optimal design solutions contributes to the implementation of experimental and theoretical studies of the change in the stress-strain state of the system "raft-pile foundation - ground between piles".

In modern conditions at construction of buildings and structures, trend of increasing loads to the ground base and using as a base weak grounds contributed to the fact, that one of the common ways to increase bearing capacity and reduce settlement, using raft-pile foundations. This foundations and their ground bases together with static, exposed to cyclic loads, which in some cases are the main, determine safety using of buildings and structures. Herewith the question of cyclic loads influence to the plate-pile foundations behavior researched not enough.

In this regard were conducted experimental (Mirsayapov & Shakirov (2014)) and theoretical researches of raft-pile foundations under cyclic loading.

2. STRESS-STRAIN STATE OF THE SYSTEM "PILE – GROUND"

Sress-strain pile base condition of raft-pile foundation is very complicated. In this bases, together deform materials with a different strength and deformation properties. Deformation development of pile base under cyclic loading will take place in the conditions of ground and piles interaction in connected conditions:

a) to the free deformation of the ground is constrained by piles;

b) to the free deformation of the piles prevents the surrounding ground.

$$\sigma_p^{max}(N) = \sigma_p^{max}(N_1) + \Delta\sigma_p(N) \qquad (1)$$

$$\sigma_{gr}^{max}(N) = \sigma_{gr}^{max}(N_1) - \Delta\sigma_{gr}(N) \qquad (2)$$

$\sigma_p^{max}(N_1)$, $\sigma_{gr}^{max}(N_1)$ – maximum stress at the first loading cycle in the piles and ground respectively; $\Delta\sigma_p(N)$, $\Delta\sigma_{gr}(N)$ – additional stresses in the pile base during the process of cyclic stressing in the piles and ground respectively.

In the pile base, pile due to its grip along the side surface with surrounding ground becomes an internal communication, preventing to the free ground deformation in the space between piles under cyclic loading. Straitened vibrocreep ground deformations leads to the appearance in the pile base more balanced internal stresses. In the ground occurs tensile stresses, and in the piles - compression stresses. Under the vibrocreep deformation difference influence between the free ground and piles, straitened vibrocreep ground deformation in the space between piles represented as

$$\Delta\varepsilon_{pl}(N) = \Delta\varepsilon_{pl}^{gr}(N) - \Delta\varepsilon_{pl}^{p}(N) \qquad (3)$$

$\Delta\varepsilon_{pl}(N)$ – additional (residual) vibrocreep pile base deformations; $\varepsilon_{pl}^{gr}(N)$ – free ground vibrocreep deformation; $\varepsilon_{pl}^{p}(N)$ – free pile material vibrocreep deformation.

Then averaged additional tensile stresses in the ground accepted:

$$\Delta\sigma_{gr}(N) = \Delta\varepsilon_{pl}(N) \cdot E_0'(N) \qquad (4)$$

$E_0'(N)$ – ground deformation modulus under cyclic loading.

For piles $\Delta\varepsilon_{pl}(N)$ elastic deformation, and therefore there are compressive stresses:

$$\Delta\sigma_p(N) = \Delta\varepsilon_{pl}(N)^* E_p(N) \qquad (5)$$

$E_p(N)$ – the pile material elastic modulus.

Efforts equilibrium equations from the additional stress state symmetrical pile base has the form:

$$\Delta\sigma_p(N) \cdot A_p = \Delta\sigma_{gr}(N) \cdot A_{gr} \qquad (6)$$

A_p – the total piles cross-sectional area in the limit field of the foundation pile base; A_{gr} – foundation ground base area.

From (6) after a number of simplifications, obtained analytical expressions for determining the additional (residual) stresses:

- in the ground between the pile space

$$\Delta\sigma_{gr}(N) = \frac{\varepsilon_{pl}^{gr}(N) \cdot E_p(N) \cdot \dfrac{A_{pl} \cdot n}{A_{gr}}}{1 + \dfrac{E_p(N)}{E_{gr}(N)} \cdot \dfrac{A_{pl} \cdot n}{A_{gr}}} \qquad (7)$$

- in piles

$$\Delta\sigma_p(N) = \frac{\varepsilon_{pl}^{gr}(N) \cdot E_p(N)}{1 + \dfrac{E_p(N)}{E_{gr}(N)} \cdot \dfrac{A_{pl} \cdot n}{A_{gr}}} \qquad (8)$$

A_{pl} – one pile cross-sectional area; n – the total number of piles in the calculated base area.

3. EQUATION OF THE MECHANICAL STATE OF THE SYSTEM "RAFT GRILLAGE - PILE - GROUND"

For an analytical description non-free deformation of the system elements, adopted calculation schemes (Fig. 1) and developed ground and pile-ground system mechanical state equations, as well as the efforts equilibrium equations. The joint solution of these equations allows to obtain the required settlement and the bearing capacity values of raft-pile foundation under cyclic loading.

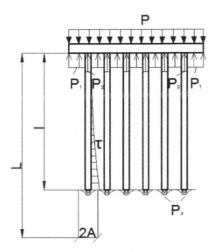

Fig. 1 Interaction design scheme of raft-pile foundation with the ground massive

To simplify the calculation, accepted design scheme which consists from the pile, surrounding it ground and the part plate grillage, attributable to one pile. The main stress-strain state components behavior of such a cell will match to behavior of the pile as part of raft-pile foundation (Fig. 2).

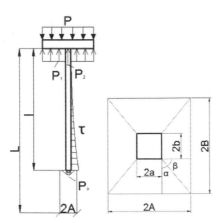

Fig. 2 Interaction design scheme of single pile with a homogeneous ground massive with the sizes 2A x 2B

The cell dimensions are 2A x 2B x L, pile dimensions are 2a x 2b x l. On the borders of a cell taken free vertical movement conditions. At the bottom of the cell accepted complete lack of movement.

For solve the task it is necessary to find the four unknown – p_1, p_2, p_3, and τ_0 (Fig. 1, 2). Using the forces equilibrium equations on the pile and the whole cell, equality movements of ground and at the heel and top piles level, obtain a system of equations:

$$
\begin{cases}
p \cdot AB = p_2(N) \cdot ab + p_1(N)(AB - ab); \\
p_2(N) \cdot ab = p_3(N) \cdot ab + K_\tau \cdot l \cdot \left(1 - 4 \cdot e^{-\alpha l}\right); \\
\dfrac{p_1(N) \cdot \beta_{gr} \cdot L}{E_{gr}(N)}\left(1 - \dfrac{l}{L}\right) + K_1 + K_2 \\
\quad = \dfrac{\omega \cdot a \cdot p_3(N) \cdot (1 - v_{gr}) \cdot k(l)}{G_{gr}(N)}; \\
\dfrac{p_1(N) \cdot \beta_{gr} \cdot L}{E_{gr}(N)} + (K_1 + K_2) \cdot e^{-\alpha l} \\
\quad = \dfrac{K_\tau \cdot l}{ab \cdot E_p} + \dfrac{K_\tau \cdot e^{-\alpha l}}{ab \cdot \alpha \cdot E_p} + \dfrac{p_3(N) \cdot l}{E_p} \\
\quad + \dfrac{\omega \cdot a \cdot p_3(N) \cdot (1 - v_{gr}) \cdot k(l)}{G_{gr}(N)} - \dfrac{K_\tau}{ab \cdot \alpha \cdot E_p}.
\end{cases}
\tag{9}
$$

Here:

$p_1(N) = \sigma_{gr1}^{max}(N) - \Delta\sigma_{gr}(N)$ – stresses occurring in the ground under the plate;

$p_2(N) = \sigma_p^{max}(N) + \Delta\sigma_p(N)$ – stresses occurring at the level of the pile top;

$p_3(N) = \sigma_{gr3}^{max}(N) - \Delta\sigma_{gr}(N)$ – stresses under the pile's heel;

$K_\tau = \dfrac{\tau_0(N) \cdot (a + b)}{\alpha}$;

$K_1 = \dfrac{k_1 \cdot \tau_0(N) \cdot (A - a)}{3G_{gr}(N)}$;

$K_2 = \dfrac{k_2 \cdot \tau_0(N) \cdot (B - b)}{3G_{gr}(N)}$;

$\tau_0(N) = \tau_0(N) \cdot e^{-\alpha z}$ – shear stresses under cyclic loading;

$\tau_0(z) = \tau_0 \cdot e^{-\alpha z}$ – shear stresses;

$\alpha = \dfrac{5}{l}$;

l – length of pile.

The solution of the system allows to find the settlement value, as well as the stresses arising in the pile trunk, in the ground under the grillage and in end of the piles under cyclic loading.

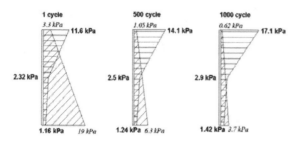

Fig. 3 Diagrams of the mobilized shear stress $\tau_0(N)$ and the limiting shear stress $\tau_z^*(N)$

Limit equilibrium zones, taking into account the rigidity of the pile material, determined by the mobilized shear stress and the shear stress limit diagrams (Fig. 3) at intersection point, which can be calculated by the formula

$$\tau_z^*(N) = \gamma \cdot z \cdot tg\varphi(N) + c(N) \tag{10}$$

$\varphi(N)$ and $c(N)$ – angle of internal friction and specific cohesion of ground under cyclic loading, respectively.

The specific cohesion of the ground and the angle of internal friction of the ground under cyclic loading are reduced (Mirsayapov & Koroleva (2016)) and they can be calculated from formulas:

$$c(N) = c \cdot m(t_1\tau_1) \cdot \lambda(t_1\tau_1) \times \sqrt{\dfrac{k(\tau_1)}{k(t)} + \dfrac{1}{1+k(\tau_1)}} \cdot c(t_1\tau) \tag{11}$$

$$\varphi(N) = 2\alpha(N) - \dfrac{\pi}{2} \tag{12}$$

Depending on the relationship

$$\tau_0(N) \le \tau_z^*(N) \tag{13}$$

There is a redistribution of forces in the ground between the lateral surface and under the lower end of the pile, as well as under the raft.

If condition (13) is not satisfied, a redistribution of forces from the ground in the zone of the lateral surface of the pile to the ground under the raft and under the lower end of the pile begins.

Experimental studies carried out at the Department of bases, foundations, dynamics of buildings and engineering geology of KSUAE (Mirsayapov & Shakirov (2014)) show that depending on the length of the pile, a different proportion of the load may occur at the level of the pile. In the case of an increase in the length of the pile, the surface of the lateral surface increases.

Stresses in the ground under the raft can be found by the formula:

$$p_1(N) = \dfrac{p \cdot AB - p_2(N) \cdot ab}{(AB - ab)} \tag{14}$$

The stresses at the top level in the pile can be expressed as follows:

$$p_2(N) = \left(\begin{array}{c} a \cdot \omega \cdot (1 - v_{gr}) \cdot k(l) \cdot (AB - ab) \\ \times E_{gr}(N) + ab \cdot \beta_1 \end{array} \right)^{-1}$$
$$\times (AB - ab)$$
$$\times \left(\begin{array}{c} P \cdot AB \cdot \beta_1 + 0{,}33\tau_0(N) \cdot E_{gr}(N) \\ \times ((A - a) \cdot k_1 + (B - b) \cdot k_2) \\ + \dfrac{\tau_0(N)}{\alpha} \cdot E_{gr}(N) \cdot l \cdot \omega (1 - v_{gr}) \\ \times k(l) \cdot \left(\dfrac{a+b}{b} \cdot e^{-\alpha l} - 4 \right) \end{array} \right) \tag{15}$$

$\beta_1 = \beta_{gr} \cdot L \cdot \left(1 - \dfrac{l}{L}\right) \cdot G_{gr}(N)$ – coefficient;

G_{gr} – ground shear modulus;

$k(l)$ – dimensionless coefficient taking into account the effect of the depth of a rigid stamp application on its length;

ω – coefficient taking into account the shape of the stamp;

v_{gr} – Poisson's ratio.

Stress under the heel of the pile can be calculated using the formula:

$$p_3(N) = \frac{p_2(N) \cdot 4ab + 4(a+b) \cdot l \cdot \dfrac{\tau_0(N)}{\alpha}}{4ab} \quad (16)$$

$$- \frac{4(a+b) \cdot l \cdot \dfrac{\tau_0(N)}{\alpha} \cdot e^{-\alpha l}}{4ab}$$

Shear stress $\tau_0(N)$ can be expressed as follows:

$$\tau_0(N) = \frac{a \cdot b (p_3(N) - p_2(N))}{(a+b) \cdot l \cdot \dfrac{1}{\alpha} \cdot (4e^{-\alpha l} - 1)} \quad (17)$$

Ground base bearing capacity in depending from the ratio (13) is estimated by conditions (Fig. 2, 4):

$$p_1(N) \le \sigma_{1u}(N) \text{ or } p_3(N) \le \sigma_{1u}(N) \quad (18)$$

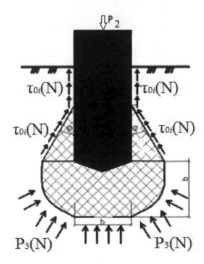

Fig. 4 Changing the stress state of "pile - ground" system under cyclic loading

The function $\sigma_{1u}(N)$ in accordance with (Mirsayapov & Koroleva (2016)) is adopted:

$$\sigma_{1u}(N) = \frac{4}{A_1} [\sigma_v(t,t_1,N) \cdot A_{sh} \cdot cos\,\alpha_1 \cdot (t,t_1,N) \quad (19)$$

$$+ \tau_v(t,t_1,N) \cdot A_{sh} \cdot sin\,\alpha_1 \cdot (t,t_1,N)]$$

$A_{sh} = b^2/(4cos\alpha_2(t, t_1, N))$ – pyramid side faces surface area (Fig.5);

$A_1 = b^2$ – cube faces surface area (Fig.5);

$\alpha_1(t, t_1, N)$ – site limit equilibrium time-varying angle;

$\alpha_2(t, t_1, N)$ – shift pad time-varying angle;

$\sigma_v(t, t_1, N) = \sigma_1 \cdot l(t, t_1, N) \cdot l`(t, t_1, N) + \sigma_2 \cdot m(t, t_1, N) \cdot m`(t, t_1, N) + \sigma_3 \cdot n(t, t_1, N) \cdot n`(t, t_1, N) + \sigma_d(t, t_1, N)$ – normal stresses;

$\sigma_d(t, t_1, N) = E \cdot \Delta\delta_d/((1+v) \cdot r)$ – dilatant stresses;

$\tau_v(t, t_1, N) = S \cdot tg\varphi_0(t, t_1, N, \tau) + c_0(t, t_1, N, \tau)$ – shear stresses at the limit equilibrium site.

The determination of the limiting value $\sigma_{1u}(N)$ is based on the calculation model described below.

The strength of the ground under cyclic triaxial compression depends on the internal friction angle change, specific cohesion and limit equilibrium plane inclination angle.

According to the results (Mirsayapov & Koroleva (2014)), failure occurs when the degree of damage by microcracks in limit equilibrium zone is critical. Ground strength reduction in time is mainly due to the cohesion forces decrease, whereas the internal friction angle varies slightly.

In the initial stage of the regime triaxial stress-strain compression heterogeneity state within the ground sample as a whole is observed. Deviator loading and long exposures under regime deviator loading is accompanied by multiple shear surfaces emergence and development and ground sample discontinuities, the position of which varies in the process of deviator increasing and in time, and therefore, the negative clay ground dilatancy (loosening) under long-term triaxial compression is localized within the limits of potential sites limit equilibrium (Mirsayapov & Koroleva (2014)). Due to the fact that the ground loosening (dilatancy) in these local areas occurs in crowded conditions (constrained by dilatancy) significant stress dilatancy in the ground around the area of loosening takes place, which is a force vertical transmission buffer zone to the pyramids area of undisturbed ground (Fig. 5). In the clay ground limit state destruction is localized in zones between consolidated pyramids and at this stage in this zone it is possible to assume that the stress-strain state of the sample is homogeneous.

Based on the proposed model (Mirsayapov & Koroleva (2011)) and the experimental results with the suggested scheme of clayey grounds inelastic deformation regime loading, according to which the strength of the Coulomb friction deviates from the limit equilibrium site and acts in the plane of purely tangential sliding physical particles. Determination of such potentially hazardous orientation areas requires consideration of the ground deformed state under regime loading.

Taking into consideration that, regardless of the heterogeneity degree of the ground elementary volume initial stress-strain state, destruction always occurs in the space of principal stresses, combining the space of principal stresses σ_1, σ_2, σ_3 and space principal strains ε_1, ε_2, ε_3 and preserving the principle of the coaxial tensor stress and strain rate (Mirsayapov & Koroleva (2011)), we assume that the Coulomb friction law relates the forces projection acting on the plane on the limit equilibrium normal to the sliding platform and to itself. Then the condition of flow for long-term and cyclic regime loading can be presented as:

$$|t| = S\,tg\varphi(t, t_1, N, \tau) + c_0(t, t_1, N, \tau) \quad (20)$$

where $S = \sigma_1 \cdot l \cdot l` + \sigma_2 \cdot m \cdot m` + \sigma_3 \cdot n \cdot n`$; $t = ((\sigma_1 \cdot l \cdot m` - \sigma_2 \cdot m \cdot l`)^2 + (\sigma_2 \cdot m \cdot n` - \sigma_3 \cdot n \cdot m`)^2 + (\sigma_3 \cdot n \cdot l` - \sigma_1 \cdot l \cdot n`)^2)^{1/2}$; $\varphi(t, t_1, N, \tau)$ – internal friction time-varying angle; $c_0(t, t_1, N, \tau)$ – time-varying specific cohesion; $l, m, n$ – direction cosines of the normal to the limit equilibrium surface; $l`, m`, n`$ – direction cosines of the normal to the sliding surface.

Spatial orientation of the site limit equilibrium is determined by the formulas (Mirsayapov & Koroleva (2011)):

$$l^2 = \frac{\overline{I_3}}{I_2 \cdot \sigma_1}; \quad m^2 = \frac{\overline{I_3}}{I_2 \cdot \sigma_2}; \quad n^2 = \frac{\overline{I_3}}{I_2 \cdot \sigma_3} \quad (21)$$

where $\overline{I_2} = \overline{\sigma_1} \cdot \overline{\sigma_2} + \overline{\sigma_2} \cdot \overline{\sigma_3} + \overline{\sigma_3} \cdot \overline{\sigma_1}$ and $\overline{I_3} = \overline{\sigma_1} + \overline{\sigma_2} + \overline{\sigma_3}$ – second and third invariants of modified main stresses tensors $\overline{\sigma_i} = \sigma_i + H(i = 1, 2, 3)$; $H = c/ctg\varphi$ – uniform compression defined by Mohr-Coulomb's hypothesis; φ – internal friction time-varying angle; c – time-varying specific cohesion under the regime long-term and cyclic loading.

Expressions for the normal cosines direction to the sliding pads are presented as (Mirsayapov & Koroleva (2011)):

$$\left.\begin{aligned}
\left(l`\right)^2 &= \frac{1}{3} \cdot \frac{3 \cdot d\varepsilon_2 \cdot d\varepsilon_3 - I_2 + \sqrt{I_2^2 - 3 \cdot I_1 \cdot I_3}}{(d\varepsilon_1 - d\varepsilon_2) \cdot (d\varepsilon_1 - d\varepsilon_3)}; \\
\left(m`\right)^2 &= \frac{1}{3} \cdot \frac{3 \cdot d\varepsilon_1 \cdot d\varepsilon_3 - I_2 + \sqrt{I_2^2 - 3 \cdot I_1 \cdot I_3}}{(d\varepsilon_2 - d\varepsilon_1) \cdot (d\varepsilon_2 - d\varepsilon_3)}; \\
\left(n`\right)^2 &= \frac{1}{3} \cdot \frac{3 \cdot d\varepsilon_1 \cdot d\varepsilon_2 - I_2 + \sqrt{I_2^2 - 3 \cdot I_1 \cdot I_3}}{(d\varepsilon_3 - d\varepsilon_1) \cdot (d\varepsilon_3 - d\varepsilon_2)},
\end{aligned}\right\} \quad (22)$$

where $d\varepsilon_1, d\varepsilon_2, d\varepsilon_3$ – main deformations increments under the regime long-term and cyclic loading; $I_1 = d\varepsilon_1 + d\varepsilon_2 + d\varepsilon_3$; $I_2 = d\varepsilon_1 \cdot d\varepsilon_2 + d\varepsilon_2 \cdot d\varepsilon_3 + d\varepsilon_1 \cdot d\varepsilon_3$; $I_3 = d\varepsilon_1 \cdot d\varepsilon_2 \cdot d\varepsilon_3$ – first, second and third deformation increments invariants.

As mentioned above, the potential sites limit state orientation in general case is not constant, but changes during inelastic ground deformation under regime long-term and cyclic loading.

Based on the above described model and experimental results (Fig. 5) the condition of strength under triaxial compression regime presented as:

$$4 \cdot \begin{bmatrix} \sigma_V(t,t_1,N) \cdot A_{sh} \cdot \cos\alpha_1(t,t_1,N) \\ + \tau_V(t,t_1,N) \cdot A_{sh} \cdot \sin\alpha_1(t,t_1,N) \end{bmatrix} \geq \sigma_1 \cdot A_1 \qquad (23)$$

The notation is shown in (19).

Based on the results of studies (Mirsayapov & Koroleva (2014)) the following scheme for the creep deformation development and long-term destruction resistance changes during the cyclic loading can be presented. Depending on the magnitude and load duration in a multiphase clay grounds two mutually offsetting effects occur - hardening due to defects healing and the thicker the particles recomposition, and the softening caused by the particles reorientation, as well as the formation and micro-cracks and macro-cracks development (Fig. 5). In cases, where softening starts to prevail over the hardening destruction and progressive creep stage occurs. At this stage of the intensive microstructure decay and the particles reorientation, while these processes do not cover the entire ground volume, but only limit equilibrium zone with low resistance value, where the development of cracks occurs.

Taking the information above into account, the equation showing the change in the specific adhesion between the ground particles is presented generally:

$$c_0(t,\tau) = K_{Ict}^M \cdot q(S) \qquad (24)$$

where $q(S)$ – function of cracks total length S; K_{Ict}^M – stress intensity factor at the crack top in the ground under the cyclic loading.

The critical crack length depends on the set of the external load T.

After some transformations and simplifications we obtain the function of ground strength reduction

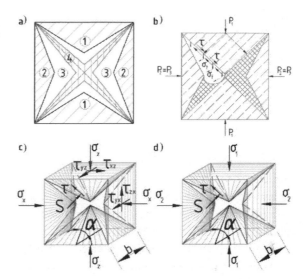

Fig. 5

a) different density local zone layout under triaxial test: 1 – vertical consolidated pyramids; 2 – fide sides consolidated pyramids; 3 – uniformed deflected state zone; 4 – dilatancy zone;

b) scheme of local zone deflected state between consolidated pyramids;

c) deflected state of volume element in spaces X, Y, Z at random moment of time under preultimate condition (stresses $\sigma_y, \tau_{xy}, \tau_{zy}$ are not shown);

d) deflected state of volume element in space X, Y, Z under ultimate condition (stresses σ_3 are not shown).

(specific cohesion) under the regime loading:

$$\eta(t,\tau_I) = m(t,\tau_I) \cdot \lambda(t,\tau_I) \qquad (25)$$
$$\times \sqrt{\frac{K(\tau_I)}{K(t)} \cdot \frac{1}{1 + K(\tau_I) \cdot C(t,\tau_I)}}$$

Then the specific adhesion between the particles, taking into account the factor of time is presented as:

$$C_0(t,\tau_I) = C_0(\tau_I) \cdot m(t,\tau_I) \cdot \lambda(t,\tau_I) \qquad (26)$$
$$\times \sqrt{\frac{K(\tau_I)}{K(t)} \cdot \frac{1}{1 + K(\tau_I) \cdot C(t,\tau_I)}}$$

where $C(t, \tau_1)$ – the ground creep volume rate;

$C_0(\tau_1)$ – the initial value of the ground specific adhesion under short-time loading; $m(t, \tau_1)$ – ground hardening function due to water-colloidal links recovery; $\lambda(t, \tau_1)$ – hardening function by restoring the structural relation-ships of ground based on a combination of various blocks under the regime loading.

Functions $m(t, \tau)$ and $\lambda(t, \tau)$ take into account the effects of micro and macro cracks development delay and effects of clay ground self-strengthening and self-healing due to the recovery of structural and coagulation relations in the early stages of loading (in blocks with low stress) or after transition from cyclic loading block to long-term static loading block.

Changing of ground internal friction angle is determined by the change in limit equilibrium sites orientation with long-term regime inelastic deformation in the process of cyclic loading, taking into account the combination of the various blocks of loading.

4. CONCLUSIONS

1. Joint deformation of the elements of the "raft – piles – surrounding ground massif" system, when piles prevent free deformation of the ground base of a raft, and free deformation of the piles is limited by the ground base of the raft, causes redistribution of forces between the elements of the raft-pile foundation in the process of cyclic loading.

Simultaneously with changes in the stress-strain state of the elements of the "raft – pile – ground" system and the redistribution of forces between them under cyclic loading, the mechanical characteristics of the ground change: the specific

cohesion between the particles, the angle of internal friction and the modulus of general deformations of the ground.

Under cyclic loading conditions, the mobilized shear stress $\tau_0(N)$ and the limiting shear stress $\tau_z^*(N)$ are not constant quantities and change as the number of loading cycles increases.

REFERENCES

Mirsayapov I.T., Shakirov M.I. (2014). Research of the cyclic loading effect on model combined raft-pile foundation construction. *Proc. of International Scien. Conference*, Moscow, October, pp 423-429.

Mirsayapov, I.T., Koroleva, I.V. (2011). Designed model of long nonlinear deformation of clay soil in a complex stress state, *Journal The News of KSUAE* №2(16), pp 121–128.

Mirsayapov, I.T., Koroleva, I.V. (2014). Computational model of the nonlinear deformation of clayey soils under complex stress state under regime loading. *Soil-Structure Interaction, Underground Structures and Retaining Walls: Proceedings, International Scientific Conference on Geotechnical Engineering* (Eds: Ulitsky, V.M., Lisyuk, M.B. & Shashkin, A.G.), pp 57–64, "Georeconstruction" Institute, St. Petersburg, Russia.

Mirsayapov, I.T., Koroleva, I.V. (2016). Strength and Deformability of Clay Soil Under Different Triaxial Load Regimes that Consider Crack Formation, *Journal Soil Mechanics and Foundation Engineering*, Vol: 53, No.1, pp 5–11.

CHAPTER 14

EXPERIMENTAL AND NUMERICAL STUDY ON PERFORMANCE OF PILED RAFT MODELS

Anh-Tuan Vu*

Geotechnical Engineering Laboratory, Le Quy Don Technical University, Hanoi, Vietnam
*vuanhtuan@mta.edu.vn

Tatsunori Matsumoto

Geotechnical Engineering Laboratory, Kanazawa University, Kanazawa, Japan

ABSTRACT: This article presents the outline of model load tests including vertical and horizontal load tests on pile foundation models in a dry sand ground at 1g field. The pile foundation models contain three piles or six piles, with or without batter piles. The performance of the foundations is investigated in different conditions of piled raft or pile group. Triaxial tests of the sand are conducted to obtain the behaviour of the sand. Finite-element simulations of the triaxial tests are carried out prior to the numerical analyses of the experiments to select an appropriate soil model and to estimate the soil parameters. After that, the numerical simulations of the experiments are conducted, and the analytical results are presented in comparisons with the experimental results. It is derived from this particular study that the piled rafts have advantages over the pile groups, and that the performance of the foundations are improved by inclusion of batter piles.

1. INTRODUCTION

Piled raft foundations have been widely recognized as one of the most economical foundation systems and applied for supporting heavy buildings (e.g. Poulos and Davids, 2005; Poulos et al., 2011; Yamashita et al., 2011). Experimental studies as well as numerical analyses on piled raft foundations have been carried out (e.g. Horikoshi and Randolph, 1998, 1999; Kitiyodom and Matsumoto, 2002; Matsumoto et al., 2004; Reul, 2004; Sawada and Takemura, 2014; Jeong and Cho, 2014; Unsever et al., 2014, 2015; Hamada et al., 2015; Vu et al., 2014, 2016).

However, in many countries, the traditional concept of pile groups is still adopted predominantly even though pile foundations usually work as piled raft foundations in reality. This situation may be attributed to lack of comprehensive knowledge about the performance of piled rafts, especially piled rafts with batter piles, subjected to horizontal loading as well as vertical loading.

In the present paper, the performance of piled raft foundations with and without batter piles is investigated through series of model load tests including vertical and horizontal load tests. Similar load tests are conducted also on the foundations with pile group condition where the raft base is not in contact with the ground surface for comparisons.

Numerical analyses of the experiments using a finite-element method (FEM) software, PLAXIS 3D, are carried out to confirm the experimental results and to obtain deeper insight into the performance of the foundations.

Outline of the experiments is described first, then the results of the experiments and numerical analyses are presented together with discussions in detail.

2. EXPERIMENT DESCRIPTION

2.1 Model ground

Dry silica sand having a relative density, D_r, of about 82% ($\rho_d = 1.533$ t/m³) is used for the model ground. Table 1 shows the physical properties of the sand. The model ground is prepared in a soil box having dimensions of 800 mm in length, 500 mm in width and 530 mm in depth. To control the density of the model ground, the model ground is prepared by 11 layers (10 layers of 50 mm and 1 layer of 30 mm). In each layer, the sand is poured and compacted by tapping so that the target relative density of 82% is attained.

The sequence of the preparation of the model ground and the model foundation is summarised as follows:

1) Place five soil layers of 50 mm (total height is 250 mm) one by one and compact until an intended relative density of 82% is attained.

2) Fix temporarily the model foundation to the planned position by the help of steel bars and clamps.

3) Place and compact five more soil layers of 50 mm and one more soil layer of 30 mm until the total height of the model ground of 530 mm is obtained.

Table 1 Physical properties of the sand for model ground

Property	Value
Density of soil particle, ρ_s (t/m³)	2.668
Maximum dry density, ρ_{dmax} (t/m³)	1.604
Minimum dry density, ρ_{dmin} (t/m³)	1.269
Maximum void ratio, e_{max}	1.103
Minimum void ratio, e_{min}	0.663
Maximum grain size, d_{max} (mm)	0.5

2.2 Model foundations

Fig. 1 shows the foundation models which are used in the experiments. The foundation models consist of three piles or six piles (with or without batter piles). They are pile groups (3PG, 3BPG, 6PG and 6BPG) if the raft base is not in contact with the ground surface, while they are piled rafts (3PR, 3BPR, 6PR and 6BPR) if the raft base is in contact with the ground surface. In the cases of the pile groups, the gap of 20 mm between the raft and the ground surface are arranged. Centre-to-centre pile spacing, s, is 80 mm, 4 times the pile diameter, D = 20 mm (s/D = 4). The pile heads are connected rigidly to the raft.

The rafts are made of duralumin with the dimensions as shown in Fig. 1 and can be regarded as rigid. The sand particles are adhered onto the raft base to increase the friction resistance of the raft during horizontal loading.

Close-ended aluminium pipes having a total length of 285 mm, an outer diameter of 20 mm and a wall thickness of 1.1 mm are used for the model piles. The upper 30 mm of the pile is embedded in the raft, resulting in the effective length of 255 mm. The pile shaft is instrumented with strain gauges, as shown in Fig. 2, in order to obtain axial forces, shear forces and bending moments generated in the load tests. Young's modulus of the piles, Ep, was estimated from bending tests of the piles. The geometrical and mechanical properties of the model pile are summarised in Table 2. The pile shaft is covered by the sand particles to increase the shaft resistance.

Table 2 Geometrical and mechanical properties of the model pile

Property	Value
Outer diameter, D (mm)	20
Wall thickness, t (mm)	1.1
Effective length from raft base, L (mm)	255
Young's modulus, E_p (N/mm2)	70267
Poisson's ratio, v	0.31

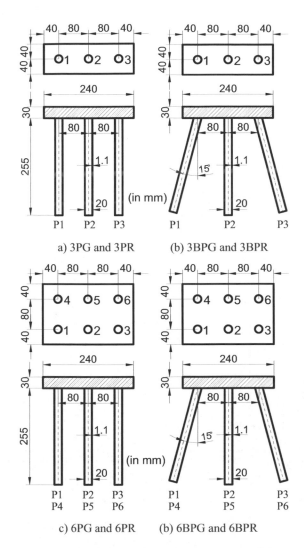

a) 3PG and 3PR   (b) 3BPG and 3BPR

c) 6PG and 6PR   (b) 6BPG and 6BPR

Fig. 1 Dimensions of the foundation models

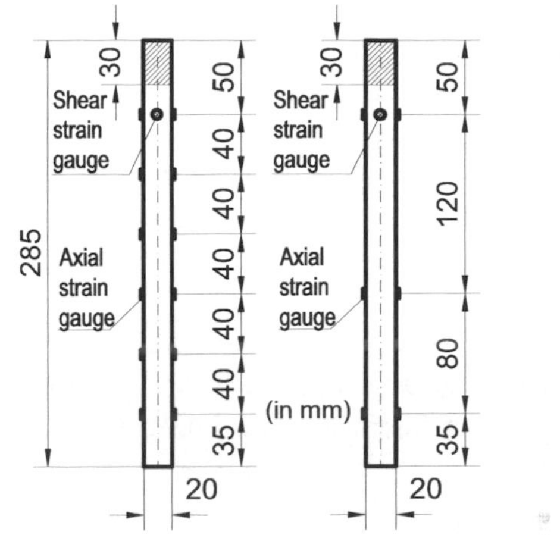

a) P1, P2 and P3   b) P4, P5 and P6

Fig. 2 Model piles

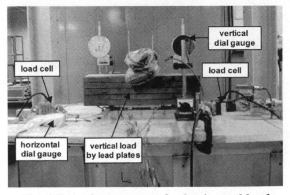

Fig. 3 Experiment set up for vertical load tests

2.3 Experiment set up and loading methods

Fig. 3 shows the experiment set up for the vertical load tests. The vertical load is applied by the help of a screw jack with a constant displacement rate of about 2 mm/min and measured by a load cell placed on the centre of the raft. The vertical displacement of the foundation is recorded by 4 dial gauges arranged at the corners of the raft.

In the horizontal load tests, vertical load is applied by placing lead plates of about 600 N and 1200

Fig. 4 Experiment set up for horizontal load tests

N on the raft in the cases of 3-pile foundations and 6-pile foundations, respectively, to simulate the dead weight of the super structure. Then cyclic static horizontal load is applied at the raft in longitudinal direction of the raft by means of winches and pulling wires (see Fig 4). The horizontal load is measured by two load cells arranged in the right (positive) direction and in the left (negative) direction. Both the horizontal and vertical displacements of the foundations are recorded by horizontal and vertical dial gauges.

3. FINITE-ELEMENT MODELLING

3.1 Triaxial tests of the sand and finite-element simulation

A series of Consolidated Drained shear tests (CD tests) of the sand under different confining pressures, p_0 = 7, 17, 27 and 50 kPa, were conducted to obtain the behaviour of the sand. To select an appropriate soil model and to estimate the soil parameters, numerical simulations of the tests are carried out. The experimental and simulation results of the triaxial tests are shown in Fig. 5 (Vu et al., 2016).

The hypoplastic model, an incrementally nonlinear constitutive model, is employed to model the sand. The early version of the hypoplastic model was introduced by Kolymbas (1985). After that, modifications and implementations of the model were proposed by Gudehus (1996), Wolffersdorff (1996), Masin (2005). The basic hypoplastic model for granular materials includes eight parameters such as critical friction angle φ_c, granular hardness hs, exponential factors n, α and β, and minimum, maximum and critical void ratios at zero pressure e_{d0}, e_{i0}, e_{c0}. A shortcoming of

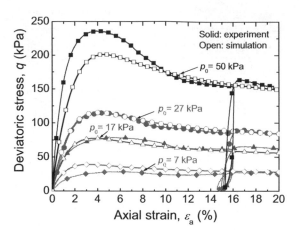

(a) Deviatoric stress, q versus axial strain, ε_a

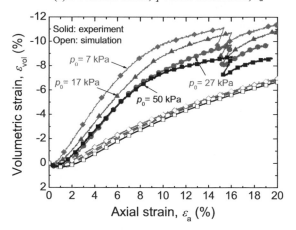

(b) Volumetric strain, ε_{vol} versus axial strain, ε_a

Fig. 5 Results of the triaxial CD tests and numerical simulations

the basic hypoplastic model is over prediction of accumulation deformation due to cyclic loading. Niemunis and Herle (1997) introduced an extended hypoplastic model to improve the performance of the basic hypoplastic model in cyclic loading. Five additional parameters were implemented in the extended hypoplastic model such as stiffness multiplier for initial and reverse loading m_R,

Table 3 Parameters of the hypoplastic soil model

φ_c (deg.)	h_s (N/mm²)	n	e_{d0}	e_{c0}	e_{i0}	α	β	m_R	m_T	R_{max}	β_r	χ	p_t (N/mm²)	e
31	2000	0.28	0.663	1.1	1.2	0.12	1.2	5	2	5×10^{-5}	0.5	1	3×10^{-3}	0.739

stiffness multiplier for neutral loading m_T, small strain stiffness limit R_{max}, parameters adjusting stiffness reduction β_r and χ. The soil parameters and the methodology for parameter determination of the hypoplastic model were presented in Herle (2000), Anaraki (2008) and Pham (2009). The parametric study on the hypoplastic model was presented in Vu (2017).

The hypoplastic model used in this research was elaborated by Wolffersdorff (1996). The soil parameters of the hypoplastic model are given in Table 3. These parameters were determined so that the calculated results match with the results of the CD tests with smaller values of p_0 ($p_0 = 7$, 17 and 27 kPa), because the effective vertical stress at the bottom of the model ground was about 7.5 kPa. Although the calculated result for the CD test with $p_0 = 50$ kPa underestimates the peak value of q, the calculated result well simulates the overall trend of the measured result. It is seen from Figure 5(b) that the calculated results underestimate the measured positive dilatancy, but well simulate the tendency of the measured dilatancy behaviours. Former researches on the hypoplastic model such as Anaraki (2008) and Pham (2009) also experienced similar results in which numerical simulation using the hypoplastic model has smaller dilatancy angle compared with the measured result (Vu et al. 2016).

3.2 Finite-element modelling of the load tests

In this research, numerical analyses of the experiments are conducted through a three-dimensional finite-element program, PLAXIS 3D.

Fig. 6 and Fig. 7 show the finite element mesh for a vertical load test and for horizontal load test, respectively. Dimesions of the model ground, the piles and the raft were presented in Section 2. Only a half of the foundation and the ground was modelled due to symmetric conditions.

The raft and the piles are considered as linear

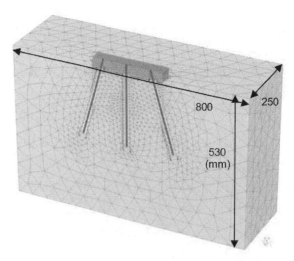

Fig. 6 Finite-element mesh for a vertical load test

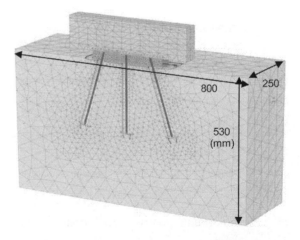

Fig. 7 Finite-element mesh for a horizontal load test

elastic materials. In order to model the pile, a hybrid model in which beam element surrounded by solid elements is used, according to Kimura and Zhang (2000). Fig. 8 shows the mechanism of the hybrid model. In the hybrid model of this paper, beam element carries a large proportion of the axial stiffness, *EA*, and bending stiffness, *EI* of the pile. The properties of the model pile, the beam pile and the solid pile are summarised in Table 4.

Table 4 Properties of the model pile, beam pile element and solid pile element

Property	Model pile	Beam pile	Solid pile
Unit weight, γ (kN/m³)	26.46	23.81	0.55
Young's modulus (kN/m²)	70.27×10^6	63.24×10^6	14.61×10^5
Poisson's ratio, v	0.31	0.31	0.31

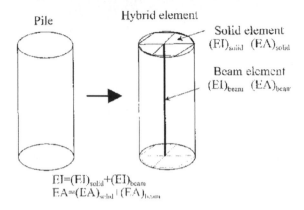

Fig. 8 Mechanism of the hybrid model (after Kimura and Zhang, 2000)

Interface elements of Mohr-Coulomb type were assigned at the raft base (in the cases of the piled rafts) and along the pile shafts. Interface cohesion was set as 0, and the interface friction angle was set at 40.2° following Unsever at al. (2015).

The analysis procedure is as follows:

Step 1: Self-weight analysis of the model ground alone.

Step 2: Setting the foundation in the ground, and self-weight analysis including the foundation.

Step 3: Analysis of loading process. In the cases of vertical load tests, incremental vertical displacement is applied to the top surface of the raft without modelling of the weight plates. In the cases of horizontal load tests, placing of the weight plates is modelled prior to the start of horizontal loading. Then, incremental horizontal displacement is applied to the raft.

4. EXPERIMENTAL AND NUMERICAL RESULTS

4.1 Vertical load tests

Fig. 9 shows measured and calculated load-settlement curves in the cases of the 3-pile foundations (3PG, 3PR, 3BPG and 3BPR). It is seen that the trends of measured load-settlement curves are simulated reasonably in FEM calculations, in which the piled rafts (3PR or 3BPR) have much higher resistance and stiffness than those of the corresponding pile groups (3PG or 3BPG), and the foundations with batter piles (3BPG or 3BPR) have higher resistance and stiffness than those of the corresponding foundations without batter piles (3PG or 3PR).

Table 5 shows comparisons between the foundations through the experimental results and the FEM results .

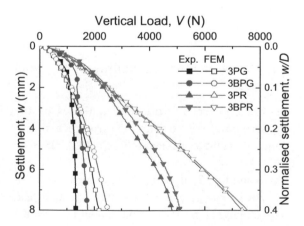

Fig. 9 Load-settlement curves of the 3-pile foundations (Exp. and FEM)

Table 5 Comparisons between the foundations in vertical loading

Vertical load	Experimental results				FEM results			
	3PG	3BPG	3PR	3BPR	3PG	3BPG	3PR	3BPR
Resistance at $w/D = 0.1$ (N)	1113	1355	2314	2505	1072	1160	2460	2520
Relative resistance at $w/D = 0.1$ (%)	100	122	208	225	100	108	229	235
Settlement at $V = 1000$ N (mm)	1.314	0.689	0.478	0.399	1.750	1.630	0.578	0.518
Relative settlement at $V = 1000$ N (%)	100	52	36	30	100	93	33	30

Fig. 10 shows the measured and calculated proportions of vertical load carried by 3 piles against normalised settlement, w/D, in the cases of 3PR and 3BPR. The proportions in the two cases are similar to each other in the measurements as well as in the calculations.

The experimental results indicate that the piles take about 85% of the load at early stage of loading, then the proportion in general decreases with the increase of w/D and finally levels off at a value of about 45% when w/D attains to 0.20. Meanwhile, in the FEM analyses, the proportion taken by the piles is about 60% at early loading stage, then gradually decreases to a stable value of about 45% when w/D reaches 0.20.

The difference in quantity between the measured results and the calculated results at the early stage of loading seems to be caused by the unintended imperfect contact between the raft and the ground surface in the experiments. As mentioned in Section 2.1 on the sequence of the model ground and the model foundation preparation, the top soil layer was compacted after fixing the model foundation temporarily. Hence the imperfect contact between the raft and the ground surface is inevitable, leading to that most of vertical load in the experiments was carried by the piles at the early loading stage (about 85%). In FEM analyses, the impecfect contact between the raft and the ground appeared in the experiments did not occur, leading to the load sharing of piles in FEM at the early loading stage is only 60%, smaller than that of the experiments. In spite of the difference in quantity, similar trends are obtained in both the measured and the calculated results, in which load

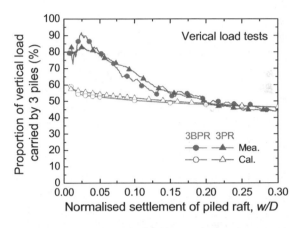

Fig. 10 Load sharing of 3 piles under vertical loading

sharing by piles is larger at the beginning and tends to decrease with increasing normalised setttlement w/D.

Fig. 11 and Fig. 12 show measured and calculated axial force distributions of each pile at various normalised settlements, $w/D= 0.01, 0.02, 0.05, 0.20$ and 0.40 in the cases of 3PG and 3BPG, respectively. The calculated results are compatible with the measured results, in which axial forces in batter piles are larger than those in the corresponding vertical piles although the differences are not considerable as those as in measured results.

Similarly, Fig. 13 and Fig. 14 show measured and calculated axial force distributions of each pile at various normalised settlements, $w/D= 0.01, 0.02, 0.05, 0.20$ and 0.40 in the cases of 3PR and 3BPR, respectively. The differences in axial forces between 3PR and 3BPR are not as obvious as

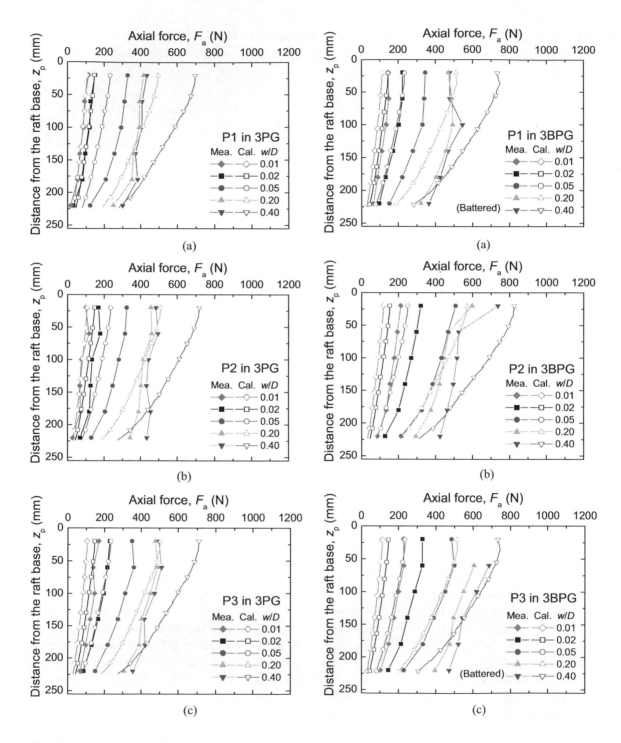

Fig. 11 Axial force distributions of piles for 3PG in VLT (Exp. and FEM)

Fig. 12 Axial force distributions of piles for 3BPG in VLT (Exp. and FEM)

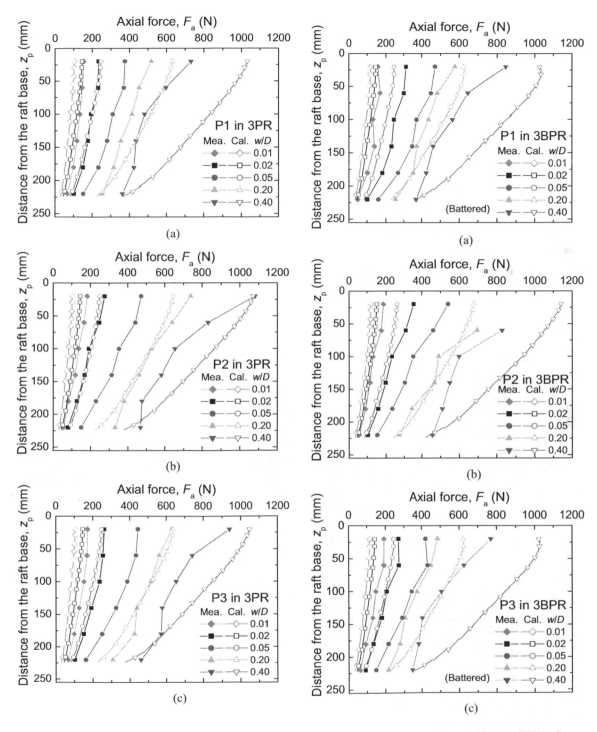

Fig. 13 Axial force distributions of piles for 3PR in VLT (Exp. and FEM)

Fig. 14 Axial force distributions of piles for 3BPR in VLT (Exp. and FEM)

those in the pile group cases (Figs.11 and 12). The axial forces in P2 (centre pile) are similar between 3PR and 3BPR. The axial forces in P1 of 3BPR are larger than those of 3PR. On the contrary, the axial forces in P3 of 3BPR are smaller than those of 3PR. It could be confirmed from comparison of the axial forces in P1 and P3 of 3PR that a small degree of eccentric loading occurred in the experiment of 3PR, leading to the above mentioned results.

It is interesting to see from both the measured and calculated results (see Fig. 11 and Fig. 13) that axial forces of the piles in 3PR are considerably larger than those in 3PG, which is mainly caused by larger pile shaft resistance of the piles in 3PR

compared with that in 3PG. It could be explained that the pressure transferred from the raft base to the ground in the case of 3PR increases the stress level in the ground around the piles, resulting in the increases of stiffness and strength of the soil, leading to the higher pile resistance of 3PR compared with that of 3PG. It can be confirmed from comparison of mean stress contours in the ground obtained in the FEM analyses of 3PG and 3PR (see Fig. 15 and Fig. 16). Obviously, the mean stress values in the ground in the case of 3PR are considerably larger than those in the case of 3PG at the same settlement.

Fig. 17 shows comparisons of vertical load-settlement curves between 6PG and 2×3PG, and between 6PR and 2×3PR through experimental results. It is seen from the curves of the pile groups that the resistance of 6PG is the same with two times of the resistance of 3PG when normalised settlement, w/D, is smaller than 0.08. After that, the resistance of 6PG is considerably larger than that of 2×3PG. As for the piled rafts, the resistance of 6PR is smaller than that of 2×3PR until w/D reaches 0.40. After that, the resistance of 6PR is notably larger than that of 2×3PR. The FEM results (Fig. 18) are qualitatively compatible with the experimental results, although softening behaviour of 2×3PR is not obtained in the FEM analysis.

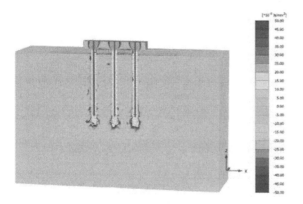

Fig. 15 Mean stress contours in the ground at
$w/D = 0.2$ from FEM analysis of 3PG (VLT)

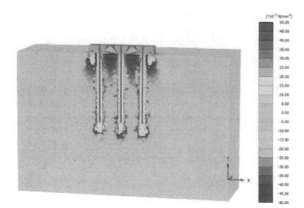

Fig. 16 Mean stress contours in the ground at
$w/D = 0.2$ from FEM analysis of 3PR (VLT)

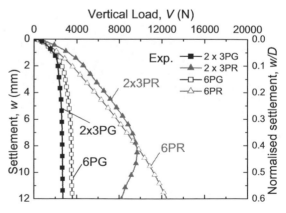

Fig. 17 Vertical load vs. settlement in the cases
of 6PG, 6PR, 2×3PG and 2×3PR
(Experimental results)

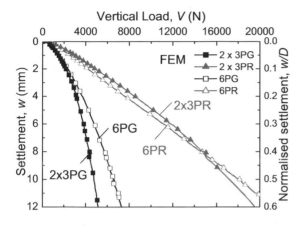

Fig. 18 Vertical load vs. settlement in the cases of 6PG, 6PR, 2×3PG and 2×3PR (FEM results)

4.2   Horizontal load tests

Fig. 19 shows the relationships of horizontal load, H, and normalised horizontal displacement, u/D, in the experiments of the 3-pile foundations. Fig. 20 shows the corresponding results by the numerical analyses. From both the experimental and numerical results, it is obvious that that the piled rafts have much higher horizontal resistances than the corresponding pile groups. It is also seen that the resistances of the foundations are effectively improved by the inclusion of batter piles in both cases of piled raft (3BPR) and pile group (3BPG).

Fig. 21 shows the measured and calculated proportions of horizontal load carried by 3 piles against normalised settlement, w/D, in the cases of 3PR and 3BPR. It is interesting to see from both measured and calculated results that the horizontal load proportion by the piles in 3BPR is larger than that in 3PR, indicating a higher efficiency of the batter piles.

Similar results are also obtained in the cases of the 6-pile foundations, in which the piled rafts have much higher horizontal resistances than the corresponding pile groups and the resistances of

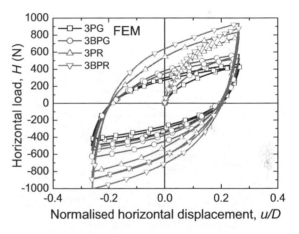

Fig. 20 Horizontal load-nor. horizontal disp. for 3-pile foundations (FEM results)

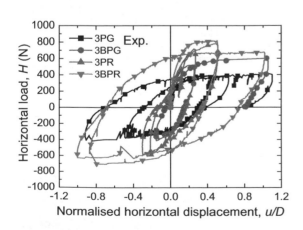

Fig 19. Horizontal load-nor. horizontal disp. for 3-pile foundations (Experimental results)

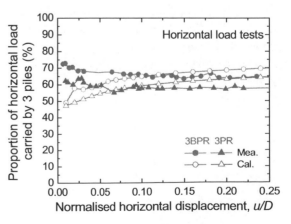

Fig. 21 Load sharing of 3 piles under horizontal loading

the foundations are enhanced by the inclusion of batter piles, as shown in Fig. 22 and Fig. 23.

It is seen from the above results that the FEM calculations simulate the experimental results very well.

Fig. 24 and Fig. 25 show the inclination of the raft vs. horizontal load during the initial loading stage for 6-pile foundations, in the experiments and calculations, respectively. The numerical results are in a good agreement with the experimental results, indicating that the piled rafts have smaller inclination than the corresponding pile groups,

and the inclination is effectively reduced by the inclusion of batter piles.

Table 6 shows comparisons between the foundations through the experimental results and the FEM results in horizontal loading.

Fig. 26 shows comparisons of horizontal load vs. normalised horizontal displacement between 6PG and 2×3PG, and between 6PR and 2×3PR at the initial loading stage according to the experimental results. Similarly, the FEM results are shown in

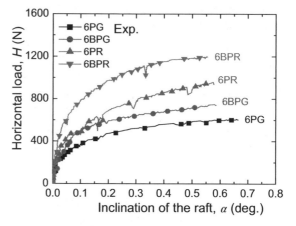

Fig. 24 Inclination of the raft vs. horizontal load during the initial loading stage for 6-pile foundations (Experimental results)

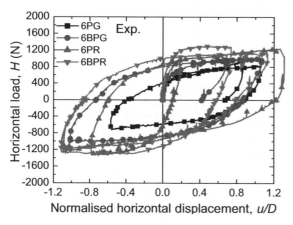

Fig. 22 Horizontal load-nor. horizontal disp. for 6-pile foundations (Experimental results)

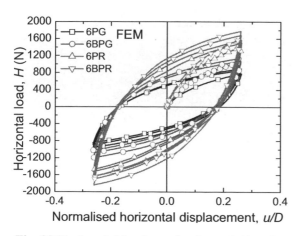

Fig. 23 Horizontal load-nor. horizontal disp. for 6-pile foundations (FEM results)

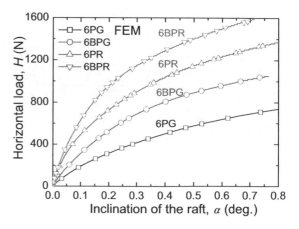

Fig. 25 Inclination of the raft vs. horizontal load during the initial loading stage for 6-pile foundations (FEM results)

Table 6 Comparisons between the foundations in horizontal loading

Horizontal load	Experimental results				FEM results			
	6PG	6BPG	6PR	6BPR	6PG	6BPG	6PR	6BPR
Resistance at $u/D = 0.1$ (N)	486	619	785	1031	465	639	856	1010
Relative resistance at $u/D = 0.1$ (%)	100	127	162	212	100	137	184	217
Displacement at $H = 400$ N (mm)	0.998	0.626	0.434	0.120	1.596	1.030	0.560	0.501
Relative disp. at $H = 400$ N (%)	100	63	43	12	100	64	35	31
Inclination at $H = 400$ N (deg.)	0.121	0.061	0.047	0.018	0.282	0.137	0.071	0.052
Relative inclin. at $H = 400$ N (%)	100	50	39	15	100	49	25	18

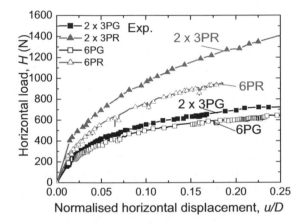

Fig. 26 Horizontal load vs. normalised horizontal disp. curves for 6PG, 6PR, 2×3PG and 2×3PR (Experimental results)

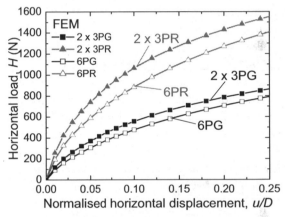

Fig. 27 Horizontal load vs. normalised horizontal disp. curves for 6PG, 6PR, 2×3PG and 2×3PR (FEM results)

Fig. 27. It is seen from both experimental and FEM results that the horizontal resistances of the 6-pile foundations (6PG and 6PR) are smaller than two times the resistances of the 3-pile foundations (2×3PG and 2×3PR), in which the difference of resistance between 6PR and 2×3PR is more prominent than that between 6PG and 2×3PG. Obviously, the influence of interaction between the raft and the piles through the ground is indicated from the results.

5. CONCLUSIONS

The following conclusions were derived from this particular research through both experimental and numerical approaches:

1) The piled rafts have much higher resistance and stiffness than the corresponding pile groups in both vertical and horizontal directions.

2) The pile foundations including pile groups and piled rafts with batter piles have higher resistance and stiffness in both vertical and horizontal directions than the foundations with only vertical piles.

3) In the cases of the piled rafts, the raft is an important member to support the load and also plays a very important role in the interaction of raft-soil-pile. The pressure transferred from the raft base to ground increases the resistance of the piles.

4) The inclination of the piled rafts due to horizontal load is smaller than that of the corresponding pile groups. The inclination of the foundations is reduced by the inclusion of batter piles.

5) The resistances of the 6-pile foundations are not equal two times the resistances of the corresponding 3-pile foundations, which are effected by interactions between the components of the foundations (piles, raft) and the ground.

ACKNOWLEDGEMENTS

The authors thank the Japanese Society for the Promotion of Science for the financial support (the Grants-in-aid for Scientific Research No. 15K06208). The authors greatly appreciate also Mr. Shinya Shimono, Kanazawa University, for his supports in carrying out the experiments.

REFERENCES

Anaraki, K.E. (2008). Hypoplasticity investigated-Parameter determination and numerical simulation. Master's thesis, Delft University of Technology, Netherlands, pp 3-12.

Jeong, S. and Cho, J. (2014). Proposed nonlinear 3-D analytical method for piled raft foundations. *Computers and Geotechnics*, 59, pp 112-126.

Gudehus, G. (1996). A comprehensive constitutive equation for granular materials. *Soils and Foundations*, 36(1), pp 1-12.

Hamada, J., Tsuchiya, T., Tanikawa, T. and Yamashita, K. (2015). Lateral loading tests on piled rafts and simplified method to evaluate sectional forces of piles. *Geotechnical Engineering Journal SEAGS & AGSSEA*, 46(2), pp 29-42.

Herle, I. (2000). Granulometric limits of hypoplastic models. *TASK Quartely: scientific bulletin of Academic Computer Centre in Gdansk*, 4(3), pp 389-408.

Horikoshi, K. and Randolph, M.F. (1998). A contribution of optimum design of piled rafts. *Géotechnique*, 48(3), pp 301-317.

Horikoshi, K. and Randolph, M.F. (1999). Estimation of overall settlement of piled rafts. *Soils and Foundations*, 39(2), pp 59-68.

Kimura, M. and Zhang, F. (2000). Seismic evaluations of pile foundations with three different methods based on three-dimensional elasto-plastic finite element analysis. *Soil and Foundation*, 40(5), pp 113-132.

Kitiyodom, P. and Matsumoto, T. (2002). A simplified analysis method for piled raft and pile group foundations with batter piles. *International Journal for Numerical and Analytical Methods in Geomechanics*, 26, pp 1349-1369.

Kolymbas, D. (1985). A generalized hypoelastic constitutive law. In *Proceedings of 11th International Conference on Soil Mechanics and Foundation Engineering*. AA Balkema, San Francisco, USA, pp 2626.

Masin, D. (2005). A hypoplastic constitutive model for clays. *International Journal for Numerical and Analytical Methods in Geomechanics*, 24(4), pp 311-336.

Matsumoto, T., Fukumura, K., Pastsakorn, K., Horikoshi, K. and Oki, A. (2004). Experimental and analytical study on behaviour of model piled rafts in sand subjected to horizontal and moment loading. *International Journal of Physical Modelling in Geotechnics*, 4(3), pp 1-19.

Niemunis, A. and Herle, I. (1997). Hypoplastic

model for cohesionless soils with elastic strain range. *Mechanics of cohesive-frictional materials*, 2, pp 279-299.

Pham, H.D. (2009). Modelling of installation effect of driven piles by hypoplasticity. Master's thesis, Delft University of Technology, Netherlands, pp 21-32.

Poulos, H.G. and Davids, A.J. (2005). Foundation design for the Emirates Twin Towers, Dubai. *Canadian Geotechnical Journal*, 42, pp 716-730.

Poulos, H.G., Small, J.C. and Chow, H. (2011). Piled raft foundations for tall buildings. *Geotechnical Engineering Journal SEAGS & AGSSEA*, 46(2), pp 78-84.

Reul, O. (2004). Numerical study of the bearing behaviour of piled rafts. *International Journal of Geomechanics*, 4(2), pp 59-68.

Sawada, K. and Takemura, J. (2014). Centrifuge model tests on piled raft foundation in sand subjected to lateral and moment loads. *Soils and Foundations*, 54(2), pp 126-140.

Unsever, Y.S., Matsumoto, T., Shimono, S. and Ozkan, M.Y. (2014). Static cyclic load tests on model foundations in dry sand. *Geotechnical Engineering Journal SEAGS & AGSSEA*, 45(2), pp 40-51.

Unsever, Y.S., Matsumoto, T. and Ozkan, M.Y. (2015). Numerical analyses of load tests on model foundations in dry sand. *Computers and Geotechnics*, 63, pp 40-51.

Vu, A.T., Pham, D.P., Nguyen, T.L. and Yu, H. (2014). 3D finite element analysis on behaviour of piled raft foundations. *Applied Mechanics and Materials*, Vols. 580-583, pp 3-8.

Vu, A.T., Matsumoto, T., Kobayashi, S. and Nguyen, T.L. (2016). Model load tests on battered pile foundations and finite-element analysis. *International Journal of Physical Modelling in Geotechnics*, published online Nov 30th 2016, http://dx.doi.org/10.1680/jphmg.16.00010.

Vu, A.T. (2017). Experimental and numerical study on behaviours of pile group and piled raft foundations having batter piles subjected to combination of vertical and cyclic horizontal loading. Doctoral thesis, Kanazawa University, Japan, Appendix 1, pp 131-149.

Wolffersdorff, P.A. (1996). A hypoplastic relation for granular materials with a predefined limit state surface. *Mechanics of Cohesive-Frictional Materials*, 1, pp 251-271.

Yamashita, K., Yamada, T. and Hamada, J. (2011). Investigation of settlement and load sharing on piled rafts by monitoring full-scale structures. *Soils and Foundation*, 51(3), pp 513-532.

CHAPTER 15

LATERAL LOAD TEST ON MODEL MONOPILE AND ITS ANALYSIS

Ya-Han Hsu
Department of Civil Engineering, National Central University, Taoyuan, Taiwan
*yhhsu1112@gmail.com

Yung-Yen Ko
National Center for Research on Earthquake Engineering, Taipei, Taiwan

Zhi-Wei Xu
Department of Civil Engineering, National Central University, Taoyuan, Taiwan

Jin-Hung Hwang*
Department of Civil Engineering, National Central University, Taoyuan, Taiwan

ABSTRACT: In order to investigate the behavior of the pile-soil interaction of laterally loaded monopile, a lateral load test procedure on model monopile was developed in this study. Static monotonic ultimate load tests and one-way cyclic load tests on monopile in dry sand were conducted accordingly. Assuming the moment distribution along a laterally loaded pile can be expressed in the form of quartic function, a regression analysis process was adopted for the interpretation of these test results. Once the moment function was obtained, the functions of shear force, pile deflection, rotation angle, and soil resistance can be calculated based on the Euler-Bernoulli beam theory. The relationships between the soil reaction and the pile deflection, the so-called p-y curves, can then be deduced. Additionally, the effect of cyclic load on the pile behavior was examined through the permanent displacement, equivalent pile stiffness and p-y curves obtained from the cyclic load tests.

1. INTRODUCTION

In recent years, the development of green energy has been a popular issue in the world. The wind power plays an important role in green energy because of its relatively low environmental impact and the efficiency in power production. In Europe, the technologies of onshore and offshore wind turbines are relatively mature, and the performance is getting better and better. In Taiwan, there are 346 onshore wind turbines installed and in operation along the west coast. However, for the lack of

territory and for the excellent wind energy in Taiwan Strait, hundreds of offshore wind turbines will be established in Taiwan in the following decades.

The monopile is now the most common foundation type for the offshore wind turbines in operation in Europe, with a share up to 80% (EWEA, 2016). Offshore monopiles may undergo the loads transferred from the superstructure due to the actions of wind, waves, flow, tides and earthquakes in the design lifetime, with loading cycles up to

$10^8 \sim 10^9$. However, the cost of foundation of an offshore wind turbine is about 15% of the total cost (Moné et al., 2015) and is considerable, and thus economization of the foundation design is essential for the offshore wind power to be profitable. Therefore, it is critical to capture the behavior of laterally loaded monopoles for reasonable design, including the cyclic load effect.

In this paper, a lateral load test procedure on model monopile is proposed. Results of static monotonic ultimate load tests and one-way cyclic load tests on monopile in dry sand according to the procedure are presented. For the interpretation of these test results, a regression analysis process to determine the parameters of the quartic function which approximate the moment distribution along a laterally loaded pile is introduced. Using the Euler-Bernoulli beam theory, the shear force, pile deflection, rotation angle, and soil resistance along the pile are also given, as well as the p-y curves, that is, the relationships between the soil reaction and the pile deflection. Moreover, the effect of cyclic load on the pile, often called "cyclic degradation", is also discussed.

2. TEST SETUP

2.1 Test Equipment

2.1.1 Movable Pluviation Device
In this study, the soil specimens were prepared by the movable pluviation device designed by Chang (2013), as shown in Figure 1. It is composed of a supporting frame, a soil funnel, a flexible pipe, a soil outlet, which allows for adjustment of the pluviation height, and two dimensional sliding rails, which enable motions of the soil outlet in both x and y directions for uniform pluviation.

2.1.2 Soil Container
The soil container used was designed by Huang (1997), as shown in Figure 2. It consists of several hollow cylinders with an inner diameter of 40 cm and a base plate made of aluminum alloy.

With different numbers of the hollow cylinders assembled, the height of the soil container can be varied from 10 cm to 60 cm, and was 50 cm in this study.

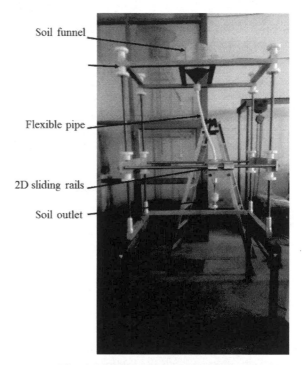

Soil funnel

Flexible pipe

2D sliding rails

Soil outlet

Fig. 1 Movable pluviation device

Fig. 2 Soil container

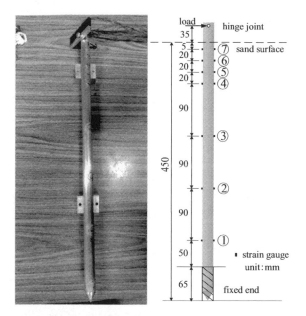

Fig. 3 Model pile and the locations of strain gauges

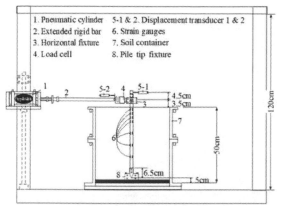

Fig. 4 Test configuration

Fig. 5 Pile end fixture

2.1.3 Model Pile

The model pile with used in this study was made from aluminum alloy with an outer diameter of 19 mm, an inner diameter of 16 mm, a wall thickness of 1.5 mm and a length of 47.5 cm, as shown in Figure 3.

2.1.4 Strain Gauge

To measure the moment along the pile during lateral load test, the strain gauges manufactured by TML with an electrical resistance of 120Ω and a length of 3 mm. The locations of strain gauges on the model pile are shown in the right of Figure 3. At each location to be measured, a total of four strain gauges were used to make a full Wheatstone bridge.

2.2 Test Configuration

The test configuration is shown in Figure 4. A pneumatic cylinder was used to apply lateral load. A load cell with a capacity of 250 lbf and displacement transducers with measuring ranges of 1 cm and 5 cm were utilized for instrumentation.

The pneumatic cylinder was fixed on the reaction frame and connected to the load cell through a rigid bar. The load cell was hinged-connected to the pile at a height of 3.5 cm above the soil surface, making the so-called free pile head condition. Two displacement transducer, Displacement Transducer 1 & Displacement Transducer 2, were installed at 8 cm and 3.5 cm above the soil surface, respectively. The pile tip was fixed to the base plate of the soil container using a pile tip fixture, as shown in Figure 5, to simulate a fixed-end condition.

2.3 Material Properties

2.3.1 Soil Specimen

The soil specimen was composed of Chunan sand from the coastal area of the middle part of Taiwan in the dry condition. The physical properties and the particle size distribution of Chunan sand were listed in Table 1 and shown in Figure 6, respectively.

Table 1. The physical properties of Chunan sand

Specific gravity, G_s	2.64
Average particle size, D_{50}	0.196 mm
Effective particle size, D_{10}	0.155 mm
Coefficient of uniformity, C_u	1.342
Coefficient of curvature, C_c	0.939
Friction angle ($D_r = 60\%$)	37°
Max. dry density	1.69 g/cm³
Min. dry density	1.36 g/cm³
Soil classification (USCS)	SP

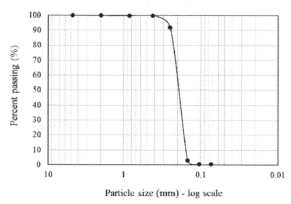

Fig. 6 The particle size distribution of Chunan sand

The soil specimens for the tests were prepared utilizing the movable pluviation device mentioned in Section 2.1 after the model pile was fixed in the soil container. The sand was pluviated layer by layer to keep constant pluviation height. Every soil specimen was 40 cm in diameter, same as the inner diameter of the container, and 50 cm in height. The relative density (D_r) of all the soil specimens was controlled to a value of 60%.

2.3.2 Model Pile

The model pile was made of 6061-T6 aluminum alloy with a Young's Modulus of 69 GPa, a density of 2.7 g/cm³ and a yield strength of 275 MPa.

In order to make the pile waterproof, epoxy was spread on the outer surface of the model pile. For the confirmation of the uniform flexural rigidity along the pile, lateral load tests of fixed-end pile without soil was conducted. The actual flexural rigidity obtained was listed in Table 2. An average

Table 2. The flexural rigidity along the pile

Number of strain gauge	Flexural rigidity, EI (N-m²)
Gauge 1	223.50
Gauge 2	228.78
Gauge 3	230.67
Gauge 4	233.30
Gauge 5	229.72
Gauge 6	220.57
Gauge 7	219.36
Average value	226.84
Theoretical value	219.11

flexural rigidity of 226.84 N-m² was adopted as representative, which is slightly larger than the theoretical value, 219.11 N-m², calculated from the specifications of the model pile.

3. TEST AND ANALYSIS PROCEDURE

3.1 Test Procedure

The lateral load tests on model pile included static monotonic ultimate load test and one-way cyclic load test. The static monotonic ultimate load tests aimed to confirm the feasibility of the test procedure designed in this study, and to observe the behavior of pile-soil interaction. Regarding the cyclic load test, the long-term action on an offshore pile in its lifetime, such as wave and tide, was simulated.

Two static ultimate load tests were performed, which were named as S1-test and S2-test, and two cyclic load tests were performed, which were named as C3-test and C4-test. Corresponding test parameters are listed in Table 3.

For S1-test and S2-test the numbers of load application stages were five and eight, respectively. In each stage, the load level was held constant for 5 minutes to stabilize the displacement of pile.

The tests were completed when the displacement measured at the Displacement Transducer 2, which was located at the same elevation as the load cell, reached 25% of the pile diameter.

Because the average period of wave load in real world is approximately 10 seconds, the frequency of the cyclic load was set as 0.1 Hz for both C3-test and C4-test. The load magnitude in the static monotonic ultimate load test when the measurement at Displacement Transducer 2 reached 1% of the pile diameter, 12.9 N, was defined as the reference load level in the cyclic load test. The amplitude of the cyclic lateral load of C3-test was specified to be 16N, which was 1.24 times of the reference load level, while the load amplitude in C4-test was 8.5 N, which is 0.66 times of the reference. The load cycles in C3-test and C4-test were 1,000 and 10,000, respectively.

Table 3. The information of tests

Test case	Measured D_r (%)	Number of load stage	
S1-test	60.2	5	
S2-test	60.9	8	
Test case	Measured D_r (%)	Load amp. (N)	Load cycles
C3-test	60.2	16	1,000
C4-test	61.9	8.5	10,000

3.2 Interpretation of Pile Response

According to Lin (2011), the moment distribution along a laterally loaded pile can be assumed to have the form of quartic function:

$$M(z) = a_0 + a_1 z + a_2 z^2 + a_3 z^3 + a_4 z^4 \qquad (1)$$

Where z is the depth along the pile, a_0, a_1, a_2, a_3, a_4 are undetermined coefficients.

Based on the Euler-Bernoulli beam theory, the first-order differential equation of the moment function is the shear force function, $V(z)$, as shown in equation (2). And the second-order differential equation of the moment function is the function of

lateral soil resistance, $p(z)$, as shown in equation (3).

$$V(z) = a_1 + 2a_2 z + 3a_3 z^2 + 4a_4 z^3 \qquad (2)$$

$$p(z) = 2a_2 + 6a_3 z + 12a_4 z^2 \qquad (3)$$

Because of the fixed pile end and the free pile head conditions in the test, the boundary conditions could be assumed as: (1) the lateral soil resistance at pile end was zero; (2) the lateral load was equal to the shear force of pile at the soil surface; (3) the moment of pile at the soil surface was equal to the product of lateral load and the distance from the point of load application to the soil surface.

Based on the data measured by the strain gauges during the static lateral pile load tests, the moment along the pile can be calculated. Then, the undetermined coefficients in equation (1) can be decided using regression analysis, and thus an optimum interpretation of the moment function can be obtained. To this aim, the least square method was used, and the Lagrange multiplier method was utilized as well to include the mentioned boundary conditions in the residual equation as constraints, as follows:

$$\overline{E} = \frac{1}{2} \sum_{i=1}^{N} [M(z_i) - M_{mi}]^2 + \sum_{j=1}^{3} \lambda_j f_j \qquad (4)$$

where $\overline{E}$ is the summation of the squares of the difference between the moment function along the pile, $M(z_i)$, and the tested moment distribution, M_{mi}, N is the number of the measurement points, f_j is the function of the boundary condition, and λ_j is the Lagrange multiplier.

With the boundary condition of the fixed-end pile that the displacement and the rotation at the pile end are both equal to zero, the functions of the pile slope, $\theta(z)$, and pile deflection, $d(z)$, can be obtained via the first-order and second-order integrals:

$$EI\theta(z) = \alpha + a_0 z + \tfrac{1}{2} a_1 z^2 + \tfrac{1}{3} a_2 z^3 + \tfrac{1}{4} a_3 z^4 + \tfrac{1}{5} a_4 z^5$$
$$(5)$$

$$EId(z) = \beta + \alpha z + \frac{1}{2}a_0 z^2 + \frac{1}{6}a_1 z^3 + \frac{1}{12}a_2 z^4 + \frac{1}{20}a_3 z^5 + \frac{1}{30}a_4 z^6 \tag{6}$$

where EI is the flexural rigidity of the; α and β are the undetermined coefficients.

The definitions of the sign of displacement, rotation angle, moment, shear force, and soil resistance used in this study are shown in Figure 7.

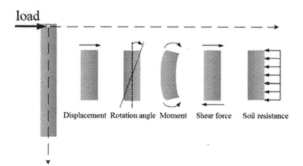

Fig. 7 The definitions of positive displacement, rotation angle, moment, shear force, and soil resistance

4. ULTIMATE LOAD TEST RESULTS

4.1 Displacement and Rotation at Pile Head

The position where the lateral load was applied is defined as pile head. The relationship between lateral load and displacement at the pile head is shown in Figure 8, while lateral load versus rotation angle is shown in Figure 9.

For S1-test, the maximum lateral load was 108.7 N, the rotational angle at pile head was 0.021 rad and the displacement at pile head was 4.36 mm, about 22.9% of the pile diameter. After unloading to zero by three unloading stages, 1.23 mm of the residual displacement at pile head was observed.

For the S2-test, the maximum lateral load was 100.3 N, the maximum rotation angle at pile head was 0.019 and displacement at pile head rad was 4.36 mm, about 22.9% of the pile diameter. After unloading to zero by four unloading stages, 1.03 mm of the residual displacement at pile head remained.

Comparing the test results of S1-test and S2-test, the difference between the two tests was small enough, which implied that this model test was repeatable.

4.2 Pile Response along the Pile

The moment functions along the pile obtained using the procedure mentioned in Section 3.2 based on the results of S1-test and S2-test are almost the same, and therefore those of S2-test are regarded as representative, as depicted in Figure 10. The moment increases as the lateral load at the pile head increases. Furthermore, the deeper the depth

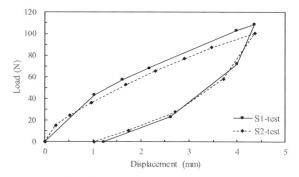

Fig. 8 Lateral load versus displacement at pile head in static monotonic ultimate load tests

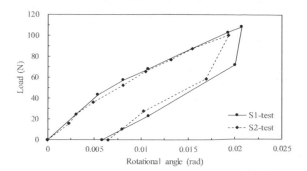

Fig. 9 Lateral load versus rotation angle at pile head in static monotonic ultimate load tests

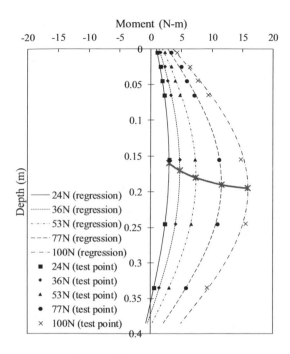

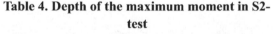

Fig. 10 Moment distribution along the pile in S2-test

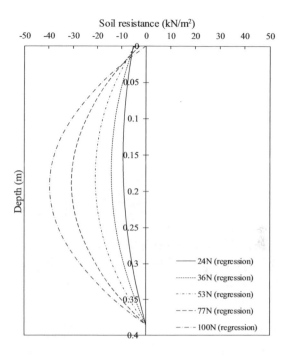

Fig. 11 Soil resistance in S2-test

Table 4. Depth of the maximum moment in S2-test

Lateral load at pile head (N)	Depth of maximum moment(m)	Maximum moment (N-m)
24	0.16	2.95
36	0.17	4.73
53	0.18	7.38
77	0.19	11.50
100	0.195	15.83

where the maximum moment occurred, the larger the lateral load, as shown in Figure 10 and listed in Table 4.

The lateral soil resistance and the pile deflection along the pile deduced from the moment function in S2-test are shown in Figure 11 and Figure 12, where the pile deflection at the soil surface was the measurements of Displacement Transducer 1 minus the displacement due to pile rotation. The lateral soil resistance increases as the lateral load

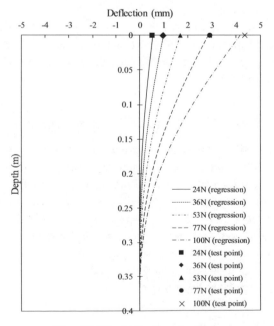

Fig. 12 Pile deflection in S2-test

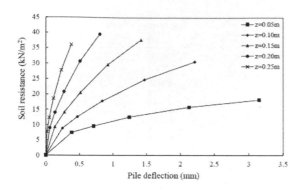

Fig. 13 p-y curves in S2-test

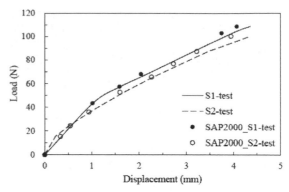

Fig. 14 Comparison of load-displacement curve at pile head in S1-test and S2-test (test versus SAP 2000 analysis)

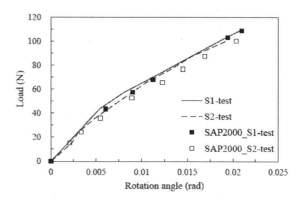

Fig. 15 Comparison of load-rotation curve at pile head in S1-test and S2-test (test versus SAP 2000 analysis)

increases, and is larger at the middle of the pile. The pile deflection also gets larger as the lateral load rises, and shows a deformation pattern of a fixed-end pile.

Based on the lateral soil resistance and pile deflection curves at different lateral loads, the p-y curve at any depth could be deduced, as given in Figure 13. The stiffness and strength of the p-y curve rises as the depth increases, implying the influence of the overburden stress and the relative density of soil on p-y curves. For a specific depth, the slope of the p-y curve decreases as the pile deflection increases, exhibiting the nonlinearity of the soil.

4.3   Validity of Test and Analysis Procedure

In order to validate the procedure of the lateral load test on model pile and the corresponding data interpretation methods proposed in this study, the finite element (FE) simulation using the code SAP2000 was performed. The Winkler beam model (Winkler, 1867) was utilized for the modeling of pile-soil system, in which the pile was simulated by beam elements, and the soil reactions are simulated by spring elements spread along the pile with the spring stiffness assigned based on the p-y curves in S1-test and S2-test.

Figure 14 and Figure 15 show the comparison of the displacement and the rotation angle at pile head obtained from the SAP2000 analysis and the static monotonic ultimate load test. It is noted that the FE simulation results are close to the test results, both for the displacement and the rotation angle at pile head. The lateral load test on model pile and the corresponding analysis procedure proposed in this study was thus verified to give an accurate assessment of the p-y curves.

5. CYCLIC LOAD TEST RESULTS

5.1 Displacement and Rotation at Pile Head

The relationship between lateral load and

displacement at the pile head in C3-test is shown in Figure 16. The hysteretic behavior of the pile and the accumulation of the permanent displacement can be observed. Figure 17 gives the permanent

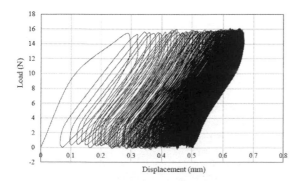

Fig. 16 Lateral load versus displacement at pile head in C3-test

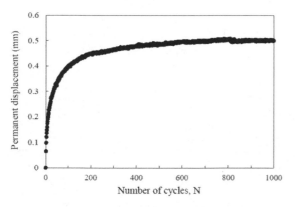

Fig. 17 Permanent displacement at pile head versus the number of cycles in C3-test

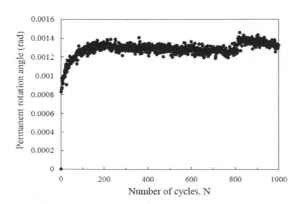

Fig. 18 Permanent rotation angle at pile head versus the number of cycles in C3-test

displacement at the pile head versus the number of cycles, showing that the accumulation of permanent displacement was quick in the first 100 cycles and then turned slow gradually. The increasing tendency of the permanent rotation angle at the pile head was similar, as shown in Figure 18, yet the instruments was disturbed at around 800 cycles, causing a sudden increase of the rotation angle. In C3-test, the permanent displacement was about 2.5% of the pile diameter, and the permanent rotation angle was about 0.0013 rad.

5.2 Secant and Equivalent Stiffness of Pile

The secant stiffness of a load versus displacement curve is defined as the slope of the outset to the peak point in each loop, shown as Figure 19, while the equivalent stiffness is defined as the slope from the very origin of the curve to the peak point of each loop, as shown in Figure 20.

Figure 21 shows that the secant stiffness of the pile in C3-test increased with the number of cycles, and it increased 50% at 400 cycles. On the other hand, the equivalent stiffness decreased with the number

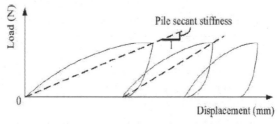

Fig. 19 Definition of secant stiffness

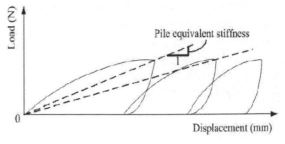

Fig. 20 Definition of equivalent stiffness

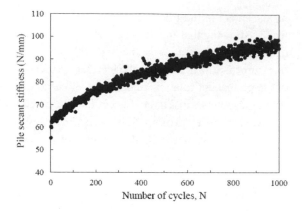

Fig. 21 Secant stiffness of pile versus the number of cycles in C3-test

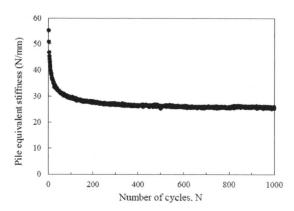

Fig. 22 Equivalent stiffness of pile versus the number of cycles in C3-test

of cycles, as shown in Figure 22, and it decreased 50% at 100 cycles.

Actually, the performance of a pile is much related to its resistance to the permanent displacement, especially for the piles used as the foundation of wind turbines, which is sensitive to displacement and tilt for operation. In this point of view, the equivalent stiffness of the pile subjected to cyclic load should be adopted in design and analysis, and it degrades with the number of cycles, which is often called "cyclic degradation".

5.3   Pile Response along the Pile

Figure 23 shows the moment distribution along

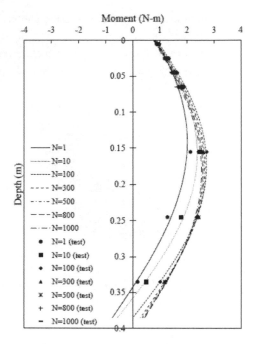

Fig. 23 Moment distribution at different numbers of cycles in C3-test

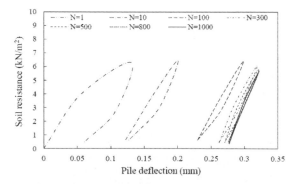

Fig. 24 p-y curves at a depth of 0.1m in C3-test

the pile in C3-test. The peak moment increased with the number of cycles and converged after 100 cycles. The moment function was then used to calculate the functions of soil resistance and pile deflection for the assessment of the p-y curves. The p-y curves at a depth of 0.1 m at different numbers of cycles are given in Figure 24, which varied with the number of cycles. Figure 24 shows the p-y curves at a depth 0.05 m, of which the slope for a specific cycle number is lower than at a depth of 0.1 m.

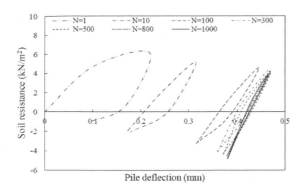

Fig. 25 The p-y curves at 0.05m depth (C3-test)

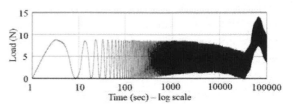

Fig. 26 Load history of C4-test

Table 5. The change of applied load of C4-test

Part	Number of cycles	Average of applied load (N)
1	0-1000	4.25
2	1000-4500	4.25-3.00
3	4500-7000	3.00-10.50
4	7000-10000	10.50-6.50

It has to be mentioned that the negative soil resistance was observed in Figure 25. That is, the direction of soil reaction was the same as that of the load applied at the pile head (see Figure 7). It is because the sand near the surface at the opposite side of the pile leaning direction collapsed during the lateral cyclic loading for its lack of cohesion, causing the additional soil pressure to the pile.

5.4 Causes of Varying Test Load in C4-test

For the C4-test, the amplitude of cyclic load was specified to be 8.5 N, and the number of load cycles was 10,000, making a long test period of 100,000 seconds at a 0.1 Hz frequency of the cyclic load. According to the load history, as shown in Fig. 26, the load amplitude actually applied was varying during the test time, especially after 10,000 seconds (1,000 cycles). According to the load history, the load period can be roughly divided into 4 parts, as listed in Table 5.

There are two possible reasons. One is that the load amplitude of 8.5 N was too small for the pneumatic cylinder used in the test, and therefore it was difficult to maintain stable load output. The other reason is the change of the ambient temperature during the long test period, 100,000 seconds, or 27.8 hours. Actually, there was no air conditioner in the laboratory, and therefore the change of the ambient temperature could be influent for the test lasts for such a long period. When the temperature

decreased, the applied load also decreased due to the decline of gas pressure in the pneumatic cylinder.

C4-test started in the afternoon, and the whole test took nearly 28 hours. From Fig. 26 it can be observed that the tendency of the variation of applied load was similar to that of the ambient temperature. Thus, the ambient temperature probably affected the applied load amplitude.

5.5 Quantification of Cyclic Degradation Effect

Long et al. (1994) conducted 34 sets of in-situ cyclic lateral load test on full-scale piles in sand. It was observed that the deformation of pile increased with every load cycle. According to the test results, the behavior of piles subjected to repetitive lateral load was modeled by degrading soil reaction modulus as a function of number of loading cycles, as follows:

$$R_n = \frac{k_{hN}}{k_{h1}} = N^{-t} \qquad (7)$$

where R_n is the degradation ratio of soil reaction

modulus, k_{h1} and k_{hN} are the soil reaction modulus of the first cycle and N^{th} cycle corresponding to the same load level, respectively, and t is the degradation parameter, which is dependent on cyclic load pattern (one-way or two-way), pile installation method and soil density. For the test situation in this study (one-way cyclic load, backfilled pile and D_r = 60%), t = 0.21 based on the suggestions of Long et al. (1994).

Using equation (7), the value of t according the results of C3-test was obtained by regression analysis, as shown in Figure 27. The value of t ranged from 0.18 to 0.22 at different depths, which is close to the suggested value.

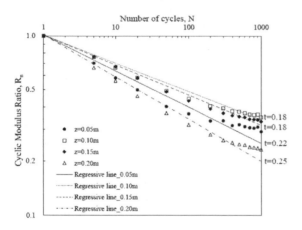

Fig. 27 The reduction of soil reaction modulus (C3-test)

6. CONCLUSIONS

In this study, a lateral load test procedure on model monopole is proposed. Accordingly, static monotonic ultimate load tests and one-way cyclic load tests were conducted, and the displacement and strain at different locations of the pile were measured. FE analysis was also performed to validate the test procedure.

Assuming the moment distribution along a laterally loaded pile can be approximated by the quartic function, the moment function can be obtained by regression analysis according to the measurement of strain gauges along the pile. Then, functions of shear force, pile deflection, rotation angle and soil resistance can be calculated based on the moment function. Thus, the p-y curves at any depth can be easily deduced.

Through the permanent displacement, the equivalent pile stiffness and the p-y curves obtained from the cyclic load tests, the cyclic degradation effect on the pile was revealed. The experimental results also supports the suggestions of Long et al. (1994) to quantify the degradation of the soil reaction modulus.

It is noted that the load amplitude in the cyclic load test may be unstable when load amplitude was small and difficult to keep constant or when there was a significant change of the ambient temperature. The model test can be improved by a better controlled loading system or by minimizing the change of ambient temperatures.

REFERENCES

Chang, Y. Y. (2013). Use of Centrifuge Modeling and Distinct Element Method to Evaluate the Surface and Subsurface Deformation of Normal Faulting and Reverse Faulting, Doctoral Dissertation, Department of Civil Engineering, National Central University, Taoyuan

EWEA (2016). *The European Offshore Wind Industry -Key Trends and Statistics 2015*, European Wind Energy Association.

Hetényi, M. (1946). *Beams on Elastic Foundation: Theory with Applications in the Fields of Civil and Mechanical Engineering*. University of Michigan Press.

Huang, J. H. (1997). Ground Subsidence Cause by the Overwithdraw Groundwater in Centifuge Model Test, Master's Thesis, Department of Civil Engineering, National Central University,

Taoyuan

Lin, C. L. (2011). Lateral Loading Test on Model Pile in Saturated Sands, master's thesis, Department of Civil Engineering, National Taiwan University, Taipei

Long, J. H., and Vanneste, G. (1994). Effects of cyclic lateral loads on piles in sand. *Journal of Geotechnical Engineering*, 120(1), pp 225-244.

Moné, C., Smith, A., Maples, B., Hand, M. (2015). *2013 Cost of Wind Energy Review*, National Renewable Energy Laboratory.

Winkler, E. (1867). *Theory of elasticity and strength*, Dominicus Prague.

Xu, Z. W. (2015). Model design and test of monopile under lateral loads, Master's Thesis, Department of Civil Engineering, National Central University, Taoyuan

CHAPTER 16

SEISMIC BEHAVIOR OF PILED RAFT IN SOFT GROUND BASED ON FIELD MONITORING

Kiyoshi Yamashita*
Junji Hamada
Tomohiro Tanikawa
Takenaka Research & Development Institute, Takenaka Corporation, Chiba, Japan
*yamashita.kiyoshi@takenaka.co.jp

ABSTRACT: The seismic behavior of a piled raft foundation combined with cement deep mixing walls embedded in soft ground was investigated based on the seismic monitoring results during the 2011 Tohoku earthquake. In order to understand real seismic behavior of the piled raft in soft ground, the monitoring results were examined focusing the effects of inertial force from the structure and action of ground movements on the foundation system. As a result, it was found that the maximum bending moment near the pile head, as well as that at the intermediate depth, were affected mainly by the lateral displacements of thick silty clay, rather than the shear force from the structure inertial force. It was also found that the DMWs restrained the amplification of the lateral ground displacements in the DMW grids.

1. INTRODUCTION

In recent years, the effectiveness of piled rafts in reducing average and differential settements has been confirmed not only on favorable ground conditions as shown by Katzenbach et al. (2000), Poulos (2001) and Mandolini et al. (2005), but also on unfavorable ground conditions with ground improvement techniques (Yamashita et al., 2011a); Yamashita et al., 2011b). Piled rafts can provide sufficient capacities against the lateral and moment loads from the structure because the loads are carried by both the piles and raft. It has become necessary to develop more reliable seismic design methods for piled raft foundations, particularly in highly seismic areas such as Japan and Taiwan.

In order to clarify the behavior of piled raft foundations under seismic loading, the lateral loading tests on model piled rafts were conducted. A large-scale lateral load test was performed by Rollins and Sparks (2002) on a group of 9 piles having a buried cap. Horikoshi et al. (2003a;

2003b) carried out static horizontal load tests as well as dynamic loading tests on model piled rafts using a geotechnical centrifuge. Katzenbach and Turek (2005) also conducted static horizontal load tests using a geotechnical centrifuge. Matsumoto et al. (2004a; 2004b) carried out a series of 1 g static lateral load tests and shaking table tests on small piled raft model, and the former test results were simulated using software developed by Kitiyodom and Matsumoto (2002; 2003). Furthermore, Matsumoto et al. (2010) carried out static cyclic lateral loading tests on relatively large-scale piled raft model to investigate the effect of the pile head connection condition. Sawada et al. (2014) carried out static horizontal loading tests subjected to relatively large moment load and rotation using a geotechnical centrifuge. However, case histories on monitoring seismic soil-pile-structure interaction of full-scale piled rafts are very limited (Mendoza et al., 2000; Hamada et al., 2015; Yamashita et al., 2016). Yamashita et al. (2012) have reported the seismic response of a piled raft with the grid-form deep cement mixing walls (DMWs) supporting a

12-story residential building at the time of the 2011 off the Pacific coast of Tohoku Earthquake (the 2011 Tohoku earthquake).

This paper presents static and seismic behavior of the piled raft system supporting the 12-story building. In order to understand real seismic behavior of the piled raft in soft ground, the static and dynamic monitoring results are examined focusing the effects of inertial force from the structure and action of ground movements on the foundation system. In addition, the monitoring data have been updated from those reported by Yamashita et al. (2012).

2. STRUCTURE

2.1 Building and soil conditions

The 12-story residential building, shown in Photo 1, is located in Toyo, Tokyo, Japan. The building, 38.7 m in height above the ground surface and

measuring 33 m by 30 m in plan, is a reinforced concrete structure with a base isolation system of laminated rubber bearings; it was completed in 2008. Fig. 1 shows a schematic view of the building and the foundation with a typical soil profile. A base isolation system was placed between the raft and the bottom floor of the building (Photo 2). The subsoil consists of an alluvial stratum to a depth of 44 m, underlain by a diluvial sand-and-gravel layer of SPT N-values of 60 or higher. The soil profile down to a depth of 7 m is made of fill, soft silt and loose silty sand. Between the depths of 7 and 44 m, there lie very-soft to medium silty clay strata. The silty clay between the depths of 7 and 15.5 m is slightly overconsolidated with an overconsolidation ratio (OCR) of about 1.5, and the silty clay between the depths of 15.5 to 44 m is overconsolidated with an OCR of 2.0 or higher. The ground water table appears approximately 1.8 m below the ground surface. The shear wave velocities derived from a P-S logging system were 110-220 m/s between the depths of 4.8 m (at the foundation level) and 43 m, and were 410-610 m/s in the dense gravel layers below a depth of 48 m.

2.2 Foundation design

Soil investigation results indicated that the loose silty sand between depths of 3 and 7 m below the ground surface had the potential for liquefaction with peak horizontal ground acceleration of 0.2 m/s2. Hence, to cope with the liquefiable sand and to ensure the bearing capacity of the raft, grid-form cement deep mixing walls, shown in Fig. 2,

Photo 1 Twelve-story building in Tokyo

Photo 2 Laminated rubber bearings

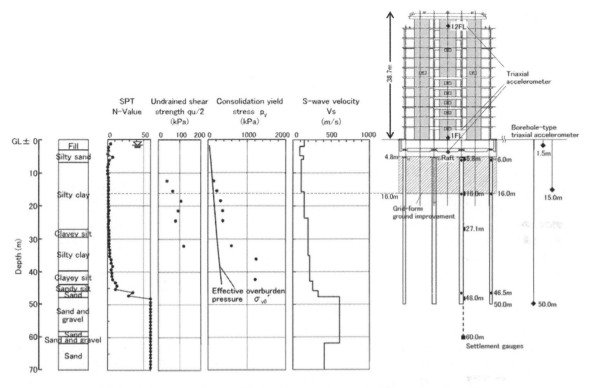

Fig. 1 Schematic view of the building and foundation with soil profile

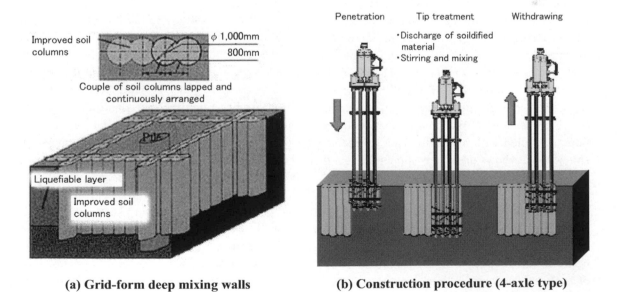

(a) Grid-form deep mixing walls   **(b) Construction procedure (4-axle type)**

Fig. 2 Grid-form deep cement mixing walls

were employed below the raft. The high-modulus soil-cement walls (typical compressive strength is 2 to 3N/mm^2) confine loose sand so as not to cause excessive shear deformation to the loose sand during earthquakes. The ground improvement execution was carried out by the Cement Deep

Mixing machine equipped with four mixing shafts (Fig. 2(b)). The spacing of the mixing shafts was 0.8 m for the diameter of mixing blades of 1.0 m. The spacing between the walls was about 6 to 9 m and the improvement area ratio (ratio of improved area in plan to raft area) was 0.25. The design standard strength of the stabilized soil was 1.8 MPa.

The total load in the structural design was 198.8 MN, which corresponds to the sum of the dead load and the live load. The average contact pressure over the raft was 199 kPa. To improve the bearing capacity of the silty soil beneath the raft, as well as to cope with the liquefiable sand, the grid-form deep cement mixing walls were extended to a depth of 16 m with the bottom being embedded in the lower silty clay below a depth of 15.7 m with an undrained shear strength of 75 kPa (OCR of 2 or higher). Furthermore, to reduce the settlement and the differential settlement to acceptable levels, sixteen 45-m-long piles, 0.8-1.2 m in diameter, were used. The pile toes reached the very dense sand-and-gravel layer sufficiently well enough to ensure the toe resistance as well as the frictional resistance. The piles consisted of steel pipe-concrete composite (SC) piles in the top portion and pre-tensioned spun high-strength concrete (PHC) piles in the bottom portion. The piles were constructed by inserting four sets of pile segments (one 12-m-long SC pile and two 12-m-long and one 9-m-long PHC piles) into a pre-augered borehole filled with mixed-in-place soil cement slurry. Fig. 3 shows the layout of the piles and the grid-form deep cement mixing walls.

In the foundation design under working load conditions, numerical analysis was carried out to obtain the foundation settlement and load sharing between raft and piles using the simplified method of analysis developed by Yamashita et al. (1998). Under seismic loading conditions, influence of lateral loading on a piled raft was examined, i.e., bending moments and shear forces of the piles were computed using the simplified method proposed by Hamada et al. (2015).

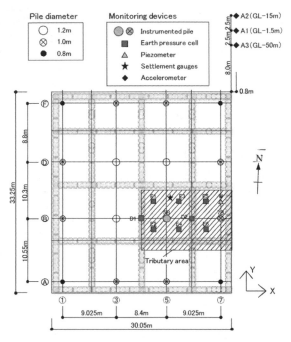

Fig. 3 Layout of piles and grid-form deep mixing walls with locations of monitoring devices

3. INSTRUMENTATION

To confirm the validity of the foundation design, field monitoring was performed on the foundation settlement, the axial loads of the piles and the contact pressure between the raft and the soil, as well as the pore-water pressure beneath the raft, from the beginning of the construction to 101 months after the end of the construction. The locations of the monitoring devices are shown in Fig. 3. Two piles, 5B and 7B, were provided with a couple of LVDT-type strain gauges at depths of 6.0 m (near the pile head), 16.0 m and 46.5 m (near the pile toe) from the ground surface (Photo 3). Near the instrumented piles, eight earth pressure cells and one piezometer were installed beneath the raft at a depth of 4.8 m. Six earth pressure cells, E1-E6, were installed on the intact soil, and two earth pressure cells, D1 and D2, were installed on the top surface of the deep mixing walls. The vertical ground displacements below the raft were measured by differential settlement gauges. LVDT-type transducers were installed beneath the raft at depths of 5.8 m, 16.0 m, 27.1 m and 48.0 m to

Photo 3 Instrumented PHC piles

Table 1 Devices in seismic monitoring

Devices	Properties
IC Card Data Logger	AD converter 24bit, Sampling 100Hz
Servo Accelerometer (Structure & Ground)	Tri-axis, Full scale: ±2000gal
Dynamic Amplifier	LVDT. Frequency Response: 20Hz
Strain gauge	LVDT
Earth pressure cell : on improved soil on intact soil	LVDT, Capacity: 500kPa Capacity: 200kPa
Piezometer	LVDT, Capacity: 100kPa
Settlement gauge	LVDT

measure the relative displacements to a reference point at a depth of 60 m, as shown in Fig. 3. The settlements of the foundation were measured at the points on the raft by an optical level, where a bench mark was set to the monitoring point of the vertical ground displacements. The measurement of the vertical ground displacements was begun just before the foundation construction excavation, late in November 2007. The measurement of the axial loads on the piles, the contact pressure and the pore-water pressure beneath the raft was begun just before the beginning of the reinforcement of the 1.5-m-thick foundation slab.

As for the observations on the seismic response of the soil-foundation-structure system, a vertical array consisting of borehole-type triaxial servo

accelerometers was installed at depths of 1.5 m, 15.0 m and 50.0 m below the ground surface to record the NS, EW and UD accelerations of the ground (8-13 m apart from the NE corner of the building), while triaxial servo accelerometers were installed on the first and the 12th floors as well as the raft to record those of the building, as shown in Fig. 1. The data acquisition system and the devices in the seismic monitoring are shown in Table 1.

4. RESULTS OF MONITORING

4.1 Long-term behavior of piled raft

Fig. 4 shows the measured vertical ground displacements near the center of the raft. The vertical ground displacement at a depth of 5.8 m, which was initialized after the immediate settlement due to the casting of mat slab, was approximately equal to settlement of "piled raft foundation". The foundation settlement reached 14.3 mm at E.O.C. The foundation settlement reached 17.3 mm on March 10, 2011, just before the 2011 Tohoku earthquake. After the earthquake, the foundation settlement increased by 0.3 mm from the pre-earthquake value to 17.6 mm on March 15, 2011. Therefore, no significant change in foundation settlement was observed after the earthquake. Thereafter, the foundation settlements varied from 16 to 18 mm and were found to be quite stable. Fig. 5 shows the settlement profiles of the raft measured

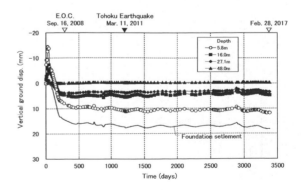

Fig. 4 Measured vertical ground displacements below raft

by an optical level 22 months after the end of the construction. The maximum angular rotation of the raft was 1/1580 rad. The increment of the foundation settlement after that time was very small, hence it is likely that the recent settlement profiles are similar to those in Fig. 5.

Fig. 6 shows the development of the measured axial loads of piles 5B and 7B. The axial load at the pile head of pile 7B decreased very slightly just after the earthquake, while that of pile 5B changed little. Unfortunately, no data were obtained at the pile toe of Pile 5B due to the disconnection during its construction. Fig. 7 shows the development of the measured contact pressure between the raft and the soil and that between the raft and the deep mixing walls (DMW), together with the pore-water pressure beneath the raft. The contact pressure between the raft and the DMW near the periphery (D2) increased slightly from the pre-earthquake value, while the contact pressure in the inner part (D1) increased very slightly. Fig. 8 shows the time-

dependent load sharing among the piles, the DMW, the soil and the buoyancy in the tributary area of columns 5B and 7B. The sum of the measured pile-head loads and the raft load in the tributary area after E.O.C. was 35-40 MN. Here, the raft load means the sum of the total load carried by the DMW and that by the soil. The sum of the measured pile-head loads and the raft load in the tributary area roughly agreed with the sum of the design load for columns 5B and 7B of 36MN.

Fig. 9 shows the load sharing among the piles, the DMWs and the soil in the tributary area versus time. The values of the ratio of the load carried by each component to the effective load after E.O.C. are shown in Table 2. The ratio of the load carried by the piles to the effective load was estimated to

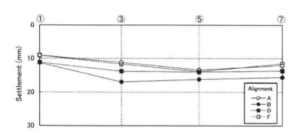

Fig. 5 Measured settlement profile (22 months after E.O.C.)

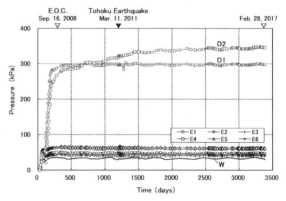

Fig. 7 Measured contact pressure and pore-water pressure

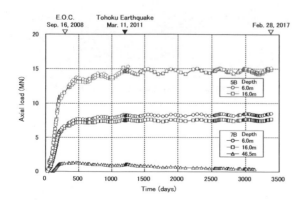

Fig. 6 Measured axial loads of piles 5B and 7B

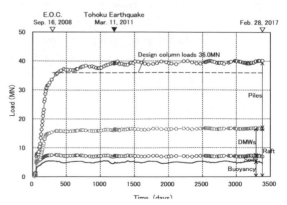

Fig. 8 Load sharing among piles, deep mixing walls and soil in tributary area

Table 2 Load sharing among piles, deep mixing walls and soil

	Sep. 16, 2008[*1]	Mar. 10, 2011[*2]	Mar. 11, 2011[*3]	Mar. 15, 2011	Apr.10,2012 to Jun.30,2014
Ratio of load carried by piles	0.646 (0.540)	0.669 (0.589)	0.660 (0.580)	0.667 (0.582)	0.663-0.672 (0.574-0.588)
Ratio of effective load carried by D.M.W.	0.283	0.264	0.266	0.266	0.268-0.278
Ratio of effective load carried by soil	0.071	0.067	0.074	0.067	0.053-0.065

Values in parentheses are ratios of pile load to total load
[*1] End of construction [*2] Pre-earthquake [*3] Near end of the earthquake (600s after start of event)

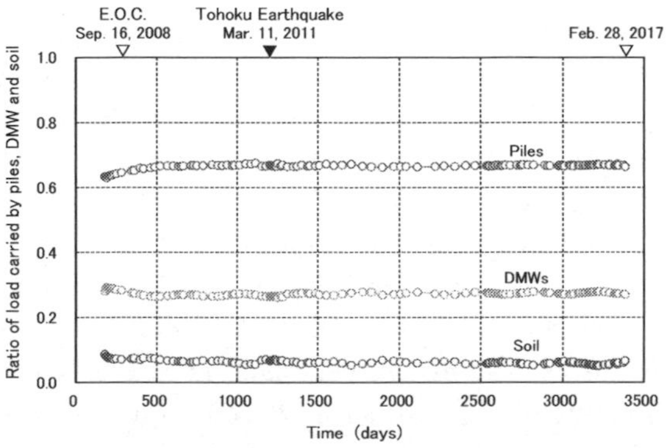

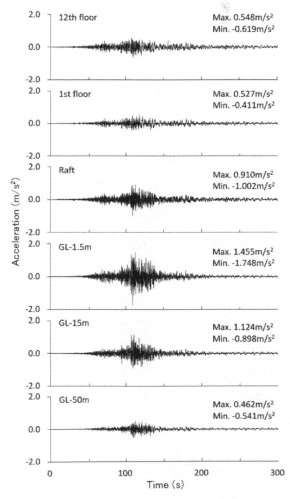

Fig. 9 Lateral load versus rotation angle at pile head in static monotonic ultimate load tests

be 0.67 just before the earthquake. At that time, the ratio of the effective load carried by the DMW was estimated to be 0.26, while the ratio of the effective load carried by the soil was 0.07. Thereafter, the load sharing among the piles, the DMW and the soil was quite stable. As a result, no significant changes in foundation settlement or load sharing were observed after the earthquake.

4.2 Seismic observations during the 2011Tohoku earthquake

The 2011 Tohoku earthquake, with an estimated magnitude of $M_w = 9.0$ on the Moment Magnitude Scale, struck East Japan on March 11, 2011. According to the JMA, an earthquake epicenter was located about 130 km east-southeast off the Oshika Peninsura at a depth of 23.7 km. The distance from the epicenter to the building site was about 380 km.

Fig. 10 Time histories of EW accelerations of ground and structure

Fig. 10 shows the time histories of the EW accelerations of the ground and the structure. A peak horizontal ground acceleration of 1.75 m/s² was observed near the ground surface. Fig. 11 shows the profiles of the peak accelerations in the NS, EW and UD directions. It is seen that the ground acceleration near the surface was dominant in the EW direction. In the EW direction, the peak ground acceleration near the ground surface was 3.2

times amplified from the depth of 50 m. The peak acceleration of the first floor was 0.53 m/s², which were reduced to 53% from those on the raft of 1.00 m/s² by the base-isolation system. Moreover, the peak acceleration on the raft was reduced to 57% from that of the ground surface motion probably because of the input losses due to the kinematic soil-foundation interaction. Consequently, the peak horizontal accelerations of the first floor were reduced to approximately 30% of those of the ground surface motions.

Fig. 12 shows the Fourier spectra of the EW accelerations of the ground motion and those of the structure response, which were smoothed by 0.05Hz Parzen window. As to the accelerations near the ground surface, it can be seen that components of the periods of 0.7, 1.0 and 1.2 s were predominant. The responses of the first and 12th floors were amplified around 3.5 s, which is consistent with the natural period of the base-isolation system against moderate earthquake motions. Fig. 13 shows a spectrum ratio for the EW acceleration spectrum at 1.5 m depth to that at 50 m depth. The predominant period of the alluvial clayey stratum is clearly seen around 1.0 s.

Fig. 11 Profiles of peak accelerations

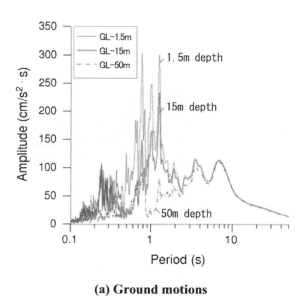

(a) Ground motions

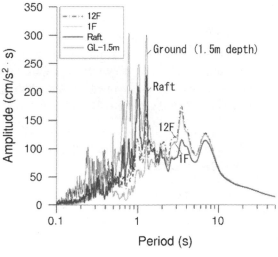

(b) Superstructure responses

Fig. 12 Fourier spectra of EW accelerations

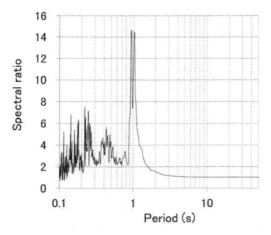

**Fig. 13. Spectral ratio of ground acceleration
(1.5m/50m depth)**

Fig. 14 shows the increments in axial loads of
the piles. The maximum amplitude for Pile 5B
near the pile head was 860 kN in compression
and 853 kN in tension, while that for Pile 7B
near the pile head was 694 kN in compression
and 1030 kN in tension. The largest amplitudes
of axial load occurred at intermediate depths
for both piles. Furthermore, the ratio of the load
amplitude near the pile toe to that near the pile
head was 1.07 in compression and 0.48 in tension,
which is considerably larger than the ratio of the
pile-toe load to the pile-head load in the static
measurements. Fig. 15 shows the increments in
contact pressure between the raft and deep mixing
walls and those between the raft and the soil.

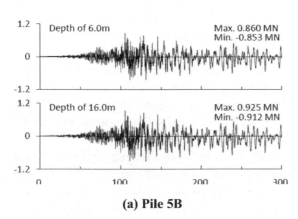

(a) Pile 5B

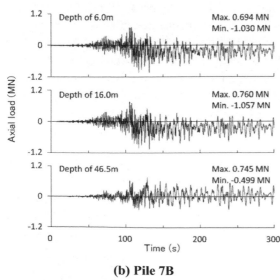

(b) Pile 7B

Fig. 14 Increments of axial loads of piles

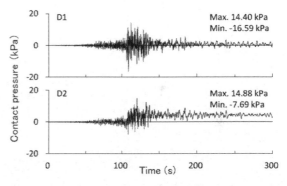

(a) Contact pressures between raft and DMWs

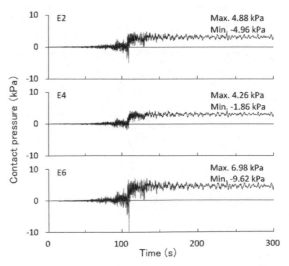

(b) Contact pressures between raft and soil

Fig. 15 Increments of contact pressures

The maximum amplitudes of the contact pressure between the raft and the deep mixing walls were significantly larger than those between the raft and the soil, as in the case of the static measurements. As for the contact pressure between the raft and the soil, the maximum amplitudes from earth pressure cell E6, near the periphery of the raft, were larger than those from E2 and E4, in the inner part.

Fig. 16 shows the pore-water pressure induced

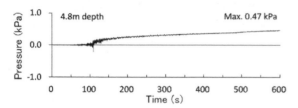

Fig. 16 Excess pore-water pressure beneath raft

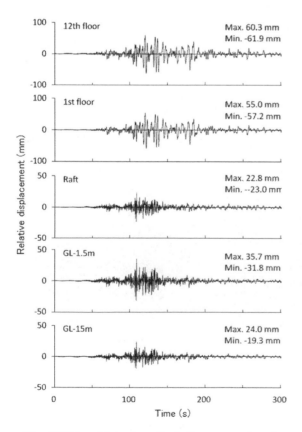

Fig. 17 Time histories of relative ground and structure displacements in EW direction

by the earthquake in the silty sand beneath the raft. While the pore-water pressure increased monotonically, very little excess pore water pressure had built up, and no liquefaction occurred in the silty sand beneath the raft. In addition, no evidence of liquefaction was observed at the site of the building.

Fig. 17 shows the time histories of the relative displacement between the ground (or structure) and that at a depth of 50 m in the EW direction. The displacements were calculated by the double integration of the acceleration records, for which components of periods longer than 20 seconds were cut off.

Fig. 18 shows the time histories for the bending moments of Piles 5B and 7B, respectively. The maximum bending moments near the pile head in the EW direction were 525 and 210 kNm for Piles 5B and 7B, respectively. The maximum bending moment at the intermediate depth (at 16 m depth) were 209 and 153 kNm, respectively, which were not so small compared to those near the pile head.

Fig. 19 shows the design interaction curves for the axial load and the bending moment of the SC pile corresponding to the allowable and the ultimate bending moments for an axial force. Fig. 19 also shows the relationship between the axial loads and the bending moments measured for Piles 5B and 7B near the pile head during the earthquake, where the bending moments are obtained by combining the components in NS and EW directions. Here, the ultimate criterion (the unit stress at the edge of the concrete reaches the compressive strength) corresponds to large earthquake loads, and the allowable criterion (the unit stress at the edge of the concrete is in the elastic condition) corresponds to medium earthquake loads. It is seen that the observed bending moments for both piles are considerably smaller than the allowable bending moment of the pile.

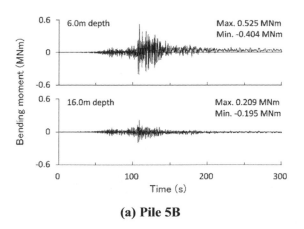

(a) Pile 5B

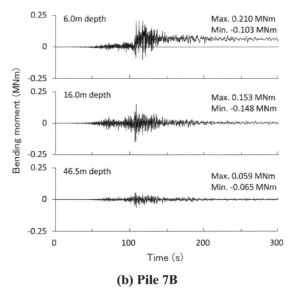

(b) Pile 7B

Fig. 18 Time histories of pile bending moment (EW)

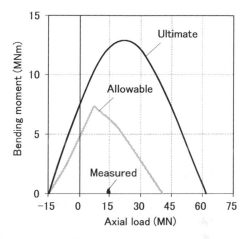

(a) Pile 5B(1.2m dia.)

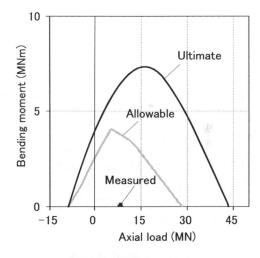

(b) Pile 7B(1.0m dia.)

Fig. 19 Design interaction curves for axial load and bending moment and measured values

5. DISCUSSIONS

5.1   Influence of seismic action on foundation

Seismic action will induce additional lateral forces in the structure and also induce lateral motions in the ground supporting the structure. These can be induced in the foundation system via two mechanisms (Poulos, 2016):

_Inertial forces and the consequent moments developed by the lateral excitation of the structure

_Kinematic forces acting on the raft and piles induced by the action of ground movements

In the following, the effects of the action of ground movements as well as the inertial forces from the structure on the piled raft system were examined based on the seismic monitoring results.

5.2 Effects of inertial force from structure on pile bending moment

Fig. 20 shows the time histories of the bending

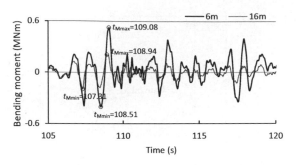

(a) Pile 5B (6 and 16 m depths)

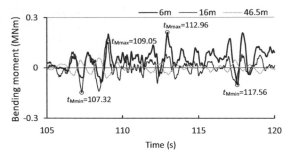

(b) Pile 7B (6, 16 and 46.5 m depths)

Fig. 20 Time history of pile bending moment (EW)

moment in the piles during 105-120 s. The bending moments at depths of 6 and 16 m were in phase both for Piles 5B and 7B, while the bending moment at 46.5 m depth (near the pile toe) in Pile 7B was out of phase.

Fig. 21 shows the time history of the inertial forces from the structure in the EW direction during 105-125 s including the peak responses. The inertial forces were estimated using the mass in structural design and the accelerations observed on the raft, the first and twelfth floors shown in Fig. 10. The weight of the superstructure above the seismic isolators and that of the raft are 152 and 41 MN, respectively (Hamada et al., 2014). Although the mass of the superstructure is much greater than that of the raft, the estimated peaks of the superstructure inertial force were slightly greater than those of the raft inertial force due to the base isolation system. As indicated by the red circles in Fig. 21, the superstructure inertial force was out of phase with the raft inertial force and also with the structure inertial force (which means the sum of the superstructure and raft inertial forces) when the bending moment near the pile head (5B) was at its maximum (t_{Mmax} = 109.08 s) shown in Fig. 20(a). However, when the bending moment was at its minimum (t_{Mmin} = 108.51 s), the superstructure inertial force was in phase with both the raft and structure inertial forces. The relation of the raft inertial force with the superstructure inertial force (during 0-150 s) is shown in Fig. 22. There appears to be a negative correlation between them and both

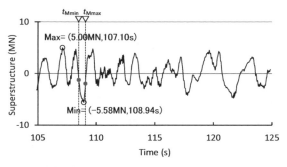

(a) Superstructure inertial force

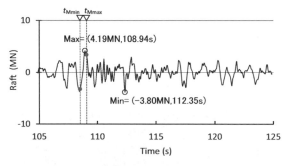

(b) Raft inertial force

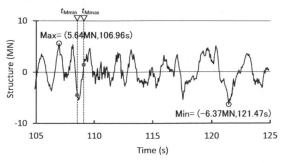

(c) Structure inertial force

Fig. 21 Time history of inertial forces (EW)

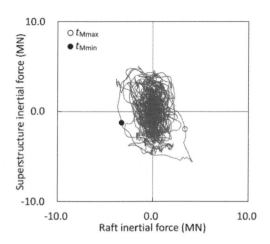

**Fig. 22 Raft inertial force vs. superstructure
inertial force**

t_{Mmax} and t_{Mmin}, respectively. This arises because
the behavior of the embedded raft (i.e., the raft
inertial force) would be affected significantly by
the ground displacements near the surface which
had strong correlation with the bending moment (as
shown in Fig. 24(a)). The maximum amplitude of
the structure inertial force was −4.5 MN at $t = t_{Mmin}$
and generated 70% of its minimum as shown in
Fig. 23(c). Thus, the effect of the structure inertial
force on the bending moment was not necessarily
significant.

5.3 Effects of lateral ground displacements on pile bending moment

Fig. 24 shows the relations of the ground
displacement with the bending moment. The
bending moments near the pile head in both
the piles had strong correlation with the ground
displacements near the surface. Furthermore, the
bending moments at 16 m depth had significant
correlation with the ground displacements at 15 m
depth. The relations of the raft displacement with
the bending moment near the pile head are shown
in Fig. 25. It is seen that the bending moment near
the pile head had strong correlation with the raft
displacement (which is approximately equal to the
ground displacement just below the raft bottom at
4.8 m depth) for both the piles.

the inertial forces tend to cancel each other. As a
result, the peaks of the structure inertial force was
comparable with those of the superstructure inertial
force.

Fig. 23 shows the relations of the inertial force with
the bending moment near the pile head (5B). It is
seen that the superstructure inertial force had no
significant correlation with the bending moment.
On the other hand, the raft inertial force was in
phase with the bending moment, and generated
81 and 86% of its maximum and minimum at $t =$

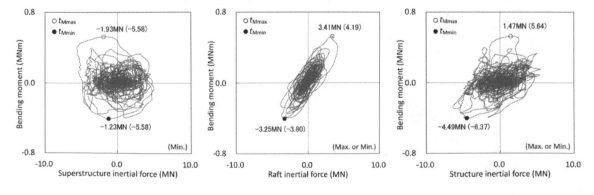

(a) **Superstructure inertial force**   (b) **Raft inertial force**   (c) **Structure inertial force**

Fig. 23 Inertial force vs. bending moment near pile head in Pile 5B(EW)

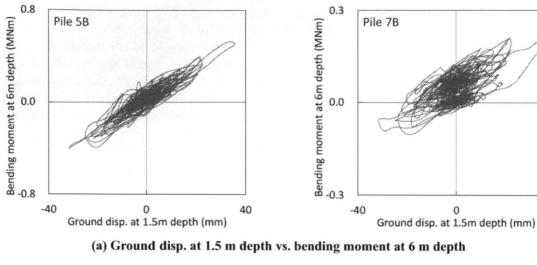

(a) Ground disp. at 1.5 m depth vs. bending moment at 6 m depth

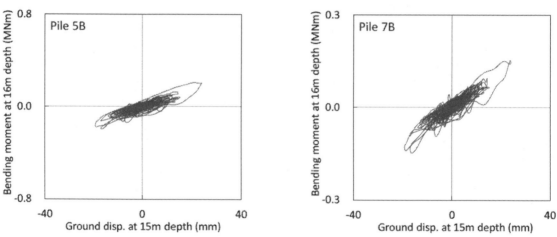

(b) Ground disp. at 15 m depth vs. bending moment at 16 m depth

Fig. 24 Ground displacement at 1.5 and 15 m depths vs. bending moment at 6 and 16 m depths (EW)

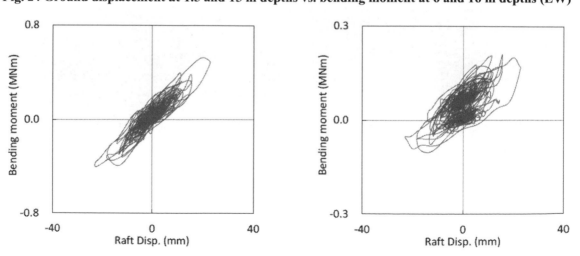

Fig. 25 Raft displacement vs. bending moment at 6 m depth (EW)

Fig. 26 shows the time histories of the ground displacements at 1.5 and 15 m depths and the raft displacement relative to the ground displacement at 50 m depth during 105-120 s including the maximum and minimum responses. It is seen that all the displacement histories were almost in phase. Fig. 27(a) shows the relation of the ground displacement at 1.5 m depth with that at 15 m depth. The ground displacement at 1.5 m depth had strong correlation with that at 15 m depth,

but the amplitude of the former was considerably greater than that of the latter. Namely, the ground displacement near the surface was about 1.5 times amplified from that at 15 m depth. Fig. 27(b) shows the relation of the ground displacement at 1.5 m depth with the raft displacement. The ground displacement near the surface had strong correlation also with the raft displacement, while the amplitude of the former was considerably greater than that of the latter. Fig. 28 shows

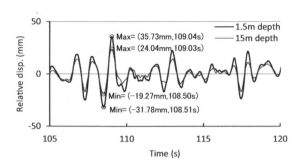

(a) Ground displacements (1.5 and 15 m depths)

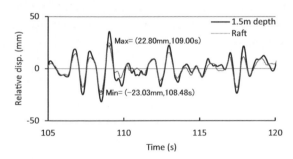

(b) Ground (1.5 m depth) and raft displacements

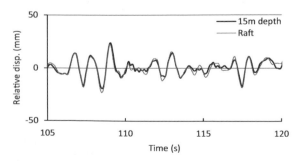

(c) Ground (15 m depth) and raft displacements

Fig. 26 Time history of relative ground displacement and raft displacement (EW)

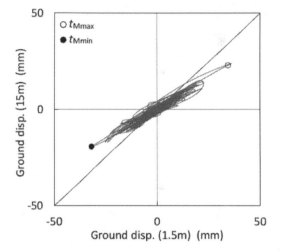

(a) Ground disp. (1.5m) vs. ground disp. (15m)

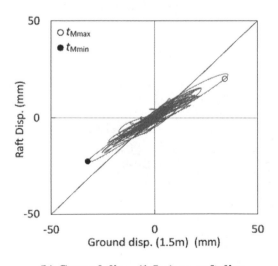

(b) Ground disp. (1.5m) vs. raft disp.

Fig. 27 Ground displacement at 1.5 m depth vs. ground displacement at 15m depth and raft displacement

the relation of the ground displacement at 15 m depth with the raft displacement. It is seen that the raft displacement was in phase with the ground displacement at 15 m depth and both the amplitudes were almost identical. This indicates that the DMWs, whose bottom reached relatively stiff clay below the depth of 15.7 m, restrained the amplification of the lateral ground displacements in the DMW grids.

Fig. 29 shows the relations of the relative displacement ($\delta S - \delta R$) with the bending moment near the pile head (5B and 7B), where δS and δR mean the ground displacement near the surface and raft displacement, respectively. Tamura and Hida (2014) have pointed out based on the dynamic centrifuge tests on a superstructure-footing model in sand that the peaks of dynamic earth pressure acting on the side of the embedded pile cap increased concurrently with the relative displacement between the pile cap and the soil. Fig. 29 suggests that the bending moments near the pile head have significant correlation with the dynamic earth pressure acting on the raft side.

Fig. 30 shows the relation of the structure inertial force with the relative displacement ($\delta S - \delta R$). Although there appears to be no significant correlation between them, the relative displacement at $t = t_{Mmax}$ or t_{Mmin} was in phase with the structure inertial force. Hence, it is likely that the dynamic earth pressure acting on the raft side and the structure inertial force acted in the same direction at the times increasing pile stresses, where the absolute value of δS was greater than that of δR.

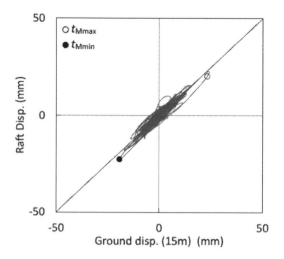

Fig. 28 Relation of ground displacement at 15 m depth with raft displacement

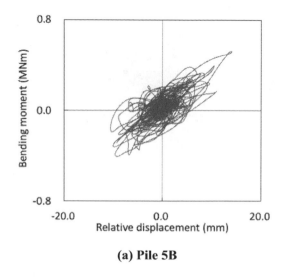

(a) Pile 5B

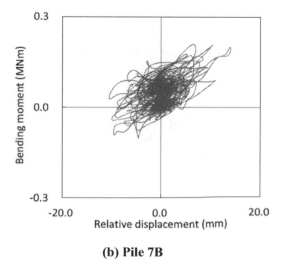

(b) Pile 7B

Fig. 29 Relative displacement (δS - δR) vs. bending moment near pile head

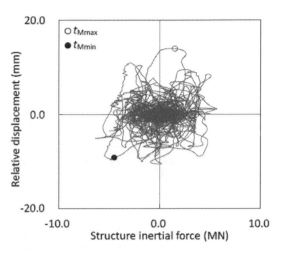

Fig. 30 Structure inertial force vs. relative displacement ($\delta S - \delta R$)

5.4 Dynamic soil-structure interaction in pile raft system

Fig. 31 shows the profiles of the EW relative ground displacements and pile bending moments at $t = t_{Mmax}$ and $t = t_{Mmin}$, together with the maximum and minimum values of the bending moment and displacement. It is seen that the bending moment near the pile head (7B) and those at the intermediate depth in both the piles were close to their maximum at t = tMmax, and the bending moments at the intermediate depth were close to their minimum at t = tMmin while the bending moment near the pile head (7B) was not close to its minimum. In contrast, the bending moment near the pile toe was very close to its minimum and maximum at $t = t_{Mmax}$ and t_{Mmin}, respectively. At that time the relative ground

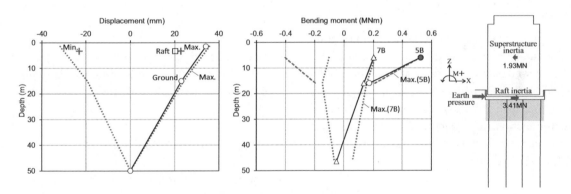

(a) At maximum bending moment near pile head (5B)

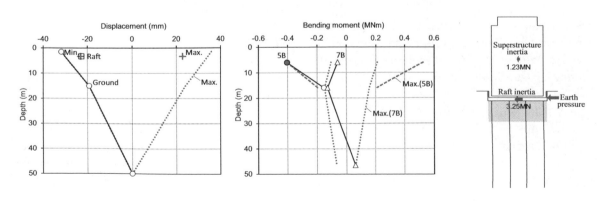

(b) At minimum bending moment near pile head (5B)

Fig. 31 Profiles of relative ground displacement and pile bending moment

displacements both at 1.5 and 15 m depths and the raft displacements were very close to their maximum or minimum. Fig. 31 also shows the schematic of foundation deformation and external forces acting on the structure which was supposed based on the monitoring data. Tamura and Hida (2014) proposed a method for estimating the phase difference between the structure inertia and earth pressure acting on the raft side. According to the method, if the natural period of the superstructure is greater than predominant period of the ground and δS is greater than δR (which corresponds to the case of the soil-structure system in this paper), the earth pressure tends to be out of phase with the superstructure inertia that is out of phase with the raft inertia. The phase differences illustrated in Fig. 31 are generally consistent with the estimation by the method, while the superstructure inertia was in phase with the raft inertia at $t = t_{\text{Mmin}}$.

Consequently, it was found that the maximum bending moment near the pile head, as well as that at the intermediate depth, were affected mainly by the lateral displacements of the thick alluvial silty clay, rather than the shear force resulting from the structure inertial force. These results are consistent with those in previous studies (Yamashita et al., 2012; Hamada et al., 2014).

6. CONCLUSIONS

Based on the examination of the seismic monitoring data on the soil-pile-structure system recorded during the 2011 Tohoku earthquake, the following conclusions can be drawn:

(1) A peak horizontal ground acceleration of 1.75 m/s^2 was observed near the surface, and the maximum ground displacement near the ground surface (relative to 50 m depth) was 36 mm. No significant changes in foundation settlement or load sharing were observed after the earthquake.

(2) The bending moments near the pile head had significant correlation with the ground displacement near the surface, and the bending moments at the intermediate depth (16 m depth) had also significant correlation with the ground displacement at 15 m depth. Thus, it was found that the maximum bending moment near the pile head, as well as that at the intermediate depth, were affected mainly by the lateral displacements of the thick alluvial silty clay, rather than the shear force resulting from the structure inertial force.

(3) It was found that the DMWs, whose bottom reached relatively stiff clay below the depth of 15.7 m, restrained the amplification of the lateral ground displacements in the DMW grids. This would be one of reasons for the fact that the bending moments near the pile head were considerably smaller than the allowable criterion in the design.

(4) It is confirmed that a piled raft with grid-form DMWs works effectively in grounds consisting of liquefiable sand and soft cohesive soil.

ACKNOWLEDGEMENTS

The authors are grateful to Mr. Y. Shigeno of Takenaka Corporation for his contribution to interpreting the seismic monitoring data.

REFERENCES

Hamada, J., Shigeno, Y., Onimaru, S., Tanikawa, T., Nakamura, N. and Yamashita, K. (2014). Numerical analysis on seismic response of piled raft foundation with ground improvement based on seismic observation records, *Proc. of the 14th Int. Assoc. Computer Methods and Recent Advances in Geomechanics*, 719-724.

Hamada, J., Tsuchiya, T., Tanikawa, T. and Yamashita, K. (2015). Lateral loading tests on piled rafts and simplified method to evaluate sectional forces of piles, *Geotechnical Engineering J. the SEAGS & AGSSEA*, Vol. 46, No.2, 29-42.

Hamada, J., Aso, N., Hanai, A. and Yamashita, K. (2015). Seismic performance of piled raft subjected to unsymmetrical earth pressure based on seismic observation records, *Proc. of the 6th Int. Conf. on Earthquake Geotechnical Engineering.*

Horikoshi, K., Matsumoto, T., Hashizume, Y., Watanabe, T. and Fukuyama, H. (2003a). Performance of piled raft foundation subjected to static horizontal loads, *Int. J. Phys. Model. Geotech.* 3 (2), 37-50.

Horikoshi, K., Matsumoto, T., Hashizume, Y., Watanabe, T. and Fukuyama, H. (2003b). Performance of piled raft foundation subjected to dynamic loading, *Int. J. Phys. Model. Geotech.* 3 (2), 51-62.

Katzenbach, R., Arslan, U. and Moormann, C. (2000). Piled raft foundation projects in Germany, *Design applications of raft foundations*, Hemsley J.A. Editor, Thomas Telford, 323-392.

Katzenbach, R. and Turek, J. (2005). Combined pile-raft foundation subjected to lateral loads, *Proc. of the 16th ICSMGE*, 2001-2004.

Kitiyodom, P. and Matsumoto, T. (2002). A simplified analysis method for piled raft and pile group foundations with batter piles, *Int. J. Numerical and Analytical Methods in Geomechanics*, 26, 1349-1369.

Kitiyodom, P. and Matsumoto, T. (2003). A simplified analysis method for piled raft foundations in non-homogeneous soils, *Int. J. Numerical and Analytical Methods in Geomechanics*, 27, 85-109.

Mandolini, A., Russo, G. and Viggiani, C. (2005). Pile foundations: Experimental investigations, analysis and design, *Proc. of the 16th ICSMGE*, Vol. 1, 177-213.

Matsumoto, T., Fukuyama, K., Kitiyodom, P., Oki, A. and Horikoshi, K. (2004a). Experimental and analytical study on behaviour of model piled rafts in sand subjected to horizontal and moment loading, *Int. J. Phys. Model. Geotech.* 4 (3), 1-19.

Matsumoto, T., Fukuyama, K., Oki, A. and Horikoshi, K. (2004b). Shaking table tests on model piled rafts in sand considering influence of superstructures, *Int. J. Phys. Model. Geotech.* 4 (3), 21-38.

Matsumoto, T., Nemoto, H., Mikami, H., Yaegashi, K., Arai, T. and Kitiyodom, P. (2010). Load tests of piled raft models with different pile head connection conditions and their analyses, *Soils and Foundations*, Vol.50, No.50, 63-81.

Mendoza, M.J., Romo, M.P., Orozco, M. and Dominguez, L. (2000). Static and seismic behavior of a friction pile-box foundation in Mexico City clay, *Soils & Foundations* 40 (4), 143-154.

Poulos, H.G. (2001). Piled raft foundations: design and applications, *Geotechnique* 51, No. 2, 95-113.

Poulos, H. G. (2016). Lessons learned from designing high-rise building foundations, *Proc. of the 19th Southeast Asian Geotechnical Conference & 2nd AGSSEA Conference*, Kuala Lumpur, 45-59.

Rollins, K.M. and Sparks, A. (2002). Lateral resistance of full-scale pile cap with gravel backfill, *J. Geotechnical and Geoenviromental Engineering*, ASCE, Vol:128, No.9, 711-723.

Sawada, K. and Takemura, J. (2014). Centrifuge tests on piled raft foundation in sand subjected to lateral and moment loads, *Soils & Foundations*, Vol. 54, No. 2, 126-140.

Tamura, S. and Hida, T. (2014). Pile stress estimation based on seismic deformation method with embedment effects on pile caps, *J. Geotechnical and Geoenvironmental Engineering, ASCE*, Vol:140, No.9, 04014049.

Yamashita, K., Yamada, T. and Kakurai, M. (1998). Simplified method for analyzing piled raft foundations, *Proc. of the 3rd International Geotechnical Seminar on Deep Foundations on Bored and Auger Piles BAP III*, 457-464.

Yamashita, K., Yamada, T. and Hamada, J. (2011a). Investigation of settlement and load sharing on piled rafts by monitoring full-scale structures, *Soils & Foundations*, Vol. 51, No. 3, 513-532.

Yamashita, K., Hamada, J. and Yamada, T. (2011b). Field measurements on piled rafts with grid-form deep mixing walls on soft ground, *Geotechnical Engineering J. the SEAGS & AGSSEA*, Vol. 42, No. 2, 1-10.

Yamashita, K., Hamada, J., Onimaru, S. and Higashino, M. (2012). Seismic behavior of piled raft with ground improvement supporting a base-isolated building on soft ground in Tokyo, *Soils & Foundations*, Vol. 52, No. 5, 1000-1015.

Yamashita, K., Hamada, J. and Tanikawa, T. (2016). Static and seismic performance of a friction piled raft combined with grid-form deep mixing walls in soft ground, *Soils & Foundations*, Vol. 56 (3), 559-573.

CHAPTER 17

MONITORING OF LOAD DISTRIBUTION OF THE PILES AND THE RAFT OF A BUILDING FOUNDATION IN BANGKOK CLAY

Pastsakorn Kitiyodom*
Geotechnical & Foundation Engineering Co., Ltd., Thailand, *pastsakorn_k@gfe.co.th

Kongpop Watcharasawe
Pornkasem Jongpradist
Department of Civil Engineering, King Mongkut's University of Technology Thonburi, Thailand

Tatsunori Matsumoto
Graduate School of Science & Technology, Kanazawa University, Kanazawa, Japan

Kasem Petchgate
Kasem Design & Consultant Co., Ltd, Thailand

Jerasak Prachgosin
International Project Administration Co., Ltd., Thailand

ABSTRACT: In Bangkok, there are many high-rise building projects with basement storey constructed in Bangkok clay. Meanwhile, the deeper basements foundations are constructed on the stiff soil, the economic advantage may be utilized by taking into account load-bearing capacity of the mat foundation (raft). This paper presents the monitoring of load distribution on the piles and the raft of a building with basement levels in stiff clay (-16 m below GL) at the Siriraj Hospital site, Bangkok, Thailand. In addition, a simplified analysis program PRAB was employed to predict the loads distribution and the settlement of the piles and the raft. It was found that the field measurements agreed well with the prediction. Although foundation of this building was designed based on pile group concept, the raft carried around 14% of total load during the construction of mat foundation.

1. INTRODUCTION

In Thailand, designers prefer to consider using pile group to support structure load from the building (Amornfa et al, 2012). The pile group mostly focus on pile capacity and group settlement without considering the presence of the raft or the mat. In fact, usually the building foundation is constructed using concrete and its bottom surface is attached to the soil beneath. Therefore, in most cases end up with overdesign of the foundation.

The use of piled raft foundations has become more popular in recent years, as the concept of combined action of the raft and the piles can increase the bearing capacity and reduce the number of piles.

Thus, the piled raft systems have been used extensively in many parts of the world e.g. England (Hooper, 1973), Japan (Yamashita et al. 1994; Yamashita et al. 1998), Germany (Poulos, 2001 and Randolph, 1994). In Thailand, the design following this concept is not yet developed. Although, the deeper basements foundations are designed by pile group concept, but in the reality the economic advantage may be utilized by considering load-bearing capacity of the raft, this issue was reported on previous studies (Watcharasawe et al. 2015).

This research was conducted to monitoring on the foundation of a high-rise (124 m in height) building with basement levels in stiff clay (-16 m below GL.) namely "Navamindrapobitr 84th Anniversary Building" at the Siriraj Hospital site, Bangkok, Thailand (Fig. 1). To investigate load sharing between the piles and the raft of the building foundation, field measurements were performed on this building foundation. The load distribution of representative piles and the raft are measured.

In this paper, monitoring results are described. In addition, a simplified analysis program PRAB (Piled Raft Analysis with Batter piles) developed by Kitiyodom and Matsumoto (2002, 2003) (Kitiyodom et al. 2005) was employed to predict the loads distribution and the settlement of the piles and the raft throughout the end of construction. In this program, the raft is modelled as a thin plate

Fig. 1 Navamindrapobitr 84th Anniversary Building (2016-2019).

elements, the piles as elastic beams and the soil is treated as interactive springs.

2. SITE DESCRIPTION AND INSTRUMENTATION PLAN

2.1 Subsoil Condition

The construction site was located very close to Chao Phraya River, Bangkok, Thailand. The subsoil profiles at the construction site, section plan of foundation, pile layout and instrument in foundation are shown in Figures 2, 3 and 4 respectively.

The subsoil profile is shown in Figure 2. The top 2.5 m thick layer is the weathered crust, which is underlain by 11.0 m thick soft to medium clay layer. A stiff clay layer is found at the depth of 15.0 m from the surface. Below the stiff clay is hard clay, the thickness is about 4m. The first sand layer is generally found at a depth of 30 to 37m. Below the upper first sand layer, there is stiff clay and further down alternating layers of dense sand and hard clay. No groundwater level was found during construction.

2.2 Site Description

The "Navamindrapobitr 84th Anniversary" Building is under construction. The construction is planned to be completed in 2019. The building is 24-storied with two basement floor having a building area of 3,079m², a total floor area of 75,683.26m², a maximum height of 124.25m, and a basement level of -15.65m below ground surface.

The pile foundation was designed using the pile group concept with a safety factor 2.5.

The piles and instrumentation layouts at the construction site are shown in Figure 4. A total of 350 piles with a length of 40m are embedded in the dense sand layer (SPT N-value of 60). A raft is placed on the stiff clay layer (SPT N-value

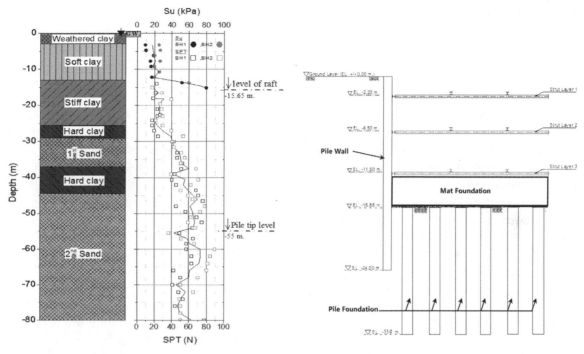

Fig. 2 Profiles of soil layer, SPT N-values and Su at the construction site

Fig. 3 The section plan of foundation at the construction site

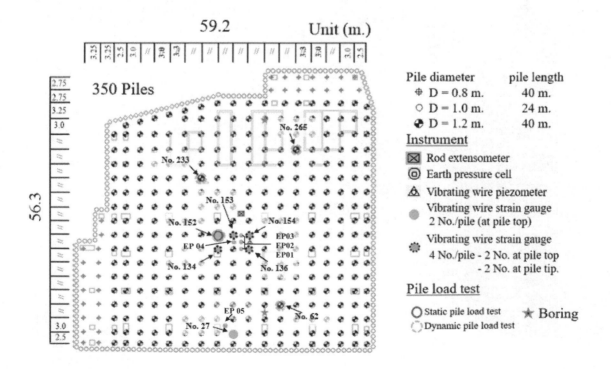

Fig. 4. Pile layout and instrument in the construction site

Table 1 Summary geometrical and the material properties of piles and raft

	Length(m)	Diam. or Thick. (m)	Young's modulus(kPa)	Poisson's Ratio, v
Bored Pile	39.5	1.2	2.65×10^7	0.2
Test pile	55	1.2	2.65×10^7	0.2
Raft		3.3	3.31×10^7	0.2

of 20) with 3.3m thickness. The piles and raft were concrete with steel reinforcing bars. The raft foundation is designed with high strength of concrete. Table 1 summarizes the material parameters of piles and raft in the analysis. Young's modulus of the pile E_p and the raft E_r was estimated based on value of Young's modulus of each type of concrete.

A pile test location of the Static and Dynamic load tests are also shown in Figure 4. The pile test was a bored concrete pile having length of 55m, diameter 1.2m.

The bore piles were constructed below the ground surface by -13 m and cut off after excavated of soil, pile No. 134, 136, 152, 153, and 154 were instrumented with vibrating wire strain gauges at pile top and pile tip. Pile No. 27, 152 were instrumented with strain gauges only at pie top.

3. ANALYSIS OF STATIC LOAD PILE TEST

In the analysis, the characteristics of foundation in the site subsoil condition and the soil resistance parameter are shown in Figure 5.

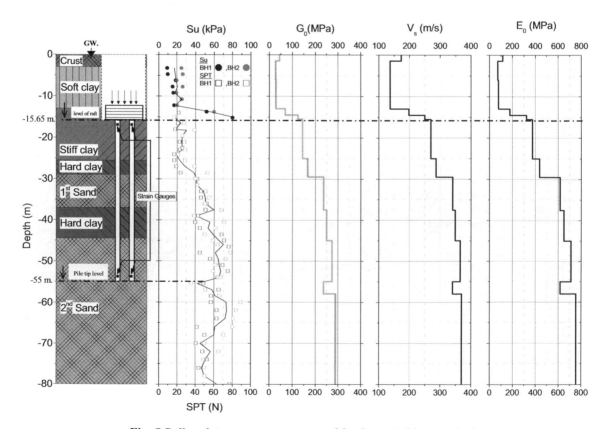

Fig. 5 Soil resistance parameter used in the matching analysis

The maximum small-strain shear modulus and Young's modulus G_0, and E_0 are considered in this analysis, the shear modulus of the soil at the maximum small-strain are determined from the given shear wave velocity, V_s, at the site.

Hence, the shear wave velocity of the soil was estimated by the observed equation as shown in Eq. (1) following Imai (1977).

$$V_s = 91 N^{0.378} (m/s) \qquad (1)$$

The shear modulus of the soil at the low strain G_0 was calculated as equation shown in Eq. (2)

$$G_0 = \rho_s V_s^2 \qquad (2)$$

Define the E_0 as maximum small-strain Young's modulus for each layer. E_0 were calculated from G_0 and Poisson's ratio, v as:

$$E_0 = 2(1 + v)G_0 \qquad (3)$$

The comparison of the calculated of PRAB and measured load-settlement curves at pile head as shown in Figure 6. It was found that the values of the small-strain Young's modulus of the soils, E_0 performed a good matching with measured data.

In addition, the static load-settlement from wave matching analysis with dynamic pile load test using numeric signal matching programs CAPWAP is also shown in the figure.

4. LOAD DISTRIBUTION OF PILES AND RAFT

In this study, the axial load of each pile in the foundation were also predicted using a simplified deformation analytical program PRAB. Due to the similarity of pile arrangement, the spacing around 2.5-2.75 in diameter. Therefore, to eliminate complexity in the calculation, only symmetric segments zone was performed in this analysis. The analysis zone as shown in Figure 7

For the analysis using PRAB, a 39m × 39m t = 3.3m. square raft with 169 piles is considered in this study, where t is thickness of raft. The bored piles have diameter (d) of 1.2m being arranged in the foundation with spacing of 2.5d and the length of pile is 39.5m at the 2nd sand layer below the ground surface.

Load acting on the pile foundation at each construction step of mat foundation are

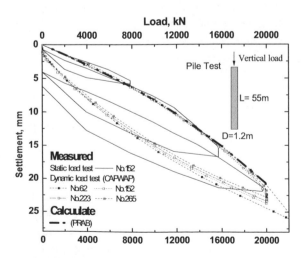

Fig. 6 Comparision of Load-settlement curves of the test plie.

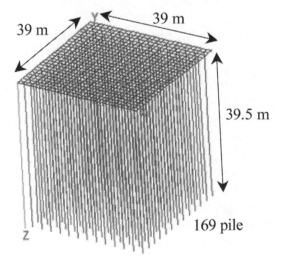

Fig. 7 A typical 3D simulation used in this analysis.

Table 2 Summary of loads at construction step of mat foundation on numerical analysis conducted

Step	Date (month)	Total Load(kPa)	Description
1	0.5	3.96	Reinforced steel of Mat foundation Layer 1.
2	0.57	39.6	Concrete Mat L1. (1.65m.)
3	1.5	43.56	Reinforced steel of Mat foundation Layer 2.
4	1.87	79.2	Concrete Mat L2. (1.65m.)

summarized in Table 2. The construction of mat foundation is distribution the weight of concrete in term of uniform load. Therefore, the Uniform Distribution Load (UDL) are performed in this analysis. It is noted that the self-weight of the raft is applied through on the plate element by using UDL step are shown in Table 2.

Fig. 8 shows the axial force distribution of calculated on the top pile at the end of mat construction. The analysis results show that the piles in the central zone are carry smaller load of structure than edge and corner piles, which is typical for a pile foundation under working load conditions. Because of the block deformation of the pile group discussed above and only small differential displacements between the piles at the centre of the raft and the surrounding soil. Hence the pile shaft loads of the centre piles are substantially smaller than the pile shaft loads of the edge or corner piles.

The comparisons between the load distributions of piles at mat construction step calculated using PRAB and monitoring value of piles No. 27, 134, 136, 152, 153 and 154 shows in Figure 9. The equivalent zone of pile location in analysis were compared with the measurement value. Increment of axial force on top of each piles are related with the construction stage. The step load of mat construction no influence on the pile base. This mean that the current weight of the structure are very small when compared with the capacity of the pile. It can be seen that analysis results are in good agreements with the measured values at each construction step.

Figure 10 shows the comparisons between the

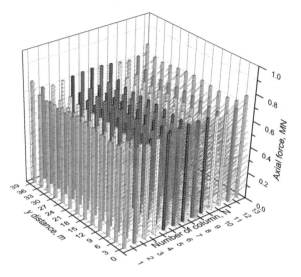

Fig. 8 Load distributions on piles in foundation

total load of building and measured value of the load carry by raft during mat construction with the calculated results. The measured earth pressure is increased with increasing in self weight of the mat. The average load carried by raft is about 14% at the end of mat construction. The calculated values show good agreement with the measured values.

5. PREDICTION OF SETTLEMENT AND THE LOAD CARRIED BY PILE AND RAFT

Figure 11 show the prediction of raft settlement calculated by PRAB. The deflection of raft in different load levels of construction are illustrated in Figures 11. For the raft in the *x*-direction at *y* = 19.5m. The calculated results show that, the settlement increase with the load of building. The analysis results also show that the deflection of the

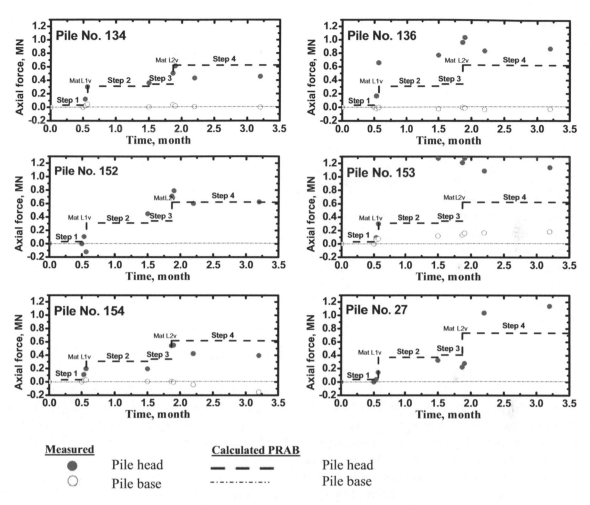

Fig. 9 Load distributions of piles in foundation

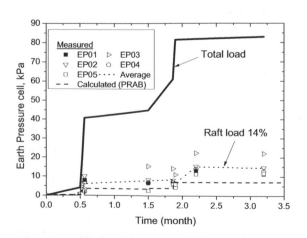

Fig. 10 Load-bearing effect of raft in foundation

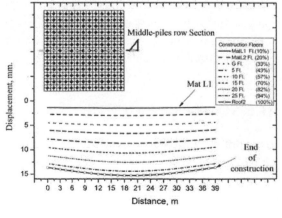

Fig. 11 Raft deflection along middle-piles row
sectionof foundation

raft increases with increasing the load of building. The differential deflection of raft with 30% load of construction is very small. Whereas, the deflection of raft at the end of construction is 1.71 mm between edge to central and overall settlement at 15 mm

Figure 12 shows the time-total load of building, measured and calculated of pile-raft foundation. The construction of building is under construction, and is plan to be finished in 2019. The raft was completed at the end of August 2016. The raft was located at 15.65 m below ground surface. Both measured values and the analysis results show that when the raft was placed on deeper soil layer, although the foundation has been designed using pile group concept, the raft is carried about 10% of the total structure load.

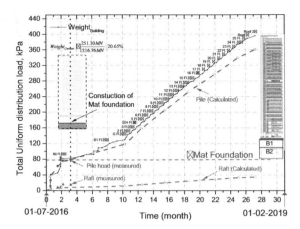

Fig. 12 Time-total load of building, measured and calculated of pile-raft foundation

Westcon co., Ltd.

6. CONCLUSIONS

This paper presents the monitoring of load distribution on the piles and the raft throughout the construction of mat foundation building. A simplified analysis program PRAB was employed to predict the load distribution and the settlement of the piles and the raft. It was found that the calculated results match well with the measurement value. Although foundation of the building was designed based on pile group concept the raft carried around 14% of the total load during the construction of mat foundation. The above results confirmed possibility of using piled raft design concept in Bangkok subsoil condition.

ACKNOWLEDGEMENTS

The authors gratefully acknowledge financial support by International Project Administration Company Limited, Thailand Research Fund (TRF) and Geotechnical & Foundation Engineering Co., Ltd. (GFE) through the TRF-Rri Project under Contract No 58I0050. Thanks, are also extended to the Siriraj Hospital, Plan Consultants Co., Ltd and

REFERENCES

Amornfa, K., Phienwej, N. and Kitpayuck, P. (2012). urrent practice on foundation design of high-rise buildings in Bangkok, Thailand, *Lowland technology international*, Vol: 14, pp 70-83.

El-Mossalamy, Y., El-Nahhas, F. and Essawy, A. (2006). Innovative Use of Piled Raft Foundation to Optimize the Design of High-Rise Buildings. *10th Arab Structural Engineering Conference*, pp. 13-15

Hooper, J.A. (1973). Observations on the behaviour of a piled-raft foundation on London clay. *Proc. Instn. Civil Engrs*, Vol: 55, pp 855- 877.

Kitiyodom, P. and Matsumoto, T. (2002). A simplified analysis method for piled raft and piles. *International Journal for Numerical and Analytical Methods in Geomechanics*, Vol: 26, 1349-1369

Kitiyodom, P. and Matsumoto, T. (2003). A simplified analysis method for piled raft foundation in non homogeneous soils.

International Journal for Numerical and Analytical Methods in Geomechanics, Vol: 27, 185-109

Kitiyodom, P., Matsumoto, T. and Kawaguchi, K. (2005). A simplified analysis method for piled raft foundation to ground movement induced by tunnellling. *International Journal for Numerical and Analytical Methods in Geomechanics*, Vol: 29, 1485-1507

Poulos H. G. (2001). Piled raft foundations: design and application. *Geotechnique*, Vol: 51, No.2, pp. 95-113.

Randolph, M.F. (1994). Design methods for pile groups and piled rafts. *Proc. of the 13th International Conference on Soil Mechanics and Foundation Engineering*, New Delhi, Vol: 5, pp 1–82.

Watcharasawe, K., Kitiyodom, P. and Jongpradist, P. (2015). Numerical Analyses of Piled Raft Foundation in soft soil using 3D-FEM. *South-East Asian Geotechnical Society Journal*, Vol: 46(1), pp. 109-116.

Yamashita, K., Kakurai, M. and Yamada, T. (1994). Investigation of a piled raft foundation on stiff clay. Proc of the 13th International Conference on Soil Mechanics and Foundation Engineering, New Delhi, pp 543-546.

Yamashita, K., Yamada, T. and Kakurai, M. (1998). Simplified method for analyzing piled raft foundations. Proc. of the 3rd International Geotechnical Seminar on Deep Foundation on Bored and Auger Piles, pp 457–464.

CHAPTER 18

USE OF GRID SOIL MIXED WALLS FOR INCREASED LATERAL PILE RESISTANCE IN COAL ASH POND

Shih-Hao Cheng*
Taiwan Building Technology Center, National Taiwan University of Science and Technology, Taipei City, Taiwan
**shcheng@mail.ntust.edu.tw*

Hung-Jiun Liao, Sin-Lan Lu
Department of Civil and Construction Engineering, National Taiwan University of Science and Technology, Taipei City, Taiwan

Der-Wen Chang
Department of Civil Engineering, Tamkang University, New Taipei City, Taiwan

Lih-Wen Quo
Taiwan Power Research Institute, Taiwan Power Company Ltd., Taipei City, Taiwan

ABSTRACT: The lateral resistance of pile foundation is often critical to evaluate the pile performance as well as to design its diameter. If an inadequate lateral resistance of the pile diameter design is performed from the analysis, additional piles or an increase in pile diameter or micro-piles are used to enhance the lateral resistance of pile. However, the move runs against the rising green consciousness. This paper aims to study the effectiveness of enhancing the lateral resistance of pile with three different sets of test results, in comparison with the traditional measures mentioned above. In the first case, as control sample, testing pile is located in untreated coal ash pond. In the second one, the pile is installed in the center of a grid of in-situ mixed wall. For the third one, the pile is constructed inside grid mixed wall, while stirring and curing took place at the depth of 2.0 m of shallow treatment. As a result, a twice and fourfold increase in horizontal subgrade reaction coefficient of pile in the second case and third case respectively is obtained compared to that of untreated coal ash stratum. Furthermore, these new measures can significantly decrease the bending moment of plies by 51% and 78%. This proves that grid mixed wall can aid in reducing the diameter of piles. More numerical results need to be done to evaluate exactly how major a change will be.

1. INTRODUCTION

Deep pile foundation is usually adapted to high-rise superstructures and bridges on soft ground or potentially liquefiable soils. The lateral resistance of pile is the most important consideration during earthquake-resistant design. Especially, when pile foundation is located in the liquefiable area, its lateral resistance during the earthquake decreases apparently. Hence, if analyses are applied at the design stage to find out some results showing the inadequate lateral resistance of pile, additional piles or an increase in pile diameter or micro-piles are used to enhance the lateral resistance of pile foundation. Although enlarging the pile diameter can strengthen its lateral resistance, it violates the term of carbon dioxide reduction. Besides, using much more potential sources of carbon emission like cement, steel materials, etc. may also require higher cost and take longer time of construction.

In general, the development of lateral resistance is at the depth of 5 to 10 times the pile diameter. Therefore, using the technique of ground improvement to increase soil strength and stiffness within the certain area in order to enhance the lateral resistance of pile is a relatively easy, potentially cost savings and time-saving treatment (Rollin et al., 2005; 2010). Many studies have evaluated the merit of grid-type ground improvement measures (e.g. soil mixing, or jet grouting wall) in increasing the lateral resistance and controlling the excess pore water pressure in liquefiable ground through field test, laboratory model test or numerical analysis and for further discussion of geometric design of grid wall (Takahashi et al., 2006; Namikawa et al., 2007; Nguyen et al., 2013; Bradley et al., 2013). But all these studies were mostly dealing with sandy soils. The properties of coal ash are different from the sand in several aspects, especially the light weight nature of ash particles. In order to provide more in-situ data to discuss the lateral resistance of pile by constructing grid mixed wall in coal ash pond, this paper has presented three sets of test result of lateral load test with steel pipe pile of 0.9 m (in diameter). These tests are all static load performed on a single pile. In the first case, as control sample, testing pile is located in untreated coal ash pond (TP1). In the second one, the pile is installed in the center of a grid mixed wall (TP2). For the third one, the pile is constructed inside grid mixed wall, while stirring and curing took place at the depth of 2.0 m of shallow treatment (TP3).

According to the test results and back-calculated analysis, if pile can be built within grid mixed wall, stirring process can take place at the depth of 2.0

m of shallow treatment, with little cement content (about 100 kg/m^3), the foundation can be formed as weak pile–raft system. In comparison with the untreated coal ash stratum, such measure has been proven in tests to increase by 88.8% of lateral resistance, 188% of initial stiffness, and fourfold of horizontal subgrade reaction coefficient (k_h) of pile. The treatment can also eliminate the bending moment of the pile and thus provide a smaller pile diameter.

2. SITE CONDITIONS AND PROPERTIES OF COAL ASH

The lateral pile load tests were performed at Taichung coal ash pond located near the coastline of a coal burning power plant in Central Taiwan. Coal ash is an end product of generating thermal power. Hydraulic fill is a common practice to take care of coal ash. Before the filling process, mortar is usually mixed at a weight ratio of 2.3 (water/coal ash) before being dumped via pipeline to the coal ash pond and becoming a reclaimed land (Figure 1). It seems a stable ground although the reclaimed land made of coal ashes is very soft soil like muds, especially for the disturbance by construction machines and other forces.

Generally, the coal ash in the pond is a layered mixture of fly ash, bottom ash, and slag due to the

Fig. 1 Hydraulically discharging coal ash

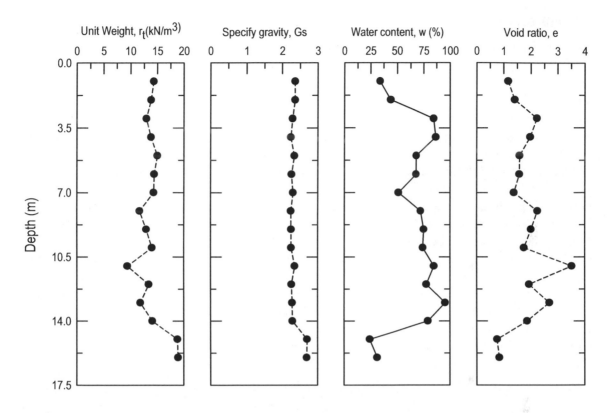

Fig. 2 Physical properties of coal ash pond

random dumping process. It looks like soil and can be categorized as silty sand. However, the coal ash is really a non-plastic material that is light in unit weight, low in gravity, with high water content and large void ratio (Figure 2). The depth of ground water table in Taichung coal ash pond is normally at 1.5 m to 2.0 m below the ground surface. A series of site investigation can be found through standard penetration test, seismic core penetration test (SCPT test), and relative density test from tube boring samples. As shown in Figure 3, based on its intensity, the rock strata of coal ash pond can be divided into three layers. The upper layer (G.L. 0~7m) is located above sea level and the SPT-N values were typically about 2~7; cone resistance (q_c) and shear wave velocity (Vs) measured by SCPT test typically varied from about 2.5~20 MPa and 175~200 m/sec respectively; the relative density obtained from this layer was typically about 25~75%. In contrast, the second layer (G.L. 7~14 m) is located below sea level and is an

extremely soft layer. Its SPT-N values normally stand lower than 2; cone resistance (q_c) and shear wave velocity (V_s) measured by SCPT test in this layer are relatively low, < 1 MPa and 90~120 m/sec respectively; the relative density obtained from this layer was typically about 5~25%, and a relatively weak layer. The third layer is below G.L. 14 m as the original seabed alluvial sand, and its properties are similar to those of the upper layer.

3. LATERAL PILE LOAD TEST

The properties, instruments and lateral load testing procedure for each testing pile were essentially the same. Driven closed-ended piles were set up to the depth of 14.5 m below ground surface by a hydraulic hammer (driving energy = 269.5 kN-m). The pile properties, instrumentation, and testing procedure are described as follows:

3.1 Pile Properties

The testing piles were 0.9 m in outer diameter (D) steel pipe pile with 12 mm in wall thickness. The steel of pipe pile conformed to ASTM A572 Grade 50 specifications and had the yield strength of 345 MPa base on the 2% offset criteria. The moment of inertia (I) and yield moment (M_y) of the testing piles were 0.0033 m^4 and 2,513 kN-m respectively. It typically extended about 0.5m above the ground surface and steel reinforcement cage was installed at the exposed pile head to maintain a good connection between the testing piles and a load actuator. Meanwhile, to avoid the deformation occurring at pile head when the lateral load was applied, the pipe pile was filled with concrete. Its unconfined compressive strength is 20 MPa, the dimension and layout of corbel should allow the actuator to apply load above the ground surface without affecting the coal ash around the testing pile.

3.2 Instrumentation

Instrumentation for the test included load cells, strain gauges, Linear Variable Differential Transformer (LVDT), and Shape Accelerometer Arrays (SAAScan). The layout of various instruments is shown in Figure 4. In addition to the load cells on the actuator which measured the total applied load, two LVDT pairs were attached to the exposed pile head so that the pile head displacement could be measured. There are 14 pairs of electrical resistance strain gauge with 1.0 m interval were attached with epoxy to the front and back inside face of test pile at 14.0 m in depth below the ground surface. The displacement of the testing pile during different applied loads was measured by using SAAScan which attached to inside face of the testing pile in active load side.

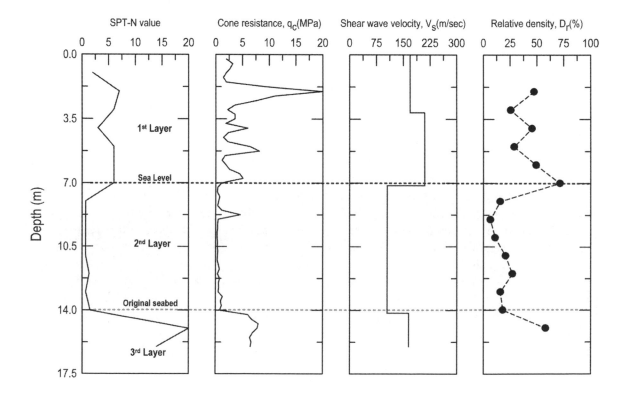

Fig. 3 Soil profile based on SPT-N value, cone resistance, shear wave velocity and relative density at test site

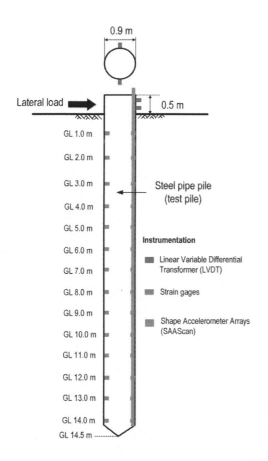

0.9 m

Lateral load

0.5 m

GL 1.0 m
GL 2.0 m
GL 3.0 m   Steel pipe pile
GL 4.0 m   (test pile)
GL 5.0 m
GL 6.0 m   **Instrumentation**
GL 7.0 m   ▓ Linear Variable Differential
GL 8.0 m   Transformer (LVDT)
GL 9.0 m   ▓ Strain gages
GL 10.0 m
GL 11.0 m   ▓ Shape Accelerometer Arrays
GL 12.0 m   (SAAScan)
GL 13.0 m
GL 14.0 m
GL 14.5 m

**Fig. 4 The layout of various instruments inside
the testing pile**

3.3. Testing Procedure

The lateral load tests were performed to gain the lateral load-displacement curves (p-y curves) under the static loading for each pile. The loading procedure was carried out with a displacement control approach and accordance with standard loading procedure: ASTM D3966-7 (2013). The lateral load tests were conducted using one or two 4,900 kN hydraulic actuators to apply load to the testing pile. In all cases, the reaction piles were located at 4.5m away from the testing pile to minimize interaction effects. Then, the load was maintained for either 10 minutes or 20 minutes depending on the load level to achieve a fixed pile displacement. The subsequent load increment was applied and the same procedure was repeated.

The specimen was under load of 12.5%, 25%, 37.5%, 50%, 62.5%, 75% and 85% of the idealized maximum load. After that, the pile was unloaded to 75%, 50% and 25% of maximum load, and at each unloading step, the load was maintained for 10 minutes. The pile was then unloaded to zero.

4. TEST LAYOUT

This paper presented three full-scale lateral load tests on single pile with and without the grid mixed wall employed to increase the lateral resistance of pile in coal ash pond. Due to the limitation of construction, all testing piles were being driven in untreated coal ash stratum under the driving energy = 269.5kN-m before lateral load tests. The driven numbers of testing piles were typically 320 to 350 when closed-ended reached the depth of 14.5m. Plain view and profiles plotting the layout of the testing pile in untreated coal ash stratum are presented in Figure 5 and Figure 6.

4.1 Testing Pile in Untreated Coal Ash Stratum

The layout of the test pile in untreated coal ash stratum for TP1 is provided in Figure 5(a) and Figure 6(a). The TP1 was intended to provide a baseline of the lateral load behavior of pile in untreated coal ash pond. To minimize the interaction effects between reaction piles and the testing pile during loading, the reaction piles were placed 1.5m above ground surface and were located 4.5m away from the testing pile. The reaction piles were also driven to a depth of 13.5m below ground surface. Typically, two reaction piles were put together in either series or parallel connection so that there will be enough loads to guarantee the reaction piles not to be moved. The movement will be a factor to estimate the accuracy of the test results.

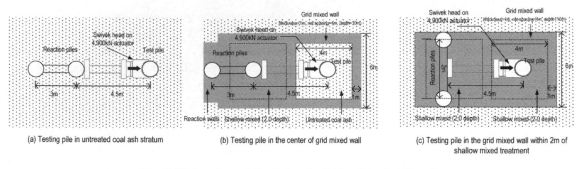

(a) Testing pile in untreated coal ash stratum   (b) Testing pile in the center of grid mixed wall   (c) Testing pile in the grid mixed wall within 2m of shallow mixed treatment

Fig. 5 Plain view of the lateral pile load test at the site

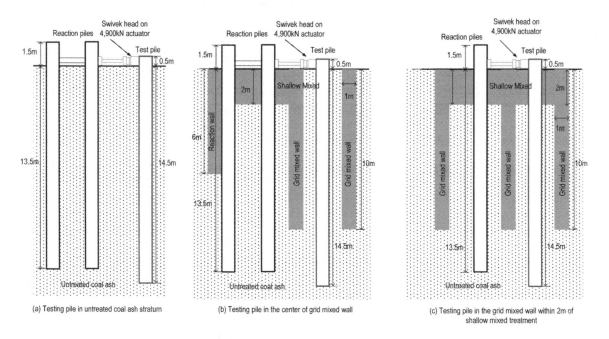

(a) Testing pile in untreated coal ash stratum   (b) Testing pile in the center of grid mixed wall   (c) Testing pile in the grid mixed wall within 2m of shallow mixed treatment

Fig. 6 Profile of the lateral pile load test at the site

4.2 Testing Pile in the Center of a Grid Mixed Wall

As shown in Figure 5(b) and Figure 6(b), the TP2 is meant to assess the effectiveness of the grid mixed wall in coal ash pond in terms of lateral resistance. To simplify the test parameters, the geometric and dimension of grid mixed wall were not being taken into account during the test. These parameters consisted of the width of grid mixed wall, the net spacing between each wall and the depth of the wall, might affect the test results. The only premises were set that the maximum lateral resistance will be no larger than ten times the pile diameter. And the depth of the grid mixed walls were around 10 m. The wall width was determined by the using of soil mixing method. WILL method was adopted in construction of the grid mixed wall and the impeller on the WILL mixing arm was 1.0m in width and designed in 3D to assure that the cement grout would be mixed evenly with coal ash. The net spacing between wall was determined by the improvement rate A_r = 50% of the test set, with a net spacing of 4m.

The design strength of grid mixed wall was set at over 1 MPa. The mix proportion of cement grout used in WILL mixing procedure was adopted by

Liao et al. (2012) test results done at coal ash pond. The binder used in the test was type I cement and the cement content per volume of treated soil was computed to be about 100 kg/m^3. Considering the injection rate as 20% in WILL mixing procedure, one cubic meter of improved soil needs a volume of 200 L/m^3 of cement grout. Since specific gravity of cement G_s = 3.0 and the cement content is 100 kg/m^3, the amount of water contained in grout is estimated to be 200−100/3 = 167 L/m^3, and the water/cement ratio should be set at 167/100 = 1.67. The unconfined compressive strength of cores of the grid mixed walls is generally higher than1.2~3.5 MPa after 28 days of curing; due to the bleeding effect and settlement of the cement particles the strength of mixed walls gradually increases with depth.

4.3 Testing Pile in the Grid Mixed Wall within 2m of Shallow Mixed Treatment

As shown in plain view and profile drawings, the testing pile was inside the grid mixed wall, while stirring and curing took place at 2m depth in the shallow mixed treatment of grid (TP3) in Figure 5(c) and Figure 6(c). The TP3 was intended to compare the lateral load behavior of pile in grid mixed wall center with and without treatment at the shallow depth of the grid. All the settings in the test were the same as in TP2.

5. TEST RESULTS AND ANALYSES

As mentioned above, all the tests were carried out in displacement control and all tests were immediately unloaded after the pile head were displaced more than 90 mm (0.1D) under the maximum lateral loading. The detail descriptions on load-displacement (p-y) curves, back calculation of subgrade reaction coefficients of pile (k_h), and displacement and bending moment along the pile depth are shown as following:

5.1 Load-Displacement (p-y) Curves

Figure 7 shows the load-displacement curves for pile head of TP1 to TP3. It demonstrates that at a pile head displacement of about 90 mm the maximum lateral load of the three tests, namely testing pile in the grid mixed wall within 2 m of shallow mixed treatment (TP3), testing pile in the center of a grid mixed wall (TP2), and untreated coal ash stratum (TP1), were 3,146 kN, 2,587 kN and 1,842 kN respectively. An increase of 55.3% in the lateral resistance was recorded when the grid of mixed wall was installed. Having added shallow treatment of 2 m, the further increase of 88.8% was obtained. Another interesting point is to evaluate the growing of initial stiffness due to the effect of shallow treatment. Prior to treatment, the secant stiffness of the load-displacement curve at a displacement of 10 mm was 39.2 kN/mm while after construction of grid mixed wall the stiffness raised to 68.6kN/mm and 112.7 kN/mm corresponding for the existence of shallow treatment. Consequently, thanks to adding grid mixed walls, initial stiffness of pile would be increased by 75% (TP2) and 188% (TP3).

It should be noted that the load-displacement curve before and after construction of the grid mixed wall in Figure 7 represents unloading to zero condition. As a non-plastic material, coal ash would form

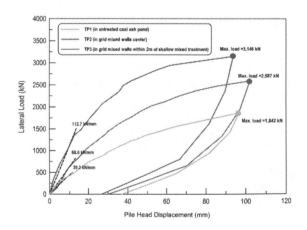

Fig. 7 Lateral load versus pile head displacement for different testing piles

a 25-35mm gap surrounding the pile itself as a mixture of soil and cement. This proves that at its second re-loading its lateral resistance is likely suffering a significant drop.

5.2 Back-calculated Analysis of Subgrade Reaction Coefficients of Pile (k_h)

Based on the analytical solution presented by Chang (1937), it suggested that boundary conditions at pile head as hinge connections that the subgrade reaction coefficients of pile (k_h) can be back-calculated from the equation (1) and equation (2) via load-displacement curves. From Figure 8 and Table 1, it can see the relationship between subgrade reaction coefficients and pile head displacement. When a testing pile is conducted in untreated coal ash stratum (TP1) and the pile head displacement are about 10mm (during normal condition) and 15mm (during seismic condition),

the subgrade reaction coefficients of pile stands at 35,800 kN/m³, and 31,200 kN/m³, respectively. When the test is implemented in a grid mixed wall (TP2), and the pile head displacement are about 10mm (during normal condition) and 15mm (during seismic condition), values for the coefficients of pile were 63,600 kN/m³, and 53,500kN/m³, respectively. As a result, the values for TP2 are approximate twice bigger than that for TP1. When the test is done in a grid mixed wall within 2m of shallow mixed treatment (TP3), and the pile head displacement are about 10 mm (during normal condition) and 15mm (during seismic condition), its subgrade reaction coefficients stands at 142,200 kN/m³ and 107,300 kN/m³ respectively. Values for TP3 are approximate fourfold bigger than that for TP1.

$$y = \frac{(1+\beta h)^3 + 0.5}{3E_p I_p \beta^3} P \tag{1}$$

$$k_h = \frac{4E_p I_p \beta^4}{D} \tag{2}$$

where: y is pile head displacement; β is the characteristic value of pile; h is the distance from load to the ground surface; P is applied lateral load; k_h is subgrade reaction coefficients of pile; $E_p I_p$ is pile stiffness; D is pile diameter.

From test results the grid mixed wall can efficiently increase lateral resistance as well as subgrade reaction coefficients of pile. In other word, under the same lateral load condition, we can effectively not only prevent the possible displacement and bending moment along the pile but also reduce the pile diameter if the subgrade reaction coefficients

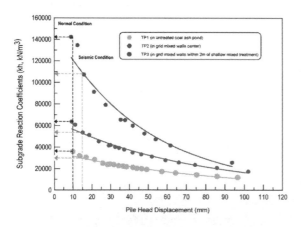

Fig. 8 Subgrade reaction coefficients versus pile head displacement for testing piles

Table 1 Back-calculated Subgrade Reaction Coefficients, Pile Head Displacement and Maximum Bending Moment under Lateral Load = 1,842 kN

Test results \ Test Pile	TP1	TP2	TP3
Subgrade reaction coefficient during normal condition(k_h, kN/m³)	35,800	63,600	142,200
Subgrade reaction coefficient during seismic condition(k_h, kN/m³)	31,200	53,500	107,300
Plie head displacement under lateral load = 1842 kN (y, mm)	88.9	44.1	24.1
Maximum bending moment under the lateral load = 1842 kN(M, kN-m)	3,365.0	1,634.4	756.2

of the foundation is increased. More numerical results need to be done to determine exactly how the measures presented in this study can reduce the diameter of pile.

5.3 Displacement and Bending Moment along the Pile Depth

During lateral load test, pile displacement was obtained from SAAScan recorded data at various levels of lateral load, and pile bending moments were determined from smoothed strain gauge data and a moment-curvature relationship derived from a sectional analysis using material and geometric properties of pile. Also, after obtained the subgrade reaction coefficients based on the presented analytical solution by Chang (1937). If the material and geometric properties of pile are given, the displacement and the bending moment along the pile depth can be estimated from the following equations.

Pile displacement along the pile:

$$y(x) = \frac{P}{2E_p I_p \beta^3} e^{-\beta[(1+\beta h)\cos(\beta x) - \beta h \sin(\beta x)]} \qquad (3)$$

Bending moment along the pile:

$$M(x) = \frac{-P}{\beta} e^{-\beta[\beta h \cos(\beta x) + (1+\beta h)\sin(\beta x)]} \qquad (4)$$

where: $y(x)$ is displacement along the pile; $M(x)$ is the bending moment along the pile; x is the pile depth.

As shown in Figure 9 and Table 1, whether the test pile is conducted in untreated coal ash stratum or within grid mixed wall, the displacement all occurred in range of 5 to 7m in depth. Also, under the same applied lateral load (e.g. 1,842 kN), the displacement of pile head in untreated coal ash stratum (TP1), comparing with that in the grid mixed wall within 2 m of shallow mixed treatment

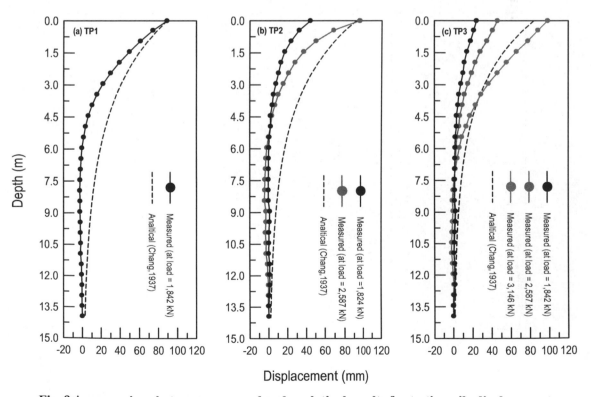

Fig. 9 A comparison between measured and analytical results for testing pile displacement

(TP3) and in a grid mixed walls center (TP2), were decreasing by 73% and 50% respectively. The equation (3) and equation (4) were established on the assumption of rigid base and homogeneous soil. Such assumption is able to meet the normal design conditions such as in TP3 when the geologic condition is relatively hard. However, the conclusion does not satisfy in TP1 when the geologic condition is relatively weak. Therefore, the bending moment could be underestimated that made the wrong estimation of the design pile diameter and the reinforcement of pile (Figure 10).

As the same figure and Table 1, it can note that for all lateral load tests the maximum bending moments occurred at the depth of 3~4.5m below the ground surface. Moreover, under the same applied lateral load (e.g. 1,842 kN), the maximum bending moment for pile in untreated coal ash stratum (TP1), contrasting with that in the grid

mixed wall within 2 m of shallow mixed treatment (TP3) and in the center of the grid walls (TP2), were decreasing by 78% and 51% respectively.

6. CONCLUSIONS

After reviewing data collected and back-calculated following three sets of lateral load tests of pile conducted at Taichung coal ash pond, the paper comes to the following conclusions:

1. Soil mixing with a cement content of 100 kg/m^3 was able to increase the unconfined compressive strength of a soft coal ash ground to 1.2~3.5 MPa after 28 days of curing and due to the bleeding effect and settlement of the cement particles, the strength of mixed walls increases with depth.

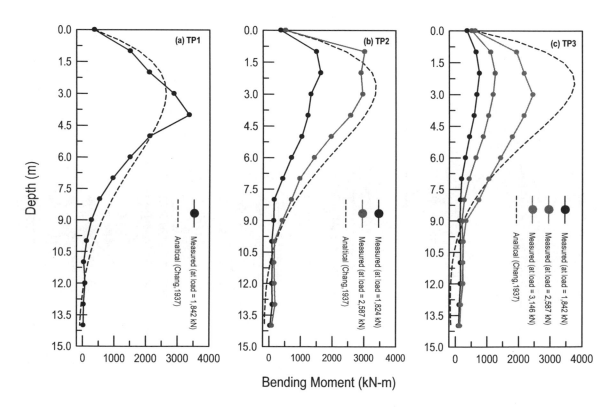

Fig. 10 A comparison between measured and analytical results of bending moment for testing piles

2. Comparing with the testing pile in untreated coal ash stratum, the pile in a grid mixed wall center will increase by 55.3% of lateral resistance, 75% of initial stiffness, and two times of horizontal subgrade reaction coefficient of pile. Testing pile in a grid mixed wall center within 2m of shallow mixed, will increase by 88.8% of lateral resistance, 188% of initial stiffness, and four times of horizontal subgrade reaction coefficient of pile.

3. The analytical solution for lateral pile behavior presented by Chang (1937) is not suitable for weak base and soft ground. It may be under estimated for the bending moment and thus made the wrong estimation of the design pile diameter and the reinforcement of pile.

4. Construction of grid mixed wall (10.0m deep, 1.0m wide, and 4.0m net spacing) adjacent to the existing pile in coal ash pond decreases the maximum bending moment by 51% (TP2) to 78% (TP3). This proves that grid mixed wall can help reduce the diameter of piles. More numerical results need to be done to know exactly how major a change will be.

5. Construction grid mixing wall could increase lateral resistance and initial stiffness of the pile. Due to consideration of its cost-effectiveness, a deep discussion in the depth of the grid mixed wall needs to be done before designing the layout.

ACKNOWLEDGEMENTS

The Authors are grateful to Taiwan Power Company for financially support this study and Diagnostic Engineering Consultants Co., Ltd. for providing equipment needed for the lateral load test of pile.

REFERENCES

Bradley, B. A., Araki, K., Ishii, T., Saitoh, K. (2013). Effect of lattice-shaped ground improvement geometry on seismic response of liquefiable soil deposits via 3-D seismic effective stress analysis. *Soil Dynamics and Earthquake Engineering*,Vol: 48, pp 35-47.

Chang, Y. L. (1937). Discussion on Lateral Pile Loading Tests.*Transactions of ASCE*, Vol: 102, pp272-278.

Liao, H. J., Cheng, S. H., Kuo, L. W., Wong, K. N., Chien, P. Y. (2012). Properties of hydraulically dumped coal ash after soil mixing improvement. *Proceeding of 4th International Conference on Grouting and Deep Mixing, New Orleans*, Vol: 2, pp 1373-1384.

Namikawa, T., Koseki, J., & Suzuki, Y. (2007). Finite element analysis of lattice-shaped ground improvement by cement-mixing for liquefaction mitigation, *Soils and Foundations*,Vol: 47, No. 3, pp 559-76.

Nguyen, T. V., Rayamajhi, D., Boulanger, R. W., Ashford, S. A., Lu, J., Elgamal, A., Shao, L. (2013). Design of DSM Grids for Liquefaction Remediation. *Journal of Geotechnical and Geoenvironmental Engineering, ASCE* Vol: 139, N0. 11, pp 1923-1933.

Rollins, K.M., Gerber, T.M., Lane, J.D., Ashford. S.A. (2005). Lateral Resistance of a Full-Scale Pile Group in Liquefied Sand. *Journal of Geotechnical and Geoenvironmental Engineering, ASCE*, Vol: 131, No. 1, pp 115-125.

Rollins, K.M., Adsero, M.E., Herbst, M.A., Lemme, N. (2010). Ground Improvement for Increasing Lateral Pile Group Resistance. *Proceeding of 5th International Conference on Recent Advances in Geotechnical Earthquake Engineering and Soil Dynamics*, San Diego , pp 1-10.

Takahashi, H., Kitazume, M., Ishibashi, S. (2006). Effect of deep mixing wall spacing on liquefaction mitigation. *Proceeding of the 6th international conference on physical modelling in geotechnics*, Hong Kong, pp 585-590.

Special Report

CHAPTER 19

RECENT TECHNOLOGY DEVELOPMENT TRENDS IN THE JAPANESE CONSTRUCTION INDUSTRY

Kenichi Horikoshi*

Technology Center, Taisei Corporation, Yokohama, Japan
**hrkkni01@pub.taisei.co.jp*

ABSTRACT: Major Japanese construction contractors run their own research institutes. As well as developing their design and construction technologies, this in-house research capability allows them to meet wide varieties of social demands and customer requirements. Like universities, these institutes carry out some basic research, but they also focus on the needs of the domestic and global construction markets as well as current social and economic conditions. Major topics of research and development at this time are i) measures to cope with major future earthquakes and other natural disasters, ii) renovation and replacement of old existing infrastructure, especially in urban areas such as Tokyo, iii) environment-friendly construction to meet corporate social responsibility, iv) application of advanced computer technology such as use of ICT and AI to enhance productivity, and v) new construction technologies required for major projects in Japan. This paper provides an overview of some typical recent developments and applications in this field.

1. INTRODUCTION

As in most Asian countries, construction technology has played an important role in improving the quality of daily life in Japan. Safe, rapid transportation systems, such as railway and highway networks, have contributed significantly to the changes we have seen in lifestyles and ways of doing business. Advanced design techniques using the latest methods of numerical analysis have brought us safer and more secure buildings and other social infrastructure. Since the dawn of time, most countries have suffered from various kinds of severe recurring disasters, such as earthquakes, volcanic eruptions, typhoons, and their consequences including tsunamis, liquefaction, landslides, floods, and so on. A developed infrastructure requires countermeasures against such natural events.

In the case of Japan, it is also very important to note that most cities are located on alluvial plains at river mouths, where the geology consists of thick layers of soft clays and loose sands. This implies that design and construction technologies related to deep foundations and ground improvement are of vital importance.

Furthermore, the rising environmental consciousness of recent times cannot be ignored by any industry. There is great expectation that the construction industry will take corporate social responsibility for minimizing the environmental impact of its activities.

Unlike construction contractors outside Japan, the major Japanese construction companies have their own research and development (R&D) institutes as well as design and engineering divisions. This is one of the unique characteristics of the construction business in Japan. The in-house research capability allows companies to expand their share of the highly competitive Japanese market, solve any problems raised on the client side, and overcome any difficulties encountered at construction sites around the world. The result is that the direction of construction R&D relates strongly with recent and future trends in the construction market and in society in general.

Accordingly, this overview of recent technology trends in the Japanese construction industry presents progress in R&D in a number of categories, including countermeasures against natural disasters, ecological and environment-friendly construction methods, and the application of advanced information and communication technology (ICT) and artificial intelligence (AI) to design and construction work. Typical examples are introduced in each category. The author belongs to the technology planning division of the technology center at a major construction company, so is well qualified to provide this overview of recent developments.

2. LATEST DATA ON JAPANESE CONSTRUCTION INDUSTRIES

It is necessary to first give an outline of overall trends in Japanese construction. The Japan Federation of Construction Contractors (JFCC) publishes an annual handbook giving the latest data on the Japanese construction industry (JFCC, 2016), and this is referred to here.

Figure 1 shows the overall trend in Japanese Gross Domestic Product (GDP) alongside investment in the construction market. It can be seen that GDP has remained almost unchanged for the past twenty years, at around JPY 500 trillion (equivalent to USD 4.5 trillion at the latest exchange rate of 111.7 JPY/USD). At the same time, investment in construction had halved by 2010 from a peak of JPY 84 trillion in 1992. Since the 2010 low of about JPY 40 trillion, investment has crept upward to about JPY 50 trillion today. This increase is attributed to rehabilitation and reconstruction work following the 2011 Tohoku Earthquake and a construction boom related to the upcoming 2020

Tokyo Olympic and Paralympic Games, and other big projects in Japan.

Figure 2 shows investment in the construction market as a proportion of GDP. Although it reached as high as 15-20% of GDP in the 1980s, investment has gradually decreased to about 10% of GDP since 1990. This is of the same order as investment in major European Countries (JFCC, 2016).

Figure 3 shows the overall trend in the number of construction companies operating in Japan and in

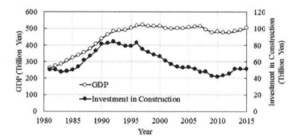

Fig. 1 Investment in construction in Japan (Data from JFCC handbook)

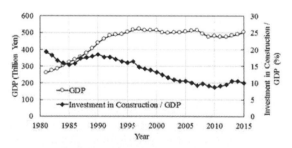

Fig. 2 Investment in construction as proportion of GDP (Data from JFCC handbook)

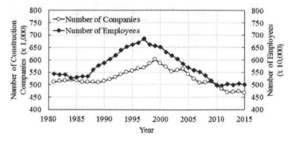

Fig. 3 Number of construction companies and employees in Japan (Data from JFCC handbook)

the total number of employees in the industry. The number of construction companies has decreased by 22% from the peak of 601,000 in 1999, while employment has fallen by 25% from the 1997 peak of 6.85 million.

The number of companies is compared with investment in the construction market in Figure 4. Although investment has increased by about 20% over the most recent four years, the number of construction companies has yet to rise. This may be attributed to the fact that having left the industry, it is not easy to return, while a rapidly aging workforce means older workers find it difficult to return and young people tend to avoid construction because it is considered difficult, dirty, and dangerous work.

Figure 5 shows the percentage of workers in different age groups. It shows the significance of rapid aging in the construction industry as compared with other industries in Japan. At present, more than one third of employees in the industry exceed 55 years old, with only about 10% being less than 29 years old.

Summarizing the data presented in this section, the following overall trends can be noted in the Japanese construction industry.

i) Though Japanese GDP has been almost constant for 20 years, investment in the construction market has fallen by almost half while the number of operating construction companies has decreased by about 22%. This has led to significant competition in a limited market.

ii) The Japanese construction market has been active over the past four years as a result of rehabilitation and reconstruction work relating to the 2011 Tohoku Earthquake and preparatory work for the 2020 Tokyo Olympics, and other big projects.

iii) Despite the upswing in activity in the

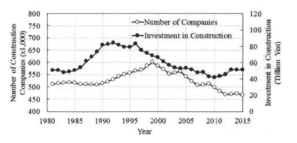

Fig. 4 Number of construction companies compared with investment in construction (Data from JFCC handbook)

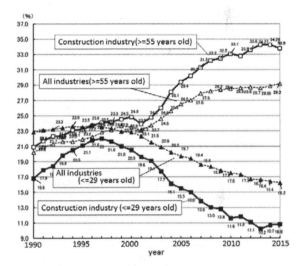

Fig. 5 Rapid aging in the construction industry (After MLIT, 2016)

industry, there is as yet no sign of increasing employment. Aging is more significant in construction than in other industries, so there is a reduced pool of potential workers. Enhancing productivity of design and construction activities is one likely solution to this problem. The latest ICT and AI should be applied to improve productivity.

To cope with this issue of productivity, the Ministry of Land, Infrastructure, Transport and Tourism has launched its 'i-Construction' campaign to promote the use of the latest ICT to enhance productivity.

As a final note, it should also be added that much of modern Japanese infrastructure was constructed in the early 1960s, prior to the 1964 Tokyo Olympics. Renewal and retrofitting of existing structures are becoming major concerns in the construction industry.

3. INTRODUCTION OF RECENT TECHNOLOGIES

Although major Japanese contractors invest in R&D, investment runs at roughly 1% of sales, which is much lower than in other manufacturing industries. This section introduces some of the technologies that have recently resulted from this investment. It should be noted that most results are the outcome of collaborative work with others such as universities, public sector organizations, and other private companies. Such alliances are necessary to accelerate the speed of research and development.

3.1 Promoting a safe and secure society

Seismic designs codes are often revised, especially following major earthquakes such as the 1995 Southern Hyogo Prefecture Earthquake and the 2011 Tohoku Earthquake. With each revision, the earthquake motion used for design has tended to become more severe, so the seismic performance of existing buildings and industrial facilities requires enhancement. As is easily understood, it is more difficult and expensive to enhance the seismic performance of an existing structure than a new one.

3.1.1 Ground improvement beneath existing structures

Seismic reinforcement of existing structures (so as to enhance public safety) has become an urgent task for civil engineers. From a geotechnical point of view, soil liquefaction is the cause of considerable damage to structures, especially in coastal areas of Japan.

An innovative technology by which the ground immediately beneath existing structures is strengthened has been developed (Ishii *et al.*, 2011). Strengthening involves two phases: horizontal directional drilling and subsequent chemical grouting.

The above-ground improvement method is used for soils that include less fines. To improve ground with a higher fines content, another technology was needed.

Figure 9 shows a ground improvement system developed to meet this need (Ishii *et al.*, 2012 and Uno *et al.*, 2016). The machine has the ability to drill both vertically and at an angle, as well as to carry out directional drilling. There is a mixing wing that remains folded during drilling; when the rod reaches the design depth, the wing opens and mixes

Fig. 6 Ground improvement beneath an existing structure

Fig. 7 Machine for horizontal directional drilling

Fig. 8 Ground improvement work beneath oil tank

Fig. 9 Ground improvement machine with foldable mixing blade

Fig. 10 Results of verification tests

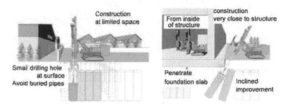

Fig. 11 Possible applications of the ground improvement technology

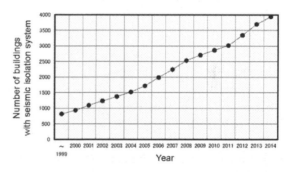

Fig. 12 Increase in number of buildings with seismic isolation systems (after JSSI, 2016)

the soil with cement slurry. Once soil improvement with the cement slurry is completed, the wing is once again folded for extraction from the ground. This technology enables soil to be improved with cement slurry with minimum influence on or near the surface on which structures stand.

Figure 10 shows the results of verification tests in which the quality of the improved soil was checked. The right-hand picture shows the improved soil mass resulting from directional drilling. With its ability to form inclined columns of improved soil, this technology was used to improve the slope of a tailing dam that suffered damage in the great 2011 Tohoku Earthquake. Other possible uses of this technology are considered in Figure 11.

3.1.2 Seismic isolation system for buildings in urban areas

The Japan Society of Seismic Isolation (JSSI) publishes figures giving the number of buildings fitted with seismic isolation systems, as shown in Figure 12. Currently, there are about 4,000 buildings in Japan equipped with such systems. Demand for seismic isolation has been particularly high since the 2011 Tohoku Earthquake.

A building fitted with a seismic isolation system requires a certain amount of clearance from neighboring buildings, typically 60cm. As a result, application of such systems to smaller buildings in built-up urban areas like Tokyo is not that easy, considering the requirement to make possible maximum use of land. To overcome this issue, a short-stroke seismic isolation system has been developed that reduces the required clearance by half, as shown in Figure 13 (Nii *et al.*, 2015 and Hibino *et al.*, 2016).

An oil damper with a two-stage damping characteristic is used, with automatic switching of the damping characteristics depending on the amplitude of the motion. The automatic mechanism is very simple and requires no power supply, so the new system works even during electricity outages.

Figure 14 illustrate the mechanism that alters damping characteristics depending on the shaking amplitude. The oil damper has an oil-flow by-pass fitted with a shut-off valve operated by a displacement detection groove. The by-pass route is active during small to medium earthquakes. But when shaking exceeds a design value, the mechanical valve closes the by-pass and the damping force increases to prevent collision with neighboring buildings. After the earthquake, the damper characteristics are manually reset.

This system has already been installed in several buildings in Japan. Figure 15 shows the example of a seismic isolation renovation project for a government office building in Shinjuku Ward, Tokyo, where the existing building was retrofitted

without interrupting use of the offices.

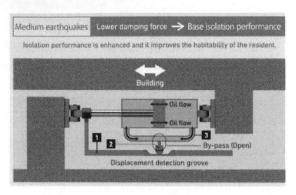

(a) Small to medium earthquakes with small shaking amplitude

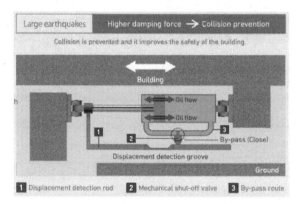

(b) Large earthquakes with large shaking amplitude

Fig. 14 Mechanism for changing damping characteristics during large earthquakes

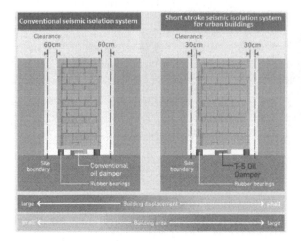

Fig. 13 Development of short-stroke base isolation system for urban buildings

Fig. 15 Government building in Shinjuku Ward, Tokyo (After Shinjuku City, 2015)

3.1.3 Seismic isolation for sensitive industrial facilities

The damage caused to semiconductor fabrication facilities in the 2011 Tohoku Earthquake was extensive, which led to the shutdown of the facilities. Moreover, toppling of expensive equipment and damage to products in mid-production can add to economic losses. To prevent such damage and losses and ensure the prompt resumption of business after an earthquake, a system of anti-earthquake measures has been developed specifically for semiconductor fabricators (see Figure 16) (Hibino *et al.*, 2011 and Komoda *et al.*, 2013). The developed system, named 'TASS Unit', is a form of seismic isolation applicable to semiconductor fabrication equipment in existing facilities. The effectiveness of the isolation system was verified by shaking table tests and in the 2011 Tohoku Earthquake.

Fig. 16 Seismic isolation system for sensitive industrial facilities

Fig. 17 Shaking table test of the developed TASS Unit system

3.2 Toward an environment-friendly society

3.2.1 Zero energy building

The shift to a low carbon society requires that the energy consumption of buildings be reduced, and even the achievement of zero energy buildings. Recently a number of Zero Energy Building (ZEB) projects and studies have come to prominence in Japan and overseas. A ZEB is a building that offers a comfortable environment for users with greatly reduced annual energy consumption (achieved by saving as much energy as possible through better insulation, solar shading, natural energy and high-efficiency equipment) and autonomous energy generating capability (such as with photovoltaic cells). Overall annual energy consumption is no more than overall annual energy generation.

Most ZEBs are constructed on spacious sites in rural or suburban areas where large PV (photovoltaic) power generation areas are available and abundant natural resources can be utilized for energy conservation.

To achieve significant reductions in energy consumption in our highly urbanized society, ZEB projects in urban areas (which are where large portion of energy is consumed) must be more heavily promoted. To this end, the so-called 'ZEB demonstration building' was constructed in Taisei Technology Center in Yokohama, one of Japan's major cities, with the aim of developing urban-style ZEBs suitable even for the central districts of large cities (Sugie, *et al.*, 2014).

Figure 18 shows some views of the ZEB demonstration building. Three major concepts were adopted in the design: 'Lively offices', 'Zero energy', and 'Greater reassurance'. Several leading edge technologies are adopted to achieve the zero energy rating.

The building's sides are finished with organic thin-film photovoltaic cells. This type of PV cell is much lighter and can be produced in more color variations,

Fig. 18 ZEB demonstration building

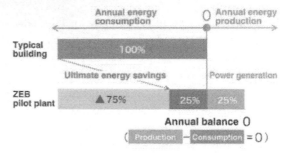

Fig. 19 Annual energy balance of ZEB demonstration building

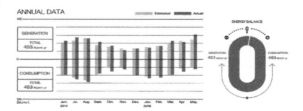

Fig. 20 First-year verification result for the ZEB demonstration building

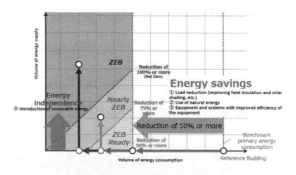

Fig. 21 Graphic definition and evaluation methods of ZEBs (After Ministry of Economy, Trade and Industry, 2015)

thereby allowing for more flexibility in design. There is also more flexibility in shape and size as compared with the more popular silicon PV cells.

Natural light is effectively brought into the offices through the use of special lighting fixtures. Besides, energy consumption is reduced through the use of low-illumination task and ambient lighting, an air-conditioning system that recovers exhaust heat, a smart air ventilation system and other systems.

Figure 19 shows the planned annual energy balance of the ZEB demonstration building. Energy consumption is reduced by as much as 75% compared with a typical equivalent building. The remaining 25% energy requirement is supplied by PV cells.

Figure 20 shows the result of the first-year verification, showing that total annual energy consumption was 463 MJ/m2yr, while total energy generation was 493 MJ/m2yr. The target of zero annual net energy consumption was successfully achieved.

On the assumption that ZEBs will become more popular, Japan's Ministry of Economy, Trade and Industry, METI, has published definitions and evaluation methods for ZEBs, as shown in Figure 21 (METI, 2015). According to this, ZEBs are divided into three categories according to the level of energy conservation and generation: 'ZEB ready', 'Nearly ZEB' and 'ZEB'. Note that the ZEB demonstration building falls into the highest category 'ZEB'.

3.3 Improving productivity in the construction industry

3.3.1 Unmanned construction system

In 1991 one of Japan's most active volcanoes erupted and generated an enormous pyroclastic flow that killed 43 people (Figure 22). The site at Mt. Unzen remained dangerous, but disaster recovery efforts had to go on, so the government decided to use unmanned construction systems for the work.

Following successful application of unmanned construction system at the Mt. Unzen site, the technology has been improved and used on many other occasions following natural disasters. These include the sites of landslides resulting from earthquakes, heavy rains and other natural occurrences. It is worth noting, also, that unmanned construction systems played an important role when the Fukushima nuclear power plant was severely damaged in the 2011 Tohoku Earthquake. Unmanned machines removed rubble and debris immediately after the accident to allow rapid and problem-free commencement of other recovery work.

Initially, the unmanned machines were controlled from a site house located at the nearest safe site to the work. Remote control of construction machinery requires particular skills that differ from those needed to operate the machines directly. Work was carried out step by step under manual control, using many monitors set up in the site house to observe the operation.

Now, more than 25 years since the first application of unmanned construction, advanced technologies related to positioning systems, monitoring systems, highly accurate sensor systems, communications, and other recent ICT and AI techniques ensure more accurate work with more automatic and autonomous control. Unmanned construction technology also contributes to reduced demand for workers.

Two autonomous unmanned construction machines are introduced here, a vibration roller and a breaker (Katayama and Ishii, 2016, Katayama et al., 2015). These machines can complete an assigned task without further human control once the initial conditions and target results have been entered.

Figure 23 shows the autonomous unmanned vibration roller. It is fitted with a number of sensors needed for autonomous operations.

Figure 24 shows the machine undergoing verification tests. After an operator enters data specifying the area requiring compaction, the machine completes the work, autonomously keeping track of the number of compactions.

Fig. 22 Mt. Unzen and aftermath of large pyroclastic flow following the 1991 eruption (https://en.wikipedia.org/wiki/Mount_Unzen)

Fig. 23 Autonomous unmanned vibration roller

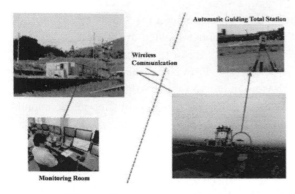

Fig. 24 Verification test of autonomous unmanned vibration roller

Fig. 25 Finishing cast concrete is hard, slow work

Since the machine accurately tracks its own position, construction work can continue even in poor visibility, such as with fog, and at night. Operational data can be linked with data from Building Information Modeling (BIM) or Construction Information Modeling (CIM) systems and linked to quality control data.

An autonomous unmanned breaker machine has also been developed based on the same concept and technology. The machine is able to detect a target object, such as a mass of rock, from a distance, approach the target, and break the up target while determining the best breaking position.

3.3.2 Automatic concrete slab finisher

Japan is suffering from a shortage of construction workers. To reduce labor requirements, an automatic finishing machine was developed for concrete floors. As shown in Figure 25, manual slab finishing just after casting is hard work for a construction worker. It is slow work in a difficult posture that places a heavy burden on the body.

An attempt was made to improve work conditions and efficiency in this concrete finishing work by developing a light-weight construction robot (Nakamura, 2016), as shown in Figure 26. The machine does the work of three construction workers. Operation is by a single worker with a controller, such as used for computer games, as shown in Figure 27, leading to a reduced workforce

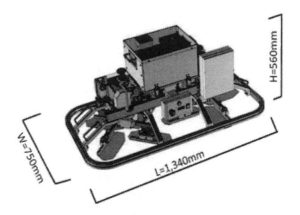

Fig. 26 Illustration of concrete finishing robot

Fig. 27 Operation of machine using remote controller

and easier work.

The machine is battery operated and weighs 90kg, of which 25kg is battery weight. Continuous operation for 3.5 hours is possible. Battery performance and weight still leave room for improvement.

Fig. 28 Typical construction site

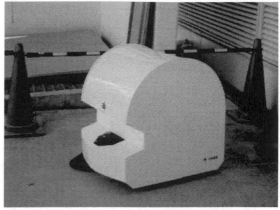

Fig. 29 Automatic cleaning machine

In addition to the types of automatic machine described above, an automatic cleaning machine for construction sites has been developed (Kato, 2016) as shown Figures 28 and 29. It is able to recognize safety cones and barriers marking off-limits areas.

3.3.3 Advanced positioning system for pile installation

Accurately marking the specified locations for piles is work that generally requires at least two people, one stationed by the measuring system (total station theodolite) and the other moving around into the exact pile positions.

An advanced positioning method named 'T-Mark Navi' that can be operated by just one person has been developed (Tanaka and Sueda, 2016). The operator wears a pair of wearable (smart) glasses that include a display system.

Figure 30 compares the operation of the system with the conventional method. A specially designed measurement device is used instead of the conventional total station theodolite. The operator carries a smart phone that communicates with the measurement device via wireless LAN and uses voice control technology to determine precise pile positions. Positioning data is visible in the display of the smart glasses, as shown in Figure 31. This system reduces the number of workers required for

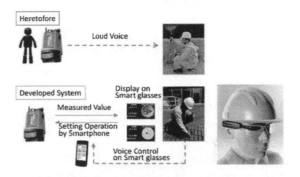

Fig. 30 Precise positioning system operated by only one person

Fig. 31 Display of positioning data via smart glasses

pile positioning by half.

4. RESEARCH ON PILED RAFT BEHAVIOR

Piled raft foundations has become much popular in Japan since Architectural Institute of Japan (2001) stated the design concept. The design approach has also become more rational and more rigorous, for example, with the use of fully 3 dimensional finite element analyses. The objective of the numerical analyses is the estimation of not only the settlement profiles but also the overall bearing capacity of foundations. Here, in this paper, the work of Watanabe and Nagao (2016), which attempted to find a method to estimate the overall bearing capacity of piled raft foundations is introduced. They clarified the bearing capacity ratios and factors which are often used in the following expressions:

$$R_{PR,ult} = \xi_{PR,ult} \left(R_{R,ult} + R_{p,ult} \right) \qquad (1)$$

$$R_{PR,ult} = \alpha_{R,ult} \cdot R_{R,ult} + \alpha_{p,ult} \cdot R_{p,ult}) \qquad (2)$$

where, $R_{PR,ult}$, $R_{R,ult}$, and $R_{p,ult}$ are the bearing capacity of piled raft, raft alone, and pile group respectively, and $\xi_{PR,ult}$ is the ratio of the bearing capacity of the piled raft to the sum of the individual bearing capacity of the raft alone and the pile group. The bearing capacity factors, $\alpha_{R,ult}$ and $\alpha_{p,ult}$ are for the raft capacity and the pile group capacity respectively. The ultimate bearing capacity was defined as the load when the settlement reaches 10 % of the foundation breadth, i.e. $S/B = 0.1$.

Watanabe and Nagao (2016) carried out a series of loading tests on model piled raft, single pile, and raft alone. Figure 32 shows the piled raft model and the corresponding ground conditions. After the tests, the load - settlement behavior and the load sharing profiles were simulated by using 3 dimensional finite element analyses and the results were compared with those obtained from the tests (Figures 33 and 34). Figure 34 shows that the results of the numerical analyses explained the experimental behavior very well.

After the verification of the above numerical approach, a series of parametric studies were conducted to investigate the effects of the foundation shape, number of piles, pile length and the ground profiles on the bearing capacity factors. Figure 35 shows the analytical models for

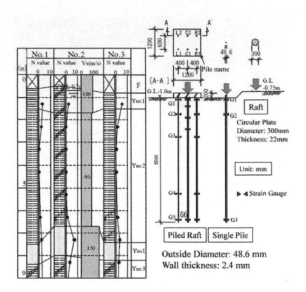

Fig. 32 Model piled raft, single pile, and raft alone with ground conditions

Fig. 33 Mesh for finite element analyses

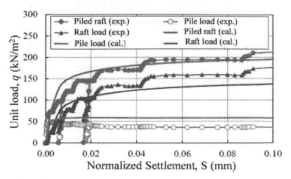

Fig. 34 Comparisons of analytical results with test results

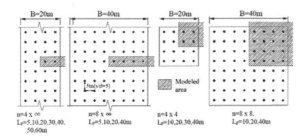

Fig. 35 Analytical model for a series of numerical analyses

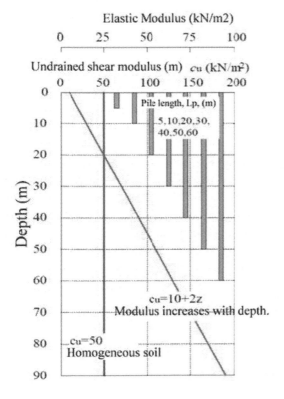

Fig. 36 Ground models used for parametric studies.

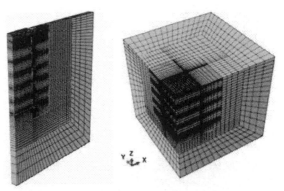

Fig. 37 Ground models used for parametric studies.

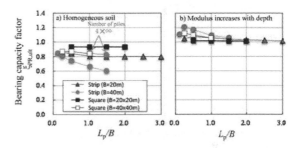

Fig. 38 Bearing capacity ratio, ξ

the pile and the Poisson's ratio were set at 25 GN/m^2 and 0.167 respectively. Figure 37 shows the mesh used for the parametric studies.

Figure 38 shows the profiles of the bearing capacity ratio, $\zeta_{PR,ult}$ The figure shows that $\zeta_{PR,ult}$ varied more for homogeneous ground. For the homogeneous ground model, the value of $\zeta_{PR,ult}$ decreases as L_p/B increases. This trend is more evident for the model with larger breadth. For the same L_p/B conditions, the ratio $\zeta_{PR,ul}$ increases by about 0.2 for the reduction in pile rows from 8 to 4.

Figure 39 and Figure 40 show the relationships between bearing capacity factors $\alpha_{p,ult}$, $\alpha_{R,ult}$ and L_p/B. Figure 39 shows that as L_p/B increases, $\alpha_{p,ult}$ also increases up to unity, whereas for the case of strip foundation ($B = 40$m), $\alpha_{p,ult}$ decreases for larger L_p/B. This phenomena is considered to be related to the ground failure patterns around the foundation. Figure 40 shows that as L_p/B increases,

strip foundations and square foundations. Ground conditions were set at as shown in Figure 36. Two Types of ground models, i.e., homogeneous ground and the ground where the modulus increases with depth, were considered. In the analyses, internal friction angle of the ground was set at $\phi = 0$ degrees, and the Poisson's ratio was set at 0.49. Pile diameter was set at 1.0 m. Young's modulus of

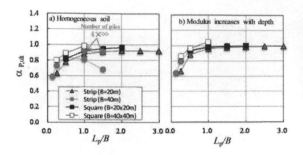

Fig. 39 Relationship between $\alpha_{P,ult}$ and Lp/B

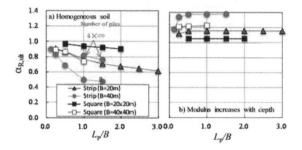

Fig. 40 Relationship between $\alpha_{R,ult}$ and Lp/B

$\alpha_{R,ult}$ decreases down to about 0.5 for the case of the homogeneous ground. However, $\alpha_{R,ult}$ can increase more than unity for the ground which modulus increases with depth. The behavior may be attributed to the phenomena the horizontal displacement of soil just beneath the raft is restricted.

Figure 41 shows the contour of plastic strain around the foundation, which shows clear difference in the failure pattern of the ground beneath the piled raft foundations depending on the pile length.

5. CONCLUDING REMARKS

This report introduces some recent R&D trends in the Japanese construction industry by exemplifying typical cases. Although these examples are taken from the author's own affiliation, the general direction of R&D is similar in Japan's other major construction companies.

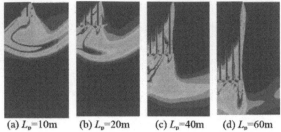

(a) L_p=10m   (b) L_p=20m   (c) L_p=40m   (d) L_p=60m

Fig. 41 Contour of plastic strain (Homogeneous ground, strip foundation, B = 40m, S/B = 0.1)

Basic research and fundamental study are always important to progress, but the immediate needs of clients and society mean that certain areas of research require urgent attention. Collaborative projects among universities, the public sector, and private companies are generally considered crucial to the efficient implementation of this R&D work.

It remains true, however, that developing a new technology and applying it on actual construction sites takes time. Even if a new method offers excellent performance gains, it must be at least as cost effective as the conventional method. The realization of new construction methods such as those outlined in this report requires that research institutes, such as those operated by Japan's major construction companies, respect all new ideas and carefully foster them until they become realistic.

REFERENCES

The technologies introduced in this paper are all posted on the website, although main sentences are written in Japanese: http://www.taisei.co.jp/giken/report/index.html. More detailed information can be obtained from the above website. Following papers are referred in this paper.

Architectural Institute of Japan (2001). Recommendations for Design of Building Foundations.

Hibino, H., Aono, S., Nagashima, I., Izumo, Y. and Ono, S. (2011). Development and application of seismic isolation system (TASS Unit). for semiconductor fabricating facilities - effectiveness of isolation as observed in the 2011 off the Pacific Coast of Tohoku Earthquake-, *Report of Taisei Technology Center*, Vol. 44, Paper #06.

Hibino, H., Maseki, R., Kurisu, A. and Kimura, Y. (2016). Base isolation and response control system using multifunctional oil dampers, *Report of Taisei Technology Center*, Vol. 49, Paper #04.

Ishii, H., Funahara, H., Matsui, H. and Horikoshi, K. (2011). Effectiveness of liquefaction countermeasures in 2011 Tohoku Region Pacific Coast Earthquake, and an innovative soil improvement method for existing structures, *Report of Taisei Technology Center*, Vol. 44, Paper #08.

Ishii, H., Fujiwara, T., Kobayashi, M., Matsui, H., Aoki, T., Tateishi, A., Suga, K. and Mikami, K. (2012). Development of soil improvement method using expandable/collapsible mixing blades, *Report of Taisei Technology Center*, Vol. 45, Paper #13.

Japan Federation of Construction Contractors, JFCC (2016). Construction industry handbook. http://www.nikkenren.com/publication/handbook.html

Japan Society of Seismic Isolation (2016). http://www.jssi.or.jp/menshin/doc/keizoku2.pdf

Kato, T. (2016). Development of the autonomic cleaning robot "T-iROBO® Cleaner", *Report of Taisei Technology Center*, Vol. 49, Paper #53.

Katayama, S., Miyazaki, H. and Aoki, H. (2015). Demonstration of the autonomy rock crash work by the excavator with a breaker - Development of the next-generation unmanned construction System - *Report of Taisei Technology Center*, Vol. 48, Paper #50.

Katayama, S. and Ishii, T. (2016). Evaluation of rolling compaction performance with autonomous control vibration roller "T-iROBO® Roller" - On site inspection of robots for the next generation social infrastructure- *Report of Taisei Technology Center*, Vol. 49, Paper #54.

Komoda, K., Yata, M., Yamazaki, Y., Ueda, T., Aono, S., Hibino, H., Nagashima, I., Izumo Y. and Kikuchi T. (2013). Efficiency of risk reduction by installation of seismic isolation system for vertical furnace, *Joint Symposium of e-Manufacturing & Design Collaboration Symposium 2013 and International Symposium on Semiconductor Manufacturing 2013*, 20130621P0054A1, pp. 1-4, Sep., 2013.

Ministry of Economy, Trade and Industry (2015). Definition of ZEB and future measures proposed by the ZEB roadmap examination committee, *Public announcement by Japanese Ministry of Economy, Trade and Industry on December, 2015*.

Ministry of Land, Infrastructure, Transport and Tourism (2016). Reference on current situation and change in construction industry *Public announcement by Japanese Ministry of Land, Infrastructure, Transport and Tourism on March, 2016*.

Nagao, T. and Watanabe T. (2015). Numerical studies o bearing capacity of piled rafts on cohesive soil - Part 3: Relationship between bearing capacity and ratio of pile length to width of foundation-, *Annual convention of Architectural Institute of Japan*, paper # 20240, pp. 479-480.

Nakamura, Y. (2016). Development of concrete slab finishing robot "T-iROBO® Slab Finisher" - Improvements of work environment and efficiency in concrete slab finishing work -, *Report of Taisei Technology Center*, Vol. 49, Paper #52.

Nii, A., Maseki, R., Nagashima, I., Kimura, Y., Nakajima, T., Aono, H. and Hosozawa, O. (2015). Development of high performance seismic isolation system for an extremely large earthquake - Development of long stroke passive switching oil damper and application study-, *Report of Taisei Technology Center*, Vol. 48, Paper #06.

Shinjuku City https://www.city.shinjuku.lg.jp/content/000144521.pdf

Sugie, D., Kumagai, T., Tabata, A. and Shimada, H. (2014). ZEB demonstration building, Technology Center, *Report of Taisei Technology Center*, Vol. 47, Paper #02.

Tanaka, Y. and Sueda, T. (2016). Development of position measurement system by using a smart glasses (in Japanese), *Architectural Design*, No. 799, pp.52-59, Aug.

Uno, H., Funahara, H., Fujiwara, T., Shibata, K. and Tateishi, A (2016). Research and development related to liquefaction countermeasures -Analysis techniques and countermeasure methods-, *Report of Taisei Technology Center*, Vol. 49, Paper #02.

Watanabe, T. and Nagao, T. (2016). Study on bearing capacity of piled raft foundations -Research and development related to liquefaction countermeasures - Vertical loading tests and three-dimensional finite element analysis-, *Report of Taisei Technology Center*, Vol. 49, Paper #30.

Acknowledgements

CIVIL ENGINEERING

Wind Engineering - Geomaterials Research - Engineering Info. &Management

TAMKANG UNIVERSITY
Established 1950

COLLEGE of ENGINEERING
http://www.ce.tku.edu.tw/main/?language=en

KGS-Astana, LLP

<u>OUR services</u>
- piles driving and installing of bored piles;
- testing of soils and all types of piles;
- design of pile foundations;
- engineering - geological surveys

Address: 2/1, Bayirkum Str.,
Astana, Kazakhstan, 010000
tel. +7 (7172) 97 83 92;
+7 (7172) 97 83 94
fax:+7 (7172) 97 83 93
e-mail: kgs-astana@mail.ru
kgs@kgs-astana.kz
URL: http://www.kgs-astana.kz/

Kazakhstan Geotechnical Society

Address:
13a, Munaitpassov Str.,
Astana, Kazakhstan, 010000
tel. +7 (7172) 34 47 96;
+7 (7172) 34 35 40
fax:+7 (7172) 34 47 96

e-mail: astana-geostroi@mail.ru
kz.secretariat.kgs@gmail.com
URL: http://kgs-astana.wixsite.com/society/issmge-kgs

⬆ Offshore Statnamic Pile Loading Test

⬅ Taipei 101 Pile Loading Test

⬇ 7500 Ton Pile Static Loading Test

PILE LOADING TEST

 台安工程技術顧問股份有限公司
DIAGNOSTIC ENGINEERING CONSULTANTS, LTD.

TEL: +886 2 8797 2111   FAX: +886 2 8797 2158
E-MAIL :decl.mail@msa.hinet.net http://www.decl.com.tw

 ## DECL SINGAPORE PTE. LTD.

TEL: +65 8322 5601
E-MAIL :admin @ decl.com.sg   http://www.decl.com.sg

New Slurry Wall Construction for Renewal of An Old Building with 3-Story Basement and 24m Long Slurry Wall

Slurry Wall Design and Construction

12m Deep Guide Wall Construction

Soil Nailing Design and Construction

9m Deep Guide Wall Construction

Pullout of 18m Long Prepakt Pile

Restoration of a Tilted Building via Grouting

SCOPE OF SERVICES

- ➢ Site Investigation Planning and Drilling

- ➢ Planning, Design and Construction of Geotechnical Engineering

- ➢ Planning, Design and Construction of Deep Excavation

- ➢ Planning, Design and Construction of Soil Improvement

- ➢ Planning, Design and Construction of Pile

- ➢ Planning, Design and Construction of Building Protection

Ground Master Construction Co., Ltd.
MICE Consultants Company, Limited

1F, No.11, Lane 295, Sec.1, Dunhua S. Rd., Taipei, Taiwan, R.O.C.
TEL：886-2-27082620   FAX：886-2-27082315
E-mail：micedps@ms25.hinet.net
http:// www.gm-mice.com.tw

TANG YUANG
CONSTRUCTION ENGINEER. INC

Limit height All Casing Pile

All Casing Pile (25)

All Casing Pile (360)

Reverse Circulation Pile

Auger Pile

Top-Down Construction Method

BUSINESS ITEM

- Reverse Circulation Pile (Large-Diameter Bored Pile)
- All Casing Pile
- Secant Pile Wall Method
- Top-Down Construction Method (Steel Pole Putting
- Auger Pile
- Sonic Integrity Testing and Analysis
- Pile Load Testing and Analysis

· COMPANY/ Tang Yuang Construction Engineer.Inc
· ADDRESS/ 2F,No.239,Nu-An Street,Tapei,Taiwan
· PHONE NO./ 886-2-2503-7469
· FACSIMILE NO./ 886-2-2515-5296
· e-mail/ ty168.ty@msa.hinet.net
· PRESIDENT/ CHENG-HUNG CHANG